Addiction and the Making of Professional Careers

Addiction and the Making of Professional Careers

Griffith Edwards and
Thomas F. Babor, editors

Routledge
Taylor & Francis Group
LONDON AND NEW YORK

First published 2012 by Transaction Publishers

Published 2017 by Routledge
2 Park Square, Milton Park, Abingdon, Oxon OX14 4RN
711 Third Avenue, New York, NY 10017, USA

Routledge is an imprint of the Taylor & Francis Group, an informa business

Library of Congress Catalog Number: 2011042491

Library of Congress Cataloging-in-Publication Data

Addiction and the making of professional careers / Griffith Edwards and Thomas F. Babor, editors.
p. cm.
Includes bibliographical references and index.
ISBN 978-1-4128-4597-7
1. Substance abuse. 2. Addicts. I. Edwards, Griffith. II. Babor, Thomas.
RC564.A26 2012
362.29—dc23

2011042491

ISBN 13: 978-1-4128-4597-7 (hbk)

Table of Contents

Part 2—Laboratory Life: The Making of Addiction Pharmacology and Behavioural Pharmacology

Part 3—Clinicians and Clinical Scientists

Foreword

A delightful feature of the international journal *Addiction* has been its regular interviews with addiction scientists, often on the verge of their retirement. The interviews contained in this volume concisely highlight the careers and hindsight perspectives of three dozen people who devoted their professional careers to the study of addiction. Together they reflect well more than a thousand years of professional endeavor. Like a detective novel, their journeys take unexpected twists and turns following the empirical clues of data, experience, and serendipity. Some of the voices are still vibrant and some now silent, but their stories live with the accumulated wisdom of a life spent in search of answers to the vexing puzzles of addiction.

Through three decades we had the pleasure of inviting many senior clinical addiction scientists to visit us at the University of New Mexico. There was, of course, the customary research colloquium, but what I always enjoyed most was the informal discussion with our addiction lab group. We asked our visitors to begin by describing how they had become involved in addiction research and treatment, and to tell us the story of how their careers had unfolded. The story was almost always one of happenstance, with an accidental quality that is also reflected in many of the stories in this volume. I cannot recall one who described setting out from the beginning to become an addiction researcher. Perhaps this is attributable in part to seniority, for in the 1960s and 70s when many of these people entered the addiction field, it was not exactly regarded to be a prestigious or wise career choice.

Once exposed, however, there was something that held the thirty-six subjects of this book in the field. The study of addiction is rarely boring and offers fascinating glimpses into human nature. The prevalence of substance use disorders is so high that one is sure to know affected family or friends, providing a personal perspective on the topic. Given mortality rates, it is a domain within which one's work can have life-or-death impact. Those who conduct longitudinal follow-up research also know what many in the public do not: that outcomes following treatment for addiction are generally quite good. If you must have a chronic life-threatening illness and could choose, addiction would not be a bad choice precisely because the prognosis for recovery is excellent. The addiction field is therefore a wonderful crucible in which to study the psychology of change.

A career-long commitment to any particular scientific endeavor can yield fruit that is unlikely to emerge from a study or two. Findings accumulate and interact leading to new, often better questions. There is time to reflect, step back and puzzle, have *aha* insights and subject them to further testing. Career scientists in addiction also attract and mentor new researchers, which is how many of the people in this volume began their own addiction careers. We are indebted to the people whose voices are heard in this volume, who devoted their careers and creativity to the enduring and worthy problem of addiction. With the accumulated science that they and others like them have contributed it is now possible, as Jaffe noted in his interview "to choose a career in addiction rather than enter into it fortuitously."

William R. Miller, Ph.D.
Emeritus Distinguished Professor of Psychology and Psychiatry
The University of New Mexico

Acknowledgments

We are very grateful to Robert West (Editor-in-Chief of *Addiction*) for the support he has given to the production of this book and for his permission to make use of material published in that journal. Chapters of commentary have been provided by leading international experts who have generously found time to help in this way. Our debt to the subjects interviewed and those who interviewed them is immense and personal. We are delighted to publish a foreword by William R. Miller who features too in this book as an interviewee. Jean O'Reilly has given splendid office support. We have much benefited from the partnership with Transaction Publishers. Grants toward editorial costs have been received from institutional sources.

Conflict of Interest Declaration

So far as they are aware, neither of the editors is subject to any conflict of interest in relation to their responsibilities for this book. No funding has been received from industry sources.

Bibliography of Interviews

Copyright Permission and Source Material

#	Interviewee	Interviewer	*Addiction* publication details
1	**Jim Orford**	Gillian Tober	Volume 106, Issue 4, Date: April 2011, Pages: 698–705
2	**Martin Jarvis**	Robert West	Volume 106, Issue 2, Date: February 2011, Pages: 260–266
3	**Michael Kuhar**	Nancy Campbell	Volume 105, Issue 4, Date: April 2010, Pages: 593–600

#	Interviewee	Interviewer	*Addiction* publication details
4	**Bruce Ritson**	Iain Smith	Volume 105, Issue 8, Date: August 2010, Pages: 1346–54
5	**Roger Meyer**	Henry Kranzler	Volume 105, Issue 10, October 2010, Pages: 1711–1720,
6	**William R. Miller**	Barbara McCrady	Volume 104, Issue 6, Date: June 2009, Pages: 883–893
7	**Rudolf Moos**	John Finney	Volume 103, Issue 1, Date: January 2008, Pages: 13–23
8	**Hiroshi Suwaki**	Griffith Edwards	Volume 102, Issue 11, Date: November 2007, Pages: 1722–1729
9	**William L. White**	Tom McGovern	Volume 102, Issue 9, Date: September 2007, Pages: 1365–1376
10	**Raphael Mechoulam**	Ruth Gallily	Volume 102, Issue 6, Date: June 2007, Pages: 887–893
11	**Nick Heather**	Robert West	Volume 102, Issue 4, Date: April 2007, Pages: 523–533
12	**Hamid Ghodse**	Andrew Johns	Volume 102, Issue 2, Date: February 2007, Pages: 197–205
13	**Walter Clark**	Raul Caetano	Volume 101, Issue 12, Date: December 2006, Pages: 1690–1695
14	**Juha Partanen**	Robin Room	Volume 101, Issue 10, Date: October 2006, Pages: 1399–1407
15	**Cees Goos**	Pail Lemmens	Volume 101, Issue 8, Date: August 2006, Pages: 1078–1085

#	Interviewee	Interviewer	*Addiction* publication details
16	**Ragnar Hauge**	Michael Blindheim	Volume 101, Issue 6, Date: June 2006, Pages: 793–800
17	**Joseph Gusfield**	Richard Madsen	Volume 101, Issue 4, Date: April 2006, Pages: 481–490
18	**Lou Harris**	Bill Dewey	Volume 101, Issue 3, Date: March 2006, Pages: 305–314
19	**M. Douglas Anglin**	Richard Rawson	Volume 101, Issue 2, Date: February 2006, Pages: 169–180
20	**Sheila Blume**	Marianne Guschwan	Volume 101, Issue 1, Date: January 2006, Pages: 31–39
21	**Joseph V. Brady**	Jerry Jaffe	Volume 100, Issue 12, Date: December 2005, Pages: 1805–1812
22	**Shanthi Ranganathan**	M.S. Jayaraman	Volume 100, Issue 11, Date: November 2005, Pages: 1578–1583
23	**Robert L. DuPont**	Barry Brown	Volume 100, Issue 10, Date: October 2005, Pages: 1402–1411
24	**Leland H. Towle**	Tom Babor	Volume 100, Issue 9, Date: September 2005, Pages: 1215–1218
25	**Malcolm H. Lader**	Griffith Edwards	Volume 100, Issue 8, Date: August 2005, Pages: 1057–1065
26	**E. A. Carlini**	Dr Joao Carlos Dias da Silva	Volume 100, Issue 7, Date: July 2005, Pages: 897–907
27	**Harold Holder**	Keith Humphreys	Volume 100, Issue 5, Date: May 2005, Pages: 585–594

#	Interviewee	Interviewer	*Addiction* publication details
28	**George Vaillant**	Thomas Babor and Griffith Edwards	Volume 100, Issue 3, Date: March 2005, Pages: 274–280
29	**Tomoji Yanagita**	Charles R. Schuster	Volume 99, Issue 7, Date: July 2004, Pages: 805–810
30	**Charles R. Schuster**	Robert Balster	Volume 99, Issue 6, Date: June 2004, Pages: 667–676
31	**Michael A. H. Russell**	Martin Jarvis	Volume 99, Issue 1, Date: January 2004, Pages: 9–19
32	**Richard Fuller**	Raymond Anton	Volume 98, Issue 11, Date: November 2003, Pages: 1485–1492
33	**Timothy Cook**	Betsy Thom	Volume 98, Issue 8, Date: August 2003, Pages: 1029–1038
34	**Conan Kornetsky**	Jerome Jaffe	Volume 98, Issue 7, Date: July 2003, Pages: 875–882
35	**Ambros Uchtenhagen**	Michael Kraus	Volume 98, Issue 4, Date: April 2003, Pages: 389–396
36	**Enoch Gordis**	Stephanie O'Malley	Volume 97, Issue 2, Date: February 2002, Pages: 141–151

Introduction: Careers Set Questions

Griffith Edwards

The misuse of licit and illicit drugs continues to cause suffering and loss worldwide on a vast scale. In response to these problems, many people devote their working lives to an attempt to prevent or ameliorate misuse of licit and illicit mind-acting substances and the consequences. The spectrum of professionals involved in that response is wide, and includes treatment personnel of every kind, research workers from many different disciplines, the voluntary sector, administrators, and the staff of relevant government, and international agencies. The judicial and enforcement sector also makes significant contributions, but it is not within the scope of this particular book. The extent, causes, and complexities of the problems caused by misuse are much commented on. But in sharp contrast to the nature, dimensions, and dynamics of the relevant response system, who works where and why within it, their motivation and training, what makes one effective in his or her career, what rewards people who enter this field and what is special about it—those questions are for the most part ignored. At worst it seems as if people who choose a professional career in the addictions are more likely to be used than valued. The optimum use of the relevant human resources seem often to have been left more to luck than been subject to intelligent planning, or based on a full understanding of the facts. One side of the interactive system of "problems" and "responses" seems to be off the map.

This book seeks to help address that imbalance. Its focus will be on the need for enhanced understanding of professional careers in the addiction field. Why do some people decide to give their life space to responding in some way to the drug problem—the *why do it* question—in a world with so many other beckoning career opportunities. How do and should we select, train, mentor, support, inspire and nurture the young career aspirant? What, then, makes for success, perhaps brilliant success, and the most effective use of talent? Is every personal case different or are their generalizable conclusions to be drawn?

Interviews as Live Material

The core material of this book derives from a series of 93 interviews that have been published in an international scientific journal, *Addiction*, over the last 30 or so years. The byline to this feature has always stated

> "In this occasional series we record the views and personal experience of people who have especially contributed to the evolution of ideas in the journal's field of interest"

Contribution to "the evolution of ideas' is indeed the touchstone for subject selection. We are seeking to interview people who have in any way shone light, made a difference, pushed at frontiers, advanced understanding. They give in each instance a personal account of what they have done and how they have been able to do it—a career declared.

Since the appearance in 1970 of the first addiction interview,[1] the journal has published interviews from a total of 40 different countries and with the count still running. Two previous books in this series [2,3] have offered collections of interviews accompanied by thematic debates. The cast has included many international leaders in this field, including such names as Kettil Bruun,[4] Vincent Dole,[5] Richard Doll,[6] Jerome Jaffe,[7] Harold Holder,[8] William Miller,[9] George Vaillant,[10] Harold Kalant,[11] and Joy Moser[12] but each and every contributor has spoken to considerable, varied, and generous accomplishment. The series has also included interviews with a Catholic priest,[13] a US senator,[14] a recovered addict,[15] an Australian Prime Minister,[16] WHO professionals,[17] and an Indian woman who established the beginnings of a national treatment system from a wing in her family bungalow[18]—the response system does indeed run broader than any one profession.

The process though which subjects are selected for the series aims at an international and wide disciplinary coverage and addiction is fortunately benefiting from advice provided by *Addiction*'s multidisciplinary and multilingual panel of 150 Assistant Editors. If the name of a candidate emerges from a trawl for nominations, there will then be consultation with senior editorial advisers in the individual's field of interest.

When the nominee's acceptance is confirmed, we will with their collaboration select and brief a suitable interviewer. The finalization of the text is likely to involve considerable further inputs from the subject and the interviewer and from the editorial office. Nothing is published until the subject is content with every last word of the product. The journal does not offer fees to either subject or interviewer but as a token of gratitude *Addiction* expects to pick up the bill for a meal for two in a good restaurant of the subject's choosing.

This introductory chapter provides a welcome opportunity for us to thank the interviewers who have for 30 years so wonderfully supported the production of these interviews. We could not at the beginning have predicted how expertly a wide spectrum of people would perform in this role. A full listing of the interviewers whose skilled contributions have given strength to the present book is given in the table of contents.

The product? What eventually goes forward for publication will at best have its subject standing out from the pages. It will be an account of a professional career coloured by personal insights, identification of role models and mentors; an account of a professional education; an account of opportunities, frustrations, joys and sorrows, and all this with an awareness of local and national contexts. We aim at a telling of human stories and at the same time the understanding of life context. Essentially, we are seeking to portray a career trajectory and a longitudinal play. The interviews are originally tape-recorded. Despite the intervening editorial process, the intention is to preserve the sense of someone talking, and we believe that these journal interviews are often able to give a magical sense of contact with the person talking. We will retain the occasional coloquillum. For people who want to conduct their interview in some language other than English we can achieve translation.

We are well aware of the time demands that these interviews put on the interviewers and the subjects, in terms of preparation, time given to the interview, and further work involved in the to and fro of the editorial work. In the event, participants usually seem to enjoy the process. We seek to ensure, however, that the final experience is one of worth confirmed. The journal's gratitude has, of course, been conveyed on every occasion but we want now to restate that gratitude very publicly. The journal is intensely grateful for the generosity of all the interviewees who have contributed to the success of this archival endeavor.

Representativeness?

With a glance backwards, we are well aware of subjects lost to interview and people whose absence from our list we much regret. The problem is an embarrassment of riches and choices have to be made.

Questions around the representativeness of the choice of subjects therefore arise and need to be examined. There is no formal sampling frame that can be accessed when addressing that question but the choice is certainly a matter of process rather than a product of editorial whim. The aim has always been on international coverage: over the last 30 years, 40 (44%) of the subjects selected have come from North America, 17 (18%) from the UK, and 36 (38%) from other countries. We suspect that this is reasonably representative of the intensity over the relevant time base of research activity across the field, but it is possible that there may have been some overrepresentation of the USA and the UK.

Questions need also to be asked about the coverage in terms of professional discipline. That issue is complex in that the base distribution of professionals will vary between countries and greatly over time. For instance, in the UK few or no psychologists, social scientists, or economists were active in the field until the early 1960s, and the lag effect results in no contributions to this series from these cadres of British professionals until relatively recently when we are proud to have published interviews with Nick Heather,[19] Martin Jarvis,[20] and Jim Orford[21] as exemplary witnesses to the contributions made to this field by British psychology. In the US, this group of researchers made a powerful entry to this specialist field much earlier, and have been strongly represented in our interviews.

Perhaps the most testing questions attach here to the representation of women in our series. Over the 30 year period we have achieved only a 7–8% representation of women among the subjects selected for interview. But we believe that the explanation probably again lies in generational realities and the lag effect. Women 30 years ago were generally not well represented among senior researchers or senior clinical staff in this field—in some countries they were probably at that time virtually unknown on that terrain. With the imbalance having narrowed over recent decades at varying paces and degrees across different countries, we would at about the present time expect to see changes in the gender distribution of this series, as represented in sequential volumes of collections. The composition of this series as represented in the present volume can perhaps be seen as holding up a mirror to a set of real-life situations which shaped leadership of the field as it evolved from its early days. The founding parents of the most influential early addiction research centres were more often founding fathers than founding mothers, with Genevieve Knupfer[22] a notable exception. On gender distribution, we can offer some data (Table 1.1) to support that interpretation. As a preliminary step towards establishing the empirical facts of this issue, we give data for two periods, 1979-1980 and 2009, showing changes over three decades in gender distribution of first authors for material published in *Addiction* and its predecessor journal (*The British Journal of Addiction*) over that period. At the earlier point, 93% of first authors were male and 7% female, while at the later point a highly significant shift had occurred to bring the overall distribution near parity—50% male and 49% female. Changes have occurred in the US and the UK, but have been even more marked in the broad "other" national category. One cannot prove a case, but these data are probably indicative.

On gender distribution, the same questions are relevant to many other professions beside addiction science. Discussion of such issues has been published, for instance, in relation to medicine in general, psychiatry, and various other subspecialties, the law, and business. There can be no doubt that in the addiction field, racial and gender discrimination has at times determined who gets their name on a paper, who is given promotion, who is invited to meetings and who wins the prizes. But on the whole we believe that *Addiction* has sought to remedy this problem rather than compound it.

Table 1.1: Gender distribution of first authors published in the British Journal of Addiction / Addiction for the calendar years 1979 and 1980 combined, and for the year 2009. Commentaries, letters, book reviews and interviews are excluded. For the former period 4, and in the latter period 6, subjects were excluded because of uncertainty in gender identification from available information.

	Years 1979 and 1980				Year 2009			
	Total	North America	United Kingdom	Other	Total	North America	United Kingdom	Other
Male	98 (93%)	48 (96%)	39 (92%)	11 (85%)	87 (51%)	53 (51%)	20 (58%)	14 (31%)
Female	7 (7%)	2 (4%)	3 (8%)	2 (15%)	82 (49%)	33 (49%)	14 (42%)	35 (69%)
Total	105	50	42	13	169	86	34	49

The Structure of this Book

As already mentioned, this book takes the 36 interviews published between 2002 and 2010 as its raw material. We decided that for purposes of presentation, these interviews could with advantage be shortened down from the originally published 6000 - 7000 words to about 3000 words. Our reason for this decision was simply to set a feasible limit to control the size of the book. The abbreviations were achieved by eliminating some detail while retaining information relating to career choice, training, and career pathway. The abbreviated statements have been checked and cleared with the interviewees wherever possible, and we are grateful for their input. We were at first apprehensive as to the possible negative consequences for the integrity of these texts. As the editorial work proceeded, we were, however, pleasantly surprised to realise that the shortened versions were emerging as statements with pace, stories, and voice of their own, rather than mere shrunken versions of the originals.

The interviews have been grouped into five sections, and in each instance specially commissioned chapters which comment on each set of interviews have been set up. We are very fortunate to have brought into partnership Peter Anderson, Ilana Crome, Jonathan Chick, Jerome Jaffe, and Kerstin Stenius. One of these authors responded to our letter of invitation to say they had not time to accept the invitation, but nevertheless the invitation was so intriguing that they would accept and make the time. They bring to this work different national professional backgrounds, but with considerable professional experience as a common feature. The commentators have been asked to focus particularly on questions around the understanding of professional career paths which they see their allocated group of interviews as illustrating. The segregation into these groups is inevitably at the margins somewhat arbitrary, and frequently one individual could have achieved recognition in more than one field of operation. We feel fortunate to have attracted these outstandingly experienced colleagues to take on the commentary responsibility. The final chapter by Babor reflects on how best the significance for the future of these life stories may be discerned.

But what we much hope is that what the interview subjects tell us, and the insights that the commentaries offer on this rich material, can in some ways enhance understanding of how to make careers in addiction more effective and more rewarding. This is not a book which can give final answers but we dare to hope that it will engage our field in inquiry, debate, and the asking of necessary questions. Addiction careers are costly investments both in cash and human terms but are, we would assert, at present grossly underinvested in appraisal of their crucial contributions to the response system, and as topics themselves for research. We hope that the lives sketched in this book will help to inform and inspire young people now making their own choices. A further and final aim of this book is to celebrate some lives well lived, what these people have given to this field, and the evolving quality and excitement of the field they have served and helped build.

Notes

1. Conversation with D. L. Davies. *British Journal of Addiction* 74 (1979) 239–49.
2. Edwards, G. (ed) *Addictions: Personal Influences and Scientific Movements.* New Brunswick, New Jersey, USA: Transaction Publishers, 1991.
3. Edwards, G. (ed) *Addiction: Evolution of a Specialist Field.* Oxford, UK: Blackwell Publishing, 2002.
4. Conversation with Kettil Bruun. *British Journal of Addiction* 80 (1985) 339–43.
5. Conversation with Vincent Dole. *Addiction* 89 (1994) 23–9.
6. Conversation with Sir Richard Doll. *British Journal of Addiction* 86 (1991) 365–77.
7. Conversation with Jerome H. Jaffe. *Addiction* 94 (1999) 13–30.
8. Conversation with Harold Holder. *Addiction* 100 (2005) 585–94.
9. Conversation with William Miller. *Addiction* 104 (2009) 883–93.
10. Conversation with George Vaillant. *Addiction* 100 (2005) 274–80.
11. Conversation with Harold Kalant. *British Journal of Addiction* 83 (1988) 1003–12.
12. Conversation with Joy Moser. *British Journal of Addiction* 79 (1984) 355–63.
13. Conversation with Monsignor Ignatius McDermott. *Addiction* 89 (1994) 791–7.
14. Conversation with Senator Harold Hughes. *Addiction* 92 (1997) 137–49.
15. Conversation with David Deitch. *Addiction* 94 (1999) 791–800.

16. Conversation with R. J. Hawke. *Addiction* 93 (1998) 1761–3.
17. Conversation with Dr. Awni Arif. *British Journal of Addiction* 81 (1986) 607–11.
18. Conversation with Shanthi Ranganathan. *Addiction* 100 (2005) 1578–83.
19. Conversation with Nick Heather. *Addiction* 102 (2007) 523–33.
20. Conversation with Martin Jarvis. *Addiction* 106 (2011) 260–6.
21. Conversation with Jim Orford. *Addiction,* 106 (2011) 698–705.
22. Conversation with Genevieve Knupfer. *British Journal of Addiction* (1988) 83, 1395–8.

Part 1—Addiction Careers and Administration at a High Level

1

Conversation with Robert L. DuPont

Robert DuPont is an American drug expert. He has played a crucial role in developing community-wide and evidence-based responses to drug problems. Throughout a highly productive professional life he has shown an ability to make things happen.

Addiction (A): Let us go back a considerable way. What shaped your decision to choose a career in medicine specializing in psychiatry?

Robert L. DuPont (RLD): When I finished the eighth grade in 1950 my family moved from a farm in Ohio to Denver, Colorado. The first thing I did was ride my bike to the neighborhood public library where, on a shelf right inside the front door, I found 20 tempting books. One was a big black book titled The Human Mind. It was a 1948 third edition of the 1930 best-seller by psychiatrist Karl Menninger.[1] I knew from the first day I opened it that I was going to be a psychiatrist. I could not imagine anything more fascinating than 'the human mind'. I had found my calling. Never wavered and never regretted the decision. It was similar to my decision to marry my wife, Helen. I knew the first time I met her that she was the one. Those two decisions were instantaneous.

A: How did you think of a career in psychiatry in those days?

RLD: I thought about medicine as a good way to help people. I was fascinated by people's stories. I was interested in literature for the same reason. That is how I thought about psychiatry then and it is how I think about psychiatry now.

A: Your family of origin?

RLD: My father was a salesman, always looking for the product that would sell itself. Early in his adult life he sold tobacco. Later he sold beer. My mother was a social worker who became a 7th grade math teacher. My parents left no doubt that having a profession improved your odds of being able to buy a house, send your kids to college and pay your bills. Because our family did not have much money the financial security of a profession was almost as attractive as the opportunity it gave for public service.

A: You took time off in medical school.

RLD: After graduating from Emory in Atlanta I went to medical school at Harvard. I had worked hard to be on the path to become a doctor, but once I was on it I was claustrophobic, thinking that this tightly circumscribed path would be too constraining for me. I went to the Dean of Students saying, 'I have to take a year off to see the world.' He let me know that I could come back to Harvard Medical School whenever I was ready. I put together the adventure of a life-time. I bought a Land Rover in Coventry, England and headed south overland for a year in Africa. I was imprisoned, and nearly executed, as a CIA spy in Guinea. When Patrice Lumumba was killed, I was almost murdered by a mob in Nigeria where I went to a rally of Africans who had congregated to protest his death. The trip left me with a life-long passionate interest in Africa and Africans.

A: I know that you later did some work with Martin Luther King Jr.

RLD: Helen, and I worked very briefly with Martin Luther King Jr. after I came back from Africa. Over the Christmas break from medical school in 1962 I got to know him, his father, his family and his church. I had tremendous respect for Dr King. When he was murdered I felt that a part of me died.

A: Much of what was going on in your life sounds like you were tending towards a career in the public service from the start. When did you make that commitment?

RLD: After I graduated from the Harvard Medical School I did a medical internship at the Cleveland Metropolitan General Hospital. Then I went back to Harvard to begin a psychiatric residency. I came to NIH to finish that residency. I came to Washington in 1966 because of the Vietnam War, thinking that I would be here for just 2 years before returning to Harvard. People laugh about my decision now, but when I was in college I thought that only dummies went to business school. Smart people went to work for the government. When I finished at NIH, at age 32, it was time for me to get my first full-time job outside of my medical training. That job put me on a life-long career path. I know this sounds crazy or arrogant or both, but I wanted my career to make a difference.

Moving into the Corrections Field

A: And that choice was . . . ?

RLD: I chose corrections. I was confident that I could make a difference in the prisoners' lives. Here you had a Harvard-trained NIH veteran who wanted to dedicate himself to corrections. That was unusual because corrections was the lowest of the low in the status pecking order then, as it is now. I stayed in Washington. The biggest factor influencing my decision was that crime had become a major political issue in Washington. Then there was the 1968 presidential election. Richard Nixon won. I was a Democrat. Everyone I knew in corrections and mental health was a Democrat. The election of Nixon that November was like death.

A: How did you find a way through?

RLD: On 20 January 1969, a bunch of new Republicans that I had never heard of came to town to take over. Nixon and his staff had to come up with good new ideas fast. One of the places they looked was corrections. That was my cue. I said let's create a task force to come up with new ideas in corrections, the best new ideas in the country

A: As a part of the initiative that you got off the ground there was this huge effort in community corrections and that was a landmark activity.

RLD: Virtually all our new initiatives were in community corrections. Ken Hardy made me the head of community corrections for the city meaning that within less than one year of my joining the department I was head of all of the city's parole and correctional halfway house services. We put in place 10 halfway houses within a year.

Crime and the Intersection with Heroin

A: Then there was the heroin use crisis that was identified in Washington thanks to your study.

RLD: The overriding question in corrections in the District of Columbia in 1969 was, 'Why is there a crime wave?' Our study showed that 44% of the men coming into the jail tested positive for heroin. We could literally correlate the rising rates of the initiation of heroin use to the rising rate of crime. That study[2] defined the modern heroin epidemic and its relationship to crime.

Developing a Community-Wide Response to Washington's Heroin Problem

A: What model of response did you develop?

RLD: My signature identity in this public health adventure was to be concerned about the heroin problem on a community-wide scale. Everybody else was interested in a few patients or small drug treatment program. For me the relevant question was not how best to get one person well, it was: 'What can the government do in a short period of time that is going to reduce heroin addiction in the whole community?' By 1 September 1969 we had started our methadone treatment program.

A: If I am correct, the program actually went from 20 clients prior to there being an NTA (Narcotics Treatment Agency) to the 2000 figure in less than 6 months.

RLD: That is right.

A: It sounds as if the treatment program was of interest to a number of prominent political figures.

RLD: Everything we did at NTA, from day 1, was big news. The most impressive visitor NTA had was Jimmy Carter. We treated 15 000 heroin addicts in our first 3 years. The monthly crime rate in the District of Columbia was cut in half in that 3-year period.

A: How quickly could you take an addict into treatment?

RLD: We always had room for another heroin addict to come in off the street.

A: How did you secure backing for the NTA methadone programme?

RLD: The first thing I did when we started administering methadone at NTA was to go to the scientific establishment for its blessing. I felt that if the National Academy of Sciences and the Institute of Medicine would officially say that this was a good treatment for heroin addiction that would be very helpful. In that initial encounter with the scientific establishment, I learned a lesson about the ability of scientists to lead in complex and controversial areas. At that time I found this experience to be profoundly disillusioning.

A: My recollection of these events is that you may well have organized the first program involving diversion from the criminal justice system, which was, in many respects, a forerunner of TASC, then called Treatment Alternatives to Street Crime.

RLD: Jerry Jaffe, the first White House Drug Czar, created TASC based, in part, on what we were doing in Washington. I was never comfortable with the image that TASC had for a time as a way of keeping addicted people out of prison. I never felt that the prison sentence was the enemy of the addicted person. I wanted to use the leverage of that prison sentence for pro-social purposes.

A: Thinking back again to the NTA experience, what were the problems involved with acquiring the large number of treatment staff needed to mount the operation in a very short period of time.

RLD: We grew to 20 treatment centers with a staff of 500 within 6 months of starting. Our prominence was a negative factor in terms of the way the rest of city bureaucracy treated NTA. From 1971 to 1973 NTA had a staff member, Jim Fair, whose only job—every work-day—was to take around visitors—20, 50 visitors a day.

A: NTA not only was significant to the field of drug abuse treatment, but it appears to have provided enormous personal satisfaction for you as well.

RLD: If I had my work life to live over again I would have stayed with NTA. Regrettably, that is an idle fantasy. NTA was unsustainable for two reasons. First, the racial politics of that time made it unsustainable. NTA was also unsustainable for personal reasons. I could not get along with some of the leaders of the government agencies that we needed to rely on. The only way I could understand it was the jealousy of other bureaucrats responding to the prominence of NTA.

Leaving NTA and the Move to the White House

A: How long did you stay at NTA?

RLD: I lasted 5 years at the top in the DC government. That is about as long as any highly visible senior bureaucrat makes it in those shark-infested waters. The average tenure of Presidential appointees is 14 months! Jerry Jaffe was named White House chief on 17 June 1971. I am deeply respectful of the outstanding job he did as the world's first Drug Czar. At the time the White House drug office was called the Special Action Office for Drug Abuse Prevention (SAODAP).

A: You went from NTA to become the second Director of SAODAP in 1973.

RLD: I was in for a variety of rude awakenings. Within a week of my arrival I had my first congressional hearing representing the federal government.

A: What kind of national database on addiction treatment was at that time available?

RLD: This time I had to present the first findings of a national survey of the nation's drug abuse treatment programs. The highly paid, high status SAODAP staff brought me a mountain of computer printouts. Because I had spent a great deal of time with treatment programs all over the country I had some knowledge of what was out there. Looking over those data I saw that these papers bore no relationship to reality. My principal job was to take the staff from 174 to 0 in 2-years. That was not the best job in government. SAODAP had been set up as a 4-year office. The Administration were not going to renew it. The excitement shifted to the National Institute on Drug Abuse (NIDA). I became NIDA's first Director. That was quite a time. Here I was the White House drug chief, the head of NIDA but also of the National Institute of Mental Health (NIMH) and the National Institute on Alcohol Abuse and Alcoholism (NIAAA). Following the formal closing of SAODAP 30 June 1975, a drug policy presence remained in the White House, with me in charge, under the aegis of a Cabinet Committee.

A: It was Carter's Secretary of Health, Education and Welfare (HEW), Joe Califano, who got you to leave NIDA.

RLD: Running a big government agency is like having a short-term lease on a classy property. You rent it for a while, it feels like your home, but before long you are out on your ear. I had been through that painful, and in some ways humiliating, process at NTA. I went through it a second time at NIDA. In the 42 years since I graduated from medical school I worked for the government just 12. They were all wonderful years.

A Fundamental Commitment to the Public Health Approach

A: How, if at all, has your thinking about drug abuse changed over the years?

RLD: My frame of reference goes beyond a local program or even a local community to the whole nation, in fact to the whole world.

A: Do you think there is sufficient awareness of the inherent dangerousness of drugs?

RLD: 'Harm reduction' is a misguided public policy because it starts by accepting illegal drug use and then seeks to normalize that drug use. That will result, down that road, in more suffering and more harm for more people.[3]

A: Over the years have you changed your perspective on methadone?

RLD: When I entered the drug field I was enthusiastic about methadone. I am much less so today. The biggest change in my thinking over 35 years in this field has been my growing recognition that the 12-Step programs are a modern miracle, the secret weapon in the war against drug abuse. The big historical event in drug abuse treatment then happening was completely lost on me in the 1960s and 1970s. It was happening at Hazelden, in Center City Minnesota, where they married professional services with 12-Step programs.

A Diverse and Continuing Sense of Personal Reward

A: Looking back, what do you see as the achievements you are proudest of in your own career?

RLD: First, I do not take my own career too seriously. In everything I have done I was one of many. I am proud to have contributed, and to continue to contribute, to a small but important part of the history of my time. In 1978, when I left the government, I founded the Institute for Behavior and Health, Inc. (IBH), a national non-profit organization. In 1982, Peter Bensinger and I founded Bensinger, DuPont and Associates (BDA). This organization has made contributions especially in work-places, and more recently in prescription drug abuse prevention. I am proud that when Joe Califano tossed me out of NIDA my insecurity led me to diversify into an entirely new field, the anxiety disorders.[4] In 1980 I was the first President of the Anxiety Disorders Association of America (ADAA).

A: And you continue in clinical practice?

RLD: I have had my own practice of psychiatry since 1969. From day one I have loved the drug issue, finding it to be deeply interesting and profoundly rewarding. The ever-changing field involves economics, politics, history, biology and even religion. Whatever you are interested in, drug abuse has it. The best part has been the people, not just experts but everyone involved, including addicted people and their families, the real 'experts' in our field.

A: Any regrets?

RLD: If I regret something, it is that I did not spend more time with the colleagues with whom I was fortunate enough to associate. I have cared deeply about the people I have known.

Notes

1. Menninger, K. A. (1948) *The Human Mind.* New York: Alfred A Knopf, Inc.
2. DuPont, R. L. (1971) Profile of a heroin-addiction epidemic. *New England Journal of Medicine,* 285, 320–324.
3. DuPont, R. L. (2000) *The Selfish Brain—Learning from Addiction.* Center City, MN: Hazelden.
4. DuPont, R. L., Spencer, E. D. & DuPont, C. M. (2003) *The Anxiety Cure: An Eight-Step Program for Getting Well,* revised edition. New York: John Wiley and Sons, Inc.

2

Conversation with Richard Fuller

Richard Fuller is an American gastroenterologist. While at Cleveland he conducted controlled trials on disulfiram which because of their methodology generalized to have wide influence. In a second phase of his professional life he directed NIAAA's clinical and prevention research program.

Addiction (A): When did you retire from National Institute on Alcohol Abuse and Alcoholism?

Richard Fuller (RF): I retired 3 January 2003.

A: How long were you at NIAAA?

RF: November 1988 to 3 January 2003. I had taken a leave of absence from Case Western Reserve University and the Cleveland VA because I was not sure I wanted to work at NIAAA but I began to enjoy it so a few months turned into almost 15 years.

Training

A: Tell me about your training in medicine and how you were attracted to the field of alcoholism.

RF: I was trained in Internal Medicine at University Hospitals of Cleveland after having graduated from Western Reserve University School of Medicine in Cleveland. I went into the Air Force for 2 years and I came back to finish my residency in internal medicine, and then in 1968 I did a gastroentrology fellowship. I would like to say that it was altruism that motivated me to treat alcoholics, but the truth is that it was for more mercenary reasons. One of the fellows the year before me had worked in night-time clinics for the city of Cleveland, which were set up to treat alcoholics. My salary at that time was $3000 per year and I had a wife and a young daughter, so I decided to moonlight—one or two nights a week. I enjoyed working with the patients and the counsellors, who were all recovered alcoholics and active in Alcoholics Anonymous. My role was to prescribe Antabuse. Although there could be a clash between Alcoholics Anonymous and pharmacotherapy. There was no training in the treatment of alcoholics. These recovered alcoholic counselors were very helpful because at least I could learn from their life experiences.

A: So the alcoholics became your educators?

RF: That is true, they did. While some AA members even today are still full of dogma and do not welcome pharmacotherapies, it is interesting that in 1968 there could be this combined effort between a physician and members of AA. I saw the recovery side and realized that it was not as bleak and dismal as I had thought from my hospital-based experiences.

A: That is actually a very valuable experience that many people in internal medicine do not have during their training.

RF: That is correct. As a faculty member of Case Western Reserve I saw out-patients often with a student or a house officer. This enabled them to see that there are recovered alcoholics who are doing well and are normal. In the city of Cleveland they had what was called a workhouse and it was, in a sense, a jail. But during the day, if you were in the workhouse and had a job, you were allowed to go to the job. If you did not have a job, they tried to find you one. Because workhouse personnel wanted to secure sobriety on the job, they prescribed Antabuse to people convicted of an alcohol-related criminal offense. Afterwards they needed some kind of ongoing treatment, so they established these clinics. There were two types of patients at the clinics, those who had been in the workhouse and others from the community were seeking treatment for alcoholism. Harold Roth, who was chief of the gastroenterology program at the VA, became very concerned that most of the patients on the gastroenterology ward were there with alcohol-related illnesses and he began to think of setting up a program to treat alcoholism. He began to talk to me about running a treatment program at the VA. He wanted a science-based program, so he encouraged me to train in clinical trial methodology. In 1969 and 1970 I studied for a Masters Degree at Case Western in biometry. I took epidemiology, biometry courses and statistical courses. The faculty tailored the program for me because I also took some graduate psychology courses and one graduate sociology course. This experience has made me open to behavioral therapy.

A: You were way ahead of your time to be doing something back then that is more common now. So how would you describe Harold Roth, was he a significant person in your development?

RF: Yes, he was a significant person because he encouraged me to do this and he was significant in other ways. Harold was a pioneer in the study of 'compliance'. When he began his studies physicians and nurses thought patients took medication as prescribed. We know differently today!

A: It is interesting how there are key people in one's career. Obviously he was one for you.

The Start of an Interest in Researching Disulfiram

RF: Absolutely. We were talking about how to treat alcoholics, and I said one thing we can do is to give them Antabuse. Harold asked, 'Does it work?'

I am embarrassed to admit this, but because it was in the PDR and approved by the FDA, I thought it worked! He challenged me and I went back and read the literature and the studies were heavily flawed. There were about 100 clinical studies at that time—only 10 were controlled and only one or two were randomized.

A: So that was the basis for your doing the disulfiram trial.

RF: I did some pilot studies and then I did a larger study that was published in the *Annals of Internal Medicine* (Fuller & Roth 1979). That study, which was conducted on 128 men, all at the Cleveland VA Hospital, addressed some of the previous serious methodological problems. That study utilized adequate controls, randomization, blinding—no previous study had been blinded. The validity of self-report, compliance, and adequate follow-up were all important issues that Harold and I tried to address. In the late 1970s there were many private programs, which kept reporting incredible results in the range of 80–90% 'success rates' with treatment in general. You know that was just not believable and I was afraid alcoholism treatment would suffer from a lack of credible results. They would call up a patient treated in a 28-day program 6 months later or send them a questionnaire. There are two problems: one is the response rate to those questionnaires was often 50%. Secondly, I was also concerned they were willing to accept what the patient told them.

A: So it is clear when you did the initial trials you put quite a bit of thought into proper methodology, design, reporting, compliance. All of those things that set a standard for clinical trials since then.

RF: While I was doing this there were other fine behavioral scientists such as Bill Miller, Dick Longabaugh, Barbara McCrady, and others who were developing first-rate clinical trials methodology.

A: Did you have discussions with them back then?

RF: No, I was doing my thing and they basically were doing theirs. The discussion developed later and we learned from each other's work.

The VA Multi-Site Disulfiram Trial

A: Tell me more about this initial trial.

RF: We found a trend toward Antabuse being effective in terms of sustained year-long abstinence. A post hoc analysis indicated that 300 patients would be needed to achieve enough statistical power to be certain of an effect. I approached the VA Cooperative Studies Program and they funded a study in which we could have adequate sample size.

A: So the VA was critical for funding this type of study at that time?

RF: Absolutely.

A: What year did you receive funding?

RF: Early 1980s.

A: How many sites were involved with this pivotal study?

RF: Nine.

A: You completed a very well-done methodological trial!

RF: I think the importance to the alcoholism treatment research field was the methodology. Now the results of that study (Fuller et al. 1986) as you know were mixed, and people interpreted it differently. We may have choosen the wrong outcome measure—total abstinence. There was no benefit of disulfiram in terms of total abstinence. In a subset of about 50% of the patients, in whom we had the very best data, there was, however, a reduction in drinking days.

A: So what was the response from the scientific and treatment community to publication of that study?

RF: Well, the one criticism of the VA Cooperative Study was that we did not give disulfiram in a supervised fashion (Chick et al. 1992).

A: What was it like being on the faculty in Cleveland and balancing family and career and that sort of thing?

RF: I never was successful at balancing career and family, I always thought I was cheating my career. My wife would tell you that I was paying more attention to my career than to my family. I worked in the golden age of academic medicine, and doctors were held in high regard. Basically I did a traditional three-prong career—practice, research and teaching. I was a member of a four-person gastroenterology group. I also conducted Internal Medicine rounds once or twice a year. I taught house staff and I taught gastroenterology to medical students. I was conducting my research. So I conducted research, clinical care and teaching. The VA was a good place because they did free up time for research.

The Transition to NIAAA

A: Tell me how the transition to NIAAA come about.

RF: There were two phases to my life. One was the phase we have just discussed and the second was at NIAAA. I had known Enoch Gordis for at least 10 years before he became the director of NIAAA. I first became aware of Enoch at an AMSA meeting (now called the American Society of Addiction Medicine). Somebody made a well-meaning, but dogmatic, statement and Enoch stood up and made this penetrating response. One of his professional goals was to bring a more scientific basis to alcoholism and alcoholism treatment. I think his life has been a testimony to that goal.

A: When he became Director of NIAAA did he invite you to join him?

RF: Not initially. He had initially sought a psychiatrist but was not successful. So he called me up and said he would like me to come down and talk about the Division of Clinical and Prevention Research that he had created. Well, at this time, I was in my mid-50s, my daughter and son were in college. If I was going to make a career change it appeared to be a good time. Enoch is a great guy to work for. I decided to go and I stayed. He created three divisions: Basic Research, Biometry and Epidemiology, and Clinical and Prevention

Research. And he wanted me to be the director of Clinical and Prevention Research.

A: How did you deploy those resources?

RF: Well, initially we had two branches; one, the Treatment Research Branch, the other was the Prevention Research Branch. The Institute of Medicine issued a report about the time I came to NIAAA called Research Opportunities in Alcoholism Treatment and Prevention (Institute of Medicine 1989). I had a grasp about the current thinking on treatment, but I did not know prevention as well. So I leaned quite heavily on that Institute of Medicine report to prepare myself to try and help move prevention research forward. I can take very little credit for anything since Congress gave us the money and the investigators had the creativity, ingenuity and the persistence to do the studies. But I will give an example where I may have made a difference. We supported two community prevention trials—one by Harold Holder (Holder et al. 1997) and the other by Alex Wagenaar (Wagenaar et al. 2000a,b). I am also very proud of the fact that during my watch Project Northland was conducted, which showed that community interventions could delay drinking in kids who had not yet started drinking (Perry et al. 1996).

The Significance of Project MATCH

A: You arrived at NIAAA around the time Project MATCH was getting ready to start?

RF: Correct. In 1990 another Institute of Medicine report came out called 'Broadening the Base' (Institute of Medicine 1990). This report suggested that treatment-matching was an important topic to study. The results of MATCH, as you know do not strongly support the argument for matching of client psychosocial characteristics to various behavioral treatments (Project MATCH Research Group 1997).

From MATCH to Combine

A: If I remember correctly, there was a major initiative to think about starting to fund medication development and clinical trials with pharmacotherapies around the time that Project MATCH was ending.

RF: MATCH was of course a major focus and then medication development took on accelerated emphasis. This led logically to the COMBINE Study to see if the two medications, naltrexone and acamprosate, combined with an effective behavioral therapy would further improve the treatment of alcohol dependence. It seemed very important to conduct a multi-site study.

Brief Intervention Research

A: Other achievements at NIAAA?

RF: Studies demonstrating the efficacy of brief interventions were initially conducted in Europe and Australia. Not every study is positive but it suggests that at least with people who are drinking more than they should (not necessarily alcoholics) a very brief intervention delivered either by a nurse or a physician can cause a reduction in hazardous rates of drinking. Michael French, an economist, has shown for every dollar spent that between 5 and 6 dollars are saved (Fleming et al. 2000). Somehow we have to get that message out to insurers and funding agencies. The more we can medicalize alcohol treatment the less stigma there will be, and it will be easier to ask for and receive treatment.

What for the Future?

A: Tell me some of things that you would like to see undertaken in the future.

RF: On the prevention side I would like to see if, once the research stops, whether the benefits from these community prevention studies decline or if they are sustained over a long period of time. I guess on the treatment side my heart is still with medication development. All the advances in neuroscience and genetics should lead to more potent medications with better efficacy than we have today.

A: What do you think is an important message for the public to have about alcoholism, alcohol abuse and alcohol dependence?

RF: I would like to see the general public aware that alcoholics can and do recover, rebuild their lives and become good citizens. Obviously this does not happen to all.

A: Now that you are officially retired do you see yourself continuing to play a role in supporting the alcohol research agenda going forward?

RF: The time has come for me to pass the baton to other able people. I am certainly willing always to offer my opinion but I have had my innings so to speak.

References

Chick, J., Gough, K., Wojciech, F., Kershaw, P., Hore, B., Mehta, B., Ritson, B., Ropner, R. & Torley, D. (1992) Disulfiram treatment of alcoholism. *British Journal of Psychiatry,* 161, 84–89.

Fleming, M. F., Barry, K. I., Manwell, L. B., Johnson, K. & London, R. (1997) Brief physician advice for problem alcohol drinkers: A randomized controlled trial in community-based primary care practices. *Journal of the American Medical Association,* 277, 1039–1045.

Fuller, R. K., Branchey, L., Brightwell, D. R., Derman, D. R., Emrick, C. D., Iber, F. L., James, K. E., Lacoursiere, R., Lee, K. K., Lowenstam, I., Maany, I., Neiderhiser, D., Nocks, J. J. & Shaw, S. (1986) Disulfiram treatment of alcoholism: A Veterans Administration Cooperative Study. *Journal of the American Medical Association,* 256, 1449–1455.

Fuller, R. K. & Roth, H. P. (1979) Disulfiram for the treatment of alcoholism: An evaluation in 128 men. *Annals of Internal Medicine,* 90, 901–904.

Holder, H. D., Saltz, R. F., Grube, J. W., Treno, A. J., Reynolds, R. I., Voas, R. B. & Gruenwald, P. J. (1997) Summing up: Lessons from a comprehensive community prevention trial. *Addiction,* 92 (supplement 2), S293–S301.

Institute of Medicine (1989) *Prevention and Treatment of Alcohol Problems: Research Opportunities.* Washington, D.C.: National Academy Press.

Institute of Medicine (1990) *Broadening the Base of Treatment for Alcohol Problems.* Washington, D.C.: National Academy Press.

Perry, C. L., Williams, C. L., Veblen-Mortenson, S., Toomey, T. L., Komro, K., Anstine, P. S., McGovern, P. G., Finnegan, J. R., Forster, J. L., Wagenaar, A. C. & Wolfson, M. (1996) Project Northland: Outcomes of a communitywide alcohol use prevention program during early adolescence. *American Journal of Public Health,* 86, 956–965.

Project MATCH Research group (1997) Matching alcoholism treatments to client heterogeneity: Project MATCH posttreatment outcomes. *Journal of Studies on Alcohol,* 58, 7–29.

Wagenaar, A. C., Murray, D. M., Gehan, J. P., Wolfson, M., Forster, J. L., Toomey, T. L., Perry, C. L. & Jones-Webb, R. (2000a) Communities mobilizing for change on alcohol: Outcomes from a randomized clinical trial. *Journal of Studies on Alcohol,* 61, 85–94.

Wagenaar, A. C., Murray, D. M. & Toomey, T. L. (2000b) Communities mobilizing for change on alcohol (CMCA): Effects of a randomized trial on arrests and traffic crashes. *Addiction,* 95, 209–217.

3

Conversation with Cees Goos

Cees Goos is a Dutch national who worked for 15 years in senior staff positions at the World Health Organization (WHO) in Copenhagen, and who was responsible for developing a regional programme on substance abuse. He helped to set up the European Alcohol Action Plan, a seminal international public health initiative.

Early Awareness

Addiction (A): Cees, most people will know you through your work for WHO Europe. But before we get to that part of your life, perhaps you can tell us how you became involved in the field of substance use and abuse.

Cees Goos (CG): I was fortunate enough to grow up in a happy family in the countryside of Holland. At home drugs or alcohol were literally far away. Perhaps a glass of jenever (Dutch gin) for the adults at special occasions, and at the age of 16 the boys in the family were invited to join in this ritual. I recall a person visiting us every now and then, a friend of the family living in the town nearby, who held a position of some importance in what I now think was a teetotallers' association or a treatment centre for alcoholics. To me, that was a very strange and alien world.

A: Other early awareness?

CG: The other early childhood association I have with substance abuse was the hushed rumours in the family at home every now and then when a neighbour had been dropped off at his doorstep the previous night after a drinking bout, which seemed to me equally strange. It was not until I had become a university student that I became genuinely interested in the use of alcohol and drugs. This was in the 1960s. Experimenting with drug taking, or other people using drugs, was something almost everybody had experience with.

A: So you became intrigued as to why people behaved in this way?

CG: Yes, I became intrigued about substance abuse early on, because around me I noticed some of my fellow students and friends, who were very much like me, being arrested for drug use, landing up in prison or, as it was called at the time, freaking out, and ending up on a psychiatric ward for a shorter or longer period of time. Throughout my life that question has kept me puzzling.

The Influence of the Environment

A: Why do people take drugs?

CG: What has impressed me always in this regard—but this may be the bias of my university education in social sciences—is the massive influence of the environment, the culture we live in, the examples within our own circles. Drug taking in the 1960s was part and parcel of the counter-culture, a movement that spread very rapidly throughout the western world. Somewhat later drug taking went beyond the counter-culture movement, and became a way of life for many who had no sympathy or even understanding of the anti-authoritarian counter culture.

A: What happens to freedom of choice?

CG: The almost universal use of cigarette smoking those days (and unfortunately even now still in many places) cannot be understood without duly recognizing the unavoidable, inescapable huge impact of the environment on the individual's choices. The freedom of choice not to smoke is just a theoretical freedom in a world where everybody smokes. The freedom to say no to drugs is only a theoretical freedom in a city district where life runs on drugs. I am a believer in shaping the environment towards a better life.

A: It sounds as if your student days were important in stirring certain awarenesses?

CG: Fantastic young years through secondary school and university, from which I graduated in 1969. An influential book was Howard Becker's Outsiders (Becker 1963).

Early Research Experience

A: How did you start out in research?

CG: Everybody used stuff, so I did too. I guess I was a normal child of my time in being keen to explore the world around me, including exotic places and exotic experiences. The difference perhaps was that my fascination for unorthodox or deviant behaviour—and its derailments—became the subject of my study as well. My university professor at the time encouraged me and a fellow student to conduct a survey on drug use among high school students, which we did. It probably was one of the first of its kind in western Europe on this scale. We had some 1500 respondents.

A: Quite a considerable undertaking for an undergraduate. Did you have any institutional support?

CG: Essentially it was performed by the two of us in about 6 months.

Setting Out on a Career Path

A: In a sense, one was not deviant using drugs at the time. How acceptable and 'normal' was it in student circles?

CG: Yes, I reckon I was part of a large minority of about 40% who experimented or used drugs recreationally. At the beginning of my professional career I worked on a project in penitentiaries for the Justice Department, and occasionally came across drug offenders, some with more or less the same background as I had had. It made me wonder, how is it that I had been lucky and they had not?

A: Was that your first official job?

CG: In the criminal justice system. For 1 year I became involved in a project aimed at improving the rehabilitation process of prisoners through investigating the lack of cooperation between community health and social services and the criminal justice system. Through this job I learned about the noise and the smell in prisons, about the devastating effects that even a short stay in a prison can have on the life of the prisoner. As an aside of this job I worked on the establishment of a local Youth Advisory Centre (JAC) to cater for the need to have better opportunities for the rehabilitation of released young offenders. Voluntary work, unpaid. At the end of the criminal justice project I decided to search for a job abroad. Via UNESCO in Paris, I ended up in the Sudan, and later Egypt, as a researcher in a global evaluation of functional literacy. After a few years, my interest in working in the substance abuse field pulled me back to my home country and I found a job as a scientist in the prevention department of the FZA, the national alcohol and drug agency.

A: A lasting career path this time?

CG: Our intention was to shift the focus away from the alcoholic patient or opiate addict to a public health perspective, which was almost totally absent at the time. It turned out as a sort of health advocacy activity, trying to influence a large audience through frequent media exposure, conferences and writing books and brochures. I witnessed a shift in emphasis from the medical, residential settings to more basic help in primary care, family and social work, things such as finding a suitable house. It was also a time of decriminalization of drug use, particularly marihuana. One day, coming to the office we found our desks being occupied by the junkiebond.

World Health Organization (WHO) Calling

A: But then you began to move in some more international directions?

GC: Yes. During my years in the FZA my bosses allowed me to conduct some work for the International Council on Alcohol and Addiction (ICAA), at the time the only international platform for non-governmental organizations (NGOs) collaborating in the field. Through the ICAA, I was asked by the United Nations Fund for Drug Abuse Control (UNFDAC) [now United Nations Office on Drugs and Crime (UNODC)] to develop and coordinate model programmes for demand reduction. It was in 1986 that I was asked by John Henderson, then WHO regional adviser for mental health in Copenhagen, to develop a regional drug prevention programme, next to the already existing alcohol one. Later on, both programmes were to be joined. Henderson made me understand that the primary task was to elaborate at a regional European level an overview of the implications of alcohol and drug-taking for public health. Staff consisted of not much more than 'half a secretary'.

A: Were you, at that time, arguing that monitoring was essential for informed decision making, much like evidence-based policy development?

CG: Quite. That was, and is still, mainstream. However, much of the sense or power of monitoring emerges only after targets have been set. With limited resources we produced two reports which, even by current standards, are not bad at all (World Health Organization 1992).

A: Would I be way off the mark in stating that the role of your Copenhagen office was a codifying one?

CG: The codifying role, which the Regional Office had through its work on Health for All (HFA), has had a tremendous influence on public health policy-making in Europe, including substance abuse. I would refer to the early initiative of WHO in the 1960s to come to the standardization of epidemiological research instruments (the so-called green series) (Smart et al. 1980, 1981).

Making Things Happen

A: What has been the impact of your WHO efforts?

CG: Probably something approaching a more appropriate ranking of alcohol problems and of prison health in the overall frame of public health; and in terms of projects, the European Alcohol Action Plan and the Health in Prisons Project, respectively. Both have set standards and models for member states to use as measuring rods. WHO creates models, standards. It has no authority whatsoever over what the member states do with the information provided. What we did well in this area is the guidance we provided on HIV risk connected to drug use (World Health Organization 1998).

A: During your stay in Copenhagen did you lose contact with the Dutch social and political situation?

CG: Certainly, even to the extent that I felt more familiar with the situation in some other member states than in my own country. I am convinced that you have to leave your national identity behind when entering WHO.

A: What about remaining true to yourself, your own personal ideas in such a position?

CG: In the Copenhagen office one probably used to have more room in this respect than in the Geneva HQ office.

Action Time

A: How did the European Alcohol Action Plan come about?

CG: Ilona Kickbusch was our department director at that time. She, Peter Anderson and I were driven by the question: with alcohol use being such an important factor affecting public health, why is it so difficult to get that point across within WHO and with the member states? Peter and Ilona together did a great deal to get alcohol onto the official WHO agenda. Without Peter this action plan would never have been released. The European Alcohol Action Plan had its roots in the Health for All (HFA) ideology, which dates back to the 1970s. The European Regional Office translated HFA into an action programme with 38 specific targets on major issues in public health to be reached by 2000. One of these targets (no. 17) was specifically about alcohol, drugs and tobacco. I think that it was quite a victory to have a separate identity for substance abuse in this framework. The European Alcohol Action Plan itself emerged later (early 1990s). It became clear that the target set for alcohol would not be reached if nothing special or specific was undertaken.

A: The plan consisted of a population approach aimed at a 25% reduction in overall consumption, and also an attempt to target high-risk behaviours. The plan was translated into the European Charter on Alcohol, which was endorsed by most European countries. It was based on ethical principles, such as the right to impartial information, protection against negative effects of alcohol, the right to be safeguarded from pressures to drink and the right to treatment for those with harmful consumption. Why did you choose this form of presentation?

CG: The idea of the Charter on Alcohol was strategic wisdom by Jo Asvall. I think the European Charter was a masterpiece. It combines wonderfully a fundamental ethical framework for alcohol policy with tangible policy guidelines.

A: Trying to convince people of the severity of the alcohol problem and the good sense of the measures to be adopted seems to be the thread in your international career.

CG: It certainly is not something which makes you popular when you advocate for protective measures in an era that is full of free market ideology. Yet I was, and I remain, sceptical about public–private collaboration when it comes to such things as food and alcohol. I think it is virtually impossible to have a real collaboration between the alcohol industry and the public health community without sizeable cost to public health.

A: Parallels with tobacco?

CG: Yes, parallels with the tobacco industry spring to mind. Not long ago we still had considerable trouble finding proof for the attempts of the tobacco industry to mislead the public and politicians. I personally know of attempts by ICAP (International Center for Alcohol Policies: the Washington-based alcohol industry lobby) to influence the WHO agenda. There have been talks at a high level in the organization about possible themes of mutual interest.

A: No communication at all between public health and industry groups?

CG: All this is not to argue that there can be no communication at all between industry and public health. As a matter of fact, I myself always insisted on having communication with the alcohol industry. Therefore, we had regular meetings with the Amsterdam Group in which we informed reciprocally on public health-related activities. I, however, never accepted their invitation to start collaboration.

A: The Gorbachov anti-alcohol campaign—that was a supply-side policy taken to the extreme?

CG: The strict measures of that campaign did have a measurable effect on consumption and damage. However, the administration failed in creating a consensus in politics and society, which is a prerequisite for long-lasting effects.

A: Is control of supply, restriction of availability the only type of measure that really works?

CG: There can be little doubt that educational efforts and public campaigns, by themselves, have only limited success.

A: What do you see as future developments in the field? Signs of a decreased political willingness to intervene are not really hopeful, are they?

CG: I think the picture is not so bleak. I foresee a gradual change towards more protection of the consumer and his or her environment: a perspective which implies a further decrease in availability, at least in well-defined geographical or psychological situations. I think we will see the development of alcohol-free realms of life, such as traffic, transportation, sports, schools. It is likely that, increasingly, workplaces will also become alcohol-free. One may acknowledge the historical and cultural roots of drinking practices, but not at the expense of young lives being ruined or even destroyed.

A: Give us, please, the formal listing of your WHO positions.

CG: I joined WHO–EURO as a staff member in 1986, first as a psychoactive drugs scientist; I became a regional adviser on substance abuse a few years later, served as acting director for health promotion and disease prevention intermittently for a period of almost 4 years, was also simultaneously coordinator for health in prisons for 5 years, and retired in 2001.

Eternal Recurrence

A: At the end of this interview, would you like to add anything we missed along the way?

CG: I have been struck time and again by the power that addiction has over people. Sad to see, but also fascinating. I have also seen people close to me lose control over their lives. Evert Dekker, for example, who used to work quite high up at the Ministry of Health, in Holland, a top civil servant, who at the end of his career developed a very serious drinking problem and who had the courage to come out in public (Dekker 1998).

A: Did you ever use tobacco?

CG: I became addicted to tobacco in the real sense, smoking even while driving a motor cycle. I quit a long time ago. Now I run for pleasure and feel good with that. Industry tells us that users are free and individually responsible, that they should and can cope without any support from so-called public health-orientated restrictive measures. That message is a fiction.

A: Any book or report which has specially influenced your thinking?

CG: What influenced me greatly at the time was the Purple Book (Bruun et al. 1975).

A: Retired from WHO, a private consultant, busy as ever, what is your current project?

CG: There are a number of issues on which I am still working, either as a consultant or as a volunteer. But to end this interview, I want to mention the names of some colleagues for whose collaboration I have over the years been specially grateful, besides those already mentioned: Griffith Edwards, Ambros Uchtenhagen, Rob van Amerongen, Klaas Brijder, Pavel Bem, Jan Walburg, Arnold Trebach, Martin Mitcheson, Jo Casselman, Rudi Mader, Franklin Apfel, Ove Petersson, Archer and Eva Tongue, Antoni Gual, Teresa Robledo de Dios, Emanuele Scafato and as a matter of fact the whole group of national counterparts of the European Alcohol Action Plan.

A: That ends the interview with Cees Goos, with him in his own modest style giving credit to others.

References

Becker, H. S. (1963) *Outsiders: Studies in the Sociology of Deviance.* New York: Free Press.

Bruun, K., Edwards, G., Lumio, M., Mäkelä, K., Pan, L., Popham, R. E. et al. (1975) *Alcohol Control Policies in Public Health Perspective,* 25. The Purple Book. Helsinki: Finnish Foundation for Alcohol Studies.

Dekker, E. (1998) *Het Beleid Beleefd Vraaggerichtheid Van Ggz En Verslavingszorg [The Experience of Policy: Demand-Oriented Mental Health Care and Addiction Treatment].* Trimboslezing 1998, jrg. VII no. 3–1998. Utrecht: Trimbos Instituut.

Smart, R. G., Arif, A., Hughes, P. H., Medina Mora, M. E., Navaratnam, V., Varma, V. K. et al. (1981) *Drug Use Among Non-Student Youth.* WHO Offset Publications, 60, 1–58.

Smart, R. G., Hughes, P. H., Johnston, L. D., Anumonye, A., Khant, U., Medina Mora, M. E. et al. (1980) *A Methodology of Student Drug-Use Surveys.* WHO Offset Publications, 50, 1–55.

World Health Organization (1992) *European Summary on Drug Abuse.* First report (1985–90). Copenhagen: WHO Regional Office for Europe.

World Health Organization (1998) *Principles for Preventing HIV Infection Among Drug Users.* Copenhagen: WHO Regional Office for Europe, World Health Organization.

4

Conversation with Enoch Gordis

After 15 years as director of an alcohol treatment program in New York City, Enoch Gordis was appointed director of the US National Institute on Alcohol Abuse and Alcoholism (NIAAA) in 1986. He met that responsibility with outstanding success. In 2003 he was a recipient of an honorary Jellinek Award.

Starting Off in Medicine—And Music

Addiction (A): I would like to talk with you about your career and achievements and the influences on your personal career path.

Enoch Gordis (EG): I think there were influences on my choosing medicine as a career. Although there were no doctors in my immediate family, medicine was a highly respected profession. But as far as getting into the alcoholism world, there really were no family influences. There was no alcoholism that I knew of in my immediate family or in close relatives. I was raised in a fairly observant Jewish family. My father was a distinguished rabbi. Although the prevalence of alcoholism in Jews is said to be low, it is probably higher than people think. Nevertheless, it was a topic remote from the Jewish culture in which I grew up. But had you asked me in medical school whether I would be entering into this world, the answer would have been, 'I don't know what you're talking about.'

A: You went to Columbia University and you are from New York originally.

EG: New York City born and bred.

A: When you entered college, what were you planning to do at that time?

EG: I began as a pre-engineering student, but by the second year, I had changed my mind to premed. It was Columbia University: the college was wonderful and the medical school was good. I ended up in internal medicine. I enjoyed the basic sciences very much.

A: Any specially memorable teachers?

EG: They had some real stars there; for example, Alfred Gilman, co-author of Goodman and Gilman's text on pharmacology, was our pharmacology teacher. When we entered the clinical years, we had famous teachers such as Dr Robert Loeb, who was the Chair of the Department of Medicine. I did not fully enjoy the clinical side of medicine until I was a few years older, when I began my residency. I had a fellowship year in the laboratory of Drs Solomon Berson and Rosalyn Yalow at the Bronx Veterans Administration Hospital. I had the chance to see, first hand, the way great scientific minds operate. This was unforgettable.

A: Berson played the violin—did you share music with Sol?

EG: Occasionally. Music is a big part of my life, too, and was, in fact, for Sol. I play the piano pretty well and the cello badly.

Working with Vincent Dole at Rockefeller

A: And after your fellowship?

EG: I then wanted to go back to research. Sol Berson introduced me to Vince and that led to a 10-year stay at the Rockefeller University laboratories with Vince.

A: So the focus in Dole's laboratory when you arrived?

EG: When I arrived in 1961, the laboratory was very much engaged in the metabolism of lipids.

A: When did Dole begin to get interested in addiction?

EG: It was around 1962. How that happened was one of the unpredictable events that shape history. Vince Dole agreed to substitute one night for a member of a committee that New York City had established to look into the heroin problem. What struck him was that everybody had opinions but nobody had any evidence. So he decided to look into the heroin issue from scratch, with no biases. The way to do that at Rockefeller was to admit some heroin addicts into the hospital and study them on Rockefeller's clinical research unit. You have to understand that Rockefeller was a very elegant place—well-manicured lawns, wood-paneled libraries, tennis court and an understated, slightly aristocratic style. So the idea of bringing heroin addicts into the sacred halls of Rockefeller was novel. There was an undercurrent of derision for the scientific direction which Vince had chosen.

A: Marie Nyswander was around at that time?

EG: Marie Nyswander joined him from Lexington. She had a lot of clinical experience and had written very perceptively about the disease concept of addiction. She knew the patients intimately and was a brilliant psychiatrist who later became Vince's wife. But she was also his scientific partner.

A: I can guess what comes next . . .

EG: But then they tried methadone. It had two virtues. It was active orally, and its effects lasted a long time. They started giving methadone in increasing doses as the patients became tolerant to it. Remarkably, the patients' conversation shifted from drugs to ordinary topics such as work, school, sports.

A: Vince was an important influence on your professional life?

EG: Vince had a very great influence on me. He and Sol Berson were the two greatest scientists I have had the privilege to work with. In the company of bright people, these two still stood out. First of all, they managed to see a lead immediately—they could smell it. The second thing is that they never let the technology dictate the question. I could never perform at a level anywhere near that. But at least, I learned what the ideal was.

Ruth Fox and the Start of a Professional Interest in Alcoholism

A: How did you move into the study of addiction while you were at Rockefeller?

EG: The whole ambience of the laboratory was in the addiction world. Marie introduced me to Ruth Fox, a distinguished psychiatrist who had been interested in alcoholism for a long time. Marie had fixed me up with Ruth because I wanted to learn something about alcoholism.

A: When you talk about both Marie Nyswander and Ruth Fox, the idea of really talking with patients and treating them as a way to understand what the essential questions are, is apparent.

Patients can nake the Hypotheses

EG: Well, from the scientific point of view, you listen to the patient and he is telling you the hypothesis. Marie emphasized that to Vince.

A: I know you ran a treatment program for many years and must have had the opportunity to listen to many patients.

EG: Yes. I left Rockefeller in 1971 and had an opportunity to establish and direct an alcoholism treatment program at the City Hospital at Elmhurst, one of the affiliated hospitals with the Mount Sinai School of Medicine. During the next 14–15 years I was responsible for the care of almost 15 000 patients and I must have seen several thousand myself. I respected the fact that unless science was the foundation of treatment and policy we were going to be in trouble. That was one of the problems in our field. We had many slogans but very little science—especially on the treatment end. I would often be surprised to find that the whole agenda of an alcoholism meeting was to trumpet some banality such as 'alcoholism is a family disease'.

Taking on the Directorship of NIAAA

A: So the reason you were sought out as a candidate for the Institute Director was because of your commitment to science as the basis for our field, and you ran a program that was well respected.

EG: I think that helped.

A: And by then you certainly had a sense of the constituency?

EG: At the time I came to NIAAA, I think it was extremely important to have a sense of the constituency, and what the impediments were. There were real problems faced by the treatment community—skepticism about treatment results, ambivalence in the public about whether alcoholism was a disease or a sin, problems with money. On the other hand, sometimes the treatment field was its own worst enemy—by taking an antiscience approach, as if AA had all the answers in 1935 and there was nothing more to learn. Outcome data was seen as unnecessary. The idea of carrying out research on patients, to many of the old-timers, was anathema.

A: So what was for you the route to NIAAA?

EG: The actual route to my being chosen to head NIAAA was just an accident—like many things in life that are important. The position was vacant—my predecessor, Bob Niven, had retired. There was an able acting Director, Loran Archer. Charlie Lieber called me at my office in Queens, New York and said, 'You know, the NIAAA Director position is open—how about you?' I was not surprised by the interview because the night before the interview I sat down with my computer and I said to myself, 'What would I ask if I were on the search committee?' and listed the questions. They asked everything I had thought of. I discussed the kinds of things we have been talking about, that we have to substitute science for the slogans. They asked me what were the biggest problems in our field. Of course, our biggest problem has not changed: we did not have a lay constituency for research, and 14 or 15 years later we still do not. It's better now, but we do not have a group supporting us like the American Heart Association. I was chosen and I was very pleased because the other candidates were excellent people. I have loved it. No job is all paradise, but the intellectual core of the work here is super. The science is interesting on every front. The chance to advance the field in a public way is also very good. I love working with the marvelous staff. It is a pleasure to come in here and be around such able people and to laugh about things together.

NIAAA and the Setting of Objectives

A: You have now been the Institute Director for 15 years?

EG: Yes.

A: In those 15 years, what were the objectives in the beginning for you and transitions after that?

EG: Originally the Institute had science as only one of its components with its meager budget. We also funded treatment programs and demonstrations. Things were changing. The Institute became much more science-oriented. But the biggest change—and that was mostly in the first years—was to change the whole image of what the field was about—that it was a field, like any other area of medicine, that it had to be science-based. The treatment community would have to be persuaded that the separation of the science from the treatment community had to end. Treatment without science is witchcraft. We had to stop claiming rates of treatment success for which there was not the slightest shred of evidence. We had to make a better effort on the research side to communicate what we are finding.

A: From then on?

EG: Nowadays we have large controlled clinical trials on one hand, major findings in human and animal genetics, neuroscience and toxicology on the other. Prevention became based on comparison trials, and we had some major conceptual advances in the field in the last 20 years. I think I can say that the efforts of the Institute have been productive in many areas. Without very, very able people around me, nothing would have happened. However, I think that one job of Institute Director is to choose directions. So its been an exciting time. The more difficult obstacles have not been to get the science going. Getting science to be recognized as an indispensable component of advances in our field by the whole community—that has been the biggest obstacle, and I think we have made some gains. Not utopia, but I think we have made some gains.

The Reputation of Addiction Science

A: Earlier, you talked about Vincent Dole being sort of stigmatized in a way by his shift into drug addiction.

EG: Yes, but that disappeared with time.

A: Do you feel as if research on addictions is now perceived as more mainstream by the larger community of researchers?

EG: Yes, it definitely is becoming more mainstream. You can see it in all sorts of ways. You see questions on addiction on the boards of Internal Medicine. There is a psychiatry subsection on addiction. Addiction research makes the science columns of the popular press and the electronic media. So there is no question, it is radically different than it was 15 or 20 years ago. Still and all, I think that if, for example, you want to do molecular biology of addiction, drugs, or alcohol—some people in the universities might tell you to choose some other route for your future. But it is certainly not the same death trap that it might have been viewed as by the academic world 20 years ago.

A: Who do you listen to when making choices?

EG: You asked me what my family influences were. Here is one. The Talmud says at one point, 'Who is wise? He who learns from every man,' and it is funny that my attitude has been shaped by that. I believe that the best people in every discipline in our research world have important things to tell us. The psychosocial research, especially prevention research, tends to be expensive, fuzzier, not as crisp as doing a study on some changes in neurochemistry. However, the fact is that rational social policy which follows from the application of science- based interventions—for example—legal alcohol levels for driving, minimum age for drinking – has already saved thousands of lives. We cannot make that claim yet for either genetics or neuroscience. The benefits of genetics and neuroscience are largely for the future. But my view that we have valuable things to learn from the best people in all disciplines has paid off. It is funny that this attitude derives from my childhood. Some of these things leave a mark.

Looking Towards the Future

A: Where do you see the future of the Institute? Or your career at this point?

EG: Well, I am 70 years old. Some people want to die at NIH if they are there, but I am not sure I am one of them. I have many interests. I might want to have a few years to pursue them again—whether it is grandchildren, music, the outdoors, and several others. Not that I want to give up thinking about this field. I think we have terrific people out there now, any one of whom would make a splendid Institute Director. It will still be important to understand the politics of this field as well as the science.

A: These days would someone's degree be important in determining whether they could be Director?

EG: I do not think one would have to preclude anybody on account of their degree from being Institute Director.

The Need to Develop a Lay Constituency

A: You have mentioned that you think one of the most important things is that we need to develop a lay constituency for alcoholism research. Do you think that is going to be accomplished in the next 10 years?

EG: Constituency groups for other diseases have generally been formed by the families of the afflicted. They demand more research to help cure their loved ones, and they are vocal in Congress, and in the media. I see several obstacles that we must overcome before we will have such a constituency. The first obstacle is the stigma attached to the diagnosis of alcoholism. Many people are ambivalent about alcoholism—they may believe it is a disease, but at the same time consider it a matter of defective character. Relatives of alcoholics are still not prepared to act together to demand more money for research.

A: Other obstacles?

EG: Another obstacle to developing a constituency for alcohol research is that the enormity of the alcohol problem is not noted by the public the way it notices the 'war on drugs'. Alcohol problems cost more and kill more than all the illegal drugs combined, and the drug most likely to kill your teenager is alcohol. The beverage industry often likes to imply that this is not so. A final obstacle to developing a lay consitutency is intellectual. There are subtle issues within the 'disease concept of alcoholism' to which our field probably has not devoted enough attention. I define alcoholism as a persistent pathological appetite for alcohol—a pathological motivational state. But even if one accepts that, the issue of volition presents ambiguities that the public senses even if it cannot articulate them. Our own thinking has to be clear for the public to be convinced.

The Need to Broaden the Public's Vision

A: Looking back on your career, what do you see as your most important contributions to the field?

EG: I suppose what I have been able to accomplish at the Institute here. To be, essentially, a lubricant for the work of the very talented scientists we support and to do my best to see that the Institute remains secure.

A: Bridging science and treatment—what success there?

EG: Where we still have problems is with the public. The public is thirsting for scientific information, but they, themselves, are wrestling with their own ambivalences about alcoholism because it's so difficult to live with an alcoholic. That dilutes goodwill and willingness to listen. I remember one month—the residents spent a month with us on the program—a resident came up to me at the beginning of his tour and said to me, 'Dr Gordis, I'm going to be frank with you. My brother is an alcoholic. He made life hell in our family. I don't like alcoholics'. But at the end of the month he told me that his vision had been broadened and that is what we must do with the whole public.

5

Conversation with Leland H. Towle

Lee Towle played a crucial role in developing the National Institute on Alcohol Abuse and Alcoholism's (NIAAA's) international activities. He did much to foster productive US relationships with the World Health Organization (WHO).

From Bench to Desk Research

Addiction (A): You enjoyed a long and productive career in the field of alcohol studies, first with the Stanford Research Institute (SRI), then with the National Institute on Alcohol Abuse and Alcoholism (NIAAA). Yet your academic training in Chemistry and Business does not seem to have prepared you for the kinds of work you performed over a 25-year period. What got you started in alcohol research administration, international relations and policy analysis?

Lee H. Towle (LHT): I started at SRI, in 1956. After 3 or 4 years doing bench research, which was interesting, but limiting given that I was not a PhD, my scientific/technical knowledge was loaned out to a project in another department. In effect, over a few years, my work moved from the 'bench' to the 'desk' and the research reports that were produced were based on information-gathering in the field rather than the laboratory. During the 1960s, I was asked to participate in a couple of European-based projects and the challenges were quite rewarding. This was the beginning of my international research and international relations interests, which ultimately became a major focus of my career. With time and growth in my capabilities in applied contract research at SRI and after some major projects that involved information/data systems development in the health and medical field, I was given the OK to establish a small program in 'health sciences research' funded by government contracts.

A: One of your first areas of focus was on the monitoring and evaluation of alcoholism treatment at SRI in the late 1960s and early 1970s. What was the role of the US government on the emergence of a viable alcoholism treatment system during this period?

LHT: It actually began in 1971 after creation of NIAAA by legislation passed by Congress. It recognized alcohol abuse and alcoholism as a major public health problem and charged the Institute with the responsibility for planning and developing programs to deal with the problem. This included establishing a viable US alcoholism treatment system.

The first Director of NIAAA was absolutely insistent that if the Institute was to be held accountable for funding these centers, then they must collect the information necessary to ensure that the centers would not only be monitored, but also evaluated. My small SRI Health Sciences Program was fortunate to receive one of the first contracts to establish a system for monitoring the alcoholism treatment centers. As we succeeded, additional contracts were forthcoming and my career and reputation in 'alcohol research' began in earnest.

The broad-based background of contract research studies at SRI was paramount to undertaking the work for NIAAA and ultimately led to my being invited to join the Institute, first as a visiting scientist and then as civil servant.

A: In 1975 you were involved in the development of a seminal report on the role of Alcohol Beverage Control (ABC) Laws on the state level in the USA. What was your perception of the influence of local and state alcohol control policies on the rates of alcohol-related problems in the USA?

LHT: Actually my involvement was rather modest over a 2–3-month period. My main job was to gather and compile information on ABC Laws as they were being implemented by the various States—the two principal categories being monopoly States and license States. The information included number of on-premise and off-premise sales outlets, taxes and prices, days and hours of operation, age for purchase, advertising, etc. My perception from working on this project was that the relationship between alcohol control policies and the rates of alcohol-related problems was not a major factor in the way in which these policies were established and implemented. Of course, social problems such as public drunkenness and DUI, and illicit or 'after-hour' sales, were to be dealt with, but health and medical problems did not seem to be of great interest.

Working with NIAAA

A: You began working at NIAAA as a Visiting Scientist in 1975. As the Institute was only a few years old at that time, you must have had a perfect vantage point to witness the evolution of a federal-level bureaucracy devoted to the prevention and treatment of alcohol-related problems. What was it like in the early years?

LHT: Yes, there were a lot of growing pains. The Institute was part of the National Institute on Mental Health (NIMH) during the first few years. The main thrust was not research at that time—it was on the establishment of the alcoholism treatment system with centers funded by individual grants for training, prevention and treatment. Funds were made available by Congress for this express purpose, and NIAAA had to create the organizational capability to do this. Then there was the external influence of the alcoholism field and some rather influential and vocal people with 'clout' in Congress. Some, but not all, were recovered alcoholics with great intentions but with sometimes misplaced ideas on where the Institute should be headed. Total abstinence as a treatment goal à la Alcoholics Anonymous (AA) was a bone of contention for a few years, as were alcohol-related problems other than alcoholism. Addiction to alcohol was avoided terminology in the early years because it implied alcohol was a drug.

Learning to work within a Federal bureaucracy was sometimes a difficult and time-consuming endeavor. Although party politics was not an issue, the Institute did have to relate to the political party in office and to the pertinent Congressional Committees and Subcommittees. Within the Institute there was also an in-house political environment, as is the case with most organizations. During the early years, the Institute seemed to have a large share of this—not always of a positive nature.

A: What do you see as the Institute's major accomplishments in research and policy during your 20 years of government service?

LHT: I think that NIAAA was not only successful, but very successful in establishing a nation-wide alcoholism treatment system—so much so that even after the direct funding of training, prevention and treatment centers was stopped, Federal funds continued to be made available via block grants to the States. Of course, this was the politics of the times, but if NIAAA had not already been responsible for establishment of the system, the block grants probably would not have had the same result. The cadre of alcohol abuse and alcoholism workers in the field is another major accomplishment, and I think we must also add to that the researchers in the field. The amount of money that has now gone into research is really quite substantial and has created a capability that was not even dreamed of in the early 1970s. The knowledge base has advanced significantly as a result of NIAAA's intramural and extramural research programs. One only needs to compare the latest Reports to Congress on Alcohol and Health with the early reports to see the growth in addiction science.

A: How did the Institute change during this period?

LHT: The 20-year period from 1975 to 1995 saw the Institute mature from one focused on building a nation-wide alcoholism treatment system to one focused on scientific research—not just in the basic sciences but also in the social and policy arenas. The whole NIAAA organization shifted from the initial Institute within NIMH, to an accepted, mature and integral part of the US National Institutes of Health (NIH). The scientific standards of NIAAA also changed substantially during this time with the whole peer-review process growing into the NIH structure.

A: What kind of influence did the NIAAA Director have on the research and policy agenda?

LHT: Substantial!!

A: Whom do you see as the most influential Director?

LHT: Tough question to answer, really. Each Director made his own unique contribution and had influence in a wide variety of ways. I do not believe that naming names would be appropriate.

Developing NIAAA's International Activities

A: When you moved into the Office of Program Development and Analysis (OPDA), you took on responsibilities in relation to policy formulation, legislative initiatives, program planning and evaluation. As an often-nameless bureaucrat in a small and somewhat obscure federal agency, what do you consider your major accomplishments?

LHT: Organizationally, I was responsible for creation of the Policy Studies and Special Reports Branch within OPDA and we designed several studies and commissioned numerous papers and reports, which served the basis for the Third Special Report to Congress on Alcohol and Health. This was such a large effort that in addition to the report that went officially to Congress, a 'technical support' report was prepared with substantially more detailed results and data from the development effort. As one example, we commissioned the first major study of the 'economic costs of alcohol abuse and alcoholism' on US society. We also made major contributions to strategic plans being put together, e.g. national plans to combat alcohol abuse and alcoholism, and had input to the Surgeon General's Report on Health Promotion and Disease Prevention. We also developed and managed the principal information systems used to monitor and evaluate the more than 400 treatment programs being funded by NIAAA. Reports were fed back to each program, to the States, and to the NIAAA staff managing the grants, as well as to the NIAAA Director.

One of my most significant accomplishments began as a relatively modest role as International Activities Officer. Initially, this was mostly a liaison role, coordinating the few international activities of the Institute and representing the Institute in meetings with other governmental levels, and with other international organizations and foreign countries. But, as time went on, this role expanded considerably and by 1981 my role blossomed into almost a full-time job as Director of International Affairs. By then, there was a substantial program of International Collaborative Research with WHO, and collaborative efforts under way or being developed with the governments of several countries, including, Japan, Mexico, Spain and Israel. NIAAA was able to have a significant input into the World Health Assembly Technical Discussions in 1982 and after much groundwork, NIAAA was named officially as a WHO Collaborating Center in 1985.

A: Up to your retirement from NIAAA, you worked as the main liaison between NIAAA and the World Health Organization. What kinds of projects did NIAAA conduct with WHO?

LHT: Liaison with WHO actually began in 1975 with preliminary consultations in 1976 that led up to the beginning of the WHO project on Community Response to Alcohol Related Problems. NIAAA provided the principal backing for this project, both in terms of funds and technical support. It was truly a collaborative research effort that involved participation of the governments and research entities in several countries, initially Mexico, Scotland and Zambia, in addition to the WHO and the NIAAA. This project included community action efforts, and led to a number of other comparative alcohol research studies.

NIAAA also had another significant role in relation to WHO. That involved working together with NIMH and NIDA in collaboration with WHO in the development of the 10th Revision of the International Classification of Diseases. This involved a wide range of activities, including meetings, consultations, technical support, and the conduct of a wide array of epidemiological and nosological studies. Through no small effort, NIAAA was also instrumental in establishing the coding of alcohol's role in casualties in the 10th revision of the International Classification of Diseases (ICD). In fact, alcohol and casualties was a major focus of NIAAA's international research efforts in collaboration not only with WHO, but also with the Addiction Research Foundation in Toronto.

A: What was the rationale for initiating these projects?

LHT: There were at least two major goals. One was to build and strengthen WHO's program of work in the alcohol field, especially in relation to cross-national studies of alcohol-related problems, and applying the knowledge gained to community action programs, such as alcohol education, prevention and interventions appropriate to the particular populations and cultures. In a broad sense, there was genuine interest in assisting the WHO in its programs of work in the alcohol field. Another was to build and strengthen NIAAA's program of international collaborations. The knowledge and experience gained via the WHO program of work led to collaboration with scientists and researchers in other countries. It also enhanced NIAAA's role in developing scientist exchange programs, the conduct and participation in international meetings and the building of alcohol research collaboration with organizations and researchers in other countries.

A: How important are public health agencies like WHO on the development of meaningful alcohol policies and the dissemination of scientific information?

LHT: This should be one of the roles of public health agencies. How well they do depends on numerous factors, money being one, of course, but knowledge and experience being another. The WHO became a leader in the field and many of the countries we dealt with looked to WHO for guidance.

A: You played a critical role in the facilitation of government-to-government contacts between the USSR and the USA at the beginning of the Gorbachev era. How did those contacts develop around alcohol research?

LHT: The problem of alcohol abuse and alcoholism in the Soviet Union was one that was very severe and highly entrenched in its society. At the beginning, contacts were initiated by the USSR by individuals who were well aware of NIAAA's position in the field in the United States. However, because responsibility for USSR's alcohol work was (apparently) situated organizationally in the psychiatric department and clinics, there was a great reluctance by the United States to respond to the overtures of these individuals because of the alleged misuse of psychiatry. The Serbski Institute was presumably at the center of this misuse and that was where, organizationally, the Soviet alcohol work was located initially. I say 'work', because at that time I don't think that a program really existed—but that, of course, was what they wanted to develop and NIAAA was seen as important toward that end. From the NIAAA perspective, the possibility of developing collaboration with the Russians was seen as a way of accessing the potentially rich but mostly unknown body of work being conducted in the USSR in the alcohol field. Initial correspondence with the Soviets was slow and deliberate, even though the political climate in the Gorbachev era was most favorable. I cannot go into the various aspects of this, but it became clear that time was needed to develop a program with the Soviets and the likelihood of this happening would be considerably strengthened if they moved their apparently nascent alcohol effort out of the Serbski Institute. During these early times, in addition to the carefully written correspondence, I had the opportunity of meeting one of the key Russian individuals at a WHO-related meeting in Edinburgh. Although our conversation was limited due to our mutual language difficulties and the fact that I could say very little officially, it became apparent that this was a very positive beginning. Over time we would eventually work together as colleagues and personally became good friends. He and I were the principals behind the eventual bilateral agreement that became the official basis for the collaboration that was developed. This happened, of course, after the first exchange meeting in Moscow between the NIAAA Director, key staff/individuals, and the Russian Director and key individuals.

The evolvement of the bilateral collaborative program of work with the Russians has been well documented, but I would just like to say that it was for me, personally, one of the greatest challenges of my career and one of the most rewarding.

A: During this period, it seems like the bi-lateral agreements and collaboration among US and Russian scientists had a political as well as a scientific agenda. Which was more important?

LHT: In my view, the scientific agenda was always the more important but satisfying the political agenda seemed to be the best way of developing the scientific agenda. Maybe 'best way' is too strong—but, at least one of the ways of building the scientific base.

Time Over Again?

A: If you could do it over again, what would you do differently in the international and policy arena?

LHT: I am not really sure that I would do anything differently, given the constraints and the rules that had to be followed. Actually, I was able to do more than might otherwise have been possible because I generally had the support of Institute Directors or was able to gain it over time. Personally, I found it most rewarding not only to manage the Institute's international program but to also participate in the collaborative research that was done with WHO and with some of the bilateral projects. In my opinion, when I left NIAAA at the end of March 1995, the International Affairs Program was strong and had contributed significantly to the field of international alcohol research. I am proud that just following my departure, I was the recipient of an NIH Director's Award. Not wanting to be boastful and feeling considerable humility in saying this here, the award read: 'For leadership shaping the direction and scientific content of the Institute's international program, enhancing the international image and credibility of research on alcohol related problems.'

6

Commentary

Peter Anderson

Addiction and the Making of Professional Careers in Administration and Government Service

In this section, there are four addiction careers in administration and government service: Cees Goos, a good friend and colleague of mine, who was responsible for the programme on 'substance abuse' in the European office of the World Health Organization; Robert Du Pont, who, amongst many other positions in US government service, became the first Director of the National Institute on Drug Abuse; Leland Towle, who, amongst many other responsibilities, led international activities for the US National Institute on Alcohol Abuse and Alcoholism (NIAAA); and, Richard Fuller who directed NIAAA's clinical and prevention research programme.

The stories of their careers should be read in their own right. In this short commentary, I reflect a little bit on how their stories relate to addictions and lessons from my own career, which I am still in the middle of, and which has ranged from UK-based general practice, global public health, research, and the interface between science and policy.

The Space of Addictions

The interest and challenge of addictions is that they occupy an integral place in their interaction with living, well-being, life and death. The last fifty years, in particular, have been characterised by important changes in people's lives and lifestyles and by strong evolutions in social structures and values. The changing nature of work and of private life, the evolution of consumption patterns, values, attitudes and beliefs of contemporary societies have all changed the place and challenges of addictions to modern society.

Addictions are an extensive feature of many societies, bringing considerable concerns. As their number has increased over the last decades, they have become a focus of social, economic and political attention, sometimes polarising societies and politics. In addition to the widely-acknowledged problem of addiction to various substances, there is a growing problem of new addictions such as gambling, eating disorders, and the use of the internet. A high proportion of all costs in many countries' health systems flow into the treatment of various addictions. In addition, there are costs of prevention and crime, which increasingly have global dimensions.

The space of addictions also allows room for everyone, stretching across the humanities and social sciences and the biological and medical sciences. Expertise in anthropology, biochemistry, cognitive science, criminology, demography, design, economics, education, engineering, epidemiology, evolutionary biology, foresight management, history, journalism, law, mathematics, media, medicine, neurobiology, political science, psychiatry, psychology, psychotherapy, public health, public management, social marketing, social policy, social psychology, sociology, technology, and toxicology, amongst many others, all have a role to play.

If you are in administration or government service, you are hopefully and probably there because you want to promote the common good. Fortunately, there is an extraordinary opportunity for action. The World Health Organization uses a summary measure, the disability adjusted life year, the DALY. DALYs are a composite measure of ill-health, adjusted for the severity of the ill-health, and premature mortality.[1] They measure the gap between current health status and what could be achieved. And, that gap is a challenge, and addiction's contribution to it enormous. Globally, out of the top ten risk factors for the health gap, alcohol is number three, and tobacco number six.[2] For both of these drugs, and, indeed, for illicit drugs, there is an extensive evidence base for highly cost-effective interventions.[3–5] And, governments, through their regulatory, legal and price instruments, and through their authoritative legitimizing functions can make a difference.

What Needs to be Done

Administration and government service can promote the public good and facilitate reducing the harm done by addictions in at least three ways: promoting basic science research on the biology of addictions, ensuring that cost effective and evidence based help is available for those suffering from addictions, and trying to influence policy in favour of the public good.

Basic science could perhaps start from an evolutionary and anthropological perspective as to why humans might get addicted to drugs and behaviours in the first place. Most addictive drugs are ubiquitous in nature, and there are likely powerful evolutionary adaptations that have moulded the biology of human response to them.[6] Human behaviour can probably only be understood in an evolutionary framework.[7] Basic science also has to include brain science, and the interactions between addictive drugs and brain function. For example, there is substantial evidence that many addictive drugs cheat the brain into thinking that addictive drugs give more benefit than they actually do.[8] In this sense, in the real world market, addictive drugs have an unfair competitive advantage that surely needs balance with appropriate regulation.[9]

Addictions are recognized disorders in classification systems of mental and behavioural disorders (for example ICD and DSM). They are also all treatable conditions. But this requires effective identification and the availability of appropriate treatment. A role of a government administration is to ensure that such treatment is available to those who need it. Further, there is extensive evidence that the provision of treatment needs to move upstream to early identification and brief advice for those at risk by virtue of their use, before they move to full blown disorders or dependence.

In general, there appears to be widespread dissonance between the harm that addictions do to societies, including the harms to people other than users, and the governance response. Governance, in this sense, can be understood as the way in which a society or organization steers itself, with stewardship of addictions needing to balance individual freedom and social responsibility, while taking into account social, economic and ethical considerations. A key role of those working in government administration is to facilitate the reduction of this dissonance through providing options and making the arguments for change in public policy.

Skills in Public Policy

What skills then are needed in public policy? First, and foremost, you need to be a good conductor. You cannot do and manage everything on your own. But, you can help steer, guide, motivate, coordinate and facilitate others to be aligned to one score sheet to help make the case for and to help implement appropriate evidence-based policy. A good conductor has a feel for what is going on, the pace needed, and what needs to come to the foreground and what needs to go to the background and when.

As with many complex issues, addictions are not alone in being riddled with vested interests, all of which require careful management. The classic hazard merchants have, of course, the greatest vested interests and try to influence policy at all levels.[10,11] People working in public policy need to understand the hazard merchants' webs of influence[12] and their tactics and strategies for derailing effective policy, and they need to know how to manage these. On the other hand, producers of risk have a role and responsibility at all levels to reduce that risk. This might require tough skills of keeping producers as producers, being responsible for their products and not producers as policy makers, which is the legitimate role of elected bodies. Sometimes, tough behind the scenes negotiations might have to take place and this may require conflict resolution skills.

People working in administration and government service have to have a wide range of competence, including management and communication skills. Addictions are highly emotive topics, and, whilst a cool and rational approach can inform policy making, sometimes emotion has to be answered with emotion. Complex issues have to be pared down to simple, and sometimes emotive issues that touch people. How does it feel to have a young son die of an alcohol overdose? How does it feel for a mother to be incapacitated through an addiction to internet gaming?

How Career Choices are Made

It is difficult to believe that a young person sets out with a definite career plan in the addictions, and chance must surely play an overriding role. This was certainly the case in my own career, when, as a trainee in general practice in Oxford University's academic practice, I was invited to undertake a small study as part of my training. One of my trainers said to me that it seems that university students drink a lot, and why did I not find out how much. And, so I did,[13] and subsequently got hooked on a career in addictions.

Reading through the four career paths in this section, two things strike one: first, if you are going to have a rewarding career, you have to take risks; and second, which is related to the first, you have to know when opportunities come your way, and also how to manage them.

People differ in their risk-taking behaviour, and this difference is also, of course, a determinant of addictive behaviours themselves. Steady conservative approaches have their value, but if you really want to reach out, sometimes bold and unknown choices have to be made to place oneself in opportunities of influence. Sometimes mistakes are made, but career choices are not fixed, and other career paths will come one's way.

And, this means being open to note the opportunities when they come. Many factors can influence the choices made when opportunities are presented: power, money, family, place, beliefs and values to name a few. Perhaps, though, the most important is: am I aligned with the mission and the values of the institution or organization with which I am going to work. Will it bring me the rewards that I am looking for?

What are the Rewards?

Although working in administration and government service can bring immediate benefit when politicians are aligned with evidence based policy that can make a true difference to people's lives, you also need to be patient and be in it for the long haul. Governments and politicians change, and whilst one administration may be counter to the public good as far as addictions are concerned, others may be more favourable. The reward is having the effective options stacked on the shelves, and then bringing them down when the window of opportunity arises.

There are always intellectual challenges, in being exposed to new disciplines, new sciences and new opportunities. Our understanding of addictions is not static, and, keeping an open mind and lifelong learning brings enormous intellectual rewards. The field is big and complicated enough, that one can never know everything.

There are also always design challenges through continuous reframing and redesigning of our understanding of addictions and our governance of addictions, which can bring enormous rewards in terms of facilitating the involvement of different sectors and different approaches to promote the public good. In the end, it is highly satisfying seeing a policy change or a new policy implemented that reduces harm to people and promotes their health and well-being. It is not the same as being a clinician, where often the rewards can be immediate. Rather, it is the longer term and gradual satisfaction of being able to influence one or more parts of a complicated jigsaw that can benefit the public good.

How Could It Be Done Better

But, how in our professional careers could we better influence the public good and how could we, ourselves, be better professionals? Key here is to be reflective and contemplative and not fixed on our own view points and prejudices. Lifelong learning for new knowledge and new skills is essential. People working in administration and government service can be viewed as change agents, but that also means that we should be open to change ourselves, always looking for opportunities for doing things better.

Doing better also means sometimes changing our career paths and working in different places and settings. It also means knowing when to stop and letting others take over. And, perhaps there can be other satisfying outcomes of retirement. Because, although, no doubt, a professional career in addictions, and certainly one in administration and government service can be highly rewarding, work is not all, and there are many other aspects of life that contribute to our own development and well-being.

Notes

1. Murray, C. J. L., Salomon, J. A., Mathers, C. D. & Lopez, A. D. (Eds.). *Summary Measures of Population Health.* Geneva: World Health Organization, 2002.
2. World Health Organization. *Global Health Risks: Mortality and Burden of Disease Attributable to Selected Major Risks.* Geneva: World Health Organization, 2009.
3. Babor T, Caetano R, Casswell S, Edwards G, Giesbrecht N, Graham K, et al. *Alcohol: No Ordinary Commodity* (Second Edition). Oxford, Oxford University Press, 2010.
4. Babor, T., Caulkins, J., Edwards, G., Fischer, D. et al. *Drug Policy and the Public Good.* Oxford, Oxford University Press, 2010.
5. Jha, P. & Chaloupka, F. (Eds.). *Tobacco Control in Developing Countries.* Oxford: Oxford University Press, 2000.
6. Hagen, E. H., Sullivan, R. J., Schmidt, R., Morris, G., Kempter, R. & Hammerstein, P. Ecology and neurobiology of toxin avoidance and the paradox of drug reward. *Neuroscience* 2009, 160, 69–84.
7. Konner, M. *The Evolution of Childhood.* Cambridge, Massachusetts: Harvard University Press, 2010.

8. Academy of Medical Sciences. *Brain Science, Addiction and Drugs.* London: Academy of Medical Sciences, 2008.
9. Anderson, P. Is it time to ban alcohol advertising? *Clinical Medicine.* 2009 9 121–124.
10. Michaels, D. *Doubt is their Product.* Oxford, Oxford University Press, 2008.
11. Richter, J. *Holding Corporations Accountable.* London, Zed books, 2001.
12. Harkins, C. Lobby Watch: The Portman Group. *BMJ* 2010; 340:b5659.
13. Anderson P. Alcohol consumption of undergraduates at Oxford University. *Alcohol and Alcoholism,* 1984, 19, 77–84.

Part 2—Laboratory Life: The Making of Addiction Pharmacology and Behavioural Pharmacology

7

Conversation with Joseph V. Brady

Joseph V. Brady was Professor of Behavioral Biology, Director of the Behavioral Biology Research Center, and Professor of Neuroscience at the Johns Hopkins University School of Medicine in Baltimore, Maryland. He is one of the founders of the field of behavioral pharmacology. In 1992 he was a recipient of the Nathan B. Eddy Award.

Addiction (A): Joe, were you interested in psychology and behavior from an early age?

Joseph V. Brady (JVB): Oh, no. My early home and school years were strongly influenced by the Catholic parochial school system of Brooklyn, New York, and by a Xaverian and Jesuit secondary and college education. When I entered Fordham, a Jesuit college, in 1940, everybody took philosophy, logic, epistemology, and for the first couple of years there was no specialization. Even through college I had no objectives in a psychological direction at all. I joined the Reserve Officers Training Corps (ROTC) while I was at Fordham. By 1942–43, the ROTC was activated, so Fordham compressed the course work and I graduated in less than 3 years. Then I was sent off to officers' training school, commissioned as Second Lieutenant and served as an infantry platoon leader. I was in Berlin by the end of the war, when orders came reassigning me to the 317th Station Hospital in Wiesbaden, Germany, which had just been designated as the Neuropsychiatric Center of the European Command, and that is what changed my life.

A: How so?

JVB: The 317th Station Hospital had been a Luftwaffe hospital, and it obviously had some psychiatric focus. When I reported in to that hospital, the Commanding General sent me over to the Chief of the Psychiatry Service, who greeted me with, 'Am I glad you're here. I've got a Major General up on the 2nd floor. I need a Rorschach on him right away.' I said, 'Yes, Sir', and ran off to the hospital library and came back the next morning to administer the first of some 500 Rorschachs that I would give over the next couple of years. I also learned the Wechsler Bellevue, the Thematic Apperception Test, the Bender Gestalt—I mastered the whole repertoire. Then the Army sent several of us back the United States, me to the University of Chicago, to bring us up to date.

A: Your interests at that time?

JVB: I thought I would get out and go to law school. My father was a lawyer, and my brother. But here came an opportunity to go to school at the Army's expense. By that time I had been made a Captain, and I had a couple of kids. So I went off to the Department of Psychology at the University of Chicago. We were to review the whole of psychology in 9 months and then take comprehensive examinations for the PhD. I was planning to get a degree in clinical psychology. But there was also another requirement. You had to pick an experiment from the literature and replicate it. I picked an experiment that Estes and Skinner had published in 1942[1] on conditioned anxiety. At the end of 9 months, I had completed my comprehensive examinations and had four rats trained so that I could measure their conditioned anxiety levels by the changes in the rate at which they performed their ongoing lever-pressing business. It occurred to me that this was really a very good model of psychiatric disorders expressed as a change in a person's rate of performance. I said perhaps electroconvulsive shock (ECS) could reverse the conditioned anxiety in these rats, so we produced full-blown tonic clonic convulsions in the animals. We had literally 'cured' these animals with the electroconvulsive shock.[2] And I was changed in terms of what I was going to do for the rest of my life. It was perfectly clear. So with all the critical course work and the dissertation done, I spent a year with Carl Rogers.

A: You wrote this up and gained your doctorate?

JVB: Yes, within 2 years. By that time the Army had assigned me to Walter Reed Army Hospital, in Washington, DC, and sent me back to the clinical service conducting Rorschachs again.

A: There was no experimental branch at Walter Reed at the time?

JVB: None whatsoever. Within a year after my arrival, Dave Rioch was hired by what was then called the Army Medical Research Institute, which was in the grounds at Walter Reed but was separate from the hospital. The idea of bringing together all these different disciplines at one place was Dave Rioch's, and Walter Reed was the first interdisciplinary neuropsychiatric research institute. Then Seymour Kety and Joel Elkes put the idea into place at the National Institutes of Health (NIH). Then NIH started awarding grants for such research. Bob Galambos, the neurophysiologist that Dave hired first, asked me to come and give a talk to him and Rioch. And with fire in my belly, I gave them the story about the electroconvulsive shock. I became the first 'Chief' of the department of experimental psychology in the neuropsychiatry division. That is one of the reasons why I have always thought of myself as the beneficiary of a fortuitous environment! In a lecture I gave at last year's meeting of the Federated American Societies of Experimental Biology, when the American Society of Pharmacology and

Experimental Therapeutics gave me the Dews Award for life-time contributions to research, I told them that I was going to present a revisionist history of behavioral pharmacology—that is, the 'great men' approach is not the way to look at the evolution of the field. This field should be viewed as the product of an interaction between methodological developments and conceptual changes.[3]

At that time, I also had an academic appointment at the College Park campus of the University of Maryland, where I established a laboratory and applied for the first behavioral pharmacology program project grant from NIH.

A: How did you, as an Army officer on active duty, come to be setting up a laboratory at a university?

JVB: This all came about as a result of a meeting of the first psychopharmacology study section at NIH. It was a very informal study section scheduled shortly after the appearance of the first tranquilizers—and after Congress had appropriated $2 million for psychopharmacology research in the NIH budget. I wrote the program project grant application from the College Park Laboratory at the University of Maryland asking for a quarter of a million dollars. As you can well imagine, that was a lot of money in the early 1950s. The reviewers ultimately agreed that the science was good and the research necessary, so they approved the first behavioral pharmacology program project grant from NIH.

A: That laboratory turned out to be an incubator for some of the early drug abuse researchers?

JVB: Heading a laboratory at the University of Maryland gave me my first chance to bring in other people on the academic track. What Schuster and Thomson discovered was that for some reason an animal was pressing the lever to obtain the infusion. I said, 'Why don't we try a drug?'. What did that do when animals started self-administering drugs? The prevailing view of alcoholism and drug abuse was that these were events that were largely the result of people being driven into this terrible life-style. Now all of a sudden we had monkeys pressing levers to obtain a drug. It is a perfect example of a methodological development producing a conceptual change: it was clearly the consequences, not the antecedents, that were maintaining the drug self-administration performance.

A: But what about the role of the 'great men'?

JVB: Well the great men are agents. They just happened to be in the right place at the right time. To hang the development of a field on great individuals is misplaced in my view. I think much of it, as an environmentalist, comes as a result of fortuitous events that occur in your life. Think of the fortuitous events that have kept me from being a lawyer!

A: When did you move your research to Johns Hopkins?

JVB: Joel Elkes, who had become Director of the Department of Psychiatry at Hopkins, invited me to join the department there in 1971.

A: You served on the President's Science Advisory Committee in 1961. How did that come about?

JVB: During the Kennedy years the White House put together a special panel to look at promising technologies for the future. Fred Skinner and I were the two behavioral representatives. By and large, Skinner avoided serving on any committees, but he evidently could not refuse. I went up to Boston and stayed with the Skinners while we spent a few days composing our contribution and talking about behavioral technology.

A: In 1961/1962 the word 'psychopharmacology' was just coming into use to describe the new area of research that you were working on, and you were involved with starting the American College of Neuropsychopharmacology (ACNP). Were problems of addiction of interest to that group?

JVB: Yes, I was one of the 'founding fathers' of the ACNP. Abe Wikler and Bill Martin were also part of the original group. The Lexington group and addiction research were well represented.

A: Not long afterward you played a central role in shaping the direction of drug abuse research for the entire country.

JVB: Several years later, I served on the very first NIMH study section on drug abuse. I replaced Jerome Jaffe, who had taken a high level job in the White House. I became the Chairman of one of those very early and very expansive drug abuse study sections.

A: Looking back, do you see some particular point in your work that led you to focus on psychopharmacology and addiction?

JVB: Absolutely. The first paper I published in *Science* was on the effect of reserpine on CER[3] and that led to my helping to set up laboratories at various drug companies—Merck, Lilly, CIBA and so on. It was the basis for the program project grant, and that is how I ended up getting Bob Schuster as my first doctoral student. It was when Bob Schuster and Travis Thompson came to my laboratory at the University of Maryland and Schuster was interested in the way a drug could be used as a discriminative stimulus that the first drug self-administration work started.

A: You continued that line of research after they left?

JVB: We took it to Johns Hopkins and it became the major driver in the laboratory there.

A: How has your abuse liability work evolved over the past 40 years?

JVB: Well, the first animals we used were rhesus monkeys. Then we got a baboon at Walter Reed and we were so impressed with that animal—its hardiness, to start with, and its relative manageability compared to the rhesus monkey. We now have had some 60 baboons in these experiments. The other direction in which that development has gone and is now being practised is extending the notion that just because a drug or a compound is self administered does not necessarily make it bad or dangerous.

A: You were also very much involved with the Committee on Problems of Drug Dependence (CPDD). Can you tell us how it evolved from a committee of the National Academy of Science into the College on Problems of Drug Dependence?

JVB: I was Chairman of the Committee around the transition time. It was still an old boys' club in 1980. It was still not a membership organization when I became Chair. I lobbied to change that. I remember arguing about why I thought the word 'addiction' was an absolutely useless term because it had too much surplus meaning.

A: Perhaps this is a digression, but could you tell us something about your involvement in the National Commission for the Protection of Human Subjects?

JVB: Last year was the 25th anniversary of the Belmont Report, the surprisingly influential product of that Commission first published in the late 1970s and immortalized as the basis for all the ensuing Federal regulations on the use of human subjects in biomedical and behavioral research.

A: You were the president of the Society of Behavioral Medicine, and the Society of Behavioral Pharmacology.

JVB: In both those cases I think the major factor was being in the right place at the right time. The Society of Behavioral Pharmacology was started because many of the people I knew who were working for the drug companies felt somewhat isolated from the academic community. In the early 1970s I was involved in the establishment of the Society of Behavioral Medicine and was its second president. The society is now 25 years old. Last year there were about 12 000 attendees at the annual meeting here in Baltimore.

A: You were also involved with the Pavlovian Society in Russia?

JVB: Yes.

A: Were you able to continue your relationship with the Russians throughout the Cold War?

JVB: Yes, but that came about mainly as a result of the space research and NASA involvement. I had a visit from Wernher von Braun from the Army Ballistics Laboratory. He came to find out whether I would be willing to put some of my 'livestock' into the nose cone of one of his rockets for an experimental space flight. I said I would be willing to give it a try. Von Braun's plan with our monkeys was a ballistic flight with recovery of the animals alive and well. The monkeys—Able and Baker—traveled 300 miles into space at 10 000 miles an hour, splashed down in the ocean and were recovered in good shape. The later chimp flight by Enoch was an orbital flight around the Earth four times and was the pre-test for John Glenn's first US human orbital space flight.

The interesting thing about this space research program and my relationship with the Russians is that throughout the whole Cold War period, the only place a live communication stayed open was in the space business.

A: In 1992 you received the Nathan B. Eddy Award from the College on Problems of Drug Dependence for your work in substance abuse. Given all the things you have done over those years, what did you choose to focus on in your Eddy Award lecture?

JVB: I focused mainly on the behavioral pharmacology of drugs of abuse—their reinforcing and discriminative functions[4]—starting with the *Science* conditioned suppression paper in the 1950s and how the people who have come since then have carried on the tradition in a much more thorough and creative way than I could possibly imagine.

A: You have had multiple and simultaneous careers—the behavior of organisms in outer space, psychopharmacology, drug abuse, research ethics. In the Department of Psychiatry at Johns Hopkins you established and headed a major division, trained and mentored students, and even served at one time as Acting Chairman of the department, and you are still active in clinical research. Can you tell us how one manages to follow so many career paths concurrently?

JVB: You just keep making responses. When an opportunity arises you have to seize that opportunity. However, I have never really felt that I did any of all these things as well as I might have done if all these other things were not going on at the same time. You do the best you can. And you keep waiting for life to get easier, but it never does.[5]

Notes

1. Estes, W. Skinner, B. F. (1941) Some quantitative properties of anxiety. *Journal of Experimental Psychology,* 29, 390–400.
2. Brady, J. V. (1951) The effect of electro-convulsive shock on a conditioned emotional response: the permanence of the effect. *Journal of Comparative and Physiological Psychology,* 44, 507–511.
3. Brady, J. V. (1956) Assessment of drug effects on emotional behavior. *Science,* 123, 1033–1034.
4. Brady, J. V. (1991) Animal models for assessing drugs of abuse. *Neuroscience and Biobehavioral Reviews,* 15, 35–43.
5. Brady, J. V. (1993) What's a radical behaviorist doing in a nice pharmacology club like CPDD? In: Harris, L. S. *Problems of Drug Dependence,* 1992, pp. 19–28. National Institute on Drug Abuse Research Monograph no. 132. NIH Publication no. 93–3505. Washington, DC: US Government Printing Office.

8

Conversation with Elisaldo Luiz de Araújo Carlini (E. A. Carlini)

Professor Carlini is a Brazilian scientist who has made important contributions to the pharmacological understanding of drug misuse. He has profoundly influenced policy responses in his own country, but has also worked with the United Nations.

From Missionary Ambitions to Clinical Pharmacology

Addiction (A): What made you choose a medical career?

E. A. Carlini (EC): One of my strongest motivations was this kind of messianic spirit that I have; I always thought that I had to do things and pay back for living. My idea was to get into a medical school and be a doctor in a missionary boat that ran along the Amazon River. I thought it would be fantastic to dedicate my life to this, simply to be a missionary doctor.

A: What made you move over to psychopharmacology?

EC: Well, I went into the Escola Paulista de Medicina (EPM), a federal public facility, in 1952 and this was a school that was not very science-minded. In the beginning of my second year in the school I made contact with two teachers who were almost the only ones to conduct scientific work wholly and exclusively. One of them was a professor of pharmacology, José Ribeiro do Vale, and the other a professor of biochemistry, José Leal Prado. Those two showed that the only means for the country to develop had to be through science, for only through science could we develop technology, and only through technology could the country stop being underdeveloped. I told them that my greatest wish was to help the general population, especially those less fortunate and underprivileged. They convinced me that if I could give my contribution to the scientific and technological development of Brazil and therefore to its economic development I would be helping, however little, thousands or millions of people who would have a better quality of life. This had a very decisive impact on me.

A: But you dedicated yourself first to the study of arterial hypertension. Tell us about that.

EC: To start working with the two teachers had already been for me a great change of plan, from wanting to be simply a physician to going into research activities. My two teachers were working in the field of experimental hypertension. The interest in psychopharmacology came when the library received the first issue of the journal *Psychopharmacologia* (now known as *Psychopharmacology*). What I could read and understand in that journal had a powerful impact upon me.

New Horizons: An Opportunity to Work in the United States

A: It was then that you received the Rockefeller Foundation Fellowship award?

EC: I spent a year working in psychopharmacology at Tulane, with easy access to a vast bibliography.

A: Where did you move to after that?

EC: I was impressed by the lines of investigation pursued at the pharmacology department of Yale University. Research work in psychopharmacology at Yale was intensive and conducted in an integrated way by three departments: psychology, psychiatry and pharmacology.

A: Even while you were in the United States you thought of returning to Brazil and applying here what was being developed out there?

EC: I had been 4 years away from Brazil and I thought the time had come for me to go back to my country.

A: You were also in the Psychiatry Department with Dr Daniel Freedman?

EC: Yes, I made a good contact with him. So I consider myself a very fortunate and privileged person as regards my background in this area. I worked with great researchers in psychopharmacolgy in those days, who were above all people full of warmth and charm. You do not have to be boring to be a scientist; you can be nice and even kind and gentle.

A Difficult Return Home to Brazil

A: Would you say that those teachers were fundamental for the development of your career?

EC: They undoubtedly molded my destiny. I came back to Brazil in 1964, 3 days before the military took hold of the country, and for 20 years we lived in a dictatorship. It was very difficult for me to cope with that situation, for during the 4 years I had lived in the United States there was much more freedom than here in Brazil. But when I arrived home there was no chance of my being hired by the Escola Paulista de Medicina. I was out of work and I took a job at the Instituto Biológico de São Paulo. I passed a test and was hired and in this job I would perform routine work, such as estimating glucose in the urine of goats.

A: So how did you find your way through those roadblocks?

EC: I went to work at the Santa Casa de São Paulo, a private faculty, which was extremely uncommon in Brazil. At the Santa Casa I created the Departamento de Ciências Fisiológicas, with the disciplines of physiology, biochemistry and pharmacology. I was Professor of Pharmacology and, at the same time, head of the department. I was able to develop a small research group. I stayed at the Santa Casa from 1965 to 1970. In 1970 there was a change of perspective and they no longer wanted to conduct research. So I was out of work again in 1970 and I went back to the Escola Paulista de Medicina and I asked them if they would accept me with my group. I came back to my old home and it is still the place at which I work.

Developing an Interest in Cannabis

A: Around this time you became interested in cannabis?

EC: We started to work with a herb that was very common in Brazil, marijuana (*Cannabis sativa* L.) and publish papers in international journals.

A: But where did this interest come from?

EC: When I began to work as a student of pharmacology at the EPM, Professor Ribeiro do Vale had a great interest in this herb. The one that interested me the most was marijuana. We began to acquire an international reputation. The studies in which I am named as the author have received more than 4000 citations.

A: Even today, with the availability of easy access to the Web, you teach your pupils to keep a constant contact with the library?

EC: Well, I try to teach my pupils. There is complete resistance and I even say that, if you do not take care, the computer makes you an 'idiot savant'.

Building Cebrid

A: You are head of one of Latin America's most important centers, the CEBRID—Centro Brazileiro de Informações sobre Drogas Psicotrópicas. What made you develop this center and how did it begin?

EC: One of the things that the few Brazilian psychopharmacologists missed greatly was that we did not have reliable information about the real dimension of the use of illicit drugs here in Brazil. This was hindering our researches and we did not have access to the papers published by Brazilian authors in Brazilian journals. Many of these journals lack continuity and others, even when indexed, are eventually lost. This was what made us go into the making of this type of resource. We managed to find what is perhaps the very first paper about drug abuse in Brazil, published in 1866 (Lima 1866). We began to see that the few available epidemiological surveys were rather limited. We decided then to conduct a new type of survey. We obtained the permission of the Ministério da Saúde to receive, from 1986 onwards, the quarterly maps of admissions due to drugs and alcohol, overdose and addiction in the whole country. We also began to study use among students.

An Interest in Ethnopharmacology

A: With these researches you have been finding out several ways of using these plants by specific ethnic groups, such as the Indians, for example?

EC: The studies on ethnopharmacology include field studies among the quilombolas, the descendants of ancient slaves, who ran away from the farms and created ghettos. Even today we have these quilombolas on land granted to them by the government, where they do not mix with the white population. They have very peculiar uses for plants, as also do our Indians. The Krahô Indians, for example, use around 150 different plants for the most distinct purposes you could imagine as regards the central nervous system, such as plants to be able to think more clearly, to eliminate bad thoughts, to prevent snoring, to have good dreams, to strengthen memory and so forth.

Speaking to Policy

A: Policy involvements both nation-wide and internationally?

EC: I believe it is part of the role of a university teacher to look at the nature of the society in which the university exists. I always had this concern and was therefore always a controversial professor. We still have to undergo profound changes to come out of cultural colonialism and also the legacy of being a country in which slavery was abolished only theoretically.

A: You became well known for this sort of activity?

EC: Yes. In 1994 I was invited by the Ministro da Saúde to be the head of the Secretaria Nacional de Vigilância Sanitária. This is a very important agency, aiming to control appropriately every health-related product in the country. That was a position requiring its holder to remain away from academic life for the duration of its mandate, a 4-year term. In 1994 I was elected a member of the International Narcotics Control Board (INCB). I was about to take up this position but could not do it, for at the same time I was appointed head of the Secretaria Nacional de Vigilância Sanitária and the INCB did not allow its members to work in an executive governmental capacity.

A: But you were elected to INCB again.

EC: In 2001 I was again a candidate and took up the position. This is a very honorable position, one that gives me great pleasure in being able to contribute to the international community.

A: You have brought to our country discussions about, for example, the classification of marijuana within the list of international conventions.

EC: One of the things that has always worried me about Brazil was the apparent contradiction between the effects of marijuana that we were hearing through interviews with users and through research studies, and what is stated in the press and is contained in Brazilian laws. We did not believe that the statement that marijuana was a terribly addictive and dangerous drug was in agreement with everyday events. Meanwhile, we were very much concerned with the issue of Brazilian law punishing with imprisonment the mere possession of any amount of marijuana. Besides, what happens here is a situation that is associated with corruption. There were cases of police officers 'planting' marijuana inside the car of an apparently well-off youngster, so as to submit him to extortion, or even of parents who managed to convince a policeman by means of bribery to avoid having him taken to jail.

A: What do you think of the way in which the 1961 UN Single Convention regulates cannabis?

EC: I never quite figured out that point of view of the 1961 UN Single Convention on Narcotics Drugs. First, I did not understand why marijuana was classified as a narcotic, nor why it is in Schedule I and in Schedule IV, along with heroin.

Harm Minimization

A: What is your view on harm reduction approaches?

EC: We believe this is something that should be accepted in Brazil. There is actually much less need for substitution treatment with methadone, for example, for cases of this type of addiction in Brazil are almost non-existent. What we believe should be implemented in Brazil is some sort of harm reduction program, such as the distribution of syringes, even though there is great resistance to that. On the other hand, in Brazil we have some parties trying to make these harm reduction measures more widespread, but in an unreasonable way, for they amplify these harm reduction interventions in such a way that their true purpose is disfigured.

A: This concern of yours for concepts, terms, guidelines and public policies has also been part of your contribution to policy formulation and consultation in the Conselho Nacional Antidrogas, the highest ranking agency in our country. What could you tell us about this experience?

EC: This is a relatively long-term experience. The issue of drug abuse in Brazil is peculiar because it is, or was, like a ship adrift, with no direction whatsoever. In 1998, by an act of the President of Brazil, he created the Conselho Nacional Antidrogas and its Secretaria Executiva, the Secretaria Nacional Antidrogas, directly under the power of the Presidency.

A: What of the future?

EC: For the future we are now at a crossroads, which is as follows. We have the CEBRID, which has a solid scientific foundation, is well known in the country and abroad and is currently a collaborating center to the WHO. This center has a group of well-trained researchers working full time. This is one of the things I always considered essential. To work in the area of research you have to commit yourself wholly, body and soul, and that takes great dedication in a country such as Brazil, where everything is much more difficult.

The Man Behind the Scene

A: I would like for you to talk about your family influences. Was there anyone who was important in your choice for a medical career?

EC: Yes. There was the influence of my maternal grandfather, who was a physician, a family doctor, back in the days when doctors took care of everyone in all age groups, and addressed every patient's needs. I remember that I was an avid reader of his books.

A: What about your family?

EC: I am married for the third time, and I have six children from all my marriages.

A: What do you do in your free time?

EC: During my free time I enjoy listening to classical music, especially Beethoven, Mozart, Haydn, etc. I remember two pieces of music that I consider real works of art. One of them, Mozart's Requiem, I heard in the Church of La Madeleine, with the Choir and Symphonic Orchestra of Varsovia. I also particularly remember listening to Bach's Saint Matthew Passion in the Saint Stephen's Cathedral in Vienna. I enjoy operas, especially Italian, among which I stress Verdi's La Traviata as my favorite, with Puccini's Turandot. Another activity that brings me much satisfaction is taking care of my dogs. I have 11 in total, three of which live at my apartment in Sao Paulo, and eight at my summer house.

A: Being the scientist that you are, you have probably travelled a great deal. I would like to know if any place struck you in particular during your leisure trips.

EC: Yes. One of the best experiences I have had outside my country was when I had the opportunity to go on the Route of Santiago de Compostela, in Spain. I have also been to Machu Pichu on two occasions, both of which have been really special for me.

Reference

Lima, J. F. S. (1866) Envenenamento de Duas Pessoas pela Trombeteira. *Gazetta Médicina Bahia,* 1, 67–68.

9

Conversation with Lou Harris

Lou Harris has played crucial and varied roles as a pioneer in the drug research field and has also done much to advance the careers of others. He has brought to pharmacological research a keen understanding of the role of the chemist. In 1985 he was a recipient of the Nathan B. Eddy Award.

Early Influences

Addiction (A): What forces directed you toward science?

Lou Harris (LH): As a kid, I was always interested in science. My parents bought me chemistry sets. I had a microscope and I had a small laboratory in the house. I was driven by curiosity about nature. I started high school in the 10th grade in 1942 and I graduated in 1944 from Boston Technical High. We were in an era that was quite unsettled due to the Second World War. I think my interests were always driven towards chemistry or medicine. As a volunteer at the Beth Israel Hospital, I was doing differential blood counts when I was only 15 years old. We were not a wealthy family, but middle-class. My father was in the wholesale produce business, so we always ate well but we were restricted in luxuries. So, I worked early on, in the family business with my father and my uncles. I was about 16 when I took a part-time job in Filenes Department Store as a bundle boy after school and worked up to the point that I was going around collecting cash from the cashiers. I started working at the Harvard Medical School in the Department of Pharmacology as an animal caretaker in 1943. I worked there continuously to 1950. I worked there until I started college at Harvard in 1950. It was quite an experience because the place was filled with people who later became extremely well-known and productive scientists. I received a great deal of laboratory experience working with many different people in the department.

A: Was a career in pharmacology your goal when you started college?

LH: No, actually towards the latter part of my stay in the pharmacology department, an organic chemist by the name of Fred Uhle came onto the scene and I had this great interest in chemistry and started working pretty much for him. At the same time, I was doyen (head technician) of the department.

A: You did not yourself serve in the military?

LH: I could not get into the military because I was so myopic. I wanted to go to college but my mother had become seriously ill, and only when she died in 1950 was I relieved of that responsibility. I applied at several colleges and was accepted at Harvard as a chemistry major. When I graduated from college, I came back to the department as a PhD candidate.

PhD Training and Early Research Involvements

A: What caused you to go from chemistry (as an undergraduate) to pharmacology?

LH: Well, the PhD in pharmacology was just natural. I continued working for the person I was working for. I worked all the time I was in college. I had to work. I had scholarship help but I had to have extra money. I was conducting clinical chemistry on the effects of anesthesia on patients with liver damage. They were mainly alcoholics that had bleeding esophageal varicies. The interesting thing about it was that we collected huge amounts of data but it was not hypothesis driven. This is not the way to do clinical research.

A: What was the project for your PhD thesis?

LH: The synthesis of lysergic acid and later the pharmacological evaluation of a number of unique substances which resulted from the chemistry. When I completed the chemical portion of my thesis, I had two publications in the *Journal of the American Chemistry Society*[1,2] but when I handed in the thesis, which was a typical organic chemistry thesis, Krayer called me in and said, 'But Lou, you're getting a degree in pharmacology. There's no pharmacology in this.' I went back to do some laboratory work, essentially isolated organ work on the guinea pig ileum and rat uterus.[3]

A: So what next, with your thesis completed?

LH: We were strapped for money. I was married as an undergraduate. By the time of my graduate studies, I had a child and was awarded a National Science Foundation (NSF) predoctoral fellowship and my wife was working. When my PhD finished, Krayer said he wanted me to carry out typical postdoctoral work. I was greatly interested in the area of central nervous system (CNS) pharmacology, a field that was expanding rapidly at that time. So, I went to Sterling.

The Move to Industry

A: Did you start Sterling in the drug abuse area?

LH: No, I started Sterling in the area of psychotherapeutic agents. It was at that time, of course, that Bill Dewey showed up as a technician. We had a major tranquilizer in advanced preclinical study, and several others were coming along. We also had some very interesting stimulants.[4]

A: So what was going on at Sterling when you arrived?

LH: Analgesics were very fascinating. We, early on, had a project team meeting to discuss the current status of the project. For decades, the chemists at Sterling were synthesizing meperidine derivatives. They had prepared more than a thousand of these compounds. We had developed test methods (tail-flick and hot-plate) that were very predictive of clinical activity. The correlations that emerged to be highest were between the tail-flick and the hot-plate tests and addiction potential (0.95).

A: How did you take things forward?

LH: At a later meeting of this project group, I presented my data and said that we were wasting our time. We were testing and bringing compounds to the clinic with a high probability that we were going to fail. The discussion came around to what direction could we go in. That was when my experience at the Mass General came into play. I told them that there were data out there showing that the narcotic antagonist nalorphine was a potent analgesic. It had also been shown in animals and man that nalorphine had essentially no opioid abuse potential. The only problem was that nalorphine had a pretty high incidence of psychotomimetic activity associated with it. My plea was if in all these years we failed to remove dependence liability from analgesia, we should be able to more easily remove the psychotomimetic activity from the analgesia. So we embarked on a new, large project.

A: Pentazocine?

LH: In his controlled double-blind clinical trial, Keats found good analgesia with a potency somewhat less than morphine with no reports of psychotomimetic activity. We were very, very excited about the compound because studies at Michigan and Lexington indicated that it had little or no dependence potential.

A: How did the cyclazocine story develop?

LH: Cyclazocine went to Lou Lasagna for the first clinical testing, which was used in postpartum pain. It turned out to be an extremely potent analgesic.[5] It had very few psychotomimetic effects associated with it at the dose they were using. We were very keen about the compound because, again, it was a very potent antagonist with little indication of dependence liability. It was at that time that Bill Martin, at Lexington, together with Abe Wickler, postulated that if you could extinguish drug-seeking behavior, then the addicts would stay off the drugs. Bill Martin proposed that what we should do was to completely withdraw heroin addicts: give them large doses of an antagonist and then let them go out in the community to test heroin injections. After repeatedly gaining no effect, their drug-seeking behavior would cease. He picked cyclazocine for this.[6] The drug was killed at that point because of the psychotomimetic activity.

Expanding Horizons

A: Despite that setback to your work?

LH: We undertook a great deal of interesting work and at one time had 12 compounds in clinical trial at the same time.

A: The next questions that attracted your attention?

LH: In the early 1960s, the federal government, under the philosophy of John Kennedy, had decided that the United States was going to wage humane warfare. What they started was called an 'incapacitating agent program.'

A: And your group became involved?

LH: When the Arthur D. Little people approached us, we started a joint program, which included cannabinoids, anticholinergics, opiate agonists and antagonists, stimulants and major tranquilizers.

The Move to Chapel Hill

A: What prompted you to leave Sterling?

LH: I was beginning to get a little restless because the only way you could advance in industry, at that time, was to go up the administrative ladder and I thought I had much more to accomplish scientifically. So I joined the University of North Carolina at Chapel Hill School of Medicine as an associate professor of pharmacology. I actually got down there the end of 1965, before Christmas.

A: What was the major research interest at that time?

LH: First of all, one of the key things we found at Sterling, which later turned out to be the key in discovering endogenous opioid systems, was the electrically stimulated guinea pig ileum. I ran a huge series of compounds and showed a very high correlation between the effects of opioid antagonists in the guinea pig ileum and analgesia in man.[7] At that time, there was very little known about receptors. We had the hypothesis of multiple receptors from Bill Martin at Lexington about the possibility of mu, kappa and sigma receptors. We expended a great deal of effort and produced a great deal of good science on interactions between opiate agonist, antagonists and the cholinergic system, the adrenergic system and the 5-HT (serotonin) systems in the brain.[8]

A: And from that base you were able to do good work?

LH: In the period 1968–69 we were doing fantastic things. No one had conducted any real pharmacology on cannabinoids and we had an excellent supply of Δ^9-THC. We discovered the phenomenon of tolerance to thus drug.[9,10]

Career Move to the Medical College of Virginia

A: So your laboratory at UNC had two major focuses—one on narcotic antagonist analgesics and one on cannabinoids?

LH: Yes. At that point, NIDA was created and came out with an announcement for center grants. At that time, I decided to move to the Medical College of Virginia (MCV). They approved the grant and that supported a very large program in the area of CNS pharmacology at the MCV.

A: That grant was funded shortly after you arrived at MCV.

LH: It permitted us to build up a large group here at the MCV. Bill Dewey came with me. Billy Martin completed his doctoral research at MCV, went to Europe and returned as a faculty member. Bob Balster and Mario Aceto, who was with me at Sterling, were recruited. In addition, we had a very close relationship with the College on Problems of Drug Dependence. In 1973, Dr Seevers was about to retire at Michigan. They asked me whether we could set up a parallel testing facility at MCV and thus we established a colony of dependent monkeys. We recruited Mario Aceto to be in charge of that program. Mario went to Michigan to learn how to carry out the work. We trained some technicians and the colony was set up. At that same time, we began to set up other testing facilities. We also started a very large graduate program.

Networks of Influence and a Lapel Pin

A: Let us discuss interactions with individuals and groups which were initiated while at North Carolina and helped to formulate the development of the department at MCV.

LH: Early on in North Carolina there was a great deal of interest in LSD and other psychotomimetic compounds. It started with LSD, but it soon grew to include psilocybin and a number of other hallucinogens such as mescaline.

A: You became interested in control issues?

LH: In 1971 the United Nations initiated the creation of the 1971 Convention on Psychotropic Substances. One of the things that was lacking in the Single Convention was all the new abused substances that were introduced in the 1960s. They initiated the Psychotropic Convention to cover all the newer substances. I think that my participation as a consultant at the WHO,[11] the FDA and the multi-disciplinary grant and testing program from NIDA had a large influence on my department. However, when I came to VCU, we created the department much as in UNC along divisional lines.

A: You also had a strong involvement with NIDA?

LH: Yes. Shortly after Bob Schuster took over as director of NIDA, he was confronted by a dramatic increase in research funding by the Institute. Bob then asked me to spend a year at NIDA.

A: Would it be true to say that over the years your department at MCV developed world leadership?

LH: I think that we were able to have a multi-disciplinary organization, but with a heavy emphasis on substances of abuse which led to our becoming one of the leading departments in the world. We were very proud of that accomplishment.

A: What about the contributions from your department in the area of drug abuse and training of future scientists?

LH: One of the strong points of the training program was that we trained people for multiple roles in research. Our graduates progress probably equally among industry, government service and academia.

A: The key to success?

LH: It was a philosophy of common purpose, shared responsibility and shared credit. I do not think we have ever become known as a single-person department.

A: Could you say a little more about how the early experiences affected this success?

LH: I think that from the early days at Harvard, from the time I was a technician there, particularly the influence of Otto Krayer and Fred Uhle on the need to have rigorous, technically sound science. Krayer once said to the medical school at Harvard, as a whole, that medicine without science is nothing. This has been a truth that we would like to stick to. And again, as a cornerstone, this idea of multi-disciplinary research, putting together the efforts of scientists and various disciplines or subdisciplines and melding it together to produce a solid body of scientific scholarly work, that has been vital.

A: Any negatives about having a department emphasizing drug abuse work as opposed to some other area?

LH: Well, I think that the big downside of this is the fact that it was very difficult at this institution to get the clinicians interested in this field. The substance abuse patient population is a very difficult one to deal with. Most hospitals and clinical departments really do not want to have anything to do with this group of sick people.

A: In your immensely busy and productive life have you ever been able to find time to do anything but push back the frontiers of science, or has leisure been the casualty?

LH: Leisure has not been a complete casualty. I enjoy golf, although I play badly and, until recently, was joined frequently by my wife. We also swim regularly for exercise and enjoy fine food, both at home and dining out. We are avid art collectors and support the work of students in the VCU School of the Arts. We like the theatre, opera and classical music. We travel extensively. Finally, through our Family Foundation, we support biomedical research and training.

Notes

1. Uhle, F. C. & Harris, L. S. (1956) The synthesis of alpha-methylamino acids. *Journal of the American Chemistry Society,* 78, 381–384.
2. Uhle, F. C. & Harris, L. S. (1957) The synthesis and cyclication of alpha-methylamino (4-carboxy-3-in dole)-propionic acid. *Journal of the American Chemistry Society,* 79, 102–109.
3. Harris, L. S. & Uhle, F. C. (1960) 4-substituted indoles as antagonists to 5-hydroxy-tryptomine and to the veratrine response. *Journal of Pharmacology and Experimental Therapeutics,* 128, 358–362.
4. Harris, L. S., Clarke, R. L. & Dembinski, J., (1963) Benzyltetrahydrofurfurylamines. A new series of psychomotor stimulants. III. The pharmacology of

d-threo-a-benzyl-N-ethyltetrahydrofurfurylamine-(zylofuramine). *Archives Internationale de Pharmacodynamic et de Therapie,* 146, 392–405.
5. Lasagna, L., Dekornfeld, T. & Pearson, J. W. (1964) The analgesic efficacy and respiratory effects in man of a benzomorphan 'narcotic antagonist.' *Journal of Pharmacology and Experimental Therapeutics,* 144, 12–16.
6. Martin, W. R., Gorodetzky, C. W. & Mcclane, T. K. (1969) An experimental study in the treatment of narcotic addicts with cyclazocine. *Clinical Pharmacology and Therapeutics,* 7, 455–465.
7. Harris, L. S. (1986) Nathan B. Eddy Memorial Award Lecture. *Problems of Drug Dependence,* 67, 4–13.
8. Harris, L. S. (1970) Central neurohumoral systems involved with narcotic agonists and antagonists. *Federal Proceedings,* 29, 28–32.
9. Dewey, W. L., Harris, L. S., Howes, J. D., Kennedy, J. S., Granchelli, F. E., Pars, H. G. et al. (1978) Pharmacology of some marijuana constituents and two heterocyclic analogues. *Nature,* 226, 1265–1267.
10. Harris, L. S., Dewey, W. L. & Razdan, R. K. (1977) Cannabis, its chemistry, pharmacology and toxicology. In: Martin, W., *The Handbook of Experimental Pharmacology Drug Addiction,* Vol. II, pp. 45. 371–429. Berlin, Germany: Springer-Verlag.
11. World Health Organization (WHO) (1977–94) *Technical Report Series.* Geneva: WHO.

10

Conversation with Conan Kornetsky

Conan Kornetsky is Professor of Psychiatry and Pharmacology at Boston University. Beginning at the dawn of the era of psychopharmacology, his work has spanned more than 50 years. He is among the last of the scientists who began their research in our field at the Addiction Research Center at Lexington, Kentucky. In 2005 he was a recipient of the Nathan B. Eddy Award.

Starting Off

Addiction (A): Conan, can you recall for us what first stimulated your interest in science?

Conan Kornetsky (CK): Actually, my earliest interests were history and what made things work. If genetics determines one's interests, the former probably stems from my maternal grandfather, who was a rabbi, and the latter from my father, whose primary position was the maintenance of the machinery in a shoe factory. But in spite of my passion for reading, and my father's repeated admonishment, 'Remember, anything you put in your head they cannot take away from you', I was not a particularly good student. In fact, when I graduated from grammar school, in Portland, Maine, the teachers recommended that I do not take the college preparatory program in high school. However, my family did not accept that advice. After high school I attended the University of Maine. I decided that engineering was the field for me. Upon completing the first year of course work I enlisted in the Army Air Corps Air Cadet program in March 1944 to be trained as a pilot or navigator. I was discharged from the Army in December, 1945, and returned to the University of Maine 2 months later.

A: And your career plans at that time?

CK: I had decided that I really did not want to become an engineer, so I switched to the college of arts and science. I found the history department much too politically conservative (I was very active in the liberal American Veterans Committee), so I sampled courses in psychology, philosophy, and sociology, finally settling upon psychology as a major.

A: Was there any clinical element in the training?

CK: A major influence on my thinking resulted from a course in abnormal psychology. We made weekly visits to the local state mental hospital for most of a semester. Patients exhibiting the classical signs and symptoms of various mental diseases were interviewed in our presence.

A: Did you at that time have opportunity to get into any experimental work?

CK: Yes. The first independent experiment that I carried out as an undergraduate was related to focusing attention. I studied the effect of auditory distraction on learning nonsense syllables. Also, because of my liberal leanings, I did a senior research thesis that looked at social attitude. I decided to compare all the seniors elected to Phi Beta Kappa with those elected to Tau Beta Pi, the national engineering honor society.

A: Was this the beginning of your interest in experimental psychology?

CK: Well, I certainly found doing these small research projects exciting. I still had no idea what I wanted to do. A philosophy professor, Dr Virtue, with whom I was friendly had previously taught at the University of Kentucky, suggested I apply there. I applied and that is where I was accepted.

To Lexington

A: At that stage you made a link with Lexington?

CK: During the first few weeks I was at the University, a position opened at the US Public Health Service Hospital at Lexington for a student to conduct IQ testing on patients. I was recommended for the position because I had taken a course in IQ testing at the University of Maine. The stipend was for board, room and laundry. The hospital was also a prison for both the incarceration and treatment of drug addicts. The room I was given was similar to those assigned to prisoners, including the iron bars; the only difference was that I had a key. I was required to administer and score three IQ tests a day, 5 days a week. It was a tremendous learning experience. I knew little about drug addiction. Even marijuana was foreign to me.

A: With whom were you working when you first went to Lexington?

CK: I first worked for Mary Daingerfield, Chief of the Clinical Psychology Department. She was a wonderful woman who taught me a lot about testing. Finding that I could not spend all my time in the evenings studying, I began to spend a fair amount of time in the Research Department of the Hospital which later became the Addiction Research Center. There I became friendly with the patients who were subjects on research projects. Harris Isbell, who was Director of Research, would make evening rounds and he became aware that I was often there, sitting and talking to the patients. He became friendly with me, explaining to me the research that was going on. At that time he was planning a clinical experiment on the effects of chronic barbituate administration and he asked me if I would like to participate.

A: How did you manage to keep up with your graduate studies at the University of Kentucky while working at the hospital?

CK: Actually, I did not. After a warning by the Chairman of the Psychology Department I had decided I really wanted to be a research psychologist, not a practicing clinical psychologist and I quickly brought my grades up to an acceptable level. But I should say that the clinical training and the contact with all types of patients had a major impact upon the way I would think about a problem.

A: And you contributed to your first published paper.

CK: Yes. It was the first published paper that listed me as an author (Isbell et al. 1950). In 1951 I published a detailed report of the psychological studies that I conducted as part of the Isbell experiment (Kornetsky 1951). About the time the barbituate experiment was completed I told Dr. Isbell that I was getting married and the present arrangement, living at the hospital, was not satisfactory. He found the funds to put me on salary, so I stopped doing IQ tests. Although I still had much to learn about drug addiction, the year I spent living at the hospital was a fantastic learning experience.

A: Around this time you met Abe Wikler?

CK: My first year at Lexington, Abe was on sabbatical leave. I was on leave when he returned from his sabbatical and in a very short time he had some animal experiments under way in which he was recording autonomic reflexes on a smoked kymograph. These long loops of paper were left hanging until they could be fixed with shellac. If you brushed up against them before they were shellacked you could destroy the data recorded on them. Well, when I returned from my leave I walked into Abe's laboratory and I brushed up against some of his kymographs. There was a screech and yell. I remember it as, 'Who the hell is this stupid ass!' Despite that first contact we became fast friends and he became my most important mentor.

A: Did you work with Wikler?

CK: At this time, the summer and fall of 1949, Isbell thought I should work with Wikler and Hill. Wikler, Hill and I met over coffee most mornings at 8:00 o'clock. It was Wikler's informal daily seminar where research ideas were proposed and discussed. At one of our early meetings I proposed what I thought was a major experiment, for it would test the hypothesis that a drug effect could be altered significantly by altering the experimental conditions. In 1949 it was somewhat radical. Abe listened, frowned. He then said something like, 'that is a stupid idea.' Abe was blunt. About a week-and-a-half later he passed me in the hall, and said that we should talk a little bit about that experiment. He told me that after some thought it was a pretty good idea. In that experiment we demonstrated that the effects of morphine would normally impair reaction-time; however, in a conflict, morphine would improve reaction-time (Hill et al. 1952b).

A: Thus you got into behavioural psychopharmacology?

CK: That is how I became involved in the field of behavioral pharmacology. We performed a whole series of experiments on the role of environmental factors on the effects of morphine, and these experiments continued after I left in 1952. The work for my dissertation, 'The effects of anxiety and morphine on the perception of painful stimuli' (Kornetsky 1954) was carried out at the hospital at Lexington.

To New York and Work on Young Heroin Addicts

A: It was quite a stroke of luck to have the opportunity to work with those remarkable researchers in the early years of the field. Why did you leave the Addiction Research Center?

CK: There were a number of factors, none because I was unhappy working in what was a fantastic research environment. The juvenile addiction study came about because there had been a dramatic increase in the number of heroin addicts under the age of 21 being admitted to the hospital at Lexington, which reflected an increase in heroin use in general by those under the age of 21. I worked with a young psychiatrict, Donald Gerard, at Lexington and at the completion of my Ph.D. in June 1952 Gerard and I were sent to New York to continue a study of juvenile addiction. We published three papers based on our research of adolescent drug abuse (Kornetsky and Gerard 1954, 1955ab).

A: Did you and Gerard work with Chein's group?

CK: Because of the widespread use of heroin by juveniles, NIMH awarded Isador Chein at New York University a large grant to study juvenile addiction. During that year in New York, Gerard and I spent a great deal of time with the Chein group. The Chein group published its comprehensive studies in a book, *The Road to H* (Chein et al. 1964). I spent one additional year in New York studiying the effects of LSD with Murray Jarvik at Mount Sinai Hospital and Gerard continued research on juvenile addiction, working with the Chein group.

Work at NIMH

A: You seem to have been a participant in many of the earliest studies in the new era of psychopharmacology. What came next?

CK: In September 1954 I moved to Bethesda, to the intramural program at NIMH, in the Laboratory of Clinical Science, in which Seymour Kety was the laboratory chief. Chlorpromazine had just been introduced and I decided I would compare the effect of this new 'wonder' drug with a variety of other centrally acting drugs, such as barbiturates and amphetamine, in normal volunteers and in schizophrenic patients (e.g. Kornetsky et al. 1957, 1959).

A: Other contacts at this time?

CK: It was at NIMH that I met Daniel X. Freedman. He was on sabbatical from Yale University and was studying some of the effects of LSD, sharing space in my laboratory. Although I was happy and excited about my schizophrenia research at Bethesda, when offered a faculty position at Boston I accepted because it would give me an opportunity to teach, continue my schizophrenia research, and build an animal behaviour laboratory.

Boston University and an Interest in Schizophrenia

A: Were you responsible for getting that interesting group of researchers to come to Boston University from NIMH?

CK: Probably. By that time I had switched my primary appointment from pharmacology to psychiatry and I had considerable influence on the research appointments that were being made. When I came to Boston University I decided that I wanted to continue my experiments in schizophrenia and to set up an animal laboratory. Although I continued to perform animal experiments with opiates, my schizophrenia research continued well into the 1970s. These schizophrenia experiments, started when I was at NIH, confirmed that there was an attentional dysfunction in schizophrenia (e.g. Orzack & Kornetsky 1966). In many schizophrenic patients there is a trait deficit in attention that is reversed by chronic neuroleptics treatment (Wholberg & Kornetsky 1973).

Drug Research with a New Focus

A: Meanwhile, how did your addiction work develop?

CK: Much of the early thinking about drugs of abuse centered on the concept that the drug use was primarily a manifestation of some sort of psychopathology. I decided that an interesting area to review would be the brain reward system that was first described by Olds & Milner in 1954. I reviewed the literature of drug effects on intracranial self-stimulation, or brain-stimulation reward, a term I prefer. I found that, with the exception of work by Larry Stein, no serious attempt to determine changes in the threshold caused by centrally active drugs had been done. Because I had been studying morphine analgesia in rats by intracerebral stimulation of a pain pathway, and using classic psychophysics to obtain a threshold, I thought I could apply this to brain-stimulation reward (Marcus & Kornetsky 1974).

A: So the method you were developing was novel and very much your own?

CK: Psychophysics was not invented by me; however, the method of determining thresholds for both rewarding and pain, application of classic psychophysical methodology independent of motor effects, were developed by my students and me (Marcus and Kornetsky 1974; Kornetsky & Esposito 1981).

A: I sense that one of your core strengths was the capacity to develop new laboratory procedures.

CK: To a degree this is true in that I modified and applied new ways of measuring the effects of drugs. Although I did not discover the phenomenon of brain-stimulation reward, I did develop new ways of measuring the reward threshold and found that all abused drugs lower that threshold, increase the sensitivity, of rewarding brain stimulation. I have use the same psychophysical techniques for measuring pain and the effects of morphine. Today there is a great deal of effort in the study of reinstatement. The concept of the role of environmental cues in reinstatement of drug use was first proposed by Wikler (1952). We demonstrated using the 2-deoxsyglucose method the effect of cue exposure on brain glucose utilization eight days after repeated cocaine administration in the rat (Knapp et al. 2002).

Current Work

A: Are you still studying opiate addiction?

CK: Currently (in 2002) I am looking at one of the classic questions concerning whether there is a maturing-out process in the abuse of opiate drugs. We are presently just beginning to compare data on brain-stimulation reward, as well as the analgesic response between old and young rats.[1]

A: For you personally, what has been the reward from a life-time spent in science?

CK: Although recognition is an important motivation for a scientist, I feel the real rewards are those that come from the actual carrying out of an experiment and knowing that what we have found is something that is unique. I used to tell students that they should make buildings and not bricks. I have come to realize that without the bricks we would have no buildings. Most rewarding has been the opportunity I have had to mentor students. In many ways I have been a student and they have been my teacher. I thank them.

A: I wonder if you can sum up your current perspective on research in psychopharmacology and addiction?

CK: We should acknowledge the importance of the early behavioral pharmacologists, many of them influenced by the behaviorism of B. F. Skinner, who provided an ideal technology for the study of drug effects on behavior in animals that appeared in the 1950s. The introduction of effective drugs for the treatment of mental illness and the development of animal models for the study of abuse liability of drugs that appeared in the 1960s were also of fundamental importance. But with few exceptions these experiments made little attempt to relate the behavior to underlying neurochemical or neuroanatomical mechanism of action of these compounds. Among the few exceptions were Wikler who used Pavlovian conditioning theory to explain the high incidence of relapse in the post-addict and related this to a variety of implied and measured neurophysiological and autonomic responses, and Larry Stein who was making use of brain-stimulation reward for the development of theories of motivation based on the role of norepinephrine. With the animal self-administration model, conditioned place preference, brain-stimulation reward models clearly established by the end of the 1970s there was a strong coming together of these models with techniques that allowed the study of the neurochemistry and neuroanatomy of the brain. Today it is rare that a paper is published that does not have at least an implied neurochemical or neuroanatomical mechanism proffered; or more up-to-date, a genetic hypothesis.

A: What is your judgement on the probable impact of this wonderful laboratory work on the world outside the laboratory?

CK: Will all this research eradicate drug abuse? I am not sure that the prevention of the initial use of abuse substances is a neuropharmacological problem. Clinical research will not eradicate drug abuse; but it will impact upon our ability to prevent relapse and to treat once dependence has occurred.

Note

1. The original interview was done in June 2002. Our results since then with aged rats indicate that the sensitivity to rewarding brain stimulation is not compromised by age and that with the procedures we use for the study of pain, directly stimulating a brain pain pathway, the threshold for aged and young rats is identical. Currently I am carrying out experiments that suggest the presence of an endogenous opiate antagonist.

References

Chein, I., Gerard, D. L., Lee, R. S. & Rosenfeld, E. (1964) *The Road to H.* New York: Basic Books.

Gerard, D. L. & Kornetsky, C. (1954) Adolescent opiate addiction: a case study. *Psychiatric Quarterly,* 28, 367–380.

Gerard, D. L. & Kornetsky, C. (1955a) Adolescent opiate addiction: a study of control and addict subjects. *Psychiatric Quarterly,* 29, 457–486.

Gerard, D. L. & Kornetsky, C. (1955b) A social and psychiatric study of adolescent opiate addicts. *Psychiatric Quarterly,* 28, 113–125.

Hill, H. E., Kornetsky, C., Flanary, H. G. & Wikler, A. (1952b) Studies on anxiety associated with anticipation of pain. I. Effects of morphine. *Archives of Neurology and Psychiatry,* 67, 612–619.

Isabell, H., Altschul, S., Kornetsky, C., Eisenman, A. J., Flanary, H. G. & Fraser, H. F. (1950) Chronic barbiturate intoxication: an experimental study. *Archives of Neurology and Psychiatry,* 64, 1–28.

Knapp, C. M., Printseva, B., Cottam, N. & Kornetsky, C. (2002) Effects of cue exposure on brain glucose utilization 8 days after repeated cocaine administration. *Brain Research,* 950, 119–126.

Kornetsky, C. (1954) Effects of anxiety and morphine on the anticipation and perception of painful radiant thermal stimuli. *Journal of Comparative and Physiological Psychology,* 47, 130–132.

Kornetsky, C. (1976) Hyporesponsivity of chronic schizophrenic patients to dextroamphetamine. *Archives of General Psychiatry,* 33, 1425–1428.

Kornetsky, C. & Esposito, R. U. (1981) Reward and detection thresholds for brain stimulation: dissociative effects of cocaine. *Brain Research,* 209, 496–500.

Kornetsky, C., Humphries, O. & Evarts, E. V. (1957) Comparison of the psychological effects of certain centrally acting drugs in man. *Archives of Neurology and Psychiatry,* 77, 318–324.

Kornetsky, C., Pettit, M., Wynne, R. & Evarts, E. V. (1959) A comparison of the psychological effects of acute and chronic administration of chlorpromazine and secobarbital (Quinalbaritone) in schizophrenic patients. *Journal of Mental Science,* 105, 190–198.

Kraus, M. A. & Kornetsky, C. (2000) Cue-induced changes in basal local cerebral glucose utilization 13 days after morphine sensitization in the Fischer 344 rat. Relevance for drug craving. *Brain Research,* 865, 194–201.

Marcus, R. & Kornetsky, C. (1974) Negative and positive intracranial reinforcement thresholds: effects of morphine. *Psychopharmacologia* (Berlin), 38, 1–13.

Olds, J. & Milner, P. (1954) Positive reinforcement produced by electrical stimulation of septal area and other regions of rat brain. *Journal of Comparative and Psysiological Psychology,* 47, 419–427.

Orzack, M. H. & Kornetsky, C. (1966) Attention dysfunction in chronic schizophrenia. *Archives of General Psychiatry,* 14, 323–326.

Wholberg, G. W. & Kornetsky, C. (1973) Sustained attention in remitted schizophrenics. *Archives of General Psychiatry,* 28, 533–537.

11

Conversation with Michael Kuhar

Michael Kuhar is a brain scientist who has made astonishingly important and original contributions to the understanding of addiction, particularly with his work on cocaine.

Early Years

Addiction (A): What forces in your early life directed you towards science?

Michael Kuhar (MK): My father, an electrician, was a big fan of science and maths. I was always very good in maths, and he encouraged that a lot. My mother suffered from depression, which got me interested in what is now called neuroscience.

A: What can you recall about your mother's illness?

MK: She was very withdrawn. I recall my father's frustration, and her inability to do simple things sometimes. She was in the hospital where they gave her shock therapy, and it worked—but it frightened her so much that she wouldn't go back for it.

A: Where did you grow up?

MK: I grew up near Scranton, Pennsylvania, and went to college at the University of Scranton. I thought that I might go to graduate or professional school after college, so I didn't want to get into debt just then. The University of Scranton was local, reasonably priced and I had a part scholarship. So I went there.

A: Your college majors were physics and philosophy, an unusual combination for a student at a Jesuit school. Why that route?

MK: Sputnik, the Russian satellite, went up in about 1957, and that captured the imagination and excitement of my generation. Being good in maths, and being from that era, I gravitated towards physics, as did many people. Philosophy as a co-major just somehow happened. I did like it.

A: When were you first drawn to pharmacology?

MK: In September 1965 I went to graduate school in physics, and that's when I decided that I wanted to go into biology. So I changed programs from physics to biophysics. I was drawn to pharmacology after that. I wanted to get into biology, preferably brain science, but I was in physics and I needed a link or a transition, and biophysics was a very reasonable transition. It was a very good department at Johns Hopkins, where I went as a graduate student in 1966. I loved the training there.

A: You went before long in the direction of pharmacology.

MK: I decided to study brain neurochemistry and neuropharmacology. I chose pharmacology for a very practical reason—I wanted to be able to get a job when I was done, and I thought pharmacology would be a more flexible degree than biophysics. Pharmacology opened the door to industry.

A: Who were your mentors at Hopkins?

MK: My main mentor was Dr Sol Snyder, who supervised my research at the hospital. When I first went to see the chairman of pharmacology, Paul Talalay, I said: 'I have no idea if you can help me, or if I should be here, but here's the direction I want to go in'. I talked about the brain, drugs and depression. And he said: 'we just hired the right person for you to work with, Sol Snyder'. And I said: 'who's he?'. He said that Sol was a bright young resident who was going to be an assistant professor the next year. I was Sol Snyder's first graduate student.

A: What was it like to work with Sol in the early days of his career?

MK: He was relatively well known because he worked with Axelrod, who later won the Nobel Prize, but at that point Sol was still finding his way. He was a psychiatrist, so he was automatically studying the kinds of things that I was interested in. He was so good that he was promoted very rapidly from assistant professor to full professor.

A: So in those first days with him, what kinds of things did you work on?

MK: I was very excited to work on the uptake of neurotransmitters such as norepinephrine, GABA [gamma aminobutyric acid] and glutamate. I was excited about doing electron microscopy, so that I could see what the brain looked like.

A: What was your dissertation topic?

MK: It was one of several suggested by Sol Snyder, my advisor. Substances that were neurotransmitters had high-affinity uptake mechanisms in their nerve terminals. Sol said: 'you know, glutamate could be a major neurotransmitter. Why don't you look for a high-affinity uptake system?'. So I did, and I showed a special nerve terminal uptake for glutamate as a neurotransmitter.[1] That, in 1969, was some beginning evidence that glutamate could be a neurotransmitter.

Entering into the Field of Neurotransmitters

A: What did neuroscience look like when you were entering it?

MK: In my experience, which of course was limited, it looked like neuroanatomy, electromicroscopy, electrophysiology. Also, neuropharmacologists were experimenting, trying to improve antidepressants, and figure out better antipsychotic drugs and so forth. After I graduated from Hopkins, I went to Yale as a post-doc with George Aghajanian, who was working with LSD and serotonin in the brain. I conducted a great deal of work on serotonin with George, partly because of its connection with LSD.

A: When you returned to Hopkins as part of the neuropharmacology group, who did you join?

MK: It was me, Sol Snyder, Joe Coyle, and at times others. My laboratory work was a continuation of things I started at Yale. When I came back to Hopkins I continued studying choline uptake. The story that I proposed was that choline uptake—unlike the uptake for dopamine, norepinephrine or serotonin—was linked to impulse flow, which made sense because it was a precursor. The more the neuron fired, the more choline it needed to make acetylcholine.

A: Was that really your first breakthrough?

MK: It was one that got me all excited; and it was probably my first unique contribution as an independent faculty member. Me and the post-doctoral fellow, Jay Simon, published the results in Nature.[2]

A: When did you first get into autoradiography?

MK: I learned autoradiography with George Aghajanian at Yale. We showed that radioactive serotonin was taken up into nerve terminals.

Moving into an Interest in Drugs of Abuse

A: When would you say that drugs of abuse become your main subject?

MK: I was interested in drugs that were abused from the perspective of their impact on the brain and the fact that they might be models for mental illnesses; but that evolved. Bob Schuster and others showed that monkeys would self-administer drugs back in the 1960s and 1970s, and that almost all the drugs that humans abused were self-administered by monkeys. That seemed like a real breakthrough. It indicated that something innate in the brain wants you to take drugs. It isn't the devil or your mother-in-law, but an innate property of the brain that makes us (humans and animals) vulnerable to take these drugs. So drug abuse was interwoven into my scientific work. In the beginning I didn't focus on it as a special topic. That evolved over some years.

From Autoradiography to Pet Scanning

A: Back in the 1970s, when you returned to Hopkins, Sol Snyder and Candace Pert and others were involved in a race to identify opiate receptors. Can you describe what it was like there when you came back? Was there a difference in the atmosphere?

MK: Yes, it was a different place from the one where I had finished my degree. I was focusing on getting my own laboratory going, getting my own research going, but it was clear that Sol and Candace and other people were very excited over this binding data that suggested they had identified an opiate receptor. It was just tremendously exciting.

A: How were you using autoradiography?

MK: One of the projects I took on, as I had just learned autoradiography at Yale, was to try to localize drug receptors in the brain by autoradiography at the light microscopic level. This gradually skyrocketed. First, Sol and Hank Yamamura and other people showed that radioactive drugs could be injected into animals, and under certain conditions the drugs would be bound mainly to receptors in vivo. I carried out autoradiography on those brains where the drug was bound mainly to receptors. Later, a graduate student and I developed another more applicable and widely used autoradiographic technique, called in vitro labeling autoradiography. This technique is still important and used prominently today. Because I had that experience, I knew exactly how to try to develop PET scanning for receptors.

A: What did you learn from the autoradiography studies that you were able to transfer into the PET work?

MK: First of all, I knew that it was possible to inject drugs into animals under certain conditions and find times when most of the drug in the brain was on receptors. That's when you want to do PET scanning. Carrying out that work, going through all the thinking and conducting a lot of experiments, even some that never worked, gave me the picture of how to do it. The importance of PET was that you could visualize the location and density of receptors in brain in living humans. It was almost unbelievable. This approach could bring studies of receptors into the clinical realm, and it did. Enter Henry Wagner, who was the head of nuclear medicine at Hopkins. He decided to bring a cyclotron and PET scanner to Hopkins and tackle the receptor imaging problem. He was a great guy, very jovial. Some thought he was not a basic scientist, but more of a clinician. Nevertheless, he was a visionary and he knew where he wanted to go. It's quite amazing that he held our group together for 5 years to write the grants, obtain the equipment, set up the equipment, build the laboratories and build the buildings. It took all that to get the PET scanning of receptors working. Well, perhaps it was some misguided youthful enthusiasm but I knew, with reasonable certainty, that it was going to work.

A: Were those early studies actually dopamine receptors?

MK: Right, the first ones that we worked on were dopamine receptors. We thought they should make a very good imaging candidate because dopamine receptors are highly clustered in one place. Also, there were enough dopamine receptor ligands such that we could find one and methylate it, and it would still keep its properties. It needed to be methylated to add a carbon-11, which was a key for PET.

A: Your 1983 *Science* publication[3] was the first report of dopamine receptor imaging in human brain, and you had started becoming involved with PET in 1978, so it was 5 years from 1978 to that publication in 1983. You started working at NIDA in 1985. At what point did you see what you were doing with PET as working on the problem of drug addiction or drug abuse?

MK: We thought PET could contribute to the problem of many illnesses: neurodegenerative diseases, psychiatric diseases, neurological diseases, behavioral disorders, all these things. We thought it was all wide open; and we could do it in people.

A: How were relationships in the laboratory?

MK: Well, we're all human beings and, unfortunately, less than perfect. That era, because of the conflicts, is one of the most difficult in my own personal memories. The opiate receptor was a big discovery, and people wanted their piece of the pie as they perceived it. The fighting for credit was sometimes bitter. Sometimes the bitterness became destructive, bad decisions were made and there were accusations of misdeeds. I was accused of not giving someone proper credit—which was untrue but nevertheless very painful. I can still feel wounded and disappointed, but I keep it in the past, which is where it should be. As human beings we are vulnerable to these things, but the discoveries were very important, couldn't be held back and fostered many positive advances.

Move to the ARC

A: Was that why you went over to the Addiction Research Center [ARC], which soon became the intramural research program of the National Institute on Drug Abuse [NIDA-IRP]?

MK: Mainly because of my desire to move ahead in my career and perhaps partly because of the distasteful political problems, I took the job at NIDA-IRP, which was just down the road from Hopkins. Dr Jerry Jaffe, the new director of the ARC and a 'mover and shaker' in the drug abuse field, offered me the opportunity to start a new Neuroscience Branch from scratch. Jaffe thought he was opening up a new kind of research at the Addiction Research Center, and he was right. We had a group of about 15 people who were the beginnings of the Neuroscience Branch. At its height, after we recruited, it had about 85 people and half were PhDs.

A: What were your priorities at the new Neuroscience Branch?

MK: One was trying to bring brain imaging to the ARC, to build up an imaging facility right there. Eventually we had a complete PET center directed by Eydie London. The other thing was to start up molecular biology. When I got to NIDA there was one person doing molecular biology. When I left there were more than 30 directed by George Uhl, so I feel that I met my major goals in my 10 years there.

A: What were you personally able to accomplish scientifically while at the Addiction Research Center?

MK: In terms of scientific accomplishments, one stands out. My laboratory published a paper in *Science* in 1987 showing that the dopamine transporter was the receptor for the addicting properties of cocaine.[4] The move to research on cocaine was partly political, in the sense that there was a great deal of money available for work on cocaine. Crack cocaine was being discovered and there was much interest in cocaine as an abused substance. For years I felt that research in drug abuse was in some ways ahead of research in other areas, because we were finding out the molecular sequelae of addiction faster than they were finding out the molecular sequelae of other diseases.

Moving to Emory

A: What kind of work did your 1995 move to Emory enable you to do?

MK: I wanted to be back in a university because I liked the freedom and atmosphere. I thought it would be interesting to work on new genes involved in drug addiction. We didn't know how many genes there were then. I think it's very likely that we still don't know all the neurochemicals involved in drug addiction. I never did accomplish as much as I wanted to at Emory, nor did I feel that I had the administrative or collegial support to do it. On the other hand, perhaps I could have done more myself. We tried to find a substitute medication for cocaine.

A: Have you developed any new scientific interests?

MK: We're working on CART (cocaine and amphetamine regulated transcript) because every time we turn around there's something new and interesting turning up,[5] so we have stayed with it. I'm also interested in mathematical modeling[6] and effects of maternal separation on drug use in offspring[7,8]—but we haven't yet been funded for that work.

A: Do you think that your most critical contributions will turn out to have to do with CART?

MK: No, I'm not sure what it will be or how that would be measured. Fortunately, my work is highly cited and that is very gratifying. My publications on transporters, receptor imaging by autoradiography and PET, cocaine analogs and CART peptides probably represent my main contributions. I think of contributions or papers as each being a 'brick' in the 'wall of knowledge.' Each finding or publication is a new brick added to the top of the wall. Eventually the wall grows and grows, and our own bricks become further down as new workers and their new bricks of discovery are added on top of our own. After a while we can barely see our bricks down there lower in the wall, but they are nevertheless there and hold up and support all the new bricks that have been laid since. I've also become interested in ethics because ethics is evolving, and it's got a very good home in science. The ethical issues I'm particularly interested in include blacklisting,[9,10] authorship and data management.

A: How do you see the field evolving?

MK: First of all, I think brain imaging is going to play a major role in figuring out what's going on in the brain, even more so than it already has. I think that molecular genetics will help us to understand the vulnerability of certain individuals to drug abuse and what is the biochemistry of vulnerability, and that's going to go a long way.

A: Tell us what you do when you have leisure time.

MK: In my spare time I do photography, some of it competitive, and I am also a movie buff, which is sort of connected to my interest in photography. I sometimes enjoy the outdoors a lot—hiking, fishing and sightseeing. I travel so much professionally that I am not someone who craves travel to faraway places. I enjoy discussion groups and my friends very much. If you peeked over my shoulder on a beach, you would find me reading popular mystery novels. I usually spend holidays with my children and grandchildren who are, like all children and grandchildren, very special.

A: Any closing remarks?

MK: Well, I'm really glad that I had my opportunities and that I made the choices I did. Experiencing the discoveries changed me. While it wasn't always easy going, in retrospect it seems worth it. Also, I feel good about the younger generation of scientists who are very competent. It is a good feeling watching them develop into leaders in the field.

Notes

1. Kuhar M. J., Snyder S. H. The subcellular distribution of free H3-glutamic acid in rat cerebral cortical slices. *J Pharmacol Exp Ther* 1970; 171: 141–52.
2. Simon J. R., Kuhar M. G. Impulse-flow regulation of high affinity choline uptake in brain cholinergic nerve terminals. *Nature* 1975; 255: 162–3.
3. Wagner H. N. Jr, Burns H. D., Dannals R. F., Wong D. F., Langstrom B., Duelfer T. et al. Imaging dopamine receptors in the human brain by positron tomography. *Science* 1983; 221: 1264–6.
4. Ritz M. C., Lamb R. J., Goldberg S. R., Kuhar M. J. Cocaine receptors on dopamine transporters are related to self-administration of cocaine. *Science* 1987; 237: 1219–23.
5. Rogge G., Jones D., Hubert G. W., Lin Y., Kuhar M. J. CART peptides: regulators of body weight, reward and other functions. *Nat Rev Neurosci* 2008; 9: 747–58.
6. Kuhar M. J., Joyce A. R. Slow onset of CNS drugs: can changes in protein concentration account for the delay? *Trends Pharmacol Sci* 2001; 22: 450–6.
7. Jaworski J. N., Francis D. D., Brommer C. L., Morgan E. T., Kuhar M. J. Effects of early maternal separation on ethanol intake, GABA receptors and metabolizing enzymes in adult rats. *Psychopharmacology* 2005; 181: 8–15.
8. Francis D. D., Kuhar M. J. Frequency of maternal licking and grooming correlates negatively with vulnerability to cocaine and alcohol use in rats. Pharmacol *Biochem Behav* 2008; 90: 497–500.
9. Kuhar M. J. On blacklisting in science. *Sci Eng Ethics* 2008; 14: 301–3.
10. Kuhar M. J. Blacklisting among scientists. *Synapse* 2009; 63: 539–40.

12

Conversation with Malcolm H. Lader

Malcolm Lader is a British psychopharmacologist who, from 1966 to 2001, directed an MRC-funded research group at the Institute of Psychiatry. He has made fundamental contributions to understanding of benzodiazepine dependence and his work gives salience to the problem. From 1983 to 1993 he was President of the Society for the Study of Addiction.

Early Experiences and Medical Training

Addiction (A): It is often useful to start an *Addiction* interview with some information on our subject's personal background.

Malcolm Lader (ML): My family was, I suppose, very poor working class. My father's family were from Leeds. My grandfather was an agricultural labourer who came off the land into a clothing factory. My mother's family came from Liverpool, again quite poor. My father was, however, professional—he won a scholarship to Leeds Grammar School and then obtained a university degree, but in the wrong subject. My grandfather wanted him to do medicine on the basis that you could always make a living in medicine, but my father refused. He went into industrial chemistry—dye stuff chemistry. Just as he was about to graduate in 1926, the German dye industry got back on its feet again so he never worked in industrial chemistry until the outbreak of the Second World War. He had short-term jobs and he always told me that his greatest ambition was to be working-class and not unemployed. He was in a reserved occupation during the war making poison gas. He got a reasonably well-paid job after that, but of course he only had half the pension years. Because he had to save hard, I was probably the poorest medical student in my year. My father seemed better off in later years and we had a car by then, but there still was not much money to spend. It is one of the reasons why I was not able to go to Oxford and settled for the local university, Liverpool.

A: What sort of experience was life at medical school like?

ML: Liverpool medical school was very orientated towards becoming a doctor—a tremendous amount of practical work. The medical students were relied upon to help run the medical services in Liverpool, which were very run down and vastly under-funded. I saw real poverty. When I was doing obstetrics in the 1950s, the most common cause for an elective caesarean was pelvic distortion due to rickets. People talk about poverty now, but they have no idea what poverty was really like then in northern industrial cities. The day I qualified I left Liverpool and came down to London.

A: Did medical school provide a stimulating peer group?

ML: Well, it might have done, but I had to come home for my evening meal and get down to studying. I suppose that is why I sailed through exams.

A: Well, you won almost every prize in sight, didn't you?

ML: Almost! and I got the first Distinction in Medicine for 10 years. But I did not have much of a social life. It was a very one-dimensional training that one received.

Postgraduate Experiences

A: But when you qualified you knew that you wanted to go on and study in London?

ML: What had happened was that I got a distinction in physiology and the professor of physiology wanted me to do a BSc. I had won enough prizes to pay for that. I did the BSc and among the many books I read there was one edited by S. S. Stevens on experimental psychology (Stevens 1951). I suddenly realized that psychology was not just lying on a couch and speculating. It could actually be an experimental subject and that started my interest in that area, but I put it on hold while I went into clinical medical training. The next thing that shaped the rest of my career was that I came down to London and got house jobs (internships), despite not having trained at a London teaching hospital. Then while wondering what to do, my fiancé Susan (now my wife) showed me an advertisement in the BMJ for research in psychopharmacology. I was also interested in pharmacology, but they were looking for people with experience that I did not have. Susan told me that the person advertising, Professor Schild, was her tutor—she was doing medicine—and she had a word with him. He remembered me, having been my examiner in pharmacology in Liverpool and he had awarded me a distinction. So I applied. He managed to stretch the grant from NIMH to cover me as well: that is how I got into psychopharmacology. Professor Schild was at University College, a refugee from Nazi Germany.

A: So you started there in 1960, and you did your PhD at University College London?

ML: Yes, and I was using the same techniques there as at the Maudsley where I was under the supervision of Michael Shepherd. I also had contact with a psychopharmacologist called Hannah Steinberg and I worked with Lorna Wing conducting research that got me an MD as well as my PhD. Then I decided that I had to get a formal psychiatric training and Michael Shepherd encouraged me in that ambition. I did my psychiatric training between 1963 and 1966 and I believe that I was Aubrey Lewis's last registrar.

A: Am I right in thinking that although you were training as a psychiatrist and you had at that stage firmly set your mind on a research career?

ML: Yes. I think the clinical side was something that I knew I had to have in order to be able to understand what I was doing in the laboratory. But I did enjoy the clinical work.

A: But somewhere you had been bitten by the bug of science?

ML: That was when I was doing the BSc in Physiology, under Professor Gregory. He just fired me with enthusiasm for the experimental method. However, I think one can overplay the experimental method. Flashes of insight are also important and the experimental method tells you how to look; the two are complementary, but there have been a lot of futile experiments done.

A: So what was the work that you did with Lorna Wing?

ML: It was on human and clinical psychopharmacology—barbiturates and benzodiazepines. We were looking at normal subjects and trying to develop methods of quantifying the drug effects other than relying only on the subjective reports.

A: So that 3-year training at the Maudsley?

ML: I thoroughly enjoyed it; I found I really had an interest in people, not just as butterflies pinned out on a board, but as humans.

A: Who were your important clinical teachers?

ML: Oh, Aubrey Lewis—he is a legend; he had a depth of knowledge and erudition that was quite outstanding. Some people found him formidable but I never did; I always found him very sympathetic. Once we met him on holiday and we spent a quite delightful day on Lake Garda, with him acting as an unofficial guide. He could set you many intellectual problems, but if you were honest with him and if you did the work, you got on well with him. When I came to read his paper on, for example, health and ill health that was a real revelation (Lewis 1953).

A: Anyone else exert an important influence at that stage of your career?

ML: Michael Shepherd was another such person, in an unusual way. Some people found Michael very disconcerting and thought he was a very difficult person to cope with. He was certainly a shy man, but in a way he had a breadth of knowledge that was even greater than Aubrey Lewis's, but without necessarily the depth. I did work with Gerald Russell on the metabolic ward. As far as research was concerned, Michael Rutter was a great influence, but he was in epidemiological rather than laboratory research. But to see him in action when I was involved in the Isle of Wight survey was just extraordinary.

Toward an Interest in Benzodiazepines

A: Tell me how you became interested in addiction?

ML: I got involved in the benzodiazepine withdrawal problem and was sucked into addictions, initially with a little reluctance, but then more enthusiastically.

A: Tell me a little about that work on benzodiazepines which was to prove so seminal.

ML: Essentially it was looking at the benzodiazepines and whether they were associated with dependence. The epidemiological interest that I had had came in because it appeared to me and one or two of my contemporaries such as Peter Tyrer, who was working with me, that there was an excessive use of benzodiazepines long-term, but at normal dose. That was, I think, the factor which was unexpected because it was a given at the time that dependence was associated with escalation of dose. We had patients who were taking benzodiazepines but still on a therapeutic dose of no more than, for instance, 30 mg a day of diazepam, and yet when they tried to stop they got withdrawal symptoms and found they were unable to stop. One of our first studies showed that a few people who had escalated would get a withdrawal reaction, but then so would the people who had not escalated the dose. We had to say essentially the textbooks are wrong: one can get a physical dependence at normal dosage. I never thought that this was an unique phenomenon. We went on and did many studies using, I think, a reasonable experimental method; we published a Maudsley Monograph (Petursson & Lader 1984).

A: There were people writing who were very sanguine?

ML: Yes, they were trying to minimize the problem. In fact, in the United States there was never quite the concern there was in the United Kingdom. My allies were the media, people such as Ester Rantzen, for example—I appeared on her programme a couple of times. The first time her programme dealt with the issue they had more letters concerning this problem than they had ever had on any other topic. What has happened is that there has been a complete change in prescription practices on this class of drugs. These followed the Committee on Review of Medicines (1980), the Committee on Safety of Medicines (1988), but what probably most influenced developments was the legal profession. Patients were starting to bring in class actions that were ultimately unsuccessful, but it got the general practitioners to think again.

The UK and Institute of Psychiatry as Work Base

A: You remained at the Maudsley Hospital and Institute of Psychiatry for your working life—you got to this campus and are here to this day?

ML: I am refusing to leave even in retirement!

A: Were you envious of people working in America?

ML: I would have liked a few years in the United States, but there were factors that kept me in this country—partly my wife's career, partly that I was able to do what I wanted to do here. I was lucky that I was taken on by the Medical Research Council on its External Staff, and I always had enough money to do the research I wanted.

A: So Petursson & Lader (1984), how did that come to be written?

ML: Hannes Petursson was among the best PhD students I ever had. He came on a scholarship from Iceland to train in psychiatry and then he wanted to do research. My regret is that I could not find a post to keep Hannes in this country. He went to back to Iceland and he is professor in Reykjavik.

A: Were you always funded by a 5-year renewable MRC Programme Grant?

ML: I had my own salary and 5-year renewable research funds.

A: Although you were a university teacher you were not burdened with a large teaching programme, were you?

ML: I do not think anyone in the Institute was.

Presidency of the SSA

A: You became president of the Society for the Study of Addiction (SSA) in 1983–93 and you are now an Honorary Fellow.

ML: When I took over the Society it was limping along. I started to draw the threads together. It seemed to me that, first, the Society should have an annual meeting. The second thing was that we had a couple of endowed lectures, and it was logical to fit those into the annual meeting. I was particularly keen that we tried to get some educational programmes going.

A: You were bringing to SSA an extraordinarily broad experience of journals and of learned societies—international as well as national experience.

ML: That is right. I was founding editor, with Peter Venables, of *Biological Psychology.* I did it for about 15 years and then handed it on.

Advisory Responsibilities

A: Then you entered into the addictions world again very importantly as a member of the Advisory Council on the Misuse of Drugs. A lot of people will not know what ACMD is; can you explain what your role was?

ML: ACMD is a statutory committee, set up by an Act of Parliament to advise the government on aspects of addiction. It does not have any executive power. I chaired the Technical Committee, which is charged with the responsibility of looking into technical matters, and in particular we would advise as to whether a class or an individual drug should be scheduled in a particular way.

A: I see that you did a 14-year stint for the Committee of Review on Medicines, and for the last 15 years you have been advising the Ministry of Defence. Is that work you have enjoyed?

ML: Once you learn the basic principle which is that you advise, and that if the ministers or the civil service do not want to take your advice, that is their business.

A: You are a famous academic traveller—one day you are along the Great Wall of China, the next down the Camberwell Road.

ML: I have been to 70 countries, but there are almost 200 in the world.

A: Looked at in the round what do you feel have been your major achievements, or your major disappointments?

ML: I think the major achievement has been to give emphasis to the need that if a doctor prescribes medication, he or she must have to think their way right through to the end and how they are going to discontinue it. It does not sound like a major achievement, but I think it is. It means that we will not be overtaken again by a benzodiazepine-type.

A: Because you describe a very hardworking boyhood, studentship, no privilege, and no money, you might become just a hard-working scientist. But you shame me with your breadth of reading.

ML: Well, remember that for my generation there was no television; wartime was very drab and quite dangerous. When I was a child I had seven jigsaw puzzles and I got so bored with doing them that I used to turn them over and do them on the blank side. But my main diversion was reading. I learnt to read in air-raid shelters. It was always one of my main passions.

Wider Interests

A: And recently you have been working for an Open University degree in law?

ML: Yes, a subject that is different philosophically and conceptually from medicine and science, and I have thoroughly enjoyed it.

A: As well as your science and your reading, you have had some propensities as a collector?

ML: I have always found works of art and antique furniture much more interesting than unit trusts which diminish in value. Most recently I have become interested in medieval herbals.

A: You moved through a very changing English society. Early on it was perhaps a rather class-bound society. Are you aware of it being a more open society now? Were you ever handicapped by not having been to Winchester or Eton?

ML: I do not know—you cannot do a double-blind controlled cross-over trial on yourself.

A: Do you think your life has been guided by any personal, ethical or value system, or a general humane Greco Roman Judaic belief in justice and truth?

ML: I have always felt sympathy for the underdog and I saw deprivation in the Liverpool slums. I have always wanted to leave the world a bit better than when I entered it, all those kinds of things.

A: You have referred several times to the Second World War—this was frightening for you as a child?

ML: It was frightening. I was 3 when it broke out. I think my earliest memory is probably about the age of 4 in 1940, holding onto my mother's hand as she chatted with the neighbours wondering when the Germans were going to invade.

A: If today a young person were to come along and say, Professor Lader, I'm thinking of a career in addictions. I have got a good BSc, I have got a clinical training—is it a sensible thing to do? How would you answer?

ML: I think that someone with that background going into addiction has to accept that they are not going to get the grant support that they would in schizophrenia or molecular biology—that is, in Britain. I think in the United States it is different. My advice would be for them to go to the best research centre to do a PhD there. The clinical side is difficult because we know the type of client. They are not the easiest people to treat. Probably the important thing is to seize the opportunities that come your way.

A: The importance of marriage?

ML: One of the most sensible things I ever did was to persuade my wife to marry me. Happily we have been a very solid couple ever since. My three daughters are a delight, but none of them is in medicine. There are also my seven grandchildren.

References

Committee on Safety of Medicines (1988) Benzodiazepines, dependence and withdrawal problems. *Current Problems,* 21, 1.

Committee on the Review of Medicines (1980) Systematic review of the benzodiazepines. *BMJ,* 2, 719–720.

Lewis, A. (1953) Health as a social concept. *British Journal of Sociology,* 4, 109–124.

Petursson, H. & Lader, M. (1984) *Dependence on Tranquillisers.* Maudsley Monograph no. 28. Oxford: Oxford University Press.

Stevens, S. S., ed. (1951) *Handbook of Experimental Psychology.* London: Wiley.

13

Conversation with Raphael Mechoulam

Entering what was, at the start, a neglected field, Raphael Mechoulam went on to pursue over the next 40 years a highly productive career in cannabis research. This interview charts a sequence of discoveries and reveals something of the dedication and intellectual daring which has characterized the enterprise throughout.

Early Influences

Addiction (A): Raphael, so often a person's later career has its roots in their childhood and the cultural atmosphere at home. Can you tell me something about your early life?

Raphael Mechoulam (RM): I was born in 1930—for my family a happy time in eastern Europe. The wounds of the First World War were not too painful any more and Hitler was still considered a demented curiosity. My father, who had graduated from one of the finest medical schools in Europe, in Vienna, was a prominent physician, head of a hospital, while my mother, who had studied in Berlin, enjoyed the life of a well-to-do Jewish family. Books, concerts, the theatre and medicine were part of my family background. I was sent to an American Grade School, where I had the only regular schooling I can remember. Then the Second World War broke out. Bulgaria joined hands with Germany. Anti-Semitic laws made our life almost unbearable. My father took a position as a physician in a village, with no running water or electricity, hoping that we would be more secure up in the Balkans. We had to move from village to village over the years. My father was sent to a concentration camp in Bulgaria, but luckily we all survived. In 1944 a communist regime was established. The new leaders, who had spent their formative years in Moscow, copied the Russian Soviet system to the last iota. I felt that my life was being swept in a flood of brain washing, but I remember with gratitude the fine teachers at the Sofia First Male Gymnasium, who did their best under very difficult circumstances. I studied chemical engineering for about a year—and disliked it. We emigrated to Israel in 1949 where I wanted to study chemistry, but had to wait for about a year as the university chemical laboratories on

Mount Scopus were surrounded by the Arab Legion. Slowly academic life improved, but looking back I realize today that I missed the challenges and excitement of a regular university education. Surprisingly, I first tasted the sweet taste of research in the Army. I was attached to a research unit and worked on various projects—mainly on insecticides, as insects had always been a scourge in the Middle East. I found the independence of research to be an addiction from which I do not want to be cured.

Entering the Cannabis Research Field

A: You published your first paper on cannabis more than 40 years ago. What led you into this field, which at the time was considered of minor interest and importance?

RM: In the early 1960s I returned to Israel from a post-doctoral stay at the Rockefeller Institute in New York, where I worked with the late Professor S. W. Pelletier on investigations on the structure of some plant triterpenes. My PhD thesis (with F. Sondheimer) in the mid-1950s was on synthetic chemistry, mostly in the field of steroids. I found research at the borderline of chemistry and biology fascinating. I believed then, and I still believe, that the separation of scientific fields is just an admission of our limited ability to learn and understand several scientific areas. In nature the border does not exist. If a leaf and a tree were able to think theywould not know the difference between chemistry and biology.

A: And back in Israel?

RM: Back in Israel I was appointed to a junior faculty position in the chemistry department of the Weizmann Institute in Rehovot. In Israel, as in the US and many countries in Europe, new staff members are supposed to choose their own research topics and then, after 5–6 years, their success (or lack of it) is evaluated and the junior staff member obtains (or does not obtain) tenure. I chose to work on several topics on the chemistry and actions of natural products. One of my topics was the constituents of cannabis.

A: Why that topic?

RM: Why cannabis? On reading the old literature on cannabis I was surprised to note that from a modern point of view the field was ripe for a reinvestigation. In the early 1960s it was almost totally neglected. There were 19th-century papers in many languages. I found and read dozens of publications in long-forgotten and obscure journals. Then I went to the more recent papers and was surprised to find that the active constituent(s) of cannabis had never been isolated in pure form and no definite structure(s) had been put forward. The reasons may have been technical. We know today that the cannabinoids—a term I coined some years later—are present in cannabis as a mixture of a large number of closely related constituents, which were difficult to separate by the methods available in the 19th and early 20th centuries. Chromatography methods were well developed at the time I started work and the availability of novel spectrometric methods looked promising for the structure elucidations. I assumed that of particular help could be an early type of a nuclear magnetic resonance (NMR) spectrometer. Luckily I was proved right.

A: Why was the cannabis field dormant at the time and why did you think that it was of importance?

RM: As the active constituent(s) of cannabis was not available in pure form there was very little modern biological and clinical work on it. And as it was an illicit substance it was not readily available to most scientists. Even if obtained legally, research with it was a laboratory nightmare. From a scientific point of view cannabis research had effectively been eliminated.

A: How did you overcome these obstacles?

RM: I was unaware of them. I went to the administrative director of the Weizmann Institute and simply asked him whether he knew somebody at Police Headquarters. Thus I obtained 5 kg of superb, smuggled Lebanese hashish. I took a bus back to Rehovot, nobody in the bus realizing that the smell from my bag was from hashish. Later we found that I had broken quite a few laws. I just had to apologize. Since then I have been obtaining hashish from the police for over 40 years, with Ministry of Health-signed documents.

Discovery of THC

A: Going back to science, how did you then proceed?

RM: First, I re-isolated cannabidiol (CBD), a major non-psychoactive constituent which had been isolated, but whose structure was only partially known. Yuval Shvo, a close friend, and I were able to establish its structure and stereochemistry using an early NMR machine.[1] The publication on CBD caused no scientific ripples. Over the years, however, interest in CBD has gradually increased.[2–5]

A: And next?

RM: In 1963 another close friend at the Weizmann Institute, Yehiel Gaoni, joined me in the cannabinoid research. Our goal was to identify the active constituent of cannabis. We needed a biologist with experience in psychopharmacology who could give us feedback on the activity of fractions and pure compounds isolated. We succeeded in enticing Dr Haviv Edery, the head of pharmacology at the nearby Biological Research Institute. He had a colony of rhesus monkeys and all the biological work leading to the isolation of the active hashish component was based on feedback from the rhesus monkeys. Repeated chromatographic separations of a petroleum ether extract finally gave us a pure although oily compound which, however, crystallized as one of its esters. The NMR spectrum and elemental analysis led to its structure and we even succeeded in preparing it from cannabidiol.[6] We named the compound Δ^1-tetrahydrocannabinol (Δ^1-THC), so that its nomenclature would parallel that of CBD. Unfortunately some pedantic chemists decided to follow the strict rules of chemical nomenclature and today Δ^1-THC has become Δ^9-THC.

A: So the neglect of cannabis research was overcome?

RM: Gradually scientists in various disciplines realized that the cannabis field was ripe for investigation and thousands of publications have since appeared on THC. It is even used as a therapeutic drug against nausea and for enhancing appetite. Surprisingly, it has not become an illicit drug—apparently cannabis users prefer their marijuana and hashish.

A: And other cannabinoids?

RM: Later we isolated six or seven new plant cannabinoids. Over the years many other groups isolated additional compounds—mostly related closely to the original cannabinoids we found in the plant. We were really surprised that from the horrendous cannabinoid soup in cannabis, only Δ^9-THC affected the rhesus monkeys.

A: How was your research funded?

RM: Originally we did not need a great deal of support. All the work was done by Yehiel Gaoni and myself. Since 1965, for over four decades, the US National Institute on Drug Abuse (NIDA) has supported our cannabis research, although I have to work hard to renew the grant every few years. I have known most of the directors of NIDA. I found that all of them were very knowledgeable in the field. I was pleasantly surprised to note that with NIDA the bureaucratic demands were minor and that once a project was approved there was no interference, either scientific or administrative, although our results and those of my colleagues did not always necessarily support the drug policy of the US federal administration.

A: What were the next steps in your research?

RM: First, Gaoni and I accomplished and published facile syntheses of almost all natural cannabinoids.[7] The next major problem seemed to be the metabolic pathways of THC.[8]

A: Other research groups also because interested in this question?

RM: It seems that about every major group in the field had the same idea. In 1970 four laboratories including mine, now at the Hebrew University Medical Faculty, reported more or less simultaneously that hydroxylation at the 11-position was the primary metabolic step. A huge amount of work was conducted on the cannabinoids over the next 15 years by my group, and by many other groups, mainly in the United States, Europe and Japan. We learned a great deal about cannabinoid pharmacology, biochemistry and clinical effects; however, their mode of action remained an enigma.

A: Why did their mode of action remain an enigma?

RM: The reasons for this baffling situation were both technical and conceptual. The conceptual problem related to THC activity had been raised by

Bill Paton from Oxford, who had pointed out that the cannabinoids belong to the group of biologically active lipophiles, and that their effects should be compared with the chronic effects of anesthetics and solvents. Hence, following this line of thought, it was possible to explain the action of THC without postulating the existence of a receptor or specific action on an enzyme or a biological system.

A: But then evidence for a receptor site came through?

RM: In 1988 Allyn Howlett, with her then graduate student Bill Devane, brought out the first evidence that a cannabinoid receptor exists in the brain.[9] We assumed that a cannabinoid receptor is not formed for the sake of a plant that has compounds that bind to it, but for an endogenous brain ligand. I decided to try to identify it.

The Discovery of Cannabinoid Ligands

A: How was that achieved?

RM: Bill Devane had by this time completed his PhD thesis and applied for a post-doctoral position in my laboratory. He wanted to learn some synthetic chemistry; I had other plans for him. At this point Dr. Lumir Hanus of the Czech State joined us. We first synthesized a novel, highly active radioactive probe and proceeded toward identification of a cannabinoid ligand using this probe.

A: Sounds difficult!

RM: The isolation problems were at first almost insurmountable. As soon as fractions which bound to the cannabinoid receptor were purified, they started to lose their activity. We know now that this was due to the lack of stability of the cannabinoid ligand. We tried to obtain a NMR spectrum. This was not simple to do on the 300 MHz machine available to us, and we ended with a curve which contained probably more impurities than actual material. However, two groups of peaks clearly indicated olefinic and doubly allylic protons in a ratio of 4 : 3. Such spectra are quite typical for polyunsaturated long-chain fatty acids. For me this was the breakthrough.

A: Exciting—what next?

RM: Some more mass spectra and a better NMR led to a final formulation of anandamide as it stands today.[10]

A: How did you name this newly discovered substance?

RM: We decided to name the new brain-derived ligand anandamide. Bill Devane was learning Sanskrit at the time and suggested 'ananda' (supreme joy in this ancient tongue). We believed that the endocannabinoid system plays a role in the formation of emotions. I looked for a suitable Hebrew equivalent but nothing came to mind. There are many synonyms for 'sorrow' in Hebrew but considerably less for 'joy'. In any case, anandamide certainly brought joy to us: it has been cited over 1800 times and its effects are studied widely.

The Complexity

A: There are numerous additional endocannabinoids known today. They act on a long list of biological targets. Can you summarize today's situation?

RM: A second major endocannabinoid, 2-arachidonoyl glycerol (2-AG) was identified in my lab and later, independently by a Japanese group. Other groups, as well as mine, have indeed identified various fatty acid ethanolamides and glycerol esters as well as fatty acids amides of amino acids. Some of the new members of this family of compounds bind to the CB1/CB2 receptors. Others do not; but new putative cannabinoid receptors are also being discovered. An orphan receptor, GPR55, has been found to bind anandamide and 2-AG, but not some synthetic cannabinoids that are excellent ligands to CB1/CB2.

A: It seems as if one is dealing with a wide family of substances?

RM: I believe that we should look at the endogenous fatty acid ethanolamides and glycerol esters, as well as the fatty acids amides of amino acids as members of a large endocannabinoid family. Most of them seem to be formed 'on demand' and their actions take place around the areas of synthesis. Hence their effects are predominantly local and specific. Their actions are ubiquitous. They are involved in most physiological systems that have been investigated—the nervous, the cardiovascular, the reproductive, the immune system, to mention a few. One of their main roles is neuroprotection,[11] but over the last decade they have been found to affect a long list of processes, from anxiety, depression, cancer development, vasodilation to bone formation and even pregnancy.[12]

A: Do you still have contact with young scientists?

RM: I still teach graduate students at the Hebrew University of Jerusalem. I have an enthusiastic bunch of young people working in my group. Most are from Israel, but a German and an American have just joined my group. At present my group is a 'mixed bag' of researchers: Moslem and Christian Arabs, observant and non-observant Jews. They work together very well indeed. It is a tragedy that Israelis and Palestinians cannot get along as well as my students do. I hope that some day we shall be able to understand fully both the chemistry and neuropsychological mechanisms of emotions, and will realize that they represent two aspects of the same phenomenon.

Notes

1. Mechoulam R., Shvo Y. The structure of cannabidiol. *Tetrahedron* 1963; 19: 2073–8.
2. Malfait A. M., Gallily R., Sumariwalla P. F., Malik A. S., Andreakos E., Mechoulam R. et al. The non-psychoactive cannabis-constituent cannabidiol is an oral anti-arthritic therapeutic in murine collagen-induced arthritis. *Proc Natl Acad Sci USA* 2000; 97: 9561–6.

3. Cunha J. M., Carlini E. A., Pereira A. E., Ramos O. L., Pimentel G., Gagliardi R. et al. Chronic administration of CBD to healthy volunteers and epileptic patients. *Pharmacologia* 1980; 21: 175–85.
4. Murillo-Rodriguez E., Millan-Aldaco D., Palomero-Rivero M., Prospero-Garcia O., Mechoulam R., Drucker-Colin R. Cannabidiol, a constituent of Cannabis sativa, modulates sleep in rats. *FEBS Lett* 2006; 580: 4337–45.
5. Carrier E. J., Auchampach J. A., Hillard C. J. Inhibition of an equilibrative nucleoside transporter by cannabidiol: a mechanism of cannabinoid immunosuppression. *Proc Natl Acad Sci USA* 2006; 103: 7895–900.
6. Gaoni Y., Mechoulam R. Isolation, structure and partial synthesis of an active constituent of hashish. *J Am Chem Soc* 1964; 86: 1646–7.
7. Mechoulam R., Braun P., Gaoni Y. Syntheses of Δ1-THC and related cannabinoids. *J Am Chem Soc* 1972; 94: 6159–65.
8. Mechoulam R. Marihuana chemistry. *Science* 1970; 168: 1159–66.
9. Devane D. C., Dysarz F. A., Johnson M. R., Melvin L. S., Howlett A. C. Determination and characterization of a cannabinoid receptor in rat brain. *Mol Pharmacol* 1988; 34: 605–13.
10. Devane W. A., Hanus L., Breuer A., Pertwee R. G., Stevenson L. A., Griffin G. et al. Isolation and structure of a brain constituent that binds to the cannabinoid receptor. *Science* 1992; 258: 1946–9.
11. Panikashvili D., Simeonidou C., Ben-Shabat S., Hanus L., Breuer A., Mechoulam R. et al. An endogenous cannabinoid (2-AG) is neuroprotective after brain injury. *Nature* 2001; 413: 527–31.
12. Pachter P., Batkai S., Kunos G. The endocannabinoid system as an emerging target of pharmacotherapy. *Pharmacol Rev* 2006; 58: 389–462.

14

Conversation with Charles R. Schuster

Charles R. ('Bob') Schuster is Professor of Psychiatry and Behavioral Sciences and Director, Substance Abuse Research Division, Addiction Research Institute, at Wayne State University, in Detroit, Michigan. He has made fundamental and varied contributions to the application of learning theory to understanding of drug taking and drug dependence. In 1990 he was a recipient of the Nathan B. Eddy Award.

Beginnings

Addiction (A): Bob, if there is an organizing principle in your career, it has been the application of learning theory very broadly to problems of drug abuse. How did you become interested in behavior and psychology, and how did you become a drug abuse researcher? Does this date back to your days as an undergraduate?

Charles R. Schuster (CRS): I would go back even further. My mother was an excellent musician and I started to play the trumpet when I was 5 years of age. My older sister Bette was a poet and a jazz lover. She went to the nightclubs in Philadelphia and met a lot of jazz musicians and invited them to come and play at our house on Saturday afternoons. We provided food and drink but it helped that Bette was beautiful. Anyway, the people who came would encourage me to play with them. I got to play with a lot of well-known guys from the big bands and by the time I was 15, I started playing in local nightclubs. So, my high school career was sort of a disaster. I did manage to be a C + student but that was because my mother was a schoolteacher as well as a musician. I had a certain amount of knowledge just because of the household that I lived in, but it certainly was not due to working hard in school. By my senior year of high school, two of my friends were using heroin intermittently. Later they got hooked on heroin and are not alive today. I saw many musicians who shot up heroin die young. That scared me out of the music business and into college.

A: So to what college?

CRS: I could not get into a regular college, so I went to a two-year community college and my grades improved. I transferred to Gettysburg College where I received excellent training in biology and experimental psychology. My first stint in graduate school was at the University of New Mexico where I got a degree in physiology and physiological psychology. I was a student of George Peterson, who had been a student of Carl Lashley. I did brain research; very little in the way of behavioral research. My master's thesis was on the behavioral consequences of severing the corpus callosum in the rat. Well, I did not ask the right questions and found nothing. I got a good grounding in scientific method and the physiology of the brain.

A: The next move?

CRS: I went to work first as an endocrine biologist at Temple Medical School. While there, I served as research assistant to a visiting professor by the name of Bernard Zondek. I learned a great deal of endocrinology from him and he pronounced when he was leaving 'Ach my boy—your future is assured—you have worked with Zondek!'. At that time, something that really did affect the rest of my life occurred. Smith-Kline & French (SKF) bought the US marketing rights for chlorpromazine from the Rhone-Poulenc Pharmaceutical Company. At that point they received a proposal from Don Bullock, a Columbia University trained psychologist, to set up a laboratory using behavioral assays to screen for new psychiatric medications. Don Bullock was given a year's contract by SKF and I was hired as his assistant. So, around 1956 I joined SKF. After 6 months of being there I was put in charge of the laboratory for several years. By that time SKF decided that behavioral pharmacology was here to stay. I went back to school to get my doctorate.

An Emerging Interest in Behavioral Pharmacology

A: After SKF?

CRS: Fortunately for me I attended a lecture Joe Brady gave in Philadelphia. He and Sherman Ross of the University of Maryland had just been given a psychopharmacology grant by NIH. Joe Brady at that time was a Captain in the army, stationed at the Walter Reed Army Institute of Research (WRAIR), but he was also a professor at the University of Maryland. Joe asked me whether I wanted to join the laboratory to get my doctorate. He offered me an instructor's salary, because I knew something about pharmacology. So I went to the University of Maryland, only to find out that they had not even considered that they needed an analytical balance to prepare drugs.

A: They were all psychologists?

CRS: Yes. One of my first big contributions was to teach everyone how to weigh out drugs, how to make drug solutions, and various kinds of injection procedures.

A: There were also a lot of neuroscientists there?

CRS: Great neuroscientists. I received training in both behavior and neuroscience. There was also a neuroendocrinologist by the name of John Mason at WRAIR. He was measuring hormonal changes in rhesus monkeys subjected to stress. The problem was how to avoid stressing the animals when getting blood samples. He developed a surgical procedure for implanting chronic jugular catheters, running them under the skin up to a pedestal that was attached to the skull. He could attach a line to the catheter and remove blood remotely. I looked at that, and I said if he could take blood out, then I could put drugs in. Suddenly I remembered the jazz musicians I had seen injecting heroin and other drugs. I wondered whether or not drugs of abuse would serve as positive reinforcers in animals. So, the first thing that I did was to see whether I could get animals to self-inject anything intravenously. I did a study with Bob Clark and Joe Brady (Clark et al. 1961). At the same time, I thought, well, I know how I can get drugs to serve as positive reinforcers in animals—I can make them a conditioned reinforcer. My doctoral dissertation was on drugs as discriminative stimuli in monkeys. I learned that Jim Weeks was able to get morphine to serve as a reinforcer in physically dependent rats. Travis Thompson (a postdoctoral fellow in the laboratory) and I decided to make monkeys physically dependent and then let them go into withdrawal, which would be relieved by an injection of morphine. Monkeys quickly learned to lever press for morphine injections (Thompson & Schuster 1964). These studies were very exciting for me. I was able to see the parallels between these animal studies and what I had observed in humans in my earlier days as a jazz musician. We had a model of human drug addiction (Schuster & Thompson 1969).

A Move to the University of Michigan

A: So what happened next?

CRS: Travis and I went to the meeting at the University of Michigan. Maurice Seevers, who was the chairman of the pharmacology department there, heard my presentation and knew that I was available. They offered me $12 000/year. I did not even ask about space; I had no idea what I was getting myself into but it looked like a great opportunity for me to work with some great guys in pharmacology. I had just gotten an NIH grant for $28 000 to study drug self-administration in rhesus monkeys and thought the University of Michigan would be a good place to do the research. So I moved to the University of Michigan in 1962, and had 5 marvelous years there.

A: Tell us about Maurice Seevers. He is quite a notable figure in addiction research.

CRS: He was incredibly influential. He had trained more pharmacologists than anyone else in the country at that time. He was a very forceful, domineering kind of gentleman. Loud, at times crude, but smart as can be.

New Opportunities at the University of Chicago

A: Why did you leave the University of Michigan?

CRS: I was contacted by Jerry Jaffe, one of the giants in the field of addiction, who at that time was a young psychiatrist at the University of Chicago. Jerry was setting up a publicly funded drug abuse treatment program for the State of Illinois. He decided that he would like to have me join him as his Associate Administrator for the state's program. Never being one to pass up an opportunity like that, I left my tenured position at the University of Michigan for a non-tenured Associate Professorship at the University of Chicago. It was the greatest move I ever made. Again, I walked into an incredibly rich environment. After Danny Friedman left Chicago to go to UCLA the psychiatry department had several acting chairs—I was the Chair for a year. Can you believe it? A non-physician, non-clinician drug abuse researcher as the Chair of Psychiatry at the University of Chicago. I did my best and the department survived. The thing that I liked about Chicago was being able to be involved with human treatment and clinical research while at the same time continuing my animal research.

A: Another important development in your research in Chicago was the establishment of one of the first human behavioral pharmacology laboratories, based conceptually on your work with animals.

CRS: Yes, I decided after a couple of years that being an administrator at the State of Illinois drug abuse treatment program was limiting to my research. So I moved out of the position and with Danny Freedman's support established the Drug Abuse Research Center at the University of Chicago. It was at that time that I started to do basic drug abuse research with humans.

A: Were you interested in marijuana research?

CRS: Another human laboratory study that stands out in my memory is one I did with Pierre Renault with marijuana smoking (Renault et al. 1971). At that time people thought that marijuana users never got high the first time they used the drug. There was a theory that initial exposure induced enzymes so that when people subsequently smoked marijuana they got high from some new type of CNS active metabolite. I was suspicious of this idea. I had seen young musicians smoke marijuana for the first time and I realized that it was probably the fact that the naive smoker did not smoke it the same way. They did not inhale as much smoke, did not hold it as long in the lung, and so forth.

From Chicago to the Directorship of National Institute on Drug Abuse (NIDA)

A: Why did you leave the University of Chicago?

CRS: In 1986, I got a call asking me whether I would be interested in applying for the job of Director of NIDA. I thought at first that it was a joke since this was during the Reagan years, and I was known as a capital L—liberal. Anyway, I was offered the position. After discussions with my wife Chris-Ellyn, we decided that I should accept the job. This was one of the most exciting and scary things that had ever happened to me.

A: Tell us some of your experiences at NIDA.

CRS: A few weeks after I arrived, I got a call from a congressperson who asked what I would do if NIDA had $60 million more a year. The NIDA budget, when I got there, was $85 million total. I called in my senior-level people and I said Okay guys, we have to have a proposal in two days to justify an increase of $60 million dollars. We got the $60 million dollar increase. That was an absolute joy, because suddenly we were able to start doing important research in new areas.

A: During that same period of time it became known that drug abuse was an important vector for HIV/AIDS transmission. Tell us a little about that problem and your involvement with it.

CRS: I felt that it was incumbent upon NIDA to research interventions that might decrease the spread of the AIDS virus among intravenous drug users and their sexual partners (Schuster 1992). The message they carried was get into treatment— but if you will not do that, do not share needles. We introduced the use of bleach as a disinfecting agent. Unfortunately, we were barred from using federal funds for needle exchange programs. I argued with my superiors about this policy, and in large measure that was one of the reasons for me ultimately leaving the position of being the director of NIDA. Another major problem was that we were limited to a great extent in talking about the use of condoms.

A: You enjoyed the NIDA experience?

CRS: The years at NIDA were absolutely phenomenal for me. It was, however, a constant battle with certain people in the government who felt only contempt for drug addicts. They looked at methadone maintenance as coddling of addicts. Maintenance was a hard sell for me. I can remember going to a White House Conference on drug abuse, I believe in 1988, and I was booed when I talked about methadone as an effective treatment for opiate addiction. It was tough. After 6 years, I decided that I wanted to go back and do research.

A: Tell me about your impact on the many scientists that worked with you, carrying forward the traditions of your mentors into the training of a younger scientist.

CRS: First of all, I was blessed to have Joe Brady as my mentor. Joe was pretty much hands off. He said, 'Okay, here is the equipment, here are the animals, do what you would like to do.' He set the occasion for me to go into the laboratory and explore—a luxury that was incredible. I attempted to follow that with all of my graduate students; I gave them a basic education in pharmacology and behavioral analysis, and taught them to critically read the literature. After that within the loose constraints of the grants that supported our research, they had to develop their own research projects. That is what made research exciting for them—they felt they had ownership of the project. My role was to guide them, not direct them. I was also fortunate to have great graduate students and postdocs. They educated me as much as I educated them.

Present Activities

A: Could you say something now about what projects you are currently working on and what research you find exciting.

CRS: Where to begin? First, I am interested in treatment service delivery. We applied to NIDA and were selected to become the Great Lakes Regional Node of the NIDA/Clinical Trials Network. I am the Director of the GLRN node, which is one of 17 spread around the country. The program is designed to take treatment interventions that have been shown to have efficacy in controlled clinical trials to see whether they are 'effective' when implemented in community-treatment programs.

A: How do you generally rate the relationship between the scientific findings and the community application in this arena?

CRS: I think there has been a tremendous gap between community treatment programs and the academic institutions where clinical research is conducted. That's why the Clinical Trials Network is so exciting.

A: What else are you doing in research?

CRS: I still am interested in human laboratory studies. Chris-Ellyn Johanson along with Kirk Frey from the University of Michigan and I have a grant to investigate the neurobehavioral toxic consequences of high-dose methamphetamine abuse in humans.

A: Another area of applied research that I know that you are currently very interested in, and where you have had a significant role over your career, is the issue surrounding the approval and regulation of medications as 'controlled substances.'

CRS: Our society uses governmental regulations as a means of controlling access to drugs that have abuse potential. Testing would probably begin with drug self-administration studies to determine whether the drug will serve as a positive reinforcer in laboratory animals. If the animal data suggest that the drug has abuse potential it would then be evaluated for its abuse potential in human laboratory and later in clinical studies. Finally, the FDA may request that the pharmaceutical company marketing the drug conduct post-marketing surveillance studies to monitor its possible diversion and abuse. My group at Wayne State has conducted several postmarketing surveillance studies (Arfken et al. 2003), and is currently monitoring the new buprenorphine products Suboxone and Subutex, which are being prescribed by physicians for the treatment of opioid dependence.

A Career in Science

A: It is very clear that you have enjoyed your work immensely and that what you are doing now is as important to you as anything that you have done in the past. Tell us a little about the experience of a career in science and where it leaves you at this particular point in life.

CRS: Throughout my career, I have followed my nose. There is no other way to put it. I have met people who have planned their careers. I sure did not. If I saw interesting things, things that have turned me on, things that excited me—I would go there. I am blessed with the fact that I had a broad enough background in pharmacology, physiology and behavioral sciences so I could move into new areas. I am not an expert in many of the areas of research that I have worked in. But I know enough about them to talk to the experts and convince them that it would be great to work together on a project. So now I am doing functional MRI, PET scanning, things that I am obviously not capable of doing myself. I see these new techniques as tools for answering questions that I think are important. That is what keeps me excited about things. There are new toys to be played with all the time and new ways of approaching some of the age-old questions. Methamphetamine abuse has come back and I am working with PET experts to study possible long-term effects on brain dopamine systems. My colleagues are doing studies to understand the human pharmacology of MDMA using very sophisticated procedures. I am lucky to work with my wife Chris-Ellyn Johanson. We enjoy science together—but she also helps me to keep my life balanced with other things—novels, art, music and boating. All of these things keep me interested and excited about life and continuing to work. When it stops being exciting, then I will consider retiring.

References

Arfken, C. L., Schuster, C. R. & Johanson, C.-E. (2003) Postmarketing surveillance of abuse liability of sibutramine. *Drug and Alcohol Dependence,* 69, 169–173.

Clark, R., Schuster, C. R. & Brady, J. V. (1961) Instrumental conditioning of jugular self-infusion in the rhesus monkey. *Science,* 133, 1828–1830.

Renault, P. F., Schuster, C. R., Heinrich, R. & Freedman, D. X. (1971) Marijuana: standardized smoke administration and dose effect curves on heart rate in humans. *Science,* 174, 589–591.

Schuster, C. R. (1992) Drug abuse research and HIV/AIDS: a national perspective from the US. *British Journal of Addiction,* 87, 355–361.

Schuster, C. R. & Thompson, T. (1969) Self-administration of and behavioral dependence on drugs. *Annual Review of Pharmacology,* 9, 483–502.

Thompson, T. & Schuster, C. R. (1964) Morphine self-administration, food-reinforced and avoidance behaviors in rhesus monkeys. *Psychopharmacologia,* 5, 87–94.

15

Conversation with Tomoji Yanagita

Tomoji Yanagita is a Japanese scientist who has for many years been a leading international figure in the study of drug self-administration by laboratory animals. He conducted postgraduate work at the University of Michigan and in his professional career did much to strengthen international understanding of the Japanese contribution in this arena.

Background

Addiction (A): Dr Yanagita, I would like you to tell me about your family, how you grew up, where you were educated.

Tomoji Yanagita (TY): I was the first son in my family. My grandfather and father were both physicians. So I was expected to be the next generation in that tradition. During my college years I was interested in physiology. As my father did, I attended the Jikei University School of Medicine, which is located in Tokyo. While I was there I became very interested in pharmacology. During the year that I served my medical internship at the Red Cross Hospital, I treated my father's patients in his office when he was away at meetings. I remember being concerned about an allergic reaction observed in the patient to whom I administered penicillin. Since that time, I became interested in the adverse effects of medications such as penicillin. So my interest in pharmacology was further strengthened by this early clinical experience. Thus, I decided that I wanted to become a pharmacologist.

A: In your medical school training at the Jikei University, was pharmacology taught in the same way as it is in the USA?

TY: Yes, almost.

A: You had a course in pharmacology? Did that include laboratory experiments as well as lectures?

TY: Yes, we had lectures and we did about eight experiments, both whole-animal and in vitro studies.

A: Do you remember any particular pharmacology professor who had an impact on your choice of pharmacology as your specialty?

TY: Yes, my boss. There was only one professor in the department, who was the chairman.

A: Who was that?

TY: Dr Nakao. I forgot to mention that my father received a PhD in pharmacology at the Jikei University. So he knew Dr Nakao well and encouraged me to study pharmacology with him.

A: Was your father a specialist or was he a family practitioner?

TY: Both. Well, my father, after taking his medical training and a PhD degree in pharmacology, entered into orthopedics. He became the vice director of an orthopedic hospital in Tokyo that was owned by a professor of orthopedics at the Tokyo University. However, when my grandfather wanted to retire he requested that my father come home to take over his medical practice. Because my grandfather's clinic was in a small city it was not possible for my father to continue specializing in orthopedics. So he became a general practitioner and took over my grandfather's clinic.

A: Was your father the oldest son?

TY: No, but he was a physician and the only family member who could take over my grandfather's clinic.

A: Do you have any brothers and sisters?

TY: Yes, I have one sister and one brother. My brother was interested in flower gardening but I requested him to enter medical school. He did so. When he graduated from medical school I wanted to be a pharmacologist and so I asked my younger brother to take over my father's clinic. My father used to say that either one of us should take over the clinic.

A: I suspect that in Japan the father's request is usually honored?

TY: Yes. But he knew I wanted to be a pharmacologist and that I was doing well in pharmacology, so he let me go into pharmacology expecting that my younger brother could take over his clinic.

A: So your brother took over the clinic at your request? Do you ever have any regrets about making that decision?

TY: Not at all. My brother has been very successful. He is doing very well as a clinician—much better than I would have done. He is quite lucky since he has been able to retain hard-working staff members and good patients. He expanded to double my family's houses and land holdings.

A: How long after you got your medical degree before you came to the University of Michigan?

TY: Six years. After my internship, I returned to the department of pharmacology at my home university, where I did a series of studies on morphine physical dependence in rats and received my PhD in pharmacology. Then, in 1960, Professor Hosoya of Keio University—a close friend of Dr Seevers, professor and chairman of the University of Michigan Pharmacology Department—recommended to my boss that I should apply for a fellowship program set up by Dr Seevers to spend a couple years studying pharmacology at the department.

A: You took your family with you to Michigan?

TY: That's right. I was the first fellow who took their family with them to the USA. The Japanese academia had a rather rigid and brutal view saying that fellows were going to study so it was not considered appropriate to take a family. I didn't care about the academia's view, so I took my wife and 6-month-old child with me.

A: You came expecting to stay only 2 years but you stayed much longer?

TY: Yes, I came to the USA in June 1960 and stayed for 5 years.

A: Tell me about your first experiences at the University of Michigan.

TY: At that time, it was impossible to use monkeys in Japan and I wanted to take advantage of the large monkey colony that Dr Seevers had for opiate research. In Japan, we couldn't think of using such animals in the laboratories.

A: Was that because of the lack of facilities or was it an ethical issue?

TY: Not an ethical problem, we simply didn't have the facilities for monkey research in Japan at that time. It was too costly and we could not obtain monkeys.

A: Were you there when the drug self-administration studies started at the University of Michigan?

TY: I arrived at June 1960, and the drug self-administration studies started in 1961. Prior to that, we had attempted to get monkeys to drink morphine and methadone. Then, by the end of 1960, we found that the drinking method had definite limitations because even the morphine-dependent monkeys refused to drink methadone or pethidine, probably due to the taste. Therefore, I understood that we had to adopt a different approach. At that time, Dr Weeks, a senior colleague in the pharmacology department who was working at Upjohn Laboratories in Kalamazoo, Michigan, developed an intravenous catheterization method in rats. One snowy day in the winter, Drs Seevers, Deneau, my laboratory mentor, and I visited Dr Weeks at Kalamazoo. We saw how he did the surgery and how he had devised a way of protecting the catheter that ran from the rat to an infusion pump. We realized later that adapting the IV catheter surgery for a monkey was the easiest part. The biggest challenge was how to have them be free to move about their cage and at the same time protect the catheter. But we finally got something that worked.

A: After you developed this system, what was the first drug that you studied in self-administration?

TY: Morphine. The next drug was cocaine. Because cocaine was a powerfully addicting drug in humans. However, it was known that it did not produce physical dependence in animals. At that time, the addicting properties of drugs were believed to be attributable to the need to avoid the aversive symptoms of the withdrawal syndrome, and self-administration of cocaine in monkeys was expected to answer this question.

A: I've seen movies of the animals you studied in the cocaine experiment. You might want to describe the movies that you made.

TY: Monkeys really were crazy to self-administer cocaine and took an injection about every 5 minutes. After the monkeys had been self-administering cocaine for a few days, they began to have convulsions. But the convulsions did not stop them from continuing to self-administer cocaine.

A: Were you surprised that there were not clear-cut withdrawal signs when animals stopped taking cocaine?

TY: I knew the results of Dr Seevers' experiment on cocaine in rhesus monkeys, but I was deeply impressed by the results that there were almost no withdrawal signs except the sleeping.

A: You continued to study other drugs in the self-administration model. Do you remember any particular drug that interested you?

TY: Well, one dramatic drug was pentobarbital. The monkeys took it quite often and became drowsy and would continue taking the drug until they fell down unconscious. After a few minutes, they would awaken and go back to the lever pressing for more drug injections.

A: Did you think when you were in Michigan that you would be able to continue primate research in Japan?

TY: No, I didn't. Dr Seevers wanted me to continue my research studies at the University of Michigan. But I told him that I felt I should go back home and contribute my experience to new drug development in Japan. Although at the University of Michigan I did research on drugs of abuse, I also learned about pre-clinical studies for new drug development including the toxicological studies that must be done in animals before a drug is tested in humans. I knew that Japan did not have natural resources such as iron and oil but did have chemical and biological technology. Therefore, I thought that Japan should try to take a leadership role in the pharmaceutical industry. Well, as you know, we have become very productive in building ships and cars and not very competitive in the pharmaceutical industry. So much for my predictions!

A: When you returned to Japan, did you keep in touch with Dr Seevers?

TY: Yes, he was very helpful to me when I returned to Japan. He arranged for me to get a subcontract from his NIH grant so that I could start a small primate research laboratory at the Central Institute for Experimental Animals in Kawasaki. To supplement the funds that Dr Seevers provided, I started a research unit that did contract studies on drug properties such as abuse liability, toxicity, pharmacodynamics and pharmacokinetics in animals for pharmaceutical industries. Subsequently, the Japanese government made new regulations that mandated drug self-administration studies with all new medications that had central nervous system effects. For over 30 years, those studies were conducted in my laboratory.

A: I have heard people in the USA say that you could not get a drug on the market in Japan unless Yanagita approved.

TY: That is not true! Only for the abuse liability of CNS-acting drugs.

A: Well, when you came back to Japan did you know that you were going to have a job? You were gone for 5 years, what did the university say about that?

TY: The university kept my position open. My boss was waiting for me to set up a laboratory and be promoted to full professorship. But when I found out that the university couldn't handle monkeys I said, 'I'm sorry I cannot come back to the university because I have this contract research program and I have to have a monkey laboratory'.

A: So you went to the Central Laboratory for Experimental Animals in Kawasaki in 1966 and you were there for how many years?

TY: For 30 years. I was there until 1996.

A: You worked there for 30 years and you had support from the pharmaceutical companies for whom you did research?

TY: Yes. But also I was supported in part by the government.Funds from the Ministry of Education were for basic research, and those of the Ministry of Welfare and Public Health were rather for applied research.Training was not our major focus, but we did have more than 10 post-doctoral fellows from Japan as well as from other countries.

A: Did you maintain a position at Jikei University during those years?

TY: Yes, I gave a lecture over there several times a year. In 1992, I became a part-time professor.

A: Why did you retire from the Central Institute? Is there an age in Japan when you must retire?

TY: There was no age limitation. The major reason was it became more difficult to maintain the laboratory. That is, because of the hard competition it became more difficult to continue the basic research and I tended to do only the contract studies. When I opened up my laboratory in 1966 it was the only contract laboratory for pharmacological and toxicological studies. In 1996, there were about 50 laboratories. When I closed my section at the Central Institute I moved all the dependence facilities and monkeys and also the lab staff in my group to where I am working today: a private contract laboratory called Ina Research, Inc. 'Ina' is the name of a city in the Nagano Province, where the company's main laboratories are located.

A: Do you go there often?

TY: Once a month for 2 days for face-to-face meetings and discussions with lab staff. Although it is only once a month, I am in daily communication by mail or e-mail. I check all study protocols, experimental data, progress reports and final reports to be submitted to the sponsors. My office is in the Tokyo office of Ina Research, Inc.

A: I would be interested in your thoughts about Dr Seevers and his role in both your life and in Japanese pharmacology. *Addiction* never interviewed Dr Seevers and it would be interesting to hear your reflections about him, as I know that you feel he was an important person in your life.

TY: Yes indeed! I think he was a kind of Uncle Sam to Japanese pharmacology. After the war, he came to visit Japan as an American delegate to provide medical education. Many people came for training, particularly pharmacologists. At that time, Japan was in the post-war turmoil and coming into a new era. So the American mission had a special importance. All Japanese people, particularly in the medical field, had the highest regard for them. Dr Seevers wanted to help Japan to be restored in medical training and research, particularly in his specialty of pharmacology. He visited Japan three times with the same mission. He thought the best way to help Japan develop in the area of pharmacology was to provide the best training for young pharmacologists in the USA. So he set up a program to provide 2 years of training in the department of pharmacology at the University of Michigan. He solicited funds from both the pharmaceutical industry and the federal government to cover the expenses of Japanese post-doctoral Fellows to study in his department. He made a major contribution to the advancement of pharmacology in Japan as well as in the USA.

A: I've been told that when Dr Seevers would come to Japan he would be treated very well because he had provided this training for so many years to so many people.

TY: Over the years, about 40 Japanese pharmacologists came to study at the University of Michigan. Most of them became professors and chairmen of pharmacology departments. They became known as the Michigan Group and were considered very prestigious. There was some degree of jealousy from those who did not get to go to Michigan.

A: The Japanese academic system is reputed to be rigid and authoritarian. What was your experience as a young academician? Has the system changed today?

TY: In a word, the chairman of a medical school department was the almighty person—'god'—and the university could not interfere with him in any way. The university appoints a professor but once appointed they cannot terminate them. The professor can award PhD degrees to those on his faculty whose research is deemed worthy of this honor. The professor also determines where you will work. If he doesn't like you, he can send you to a low-prestige place to work. The absolute authority of the professor is a long-observed tradition in Japan. The competition for becoming a departmental chair is intense. Universities compete to get one of their faculty members appointed. This extends their sphere of influence. Usually, the top-ranked university has the prestige to recommend who will become the next chair in other universities. But things changed a lot. Nowadays, it's not quite this way. If a chair is too authoritarian, promising young researchers will not go into that department. Times have changed since I was a young pharmacologist.

A: Dr Yanagita, you have had an incredible career of over 45 years as a pharmacological researcher, scholar and policy maker. In retrospect, are there things that you would have liked to do differently?

TY: Well, I was not certain whether I should go into medical practice or do pharmacological research. But pharmacology was certainly fun! I would have got bored treating patients with common diseases every day. And I never regretted this decision. I have had very good fortune. The fact that I could go to Dr Seevers' laboratory and do drug dependence studies was marvellous luck. I was able to support my research here in Japan for over 45 years. So I have no regrets. I am quite satisfied.

A: Do you intend to stop working soon?

TY: Not totally. I am, again, very lucky that I can work as much as I want, sometimes a little more than that, but generally I do as much as I want to do. Yes, so long as I can work I will continue to work. Fortunately, I have a good staff. They are good people and seem to be happy with me and give me all kinds of privileges. So I work for Ina Research, Inc., half of the time and the other half of my time I spend in scientific activities, public service, writing and working with professional societies.

16

Commentary

Jerome H. Jaffe

Laboratory Life: Addiction Careers in Pharmacology and Behavioural Pharmacology

The Background from Which Addiction Scientists and their Science Emerged

Each of the nine individuals whose interviews comprise this section devoted at least part of their careers to work in the laboratory, but most of them also made contributions to other aspects of the field of addictions. Over the past 50 years, I have had the good fortune to know eight of them personally and to have worked or collaborated with six of them. In this connectedness I do not believe I am exceptional. Such collegial relationships were common in the early days of addiction studies, a field that largely developed in the second half of the twentieth century. They all entered this field in its infancy or early adolescence when the total number of participants worldwide was relatively small. There is no common thread in their backgrounds that would have predicted their interest in the pharmacology or psychology laboratory, but there is no doubt that the environment of the early years of the field shaped their longer term career choices and their interconnectedness.

Throughout the first half of the twentieth century the few researchers and clinicians interested in addicting drugs and the treatment of those who developed problems with their use, with a few notable exceptions, were based in the traditional academic departments of pharmacology, neurology, psychiatry, and psychology. One very notable exception was the US Public Health Service Addiction Research Center (ARC) at Lexington, Kentucky, where the researchers were actually government employees, some of them in the commissioned corps of the Public Health Service.

Work began at the ARC in 1938. There were rarely more than a handful of clinicians and researchers there, but they included such people as Harris Isbell, Abraham Wikler, and William Martin, whose research and writings laid a foundation that continues to influence the field to this day. In their work assessing the abuse potential of new analgesics being developed by the pharmaceutical industry, these researchers collaborated closely with the Department of Pharmacology at the University of Michigan headed by Maurice Seevers, which maintained a colony of opiate-addicted monkeys and where new compounds from industry were screened. ARC researchers and those from industry and the University of Michigan, as well as guests from academia and government agencies, exchanged ideas and presented findings at the yearly meetings of the Committee on Problems of Drug Dependence (CPDD) of the National Academy of Sciences National Research Council. The CPDD was not a learned society, but rather a committee of 10 to 13 scientists established in 1929 by the National Research Council to explore the problem of addiction. Under the influence of its Executive Secretary, Nathan B. Eddy, it adopted the goal of discovering a non-addicting analgesic. In the 1980s it evolved into an independent learned society, changing its name to the College on Problems of Drug Dependence, and opening membership to scholars who had made contributions to the field. It thus became comparable to the UK-based scholarly organization, the Society for the Study of Addiction, founded nearly a century earlier, in 1884.

In the late 1950s, two quite distinct developments began to exert profound effects on the field of addiction studies. One was the dawning of the era of psychopharmacology which changed the treatment of the mentally ill, opened new vistas for research, and elicited government support for such research. The other development was the emergence of an epidemic of illicit drug use (heroin, cannabis, LSD) that was experienced most acutely in the US, but was felt elsewhere as well. Some countries responded only with new anti-drug laws, but some also came up with support for more research.

In 1961, a group of researchers in the US founded another learned society for a new field, the American College of Neuropsychopharmacology (ACNP). Abraham Wikler, Harris Isbell, Conan Kornetsky, Daniel X. Freedman, Jonathan Cole, Murray Jarvik, Joseph V. Brady were among its earliest members. For a brief period addiction studies appeared to be evolving into a subtopic of psychopharmacology, or at least many of those interested in addiction viewed themselves as psychopharmacologists. All of the Americans discussed in this section are members of the ACNP; Yanagita is a foreign corresponding member. In 1966, the National Institute on Mental Health (NIMH) in the United States established a Psychopharmacology Research Branch and appointed Jonathan Cole its Chief. For the most part, this became the funding vehicle for much of the research in both the addictions and psychopharmacology.

At about that time, the Committee on Problems of Drug Dependence recognized that its concerns needed to expand beyond the development of non-addicting analgesics and the attendees at the annual meetings began to change dramatically. They now included clinicians interested in the treatment of addiction and government officials from a number of agencies. At the 1963 meeting held at the University of Michigan, Charles R. Schuster and Travis Thompson presented their findings on opiate self-administration. I attended both the 1963 and 1964 meetings at the invitation of Murray Jarvik. A partial list of attendees at the 1964 meeting whose names would be familiar to people in this field includes Vincent Dole, Conan Kornetsky, Tomoji Yanagita, Louis Harris, John Ball, John O'Donnell, Julius Axelrod, and William Martin. Members of the Committee present included Dale Cameron (who was later to head the WHO Section on Drug Dependence), Harris Isbell, Jonathan Cole, Maurice Seevers, and of course Nathan Eddy. The 1964 meeting was notable also for the attendance of Dean F. Markham, a Special Assistant to the President for Narcotics and Drug Abuse, and Henry Giordano, Commissioner of the Bureau of Narcotics. In 1964, Dole successfully defied the agency's demand for oversight of methadone maintenance. It is not known whether Dole and Giordano exchanged greetings.

This brief sketch of the state of the field in the early to mid-1960's is relevant since that is when eight of the nine men discussed in this section entered it and the trajectories of their lives were powerfully influenced by the institutions, economic resources and major actors who strode the stage at that time.

The Actors of a Founding Era

As a graduate student in psychology at the University of Kentucky in the 1940s, Conan Kornetsky was working part-time at the US Public Health Service Hospital at Lexington. A chance meeting with Harris Isbell, the Director of the Addiction Research Center (ARC), which was located on hospital grounds, led to Kornetsky's participation in one of the classic studies of barbiturate addiction. He also collaborated with Abraham Wikler on studies of the effects of morphine on anxiety. The barbiturate studies were eventually accepted as his doctoral thesis. Isbell arranged for Kornetsky's appointment to the Public Health Service and sent him to New York City to study the epidemic of heroin use among adolescents that had emerged following World War II, and where he also collaborated with Murray Jarvik on an early study of LSD. His next assignment brought him to the intramural program of the National Institute on Mental Health (NIMH) where he developed an interest in attentional impairment in schizophrenia and also a lasting friendship with Daniel X. Freedman who was conducting studies of LSD there. After moving into academia, at Boston University's Department of Pharmacology, Kornetsky continued his interests in schizophrenia and opioid dependence with work at both the laboratory and clinical levels. He was one of the founding members of the ACNP in 1961.

The next step in Kornetsky's career illustrates the close linkage at the time between some seminal developments in neuroscience, psychopharmacology, and addiction sciences. He noted that the literature on brain self-stimulation reward behavior, pioneered by Olds and Milner in 1954, contained little on how psychoactive drugs affected the thresholds for such self stimulation. Kornetsky set out to use the classic psychophysics method of limits to determine threshold changes. In a series of experiments carried out by Kornetsky and his many graduate students it became clear that virtually all drugs with abuse potential lowered these thresholds. The method has become standard and is used by many laboratories throughout the world. Perhaps what is most remarkable about this very early entrant into the fields of psychopharmacology and addiction science is that more than 60 years later he still gets up each morning eager to get to work in his laboratory.

Like Kornetsky, Joseph V. Brady was a founding member of the ACNP in 1961. Brady's distinguished career in addictions stemmed mostly from what he has called "the fruits of a fortuitous environment." A commissioned officer in the US Army when he completed doctoral training in clinical psychology at the University of Chicago, Brady was assigned to clinical duties at Walter Reed Army Hospital in Washington, DC, but he was quickly recruited to be Chief of Experimental Psychology for a new interdisciplinary neuropsychiatric research group being formed by David Rioch. He also got an academic appointment at the nearby University of Maryland, College Park campus. In the mid-1950's, Brady demonstrated that reserpine could alter conditioned fear in monkeys. This marked his entry into psychopharmacology, but not yet the start of his interest in addictions.

With funding from the NIMH Psychopharmacology Research Branch, Brady established a behavioral pharmacology laboratory at the University of Maryland. Bob Schuster, who was working as a laboratory associate at a pharmaceutical company when Brady lectured there, became the first of his many graduate students who would go on to distinguish themselves in behavioral pharmacology.

In 1971, after retiring from the Army, Brady moved his laboratory to the Johns Hopkins Medical School Department of Psychiatry, bringing with him the methodology of drug-self-administration and a colony of drug-self-administering baboons. He also developed a Division of Behavioral Biology that consistently produced outstanding researchers. As Professor in both the Departments of Psychiatry and Neuroscience (founded by Solomon Snyder and where Michael Kuhar was a professor) Brady was a bridge between these disciplines and between Johns Hopkins medical school and the staff of the Addiction Research Center, which completed a move to Baltimore from Lexington in the early 1980's.

In one of his simultaneous careers Brady has also studied human behavior during prolonged space flight. His association with the US space agency (NASA) began in 1959 when he trained Able and Baker, the first monkeys to go into outer space and return safely. More than 50 years later he is still conducting research for NASA.

What is most remarkable about Joe Brady, (besides his sense of humor, intellect, energy, competence, and longevity in the field), is his capacity for friendship, which includes an ongoing relationship with his first graduate student.

When Bob Schuster joined Joe Brady's behavioral pharmacology laboratory at the University of Maryland in 1960 he brought with him knowledge acquired as a lab assistant in the pharmaceutical industry. While in Brady's lab, Schuster and Travis Thompson developed a method for drug self-administration in the monkey that allowed for an exploration of the environmental factors affecting drug use and dependence. Leaving his mentor with a new set of laboratory methods (which Brady moved to Johns Hopkins a few years later), Schuster joined Maurice Seevers' department of pharmacology at the University of Michigan, where his research was supported by grants awarded by the National Institutes of Health (NIH), and where he got to know Tomoji Yanagita. In 1968, I persuaded Bob to come to the University of Chicago. Daniel X. (Danny) Freedman, Chairman of Psychiatry there, had recruited me to the department. I was also heading drug treatment programs for the State of Illinois while trying to continue carrying out meaningful and publishable research. Bob came to Chicago and successfully established drug self-administration models while collaborating with me on clinical research on the treatment of opioid dependence. He built a very productive research group exploring drug abuse in both animals and humans. The number of successful addiction researchers who got their start under his mentorship is remarkable.

In 1986 Schuster took a hiatus from academia when he was named Director of the National Institute on Drug Abuse (NIDA), a post he held for 6 years. Those were not easy years. It was a time when within the US federal government the view of drug use as a moral issue was again in vogue. Bob was criticized not only for any advocacy of harm reduction measures, but even for methadone treatment, which the government had strongly supported since 1971.

Schuster returned to academia and continued to be a productive researcher and mentor and an influential presence and voice in all matters relating to our field until his sudden death in February of 2011. His particular focus in recent years had been on the abuse liability of prescription drugs

It is not surprising that after completing medical training Tomoji Yanagita still wanted to be a pharmacologist. He came from a family of physicians; his father also had a doctorate in pharmacology. In 1960, after earning his PhD with studies on morphine dependence, Yanagita accepted a fellowship at Maurice Seevers' pharmacology department at the University of Michigan. One of the giants in the still nascent field of addiction studies, "Mo" Seevers had devoted himself to advising the Japanese on the modernization of their medical teaching and established a series of fellowships for Japanese physicians and researchers. While at Michigan, Yanagita ingeniously adapted for monkeys the intravenous self-administration system used in rat studies by Weeks at Upjohn. This allowed for the study of self-administration of a wide range of drugs. (It was shortly thereafter that Bob Schuster joined the group at Michigan.) Upon his return to Japan in 1966, Yanagita established a primate research laboratory that conducted studies, including abuse liability, for the pharmaceutical industry.

Not covered in the synopsis of Yanagita's interview is a role he played in profoundly influencing the treatment of opioid dependence throughout the world. Yanagita served as Chairman of the WHO Expert Committee on Drug Dependence in 1988, (Hamid Ghodse was Vice Chairman, I was Rapporteur), when the scheduling of the partial agonist buprenorphine was being considered. To the consternation of some and the approval of others, the WHO Committee recommended control of buprenorphine, but under the 1971 Psychotropic Convention, rather than under the more restrictive 1961 Single Convention. This decision proved to be important, if not critical, to the further development and widespread use of buprenorphine in the treatment of opioid addiction, and it was achieved in no small measure by Yanagita's diplomatic skill and scientific stature.

For E. A. Carlini the fulfillment of an early dream of public service to the people of Brazil led through the pharmacology laboratories of two medical school mentors who convinced him that he could be of greater service as a researcher than as a missionary doctor along the Amazon. *Psychopharmacologia,* which published its first issue in 1959, led to his subsequent interest in psychopharmacology and to several years of post-doctoral work in the US, the last few of which were spent at Yale where there was an interdisciplinary programme involving the departments pharmacology, psychiatry, and psychology (funded, to the best of my recollection, by the Psychopharmacology Research Branch of NIMH). Among the stars of that programme with whom Carlini formed a warm relationship with was Daniel X. Freedman who was newly returned to Yale from his studies of LSD at the intramural program of NIMH.

Carlini returned to Brazil in 1964 where he created an interdisciplinary (physiology, biochemistry, pharmacology) research group modeled loosely on what he had experienced at Yale. In 1970 he returned to the Escoli Paulista da Medicina where he had first trained and undertook his now widely read studies on cannabis, and later carried out ethnopharmacologic studies of plants used by indigenous tribes. He also began to transition into less laboratory-based public service, first, establishing the Brasileiro de Informacoes Sobre Drogas Psicotropicas, and later undertaking periodic gathering of epidemiological data on drug use among students and admissions to treatment for drug and alcohol problems in Brazil. In 1994, the transition to positions dealing with general public health reached fulfillment with Carlini's appointment as head of the Brazilian health agency charged with controlling "every health related product in the country." From these various posts he has been able to advocate for greater efforts in Brazil for harm reduction, for less Draconian penalties for cannabis, and also perhaps its eventual removal from the 1961 Single Convention.

Lou Harris started out wanting a career in academia. He had worked his way through Harvard and earned a PhD in pharmacology from Harvard Medical School, but economic necessity sent him into the pharmaceutical industry at Sterling in 1960. His research group there developed both pentazocine and cyclazocine, a long acting opioid antagonist. Cyclazocine was sent to Bill Martin at Lexington for testing. Wikler and Martin proposed that prolonged blockade of opioid reinforcing effects could lead to extinction of opioid self-administration. (I carried out the first clinical trials of cyclazocine in ambulatory heroin addicts in New York in 1964 and this probably was a factor in my move to Chicago.)

In 1965, Harris accepted an academic appointment at the University of North Carolina School of Medicine. There he developed a research group that focused on opioid and cannabis pharmacology, which later moved to the Medical College of Virginia. By 1971, when I became head of the White House Special Action Office for Drug Abuse Prevention (SAODAP), Harris was already a major figure in addiction research. In my SAODAP role, I was able to influence an expansion of the research activites at MCV by increasing funding to NIMH for research that allowed Harris's group to receive an addiction center grant, and when it appeared that the monkey colony at Michigan might not be maintained when Mo Seevers retired, I urged that a second monkey colony be established at MCV.

In addition to heading a department that emphasizes studying the pharmacology of drugs that are abused, Lou Harris has been a respected consultant to the World Health Organization Expert Committee on Drug Dependence and to several federal agencies in the US. As further illustration of the close relationships among the early leaders in our field, Lou Harris spent his sabbatical year in Washington helping Bob Schuster, who that year had assumed the directorship of NIDA.

Soon after he completed medical training, Malcolm Lader sought further training in research. In 1960, he got a research position in psychopharmacology in a laboratory that had received NIMH funding (presumably from the Psychopharmacology Research Branch). Lader earned his PhD and then undertook training in psychiatry at the Maudsley Hospital and the Institute of Psychiatry. He became interested in exploring the question of benzodiazepine dependence. His demonstration that dependence could develop at relatively normal dose levels had a major public health impact, changing the way these drugs are prescribed. It was his gateway into addictions.

Organizations and meetings devoted to an area of interest where clinicians and researchers can interact play a critical, if not essential, role in the evolution of a disciplinary identity. In the US, the CPDD played such a role.

In the UK, the Society for the Study of Addiction (SSA), a learned society originally established in the 19th century, had languished through most of the 20th century. Lader's role in reinvigorating the SSA and instituting its annual scientific meeting was a major factor in the growth of addiction studies as a discipline in the UK. He became President of the SSA in 1983 and held that post for a decade. Lader also chaired the Technical Committee of the UK Advisory Council on Misuse of Drugs, the body responsible for recommending the scheduling of drugs. Lader no doubt has known and interacted with most of the players on the international addictions stage. He remained at the Psychopharmacology Unit at the Institute of Psychiatry for his entire professional career.

Thinking that it might open the door to a job in industry, Michael Kuhar shifted his interest from physics to pharmacology and went to Johns Hopkins for graduate studies. There he had the good fortune to work with Solomon Snyder, who had recently joined the faculty after his post-doctoral studies in Julius Axelrod's laboratory at NIH. Snyder was continuing the study of neurotransmitters and their receptors pioneered by Axelrod. Axelrod also was interested in mechanisms of tolerance and had published several papers on that subject in 1960's, and had presented a theory of tolerance at the 1966 meeting of the Association on Research on Nervous and Mental Diseases (ARNMD) organized by Abe Wikler. Snyder's lab received a large Center grant as part of the SAODAP initiative to expand addiction research, funding that led to the successful identification of the opiate receptor.

After a post-doctoral year at Yale where he developed expertise in autoradiography, Kuhar returned to Johns Hopkins and conducted work on choline of such importance that it earned publication in *Nature*. Kuhar got independent funding in 1972. His work on the distribution of opiate receptors was published in *Nature* in 1973. He then expanded his range of skills to include work with PET scanning to image receptors in the living brain and was part of the group that, in 1983, first reported on the imaging of the dopamine receptor in human brain.

In 1984 I became Director of the Addiction Research Center. I believed that the ARC's research activities needed to expand to give greater emphasis to neuroscience and molecular biology, and I persuaded Kuhar to move from Johns Hopkins to the ARC to establish a new neuroscience branch. He quickly developed a collaboration with Steve Goldberg who studied drug-self-administration in monkeys and they showed that the reinforcing effects of cocaine were due to its inhibition of dopamine uptake.

After 10 years at the ARC and a remarkable record of scientific accomplishment, Kuhar accepted an endowed chair at Emory University in Georgia where he has continued his outstanding record of scientific output, the most recent being the discovery of CART, a new neuropepetide that modifies the actions of dopamine.

Kuhar's activities outside the laboratory have included co-editing two encyclopedias on drug and alcohol dependence for the general public, the presidency of the CPDD, and the establishment and presidency of the International Drug Abuse Research Society.

In another part of the world, Raphael Mechoulam's curiosity about the chemistry of plant products led him, in the early 1960's, to explore the active constituents of cannabis which up to that time had not been isolated in pure form. Fortuitous relationships with Israeli regulatory officials gave him access to the hashish he needed for his work. Such cooperation between drug law enforcement officials and academic researchers is often a critical element in advancing both basic and clinical research on controlled substances. Critical, too, is financial support. In Israel this was minimal, so in early 1963 Mechoulam applied to the NIMH in the US for a grant but was turned down because, he was told, cannabis use was not an American problem. As he tells the tale, shortly afterwards, a US Senator telephoned NIMH to ask about marijuana's effects on the brain (his son had been smoking it), but no one there could tell him anything about it. Mechoulam then received a call from Daniel Efron, who worked for Jonathan Cole, head of the NIMH Psychoparmacology Research Branch. Efron came to Israel; Mechoulam received a grant; and Efron took a supply of pure THC isolated by Mechoulam's research group back to the US to give to other researchers. Some of this probably went to Lou Harris's group at the University of North Carolina. Mechoulam's work was supported by NIMH and later the National Institute on Drug Abuse (NIDA) for the next 40 years. This support may be some of the most cost-effective funding these agencies ever made; it resulted in an explosive expansion of knowledge about cannabinoids and the discovery of the endogenous ligands for the cannabinoid system, endocannabinoids. This body of knowledge has already had applications far beyond the addictions field.

The Future for Addiction Careers

The field of addiction studies has changed dramatically in the 40 to 50 years since these 9 men began their distinguished careers. It is now possible to choose a career in addiction studies rather than enter into it fortuitously. The change was driven by a confluence of interacting events and developments that occurred mostly in the 1960s through the early 1970s and included epidemics of illicit drug use (heroin, cannabis and LSD) in the US and Western Europe and a growing realization that law enforcement responses could not contain the growth of drug use or its consequences. These events and developments interacted with a growing demand by former alcoholics to see alcoholism treated as a distinct disorder, new ways of treating opiate addiction (methadone maintenance, therapeutic communities, opioid antagonists) that shattered long held views of its incurability, and new optimism that further research could lead to even more effective approaches to treatment and prevention. By the late 1960s these developments had begun to elicit a trickle of government support for research and treatment. In 1970 in the US the National Institute on Alcohol Abuse and Alcoholism (NIAAA) was established as part of the Public Health Service. New professional societies concerned with alcohol research and treatment came into being and older ones dealing with drugs, such as CPDD, expanded and developed new vitality.

President Richard Nixon's 1971 decision to establish a special White House office on drug abuse to expand and coordinate treatment, research and training was precipitated by reports of heroin addiction among US servicemen in Viet Nam. He appointed me, an academic psychiatrist and researcher trained partly at Lexington, as his "drug czar" and gave me carte blanche and a multimillion dollar budget to shape a national response. New academic research centers were established, new researchers entered the field, and still other professionals found roles in the expanding treatment and training activities. The National Institute on Drug Abuse (NIDA) was established in 1973. Similar investments in research and treatment were made in other countries within a few years. A decade later when the HIV epidemic was linked to injection drug use a new infusion of resources found its way into the expanding field of addiction research and treatment. By the early years of the 21st century NIDA and NIAAA had combined research budgets in excess of a billion dollars.

Along with the growth of clinical, research and training activities the infrastructure that supports these activities also grew. In 1964 there were only four learned journals devoted to drug and alcohol studies. By 1991 there were 29 such journals and more have since begun publication. Equally dramatic has been the rise in the proportion of addiction related articles published in journals of psychiatry, pharmacology, and psychology, and the growth worldwide of national and university-based research institutes and centres focused on addiction, a disproportionate number of them located in the US (Babor 1993).

A sign that addiction studies is evolving into a field distinct from the parent disciplines in which the early entrants trained is the establishment of endowed university chairs in addiction studies or addiction research. Although these are now typically located within traditional departments, the idea of a distinct department is not farfetched. Generous funding now supports national and international meetings devoted to research and treatment dealing with drug and alcohol problems, meetings that have become so numerous that a well funded and enthusiastic attendee could go from one to another with no need for a place to call home. These meetings have allowed and supported national and international collegial relationships. When clinicians and researchers give priority to attending addiction related meetings rather than those of their parent discipline, it may be a sign of their primary professional identity.

It now seems improbable that funding of the addiction research enterprise will be so generous in the future as it has been over the opening years of the 21st century. But when a scientific and clinical infrastructure achieves a critical mass and collegial relationships now enjoyed by the field of addiction become established, – what Babor (1993) has described as the invisible college – it is likely to survive fluctuations in economic support. What is more difficult to predict even now is the degree to which the field will continue to maintain its current coherence, where those most concerned with clinical and policy issues and the neuroscientists who are employing ever more technically sophisticated methods to study the molecular and genetic underpinnings of the addictive process, see themselves as part of a single field of study.

Reference

Babor T. F., Beyond the invisible college: a science policy analysis of alcohol and drug research. In: Edwards G., Strang J., Jaffe J. H., editors, *Drugs, Alcohol, and Tobacco: Making the Science and Policy Connections.* Oxford: Oxford University Press; 1993, pp. 48–69.

Part 3—Clinicians and Clinical Scientists

17

Conversation with Timothy Cook

From 1966 to 1974, Timothy Cook was the first director of Rathcoole House and the Alcohol Recovery Project (ARP), a pioneering British initiative that aims to help the homeless drinker. He came to this field after earning a law degree at Cambridge. His work at the ARP contributed to changes in the public handling of the drunkenness question.

First Steps

Addiction [A]: A bit about your background.

Timothy Cook [TC]: I was born in 1938, educated at Loughborough Grammar School and then studied law at Cambridge University. I lectured in law for a year at Sheffield University but then enrolled in a new postgraduate criminology course at the Cambridge Institute of Criminology. It was there that I became very interested in the practical issues concerning the treatment and containment of offenders rather than more theoretical criminology. On completing that course I secured a job as assistant warden at Norman House in north London, a hostel for homeless ex-prisoners. It had been founded by Merfyn Turner, who was a great influence on me. I worked there for 2 years and I learned a great deal both about myself and about the world of prisons and prison after-care. I then spent 2 years, 1964–66, as a prisoner welfare officer at Blundeston prison in Suffolk. This was run by a very inspiring governor, Eric Towndrow, another great influence on me. What I soon discovered both at Norman House and Blundeston was the number of men with serious drinking problems going through the prison system.

A: So that was a serious introduction to the world of drinking problems?

TC: At Blundeston we started an Alcoholics Anonymous group. I remained in touch over 20 years or more with several men from the group who never drank again after they left prison. So I found myself becoming increasingly interested in drinking problems and responded to an advertisement for a warden at Rathcoole House. I moved into Rathcoole in south London on 1 May 1966.

A: Did you have GPs or other doctors involved at Blundeston?

TC: There was a visiting GP but no psychiatric services and certainly nothing in the way of treatment to address alcoholism. The prison was run on very therapeutic lines and a lot of time was spent talking with individuals, a third of whom at least had serious drinking problems.

A: Was there a moral approach in society in those days to men with drinking problems?

TC: Generally, drinking too much was not regarded as too terrible. Such people were seen as characters, very amusing and everyone shut their eyes to the problems they were causing for others. For the public drinkers such as the drunk on the streets they undoubtedly were seen as the 'undeserving poor'.

A: The other thing that was happening at that time was that the disease concept came to the UK in the early 1950s.

TC: Certainly during most of the 1960s the primary model was the disease model. To some extent it helped alcoholics feel less bad about their drinking and was a valuable corrective to the notion of them being undeserving. But then the sociological perspective emerged and passionate arguments developed about the disease model. I tended to be much more pragmatic. It wasn't helpful to operate from a model mainly because the patterns of the men's drinking and their responses to Rathcoole were so very different. I recall one man who came to Rathcoole and said, 'I just want to stop drinking.' He went to AA, left the house after a year or so and 30 years later he died from natural causes with I'm told one of the biggest funerals AA has ever seen. It seemed scarcely relevant to agonize about a disease model.

A: Professional help at Rathcoole?

TC: Medical help was provided by an excellent GP, Dr Benno Pollak, and a psychiatric registrar from the Maudsley hospital came on a weekly basis.

Beyond the Dickensian: Rathcoole House Established as a Centre for Homeless Drinkers

A: Can we set the context within which Rathcoole was emerging? Can you tell us something about what their approach was?

TC: Following the establishment of Norman House in the 1950s, which was the first ever prison after-care hostel, a few smaller hostels had developed in London. But the core provision for homeless men and women in the big cities was large lodging houses and government reception centres. Some had dormitories for a hundred people. The Camberwell Reception Centre, run by the Department of Health and Social Security, was the largest and took up to 900 people. The lodging houses run by bodies like the Salvation Army were extraordinary places. However humanely they were run, the amount of care and attention that could be given to any individual was minimal. There were a few inspired staff at Camberwell but they were working in impossible conditions. In contrast, a place like Rathcoole, taking 10 people in a well-furnished house, was a totally different concept.

A: So Rathcoole was quite an important new development?

TC: Yes. These men were crude spirit drinkers, homeless, absolutely the archetypal skid-row alcoholic.

A: Who initiated this?

TC: Until 1963, the after-care of prisoners was in the hands of voluntary organizations. It was then made the responsibility of the Probation Service. The Home Office established a committee, chaired by Lady Reading, to examine the residential provision for homeless discharged offenders. Griffith Edwards submitted proposals to that committee for tackling the problem of the chronic drunkenness offender. There is no doubt that Lady Reading, a dynamic and powerful figures, was impressed by Griffith Edwards and his ideas. When the Carnegie Trust gave the Home Office Committee funds for a special After-care Trust to promote four new projects, the Edwards' proposal was chosen as one of the four. Rathcoole opened on 1 May 1966. It is hard to imagine today that personalities, policies and funds could so perfectly come together.

A: So what were the practical issues that then emerged?

TC: Within a month the house was full. There were two key issues that emerged immediately. Firstly, should residents be made to get a job? Secondly, if residents drank what should our policy be? I decided, and the committee agreed with me, that it should not be compulsory to go to work. Men needed to stay sober in their own individual ways. A much bigger problem was whether men should be evicted once they began drinking. Initially we took a tolerant approach. If they came back drunk I would probably take them to the Camberwell Reception Centre or tell them to go away and return in the morning when they would be re-admitted. Some of course disappeared forever. This 'policy' led to considerable confusion as to our purpose. We decided that we had to engage the residents much more in developing an appropriate policy. This was the key development in the history of the house in my time. As a whole group we decided that the policy should be 'if you drink you are out' and there was to be no immediate re-admission.

A: So, they went out to work and were expected to be alcohol-free. What else did the treatment approach consist of?

TC: The core of what we were trying to do was to engage the men as much as possible in the responsibilities of the house. This began in quite small ways but gradually expanded during the initial years.

A: House meetings?

TC: There was a weekly house meeting, which the psychiatrist attended but which was in no way a treatment group; it was often much more to do with the practical issues in the house.

A: The house seems to have worked on cultivation of self-responsibility?

TC: We certainly tried to develop the theme of responsibility as far as possible. I referred earlier to the whole house being involved in deciding on the policy of 'if you drink you are out'. Then I was married in 1967 and went to live in the second house, which was just being opened, so we took the opportunity to gradually phase out residential staff at Rathcoole. Within 2 years there were no residential staff at all. We were all eventually convinced that in fact there were fewer problems with drinking than previously. We then took this a stage further by having all prospective residents interviewed by the house as a group and the admission being determined by that meeting.

A: What was the GP's role?

TC: This engagement in responsibility was backed up by the men being given a great deal of personal attention and nowhere was this better demonstrated than by the support and interest of the GP, Dr Benno Pollak. On admission to the house Dr Pollak gave each man over an hour's medical examination with blood tests and all the works. There was also an interview and assessment by the psychiatrist. But behind all this lay employment. Despite a lifetime of drinking many of them were very keen to get into work and saw that as the backbone of their recovery.

A: But in other places were they getting counselling?

TC: There was advice, support, argument and discussion far into the night with individuals, but that would not be recognized by anyone as counselling. As far as the homeless alcoholic was concerned, much of the work focused on how to get them to the facility in the first place and what to do when they were sober. Trying to cope with a sober life and more independent living was a huge challenge for them, and that was why AA was so powerful for some of them.

Expanding the Facilities

A: You said you moved to another hostel?

TC: After Rathcoole had been running a year it was clear that some men were doing extremely well. We had two who had been there virtually the whole year. When I married in March 1967 it was not possible to live in my one room/office. The committee bought a house near Clapham Common and Margaret and I had a flat at the top of it. The men who had done well at Rathcoole moved into it. About a year later we bought another house with independent bedsits not far away. So within 3 years we had two hostels and a group of independent flats but exactly the same number of staff that began in 1966. All these facilities are still operational, and of course many more.

A: It grew quickly in a sort of progression?

TC: In 1968 we developed the notion of the 'shop front', a concept and service that is now part and parcel of the provision. We obtained a very generous grant from the City Parochial Foundation, which was sufficient to open up three shop fronts and appoint a research worker. The shop fronts opened in 1970 and from then on we were called the Alcoholics Recovery Project (ARP).

Making the Research Connections

A: There was some research done at Rathcoole?

TC: There were two aspects to the research. There was a detailed analysis by Jim Orford and Shirley Otto, two psychologists at the Addiction Research Unit, of a number of alcoholic hostels including Rathcoole (Otto & Orford 1978). We wrote a paper for the *BMJ* and Dr Pollak and I wrote various papers for other journals (Cook, Morgan & Pollak 1968). We had a passionate interest in writing about the work, and the close links with the Addiction Research Unit certainly encouraged that. I have always believed that the voluntary sector is poor at writing about its work so that a lot of important experience is lost as a result. With the funding from the City Parochial Foundation we appointed Peter Archard as a research worker, who decided to undertake a major participant observation study with the drinking school on Camberwell Green. He wrote two books from this study (Archard 1975), one that was essentially the publication of his PhD (Archard 1979).

A: Were you aware at the time of any sort of effects of the research on policy or practice?

TC: The overall success of the early years at Rathcoole helped push the Home Office into establishing the habitual drunken offenders working party, which began meeting in June 1967 and reported in 1971 (Home Office 1971). This climate had been helped by a 3 day international symposium in 1968 on the drunkenness offence (Cook, Gath & Hensman 1969). We had lots of discussions with the civil servants responsible for drafting the famous DHSS circular 21/73, Community Services for Alcoholics (Department of Health and Social Security 1973).

The Habitual Drunkenness Offending Working Party

A: Can you tell me about the habitual drunken offenders working party?

TC: Everyone who had been involved in setting up Rathcoole knew that even if it was 100% successful, a much more strategic approach was needed. Lady Reading undoubtedly took that view and with the evidence emanating from the Addiction Research Unit as well as the first practical demonstration of what might be done from Rathcoole, there was a strong argument for looking at this problem much more widely. I recall a supper meeting at Lady Reading's house with a few of us and the then Home Secretary, James Callaghan, and—behold—the working party was established. The eventual report was remarkably thorough and humane and owed much to the chairman, Terry Weiler. Funds were made available to help alcoholics and circular 21/73 was issued (DHSS 1973).

Moving On

A: So you left the alcohol field in 1974?

TC: Yes. I left to do an MA in social policy and public administration at Brunel University. I had spent nearly 9 years in a very exciting but highly specialized field and I needed to broaden my horizons. While on the course the book I had written about the ARP, Vagrant Alcoholics (Cook 1975), was published. I was part of an exciting, rewarding and deeply fulfilling venture. Much was achieved and anything seemed possible. Fortunately, during my time at the foundation I saw many people equally enthusiastic about their current role in the voluntary sector.

A: By the time you were leaving in 1974 the Kessel committee (DHSS Advisory Committee on Alcoholism 1978) was starting, of which you were a member.

TC: I have two strong abiding impressions. First is that the committee was quite often gripped by strong arguments between the different medical members. The second was that it really did not see itself sufficiently as a committee geared to see that action took place.

A: What did you do after 1974?

TC: I have always remained interested in the alcohol field but not contributed in any significant further way. After the Brunel course I went to Cambridge House, a settlement in Camberwell, and from there I went in 1978 to be the director of Family Service Units, a national organization concerned with disadvantaged families and communities. In 1985 I went to my last job, as Clerk of the City Parochial Foundation, established in 1891 to benefit the poor of London.

A: Would you advise a young person to go into this kind of work now?

TC: There is a freedom and excitement about the voluntary sector that I experienced and then saw repeatedly in others when I was at the foundation. Young people see this too and scarcely need advice to go into it!

The Mystery of Recovery

A: You still seem to be working through what the ARP experience meant for you.

TC: I will finish by describing a meeting I had recently with Bernie McGovern, who was a resident in one of the houses in 1970, stayed for 2 years, left and after a time returned to Scotland, married and has stayed sober for 30 years. I recently re-established contact with him and he came down to London to stay with me. Naturally, we reminisced about the good old days. He then mentioned a particular incident that I'd never heard about and that illustrated a quite profound point about the recovery of the alcoholic and the limited role that perhaps we play in it. He said that after 6 months at the house he walked into a pub on Clapham Common, and went up to the bar. When asked what he wanted he walked to the door, but returned to the bar a second time and a third. He finally ordered an orange juice but before he could drink it he walked out. That was the closest he ever came to drinking again. He is not easily able to explain why he went into the pub and why he left. For him it was the critical moment in his recovery. I never heard about this event until now. Recovery is a huge battle with many such defining moments, and although statistically Bernie goes down as one of the great successes it is hard to know just what part we played. So for me almost 40 years after I moved into Rathcoole House the mystery of recovery remains, and I am glad that it does.

References

Archard, P. (1975) *The Bottle Won't Leave You.* London: Alcoholics Recovery Project.

Archard, P. (1979) *Vagrancy, Alcoholism Social Control.* London: Macmillan.

Cook, T. (1975) *Vagrant Alcoholics.* London: Routledge and Kegan Paul.

Cook, T., Gath, D. & Hensman, C. (1969) *The Drunkenness Offence.* Oxford: Pergamon Press.

Cook, T., Morgan, H. G. & Pollak, B. (1968) The Rathcoole experiment: first year at a hostel for vagrant alcoholics. *British Medical Journal,* 1, 240–242.

Department of Health and Social Security (DHSS) (1973) *Community Services for Alcoholics.* Circular 21/73. London: HMSO.

DHSS Advisory Council on Alcoholism (1978) *The Pattern and Range of Services for Problem Drinkers.* London: DHSS and Welsh Office [Kessell committee].

Home Office (1971) *Habitual Drunken Offenders.* London: HMSO.

Otto, S. & Orford, J. (1978) *Not Quite Like Home.* London: J. Wiley.

18

Conversation with Hamid Ghodse

Hamid Ghodse obtained his medical training in Iran before qualifying in psychiatry in the United Kingdom. He went on to establish an important addiction centre at St George's Hospital, London and made many personal contributions to the research literature and he is the author of a standard textbook. His influence has, however, also been international and he has been president of the United Nations International Narcotics Control Board. He is an internationalist par excellence.

From Tehran to Tooting

Addiction (A): On looking through your publications, the first was in 1964; a guide-book in basic sciences for university entrance in Iran. Some years later we find you in Tooting with more than 300 publications to your name—so let us examine the journey from Teheran to Tooting.

Hamid Ghodse (HG): I am one of nine and I am the eldest son of that family. My father was a civil servant, and my mother a teacher and later in life a headmistress, and she then had her own private school under her own name. The family had strong educational interests.

A: What sparked your interest in medicine as a subject?

HG: My nickname was 'Doctor', possibly because I was quite chubby like one of the local doctors. I was always fascinated with biology. My strongest interest was biological science. So I very much enjoyed my time as a medical student, from 1959 to 1965. Even before I went to medical school, I was interested in behavioural science and psychology. I was known among my friends and family for reading such authors as Dostoyevski, Rousseau, Sartre, Freud and Konrad Lorenz.

A: How was psychiatry taught in your medical school—was it inspiring?

HG: Not at all. Our psychiatric training was very brief and limited.

To the United Kingdom and a Training in Psychiatry

A: You went on to complete your MD in 1965, on 'The physical and mental complications of non-sterile deliveries at home'.

HG: At that time, I was not sure whether to follow a career in psychiatry or obstetrics. I therefore chose a thesis which allowed me to study both. I was also fortunate in having a very good supervisor.

A: Why England, and what were your medical aspirations?

HG: I first came to England in 1957 as a Boy Scout, attending the Jubilee Jamboree in Sutton Coldfield. This was the centenary of Baden-Powell's birthday and the fiftieth anniversary of the Scout organization. I was one of the few scouts from Iran and for the first time we left our country to participate in a meeting of 84 000 people from all over the world. During that period a family at Neath in South Wales invited me to stay with them for a week; our friendship started from there and subsequently, most years up to my graduation, I used to stay with them for the summer holidays. They treated me like one of the family. When I qualified, I felt Britain was the natural place for my postgraduate studies because I already had my adoptive family in Wales.

A: Were you intent on studying psychiatry at that time?

HG: By that time I knew that I wanted to become a psychiatrist. I first worked as a senior house officer at Morgannwg Hospital in Bridgend, South Wales. It was an excellent psychiatric hospital and I learned about medicine in the United Kingdom.

A: What led you to further studies in London and who were your main influences?

HG: The late Professor Linford Rees was Professor of Psychological Medicine at St Bartholomew's Hospital in London and I knew his family in Wales. He suggested that I should apply for the psychiatric training rotation at Hackney and Barts. I was very lucky and got the job. Professor Linford Rees was truly in a class of his own as a clinician and I always looked up to him. He was not only a wonderful teacher and a wise mentor but also such a genuinely nice person to get to know. I was considered a member of his family and I spent every Christmas Day, in the years before my marriage, in Linford's house.

A: Did you then start to develop an interest in drug and alcohol problems?

HG: At the end of the 1960s there was tremendous concern at the apparent increase in drug misuse, and particularly of heroin, in London. Any doctor could prescribe heroin and even cocaine to addicts, and of course some private doctors acquired a reputation for being a 'soft touch' and for giving the addict whatever he or she asked for. The Misuse of Drugs Act 1967 limited private prescribing, and also led to the opening of the drug dependency units, or 'DDUs'. One of the first was at Hackney Hospital, which was part of the Barts group of hospitals in north-east London, in 1968 and it was part of my training to work there.

A: Did the staff in the DDUs really know what they were doing at that time?

HG: At first we had little experience. Some patients were on huge doses of heroin and cocaine and stimulants. I can remember assessing patients on prescribed daily doses of many hundred mg of heroin and perhaps 3–400 mg cocaine. It was reported at the time that one doctor prescribed 6 kg of heroin for his patients in 1 year. Those first patients we treated in a haphazard way on a trial-and-error basis.

A: Why were you attracted to working with those patients at that time?

HG: When I started treating addicts, I developed a strong interest in these complex human behaviours. Drawing on my background in biological medicine, I started to develop some lines of research.[1] I questioned addicts about their diet and life-style and measured glucose tolerance and other endocrinological effects of opioids in heroin-dependent patients.[2] This work eventually formed my PhD thesis. I was lucky to have worked with a very friendly and highly academic consultant, Dr John Reed.

A: What were your thoughts about a future psychiatric career and your next steps?

HG: Well, in 1971, I had moved from the St Bartholomew's rotation to the Maudsley. Entry to the Maudsley was very competitive. This proved to be an excellent start to a comprehensive training and I passed the Diploma in Psychological Medicine in 1974. I then moved to the Institute of Psychiatry (IOP) as a research psychiatrist. I was attracted to an academic career.

A: At that time Dr Aubrey Lewis was still at the Institute—he retired in 1966 but carried on as an Emeritus Professor.

HG: Aubrey Lewis had retired when I was there. On a few occasions he asked for my help in relation to some long letters written in Persian. The late Sir Denis Hill was encouraging me. As for my contemporaries, a number of them are very eminent leaders in their field. The atmosphere of the junior common room was very supportive but it was also, I think, a very competitive environment.

The Addiction Research Unit

A: You then went to the Addiction Research Unit (ARU)?

HG: When I first wanted to go to the Institute after I finished my general training in psychiatry, I was encouraged to join a UK/US project in the psychiatry of old age. Then a position in the Addiction Research Unit emerged and that was my preference, especially as I was already doing my PhD in that field.

A: What research did you join at the ARU and who were you working with?

HG: This was another opportunity to meet and work with a man (Griffith Edwards) who influenced not only my future career but also my way of looking at and approaching research. The whole of the environment of the ARU was multi-disciplinary, but predominantly with a social and behavioural orientation and with a number of high flyers among young psychologists and sociologists. I became more familiar with the social sciences and I learned a great deal about the social aspects of human behaviour. Griffith has remained a life-long teacher and family friend.

A: Your papers then reflect a developing interest in drug use, for example overdoses, drug users attending accident and emergency departments, and then mortality.

HG: That arose from interests within the ARU; I gradually got into the epidemiological aspects and surveys. I devised a survey of the London casualty units. This led on to a body of work that became, in a way, classical studies on the medical impact of drug misuse. I studied nearly 70 casualty departments in Greater London. We were interested in any presenting problem related to drug misuse. We were a little surprised to find that across all those London casualty units, there were something like just under 2000 presentations a month, related to drug misuse.

A: This work was very influential?

HG: The methodology actually became an integrated part of the casualty department's monitoring system. Subsequently, the methodology was adopted by the World Health Organization as a practical means of monitoring the impact of drug abuse and related problems in A&E departments in many other countries. There was a further impact, in that the Department of Health recognized that emergency services for drug misusers were scarce. Because we repeated the surveys over subsequent years, we started to pick up changes in doctors' prescribing habits and noticed increasing problems relating to the misuse of prescribed barbiturates. In the light of research findings, and with funding from the Department of Health, the Campaign on the Use and Restriction of Barbiturates (CURB) started to help doctors to reduce the prescribing of barbiturates. We conducted a study of more than 1400 A&E department staff on how they responded to drug addicts.[3]

A: Who were your academic colleagues at the ARU at this time?

HG: There were a number of excellent colleagues—the culture was very helpful in many ways in forging relationships with other disciplines and the ARU provided me with the opportunity to work with psychologists, sociologists, statisticians and clinical and basic scientists such as Jim Orford, Gerry Stimson, Ray Hodgson, Margaret Sheehan, Edna Oppenheimer, Bram Oppenheim, Ilana Crome, Michael Russell, Gloria Litman and Herb Bloomberg and David Robinson—all of whom are pioneers in various aspects of addictive behaviour. Griffith was able to attract scientists and researchers from different disciplines into the field of addictions and created an environment that nurtured and fertilized ideas so that it became a centre of excellence in the field. This was a golden era of the research in addictions in the United Kingdom. We interacted in different ways, with easy access to each other's opinions; it did not feel competitive at that time, but very supportive. But one day I had a letter inviting me to apply for the post of consultant and senior lecturer in the psychiatry of addiction at St George's and St Thomas' Hospitals. At that time, St George's Hospital was at Hyde Park Corner in central London, and had a small psychiatric out-patient and associated addiction clinic at St George's, Tooting. There was also a DDU at St Thomas' Hospital, including an in-patient addiction treatment unit at Tooting Bec Hospital in south London. I joined Dr Thomas Bewley, who looked after the out-patients at St Thomas'. I worked in St George's out-patient department and we shared the in-patients at Tooting Bec. Thomas, who subsequently became the Dean of the Royal College of Psychiatrists and then President, was an excellent clinician and medical politician. It was an excellent opportunity to work with such an experienced senior consultant colleague and I learned a good deal from him. St George's had a very comprehensive academic department of mental health sciences. Influential within it was Professor Arthur Crisp, an internationally renowned authority on eating disorders.

A: At that time, London and many other cities experienced a marked increase in the numbers of heroin misusers. How did that impact on your clinical work?

HG: We could admit patients with very complex needs to the in-patient unit. The Tooting Bec unit was the only unit in the country which had no restrictions on admission. It was truly a medico-psychiatric ward providing most types of treatment.

A: But then you established an in-patient unit at Springfield Hospital.

HG: Tooting Bec Hospital, which was a big mental hospital with more than 1000 beds, was due to be closed and the patients cared for in community settings. This was a very positive step for most patients but not for severely dependent drug misusers with severe behaviour problems. I had to take the case to public debate. I succeeded in saving the unit by transferring it to the nearby Springfield Hospital.

A Very Successful University Department

A: And your addictions base then developed further and greatly?

HG: When I started as a consultant at St George's the addiction team had half of my time, a few sessions of a medical assistant, a nurse and a part-time secretary. When I left St George's, addiction services comprised a university department of addictive behaviour with over 200 staff, 85 of them in the academic department and others in 10 community-based clinics, out-patient units and outreach, and in-patient units together with a dedicated alcohol service. The staff included three professors, two readers and eight senior lecturers and eventually the research and development income of our addiction department exceeded that of the rest of mental health. These achievements were due to the dedication and hard work of all staff.

A: One of your research interests at that time involved a novel method of assessing opiate dependence. Could you describe this for us?

HG: I was always searching for a better assessment tool for the accurate diagnosis of dependence on psychoactive drugs. After conducting a pilot study with some encouraging results, I discussed the project with a good friend and colleague, Professor Steven Smith, who was in charge of the department of pharmacology at St Thomas' Hospital and medical school, and he agreed to help me with the development of the opiate addiction test. The test involved the objective measurement of the pupils of both eyes. With Dr Dan Taylor, we developed a dedicated video-computer based binocular pupillometer. It was exhibited at the Millennium Dome in 2000, it won the Trade and Industry SMART and SPUR Awards, and was also the runner-up for the Aneurin Bevan NHS Award.[4]

Presidency of the UN International Narcotics Control Board

A: Moving to your international activities, you are the current President of the International Narcotics Control Board (INCB).

HG: The International Narcotics Control Board is the independent and quasi-judicial United Nations control organ for the implementation of the United Nations drug conventions. It was established in 1968 by the Single Convention on Narcotic Drugs, but there had been predecessor organizations under the former Conventions since the time of the League of Nations. In brief, the Board is the guardian and the watchdog of the International Drug Control Conventions.[5]

A: When we consider the current role of the INCB, many of the international conventions controlling drug misuse are some years old—for example, the Single Convention dates from 1961. Do these conventions and treaties still have relevance today?

HG: More relevant today than at that time. You can therefore see that the opiate addiction situation today, although it is serious, is in no way comparable with the addiction epidemic that prevailed when narcotic drugs were available without restriction. The situation is the same for psychotropic drugs during the 1950s, 1960s and 1970s. The international drug control measures have played an important part and will continue to do so in the reduction of the problem.[6]

A: Now looking through your papers there are one or two you have published with a certain Dr Barbara Ghodse, who is your wife. Could you say something of the influence of family on your work?

HG: Oh very much so. I think Barbara has always been extremely helpful; not only has she been an excellent supportive wife, but a very good mother for our three children. She is a qualified doctor. She is now a Health Service manager.

A: How did you maintain your enthusiasm over many years of scientific and clinical work?

HG: Of course addiction work can be frustrating, but at the same time the way in which I look at it is very much in a professional, clinical manner. If somebody misuses drugs or alcohol and acquires a health problem, they need a medical response that is not judgemental. It is important to de-stigmatize the state of addictions. The first thing an addiction doctor needs, in addition to a professional objective perspective, is a compassionate view of the condition. Colleagues remain very important to me. I consider them to be my greatest asset, people that I can turn to for inspiration, for reflection and advice on difficult research questions.

A: I am aware that some colleagues have said that, in working with you, it is as if you are a village elder. You appear to know everything that is going on in your own village.

HG: Well, that description is quite right.

Notes

1. Ghodse A. H. Increased serum growth hormone levels in absence of acromegaly. *Br J Psychiatry* 1977; 1: 1381–2.
2. Ghodse A. H, Reed J. L. Gastric emptying, glucose tolerance and associated hormanal changes in heroin addiction. *Psychol Med* 1984; 14: 521–5.
3. Ghodse A. H. The attitudes of casualty staff and ambulance personnel towards patients who take drug overdoses. *Br J Psychiatry* 1978; 12: 341–346.
4. Ghodse A. H., Greaves J. L., Lynch D. Evaluation of the opioid addiction test in an out-patient drug dependency unit. *Br J Psychiatry* 1999; 175: 158–62.
5. Bayer I., Ghodse A. H. *Evolution of International Drug Control, 1945–1995. Bulletin on Narcotics.* Austria: United Nations; 1999, p. L1 (1) and (2).
6. Bucknell P., Ghodse A. H. *Misuse of Drugs,* 3rd edn. London: Sweet and Maxwell; 1996.

19

Conversation with Nick Heather

Nick Heather is a British psychologist who has made notable and innovative contributions to this field. He has, over a distinguished career, developed and directed three research centres but has still found time to play the piano.

Early Days

Addiction (A): You were born in 1938. What are your earliest memories?

Nick Heather (NH): I was in London during the blitz and my earliest memories are of blackout curtains, air-raid sirens and going down into our Anderson shelter (a kind of primitive bomb shelter people had in their back gardens).

A: Did you stay in London throughout the war?

NH: No. Towards the end, my family went up to North Wales where we had relatives. We moved because of the V2 rocket scare. It was quite a change moving from London to this little village called Rhuddlan, near Rhyl. But my first clear memories are from there, such as going to school for the first time.

A: What was your family background?

NH: My father was manager of a busy off-licence in Wood Green, north London. I think he probably fitted Jellinek's description of the 'delta-type' alcoholic. That is the type who does not lose control, but drinks heavily every day, such as what we think of as the continental or French kind of alcohol dependence. My father managed to do his work very efficiently, but most nights would be drinking extremely heavily with his friends. There was obviously a high occupational risk factor there. I have often thought about whether this was why I developed an interest in alcohol problems. I simply do not know. It might have been something I just stumbled into. But I was very deeply affected by his drinking at the time; I was ashamed of the fact that virtually every night he would be drunk. He was very generous and warm, and certainly a very intelligent man.

A: Your mother?

NH: My mother was a housekeeper and a wonderfully kind and sensitive person. Some people regarded her as little short of a saint because of her kindness to people. She gave me a lot of love and a good upbringing.

A: Was your family religious?

NH: Not particularly. And I certainly am not. I would probably call myself agnostic, for want of a better word. I am also quite impressed with the more positive kind of atheism espoused by Richard Dawkins.

A: Your views on AA?

NH: I do not think we completely understand why it achieves the success that it does. I have found it difficult to reconcile a rational, scientific approach with 12-Step ideology.

A: This is a trivial issue, but reading through your CV I see that your name is actually Brian, so why Nick?

NH: When my mother came back from hospital with me I had a lot of black hair and was very ugly, apparently, so my father said I looked like 'Old Nick' and it stuck.

Moving Towards an Academic Life

A: You came into academic life rather late; can you tell us how that happened?

NH: Having passed the 11+, I went to a school called Latymer in Edmonton, north London, which was an ordinary grammar school at the time. I did quite well, but left at 16 after gaining good 'O'-levels. Going to university was something other, better-off people did. Also, I was a little wild and got into one or two scrapes, so the school did not exactly encourage me to stay on. I found jobs doing clerical work, which was very tedious, and I stuck them out until National Service.

A: National Service was compulsory at that time, wasn't it?

NH: Yes, I caught the end of it in 1957. I did most of my time in Germany as a signals operator in the Royal Air Force.

A: And then?

NH: Afterwards, I returned to the same type of work: trainee sales representative. After a year of that, I thought there must be more to life than this and the year was magically 1960. I had read a little of Jack Kerouac (On the Road) and something was in the air, so I dropped out. I cashed in my small superannuation and went down to Eastbourne for the summer and worked at washing-up in hotels, labouring jobs and being a deck-chair attendant, where I met some university undergraduates. One chap persuaded me that I might have the ability to go to university. So I went back home and studied 'A'-levels by correspondence course. I was helped by knowing somebody who did the same thing and who had a similar working-class background. I chose to study psychology and obtained a place at University College London.

A: How did you hear about psychology, as at that stage it probably was not on the radar of most people thinking of university?

NH: I do not think that is true. It was certainly on my radar.

A: Did you enjoy your studies?

NH: UCL was supposed to be one of the best places to study psychology and probably still is. I enjoyed my undergraduate days enormously and it really changed my life. I did not work very hard—remember it was London in the 1960s and a great deal was going on outside the lecture room—but I managed to get a 2/1.

Finding Meaningful Directions

A: When you graduated, what happened next?

NH: I started a PhD at UCL under Bob Audley on 'random walk' models of decision-making processes. I did 2 years of this and gave it up. This particular research seemed to be utterly meaningless to me at the time. I obtained a job lecturing at West Ham College of Advanced Technology (now the University of East London) but I became fed up with that, too. So I dropped out again and went to Morocco. It was when I came back that I decided to study clinical psychology. I thought that with clinical psychology I would be doing something more tangible, more about human life. I was accepted at the MSc course in clinical psychology at the University of Leeds.

A: The concept of randomness might be something that could be applied to your early career path.

NH: I do not think it was random. I think I was looking for something relating to psychology, but in a way that made it meaningful for me. This is reflected in my first book, which was called Radical Perspectives in Psychology,[1] a kind of distillation of objections to academic psychology and psychiatry around in the 1960s. This gave me the confidence that I could write books and perhaps contribute to ideas.

A: With the benefits of the many years since then, how far do you feel that these criticisms remain valid?

NH: Well, I think many of them have been answered, to some extent, because this was before the cognitive revolution in psychology and we were in the 1960s, still talking about rat psychology. In fact, one of the radical magazines around at the time was called Red Rat.

A: Was this movement political?

NH: Not in the active sense but it took the view that mainstream psychology and psychiatry supports the status quo and existing power arrangements and prevents people from asking questions about social injustices, etc., not such an outlandish idea it seems to me now.

A: So, next. . .?

NH: After gaining my MSc in clinical psychology my first job was at the University Hospital of South Manchester. I was the only full-time psychologist serving this huge psychiatric hospital and I was very busy conducting psychometric testing and behaviour therapy of all kinds. The big influence on me at the time was personal construct theory and I came under the spell of Don Bannister, who was absolutely brilliant. I had a chance to continue repertory grid research in Manchester, when Brian Hore asked me to take part in a project which was trying to understand the psychological changes taking place during group therapy for alcoholism. That was also my introduction to alcohol studies.[2]

A: You did not stay at Manchester very long.

NH: After 2 years at Manchester, Reg Beech came in to head the psychology department and he wanted to bring in his own people, so to gain promotion I had to move on. I met Frank McPherson at a conference and he told me about a job in his clinical psychology department in Dundee, so I went up there. That job was half-time working in prisons and young offender institutions and half-time in regular adult clinical psychology.

A: And you then took up working towards a PhD again?

NH: Yes. I continued using repertory grid techniques, trying to test various theories of delinquent values. I had always been interested in sociology and for a while had been a member of the National Deviancy Conference, quite famous in the history of sociology in the United Kingdom.

Moving Towards Addictions

A: Did this work have any relevance to addiction?

NH: I started to conduct some work on the acute effects of alcohol on people's world-views using repertory grid techniques. And then I became caught up with the controlled drinking issue. So that is when I became really immersed in alcohol studies.

A: You mention your interest in the controlled drinking controversy. How did that start?

NH: David Davies, who was running the Alcohol Education Centre at the time, convened a meeting on 'Resumed Normal Drinking' at the Crichton Royal Hospital in Dumfries in 1976. David had, of course, begun the whole controversy with his 1962 paper. I suppose it was the radical quality of the claims about the controlled drinking goal that attracted me. So I then applied to the Medical Research Council (MRC) to carry out a randomized controlled trial of a cognitive–behavioural treatment for people suitable for the controlled drinking goal and was delighted to get it—my first grant ever. I was lucky enough to be able to employ Ian Robertson as assistant on the project. Collaboration with Ian was to prove very important to my career.

A: You became involved in the New Directors Group around this time?

NH: The Crichton Royal meeting became an annual event at various locations and quickly turned into the New Directions in the Study of Alcohol Group. After a year I became Chair, a position I held until I left for Australia.

The focus on controlled drinking soon expanded to become a more general critique of the disease concept of alcoholism—something I regarded at the time as a very dumb idea and still do.

Into the Study of Interventions

A: Then you published with Ian a rather important book.

NH: I suggested to Ian that we write a book on the whole controlled drinking issue.[3] Perhaps the main conclusion of the book was that, although the controlled drinking goal did have a place in the specialist treatment of those with relatively serious problems, its most important application was in community-based services offered by generalists and mainly as a form of early intervention.

A: How did you take the community intervention idea forward?

NH: We began looking around for ways in which these community-based interventions could be developed. I received a grant from the Alcohol Education and Research Council to employ Steve Baldwin to develop and evaluate 'alcohol education courses' for young offenders. Ian and I also collaborated with the Scottish Health Education Group (SHEG) to develop and test a self-help manual for problem drinkers.[4]

A: And then?

NH: Probably the most important application of the controlled drinking goal at the time was brief intervention given opportunistically by GPs and other primary health care staff. We collaborated with SHEG again to produce a screening and intervention pack for GPs (DRAMS).

A: Did you have any job security at this time?

NH: No. In 1979, I had moved over to the university from the National Health Service (NHS) on soft money. I began to attract funding from various sources and to employ a small group of researchers, the Addictive Behaviour Research Group, but I remained on soft money all the time and this was not very comfortable.

The Move to Australia

A: Then came your move to Australia.

NH: In 1986 I applied for the post of Director of the National Drug and Alcohol Research Centre (NDARC) at the University of New South Wales and was offered the job.

A: That research establishment arguably has contributed to Australia being a major force in the field of addictions.

NH: Yes, I agree. Setting up the centre was probably the most exciting period of my career. At the beginning we had some trouble in identifying a suitable Deputy Director. In the end I was able eventually to persuade Wayne Hall to take the job. He turned out to be someone of extraordinary gifts in research and scholarship.

A: How long were you in Australia?

NH: Six-and-a-half years. I left in January 1994. I would say that NDARC is now one of the leading research centres in our field in the world and I am very pleased to have played a part in all this achievement.

Back to the UK

A: Then you came back to a post in Newcastle.

NH: There were many things that influenced my coming back. I never got over a feeling of some home-sickness and I realised how British I really am.

A: So what have you been doing since you came back?

NH: I set up the third research group of my career, called the Centre for Alcohol and Drug Studies. I also worked with Tim Stockwell and Timothy Peters to edit a large handbook on alcohol and its problems.[5]

A: And you became involved in a major multi-site treatment trial?

NH: There have been two major projects since I came back to the United Kingdom. One is the UK Alcohol Treatment Trial. Shortly after I returned from Australia in 1994, MRC convened a meeting, chaired by Griffith Edwards, on what was needed in research on treatment for alcohol problems in the United Kingdom. A group of us got together and submitted an application which was eventually accepted. This was the largest clinical trial of treatment for alcohol problems ever carried out in the United Kingdom. It was a great chance to work over an extended period with friends and colleagues whom I have known for a long time.[6,7]

A: And your other large project since returning home?

NH: The other large project was working with the World Health Organization (WHO) to try to implement brief interventions in routine primary health care across Europe and Australia.

Retirement So-Called

A: When did you formally retire?

NH: In 2003. I was given an Emeritus chair and a room at Northumbria University.I am trying to slow down but it is difficult, partly because this just happens to be an interesting time for alcohol studies in the United Kingdom.

A: For readers who want to know a little more about Nick Heather the person, would you mind telling me who are your heroes?

NH: In the addictions field, I would have to say Bill Miller because he has made seminal contributions to our field in so many ways. Outside addictions, my choice of heroes would have to be a toss-up between Thelonious Monk and Jimmy Greaves.

A: Why Jimmy Greaves?

NH: His calmness and composure in front of goal. He was the greatest goal-scorer I have seen and I have seen a few.

A: You mention the jazz musician Thelonious Monk. You play jazz piano yourself, I believe.

NH: Yes, jazz is my other great passion in life and Thelonious is my main man. When I was at University College I was the pianist in a rhythm and blues band, with some good musicians, and since we could not find a singer, I did that too. Now, I still play quite a bit, just for my own satisfaction.

A: How would you like to be regarded by people in the field?

NH: As somebody who has made a contribution to the understanding and treatment of addictions in general and alcohol problems in particular—simple as that.

Notes

1. Heather N. *Radical Perspectives in Psychology.* London: Methuen; 1976.
2. Heather N., Edwards S., Hore B. D. Changes in construing and outcome of group therapy for alcoholism. *J Stud Alcohol* 1975; 36: 1238–53.
3. Heather N., Robertson I. *Controlled Drinking.* London: Methuen; 1981.
4. Robertson I., Heather N. *So You Want to Cut Down Your Drinking? A Self-Help Manual for Controlled Drinking.* Edinburgh: Scottish Health Education Group; 1983.
5. Heather N., Peters T., Stockwell T., editors. *International Handbook of Alcohol Dependence and Problems.* Chichester: John Wiley; 2001.
6. UKATT Research Team. Effectiveness of treatment for alcohol problems: findings of the randomised UK Alcohol Treatment Trial (UKATT). *BMJ* 2005; 351: 541–4.
7. UKATT Research Team. Cost-effectiveness of treatment for alcohol problems: findings of the randomised UK Alcohol Treatment Trial (UKATT). *BMJ* 2005; 351: 544–8.

20

Conversation with Martin Jarvis

Martin Jarvis is a British psychologist who has made large and varied contributions to tobacco research and to related policy advice. He was a founding member of Michael Hamilton Russell's highly influential London-based nicotine research group.

Finding a Career Path

Addiction (A): Tell us something about your early life.

Martin Jarvis (MJ): I was born in Norfolk just before the Second World War, and I can vaguely remember taking refuge in a shelter in the front garden when Norwich was bombed. The family moved to Rickmansworth on the outskirts of London when I was 9. I was fortunate to start at Watford Grammar School in 1950, the same year as an inspirational headmaster, Harry Ree, arrived.

A: How did you get into the field of smoking?

MJ: It was a long and tortuous route, first getting into psychology, and then into smoking. At the age of 13 I had to choose between having to do languages and science at school and I opted for languages, which meant Greek and Latin, and before long there I was at Cambridge translating Shakespeare into Greek iambics—which I loved. When I left Cambridge in 1961 with a Classics degree, I had no sense of where I was heading or what I wanted to do. But some good friends were psychologists, so I became interested in psychology and decided to do a part-time degree at Birkbeck. Initially I was working at the Bank of England, which again showed what little I knew about what I was all about and where I was going. I was in what they called the 'Economic Intelligence Department'! After that I worked at the Institute of Psychiatry (IOP) as a research assistant to John Steiner, a psychiatrist who also had a PhD in experimental psychology, on a project on risk-taking behaviour.

A: How did you get to work at the Institute?

MJ: I was friendly with Peter Bryant, a child pyschologist who went on to become professor at Oxford, and also Bernie Spain, who was a clinical psychologist who had just completed her Maudsley training. One of the good things about my job there was that it introduced me very early on to laboratory computers, which were then in their infancy. I started work at the Institute in 1963.

A: And when you graduated?

MJ: I completed the last year at Birkbeck full time. I graduated from there in 1968 and came to UCL's physiology department and began to work on averaged evoked potentials. But it was not clear to me that it was going anywhere useful and so in 1970 I went back to the Institute, this time to work on cognitive abilities of chimpanzees.

A: Had you decided at that point that you wanted to be a researcher?

MJ: Yes, absolutely; I enjoyed research but I had no sense of a career trajectory. I was doing stuff that I enjoyed but I did not have any grand vision.

A: Your work with chimpanzees?

MJ: By 1976, although it was still enjoyable working with chimps, I decided that I really needed to think about my career. I decided to undertake a training course in clinical psychology; so I did that from 1976 to 1978.

A: This was at the IOP?

MJ: Yes. That was the clinical psychology training course which was probably the most sought-after. I was lucky to get in, but I had to cash in my pension to fund those 2 years. It was a 2-year MPhil course in those days. I met many good people. Jane Wardle was one of my teachers, and on my course there were all sorts of bright and interesting people: Joanna Collicut, who eventually became a vicar and wrote a riposte to Richard Dawkins' *The God Delusion* called *The Dawkins Delusion*, Ian Robertson, who went on to a career in neuropsychology, Susan Michie who is now a prominent health psychologist, and numerous others.

Entering the Smoking Field

A: What next?

MJ: This is where fate takes a hand. Just as I was completing that course, Mike Russell, who had been working at the Institute and whom I had known for several years, had received a Medical Research Council (MRC) programme grant to study pharmacological and behavioural issues in cigarette smoking. That sounded like a very interesting opportunity, because it combined research and clinical work. I joined Mike's group in 1978, with my initial remit to be involved in the smoker's clinic helping smokers to stop. My very first project was a collaboration with Martin Raw, the other psychologist there, to run a randomized controlled trial on nicotine chewing gum for smoking cessation.

A: That was one of the first studies conducted under the programme grant?

MJ: It was. This was the first blinded randomized trial. We gained very clear evidence.[1] We found that a doubling of 1 year sustained quit rates from something like 14% on placebo to 32% on active gum. It was a very fortunate time to join Mike's group. He had been working on smoking since 1969 but things really started to take off at that time. I would say that he invented the world of smoking research in those years.

A: That was in the early 1970s?

MJ: He hired Colin Feyerabend to develop the assays—I think in 1973. Colin had a blood nicotine assay ready by 1975 and the cotinine assay came along a year or two later. What underlay it all was Mike's vision and understanding of the importance of nicotine in smoking. He had been working on nicotine gum from the early 1970s and had been highly instrumental in persuading the pharmaceutical company LEO to develop a commercial product. I was very fortunate to inherit a great deal of this work. The gum needed testing, the assays for characterizing intakes were there, and I just loved this area. From that moment on there was no question of where I was going to work—this was definitely a beautiful fit for what I wanted to do.

A: What about evaluating the breath test for carboxyhaemoglobin?

MJ: At the time we were using blood samples for measuring carboxyhaemoglobin (COHB) as an indicator of smoke intake. Then along came expired air carbon monoxide devices (the so-called Ecolyzer) and I was asked to carry out a study comparing blood COHB with expired air carbon monoxide (CO). The study showed that expired air CO was a pretty serviceable way of estimating COHB and CO intake from smoking.[2]

A: You also conducted the first study showing precious little relationship between the cigarette yields printed on the cigarette pack and what smokers actually got from their cigarettes.

MJ: This study had a big influence on me, and on the field subsequently, in that we quickly became aware that the nominal yield of the brand people were smoking bore little relationship to the blood nicotine level we observed. We published that study in 1980 and the world seemed massively uninterested.[3] The dose smokers get is determined not by the product, but by the smoker's needs.

A: The inferences you drew from that study?

MJ: Our research persuaded us about the controlling role of nicotine in smoking behaviour. There was the story about how nicotine replacement helps people to quit, so giving people nicotine makes it easier to stop; and there was the story about how people seemed to self-titrate their preferred nicotine dose from cigarettes. Another story is that we were looking at nicotine intake from other products, particularly nasal snuff and cigars and pipes—all this pointed in the direction of the controlling role of nicotine. At that time we were considered crazy nicotine advocates who were completely out on a limb.

A: Around this time, Mike's research group were developing an important investigation of laboratory measurements?

MJ: I was becoming increasingly interested in the application of measures of dose. We had blood nicotine, we had cotinine, we had CO and I wanted to look at all these measures in the same study to see how they all stacked up, one against the other, as indicators of smoking intake. First, we determined which of these measures identified smokers. Cotinine stood out as the best measure.[4] We also found a clear relationship between cotinine levels in blood, urine or saliva and the non-smokers' self-report of how much they were exposed to other people's smoke. This was perhaps the first study that had shown that you can quantify real-life passive smoking by measuring some biomarkers.[5]

A: You also conducted some studies on nasal snuff, I think.

MJ: We looked at how snuff stacked up as a way of getting nicotine into people. But then Mike got wind of a snuff-taking club in Somerset whose members would do odd things, for instance, taking as much snuff as you could in a minute without sneezing. We took before-and-after blood levels from daily snuff users and naive snuff users. Most interestingly, we charted blood nicotine levels in users who were taking snuff under competition rules, and in these individuals we saw some absolutely astonishing increases in blood nicotine levels. We showed that regular daily snuff users have blood nicotine levels which are remarkably similar to cigarette smokers—it showed that this route of nicotine delivery had considerable potential for giving people the kind of nicotine doses they seemed to want.[6]

A: So already you were thinking about harm reduction.

MJ: Very much so. Mike had enunciated a deep truth about smoking in one of his earliest papers when he said that 'people smoke for nicotine but they die from the tar'.

A: And this focus on nicotine also led to the idea of a high nicotine, low-tar cigarette?

MJ: I think Mike had a perception that nicotine was the key to understanding cigarette smoking right from the beginning of the 1970s. Mike Russell was a fabulous researcher and a wonderful person to work with—encouraging, very supportive, did not suffer fools gladly, did not take prisoners, and very, very helpful in developing my career. The tobacco group was growing quite rapidly through the 1980s. When I joined, Martin Raw was already in post along with social psychologists Steve Sutton and Dick Eiser. Mike's interests were wide-ranging; he was not just 'it's all the nicotine, stupid'.

A: The team was mainly psychologists, then?

MJ: It was indeed, and we were soon joined by Robert West, John Stapleton, Peter Hajek, Ann McNeill and Gay Sutherland. Jonathan Foulds came along a few years later. Virtually all were psychologists and it was a very congenial and strong research group. I was becoming increasingly interested in the epidemiological aspects of smoking behaviour. I was eventually successful in persuading our national surveys of school children's smoking to incorporate saliva sampling, thinking that that would help give us a window into passive smoking effects as well as active smoking.[7] We were able to show things such as how the mother's smoking has a big impact on children and the added effects when both parents smoke.[8]

A: So by now you were reaching beyond clinical samples?

MJ: Yes. In another study in a sixth-form college in 1986/87, we managed to take saliva samples from about 900 16–18-year-olds and asked them to complete questionnaires about their smoking. We followed them over the course of a year, and were able to chart how smoking intake develops in novice smokers over a relatively brief period. Somewhat later on, when the Health Survey for England (HSE) was first planned, we agitated strongly for them to include cotinine measures in their basic design of the survey and we were successful in achieving that from 1993 onwards. That was instrumental in gaining a truly epidemiological perspective on both active and passive smoking effects in large samples of the general population.

A: And the HSE has been rich source of data?

MJ: It has proved enormously valuable. It has helped us to track passive smoking and its determinants in the general population and to map how exposure levels have declined over a period of years.[9] We were able to show that if you come from a more deprived background, not only are you more likely to be a smoker, but also you will take in a much higher nicotine dose than a more affluent smoker.[10]

Moving to University College, London (UCL)

A: Going back to your career, when Mike retired you transferred to University College London.

MJ: Well yes, Mike had programme grant support from the MRC, but he was also very aware of the need to try to gain longer-term secure funding. We were all living on grant money. So there were some negotiations with the Imperial Cancer Research fund which led to them setting up what was called the Health Behaviour Unit (HBU) to work initially on smoking, but with the intention that it would broaden to cover other behavioural issues important for cancer. That was a key development, in that it brought us under the wing of one of the most important scientific funders in the United Kingdom, associated with some very good people including Richard Doll and Richard Peto on the epidemiological side. That started in 1988, while we were still at the Institute, but as Mike approached retirement there was a feeling among many of us that the group's position at the IOP was not ideal. This was the age when mission statements were becoming more of a dominant feature. We were in the late flowering of the Thatcher years and the hospital obviously felt that it had to focus more on its core psychiatric mission, and smoking was not perceived as a core feature of the Maudsley's remit. So in 1996 we came to UCL, finding a home in Michael Marmot's department where the unit has been allowed to flourish. Another crucial element occurred in 1991, when Jane Wardle joined the Health Behaviour Unit with a view to developing the non-tobacco side of the research. She has been a huge force for the success of the unit. Jane took leadership of the HBU in 1995 when Mike was about to retire and has taken it forward through the years at UCL.

A: So having got up to UCL you are now in a department of epidemiology, although you are a psychologist. In some ways you had found a department which reflected some of your major interests: measurements of cotinine in very large data sets and working with population data.

MJ: Yes, although the nicotine gum trial was not the end of my involvement in nicotine replacement therapy (NRT) treatments. A year or two later we pioneered the nasal spray and conducted the first trial in the 1980s.[11] Certainly my personal interest shifted more towards the epidemiological scale of research.

A: The passive smoking issue then became very topical. You were on the Department of Health Scientific Committee on Tobacco and Health?

MJ: Yes. I think where Mike was so successful was in mapping out a research agenda and setting out the key findings in relation to nicotine. One area where he was less successful was becoming involved in the policy process. Partly that was because he could be somewhat impatient with the powers-that-be. So I think the generation of us that trained under Mike was perhaps more keen to take smoking issues from the simply scientific arena into the policy arena. In the 1990s I became a trustee of Action on Smoking and Health (ASH) and have tried to influence to some extent how they understood and approached smoking issues. I also joined the government's Scientific Committee on Tobacco and Health. I think that has been productive in bringing some of the scientific understanding of smoking, and particularly nicotine, into aspects of government policy, and it was certainly productive in terms of bringing the passive smoking issue more to the fore.

A: And you became adviser to a Parliamentary Committee?

MJ: In 2000 I was lucky enough to become the Specialist Adviser for the Health Select Committee's enquiry into tobacco smoking and the role of the tobacco industry. The Health Committee's report was very timely in terms of issues to do with the industry, advertising bans and smuggling.

A: You were also integral to the development of a policy which banned smoking in public places.

MJ: Yes. In 2004, I was the Health Committee's Specialist Adviser into their inquiry into smoking in public places, which coincided with the progress of the Bill to ban smoking in public places going through the Commons.

A: In Britain and America we seem to be stuck at a prevalence of around 20% and many people are talking about harm reduction. Do you think harm reduction is now one of the key battle-grounds?

MJ: To me it is a no-brainer—certainly we should be encouraging people not to start smoking, and those who have started to stop; we should also be thinking about how we can make tobacco less harmful for people who will not, or cannot, give up. I suspect that the future of harm reduction lies with pure nicotine products which are much better nicotine delivery devices than the current generation. There are also large research agendas in understanding more clearly how nicotine controls cigarette smoking. There are many things we do not understand—we do not understand much about the individual's career over time, how or if nicotine preference and dose can change within an individual over time—extraordinary omissions—so there is a huge research agenda out there.

Notes

1. Jarvis M. J., Raw M., Russell M. A. H., Feyerabend C. Randomised controlled trial of nicotine chewing-gum. *BMJ* 1982; 285: 537–40.
2. Jarvis M. J., Russell M. A. H., Saloojee Y. Expired air carbon monoxide: a simple breath test of tobacco smoke intake. *BMJ* 1980; 281: 484–5.
3. Russell M. A. H., Jarvis M. J., Iyer R., Feyerabend C. Relation of nicotine yield of cigarettes to blood nicotine concentrations in smokers. *BMJ* 1980; 280: 972–6.
4. Jarvis M. J., Tunstall-Pedoe H., Feyerabend C., Vesey C., Saloojee Y. Comparison of tests used to distinguish smokers from nonsmokers. *Am J Public Health* 1987; 77: 1435–8.
5. Jarvis M., Tunstall-Pedoe H., Feyerabend C., Vesey C., Saloojee Y. Biochemical markers of smoke absorption and self reported exposure to passive smoking. *Epidemiol Commun Health* 1984; 38: 335–9.
6. Russell M. A. H., Jarvis M. J., Devitt G., Feyerabend C. Nicotine intake by snuff users. *BMJ* 1981; 283: 814–7.
7. Jarvis M. J., Goddard E., Higgins V., Feyerabend C., Bryant A., Cook D. Children's exposure to passive smoking in England since the 1980s: cotinine evidence from population surveys. *BMJ* 2000; 321: 343–5.
8. Jarvis M. J., Russell M. A. H., Feyerabend C., Eiser J. R., Morgan M., Gammage P. et al. Passive exposure to tobacco smoke: saliva cotinine concentrations in a representative population sample of non-smoking schoolchildren. *BMJ* 1985; 291: 927–9.
9. Jarvis M. J., Mindell J., Gilmore A., Feyerabend C., West R. Smoke-free homes in England: prevalence, trends and validation by cotinine in children. *Tob Control* 2009; 18: 491–5.
10. Jarvis M. J., Wardle J. Social patterning of health behaviours: the case of cigarette smoking. In: MarmotM., WilkinsonR., editors. *Social Determinants of Health,* 2nd edn. Oxford: Oxford University Press; 2005, p. 240–55.
11. Jarvis M. J., Hajek P., Russell M. A. H., West R. J., Feyerabend C. Nasal nicotine solution as an aid to cigarette withdrawal: a pilot clinical trial. *Br J Addict* 1987; 82: 983–8.

21

Conversation with Jim Orford

Jim Orford is a psychologist who has made many original contributions to addiction research and to exploring the meaning of addiction as a concept. His book, Excessive Appetites, *has been widely influential.*

Early Days

Addiction (A): Start out by talking about your childhood and your memories of what it was like.

Jim Orford (JO): I had a very safe, comfortable, loving, modest, post-Second World War London childhood. I was an only child so I was very influenced by the things my parents were interested in, including their memories of the war. I was born in 1942, so the war was still going on. My father was in the Army, and was away for most of the first 4 years of my life. It was a period of austerity when they got back together again; we were on rationing and there was not much money around. But the memories of the war they shared with me were very positive: what a tremendous spirit there had been—the Dunkirk Spirit was very important. They were Conservative in their politics; Churchill was the great hero. It was a source of some regret to me later on in life, though, that I did not share my parents' politics in the slightest, nor my mother's religious faith. Otherwise I was very influenced by them both. For one thing, I have inherited a love of words and of writing from my mother. Writing was her passion. She had some articles and poems published, and three historical novels. My father also had an artistic passion which unfortunately I did not inherit. He was a local government chief officer, in what was then called O&M—Organization and Methods—but it was his water-colour painting that he loved. He taught it to others, sold pictures regularly and exhibited. So, in their modest way, they were both very talented.

A: And presumably they had an influence on the school that you went to.

JO: They sent me to a 'minor public school'—I think that is how, in the crazy British system of education, it would be classified. I was one of the scholarship boys who went from the local area to this otherwise private school. My parents cared very much about my schooling, and I am indebted to them for that. After that I don't think they had much influence because neither of them had been to university themselves, and they just felt it was beyond what they knew about.

A: By this time presumably your academic life had set out in a particular direction.

JO: I could have gone on the science or the arts side, but I got best marks in the science subjects and I enjoyed science. I was successful in winning one of the university scholarships that British Petroleum were offering on the understanding that I would go back and work for them afterwards as a chemical engineer. Once at Cambridge things changed. My experience there was not altogether positive. I came away rather anti-Oxbridge.

A: OK, say more about that.

Entering Psychology

JO: I see British education generally as being pretty elitist and unequal and Oxbridge is the pinnacle of it. My college, like my school, was all male and the servants treated students like young gentlemen. One aspect of the Cambridge system which I was very grateful for was its flexibility. I was able to change to psychology. Psychology was such a minor and early subject in those days, you could study a little bit of it—I did one-third of my second year and the full third year—and still finished up with a qualifying psychology degree.

A: Why psychology?

JO: I had never met anyone who was a psychologist and I don't think I had ever read a psychology book. I simply went into psychology because I needed to find something that looked interesting that enabled me to stay at university but to drop out of the main scientific subjects. But I loved psychology; the subject matter fascinated me from the outset and, unlike chemistry, everything was debated and challenged. This was what I had hoped university would be all about.

A: So you finished Cambridge with a degree in psychology.

JO: I also finished with a wife and a baby, which was another major transition. Judith had been studying nursing at Guys Hospital in London, and she gave that up and moved to Cambridge.

A: Were you at that time changing in your belief systems?

JO: I was changing in my social and political outlook on life. I was very interested in politics, but it was a struggle to give up the Conservatism I was brought up with. Getting married and having a baby clinched it. I realized for the first time in my life what it was like not to have much money, but to have responsibilities for a family.

A: You finished university with a commitment to go and work for British Petroleum?

JO: I had dropped chemistry so I could not do that. I gained a place at the Institute of Psychiatry, Maudsley Hospital, in London, funded by a health authority in north Manchester. It was to take a course for 1 year, which enabled me to qualify as a clinical psychologist in those days.

A: Then you presumably had a commitment at Manchester you had to fulfil if they had sent you off to train in London.

JO: Yes I went back to Manchester for 1 year. I became involved, not by my own choosing, because I was still a 'probationer' clinical psychologist, in a programme of aversion therapy for sexual disorders and the principal so-called sexual 'disorder' that was treated in this clinic was homosexuality. It was in the very last years before the Wolfenden Report in Britain and the law changing in the 1960s that legalized homosexual behaviour in private between consenting adults. It was a time when behaviour therapy was fairly new and psychologists thought of themselves as doing something quite radical, even progressive, strange as that may seem now, since instead of defining homosexuality as an illness or disorder, we saw it as a form of behaviour. There was great excitement at that time about behaviour change. One positive thing that I did carry forward from that year, and which has been of influence in my career ever since then, is something about how people change. I came to the conclusion that in behaviour therapy it was not the behavioural methods that were changing people, but that actually what people were going through was a symbolically very important series of events. I finished up quite convinced that what was more likely to have an impact was not the stimulus–stimulus or stimulus–response associations, but rather going through the experience of coming to see experts who claimed they could change an important aspect of behaviour. That has carried through to my ideas about how people change if they have an alcohol or other addiction problem; why I think that some of the processes of change are much more general than the specific theoretical treatment rationales suggest. I was very influenced at the time by Jerome Frank's book, *Persuasion and Healing*,[1] about general change processes.

To the Addiction Research Unit

A: How did you come to go back to London?

JO: I wanted to do a PhD but I couldn't find anyone who was keen on having me. Then I had a message one day to telephone someone called Griffith Edwards, whom I had never heard of before but who subsequently turned out to be one of the major influences on my life. He said he was looking for a psychologist to join his new team. At that stage I would have gone almost anywhere to do a PhD on almost anything. I went to meet Griffith and Sally Guthrie, who played a significant role at that stage in my career, because she and I wrote one of the early papers on wives coping with their husbands' alcohol problems, which became the subject of my PhD and has been an interest of mine ever since.

A: Which was the first project you worked on?

JO: The project we called the Family Study. This was what turned out to be the famous treatment versus advice study which people even mention to this day. Griff was always very good about authorship. I was the first author on the Maudsley Monograph that we wrote about it later and he was first author on the main paper.[2] I have always explained to people when they ask how the project arose that it was Griff's idea. The idea was that the study would compare treatment as usual as given by him and his team at the Maudsley Hospital, versus simply one session of advice to abstain following a full assessment. The second main facet of the study was studying the influence of marriage on treatment outcome.

A: You are seen as the person who initiated that interest in family coping. Tell me about that.

JO: We agreed early on that we should look at that. One of the people who influenced us at that point was a leading social psychologist from the London School of Economics, Bram Oppenheim, who was a consultant to the unit and who became my PhD supervisor, jointly with Griffith. I sometimes think, oh no, am I still working on this after all this time? It does make you think, do you get very far really in a whole career?

A: What are the most pleasing achievements of your career?

JO: What immediately comes to my mind is my book *Excessive Appetites*.[3] I think at the time it was genuinely doing something that was needed and was pulling things together in a new way. I think it is part of something bigger, part of the whole teaching, lecturing, influencing side of my career. Besides research, which is my greatest love, that has probably been the most satisfying general aspect. The other is writing. It was interesting the way my first book[4] came about. It was another of these out-of-the-blue things. Hans Eysenck was editing a series and was stuck for someone to write a book on social psychology applied to mental illness. He asked me because I had given some lectures to trainee psychiatrists on that subject. I am a great believer in out-of-the-blue things, actually. I have not been someone who has planned and sometimes I think I could have achieved a great deal more if I had been. Anyway, I wrote that little Penguin book and I enjoyed it and found I could do it. I have never looked back about writing and it has become more and more of a part of what I do. I now think of myself, more than anything else, as a writer.

A: Say some more about your time in London.

JO: The experience of being in the Addiction Research Unit (ARU) with Griffith Edwards was a tremendous one. I think of Griff as a towering figure in the field. He started off so many good things. The whole treatment versus advice thing was a brilliant idea, fantastically bold for its time. He had also become involved in a big way in the movement, which was very strong at the time, of small therapeutic houses, or hostels, for men with drinking problems. It was also in the spirit of the times; it was the 1960s, influenced by the Therapeutic Community ideas of Maxwell Jones and others. It was very much the idea that they were looking after themselves in the house, rather than other people looking after them. He said: 'You have got to come and meet these people'. So there I was one evening, as a young clinical psychologist who had been conducting aversion therapy in a laboratory in Manchester, sitting round with these men telling me what they were doing, living together and trying to overcome their drinking problems. That was a new experience for me. I also remember, early on, asking Griff what books I should read. He suggested two. One was Jellinek's *The Disease Concept of Alcoholism*,[5] which I thought was very interesting. The second book he recommended was Pittman & Snyder's *Society, Culture and Drinking Patterns*,[6] which was completely new to me and very exciting; and of course, Griff was so well connected internationally. There were constantly people coming through the unit who came from the States and other parts of the world. It was helping to give me a social, cultural and international outlook.

A: Other activities and influences at the ARU?

JO: There was a great crowd of people there, including, to mention only some, Celia Hensman, Seta Waller, David Robinson, Gloria Litman, Shirley Otto, David Hawks, Ray Hodgson, and others who were associated very closely with the unit such as Tim Cook, Judith Harwin, Terry Spratley, Marcus Grant and David Davies. It was a very exciting place to be and Griff was so generous with me. At a very early stage he arranged for me to give a keynote talk at an international conference in Sydney, and a little later, one in Washington. He and I travelled to Australia together, spending an hour with Mother Teresa in Kolkata on the way.

Moving on to Exeter

A: So you moved on after 10 years at the ARU?

JO: After finishing my PhD I was looking around for other things and found a job in Exeter. Jim Drewery, who had been my PhD external examiner and who had been working on interperson perception and 'alcoholic marriages', was there. Exeter was a totally new phase in my life, because I moved from being a full-time researcher to be the academic half of a two-person team, directing a new clinical psychology postgraduate course. That threw me into being a university teacher. After a few years Jim Dewery retired and I took over as sole course director. It was a very busy time. I was there for 17 years. The clinical side fitted in with the community psychology interest that I had started to develop at the ARU. While I was in Exeter, a whole set of community mental health teams and a community alcohol team were developed, and I became involved in the latter. For a few years we had a really exciting experiment in delivering a community-based service. During that period I wrote my first book on community psychology, *Community Psychology: Theory and Practice*.[7] Certainly, helping develop community psychology in

Britain and later more generally in Europe is one of the things that I would put high on my list of things that I am pleased to have done.

A: And what about your research?

JO: Around that time, the mid-1970s, the New Directions in the Study of Alcohol Group got started. The hot issue was whether it was possible for people who had serious alcohol problems to control their drinking. One of my successful grant applications was on that topic. They were amongst the things that kept me engaged in the alcohol studies field.

A: Had you started to work with those other behaviours that you address in *Excessive Appetites* before you left Exeter?

JO: Gambling, yes. In fact, gambling has become a big interest of mine in its own right over the years. A number of things happened towards the end of my time at the ARU. I conducted a small study, which was never written up, in which I interviewed a number of people with alcohol problems who also seemed to have problems with their gambling. I also became involved with a group of professional people in London who were interested in problem gambling. I started to read more about the subject and was becoming quite convinced about gambling addiction. Reading around I also discovered a whole fascinating literature about sexual addiction, largely men writing about nymphomania, women's excessive sexuality. And there were people writing much more recently about something they were calling hypersexuality, so I wrote a paper, which was published in the *British Journal of Addiction*, raising the question: is this an addiction? Then I found that people were starting to write about binge eating. Then I began to read more about the drug field. For example, at that time Virginia Berridge[8] was starting to publish her work on the history of opium-taking in the 19th century. I realized there was something to put together here, that addiction was much more of a general thing than simply one or two of the very familiar substances, and that there was a whole psychology to be written about that. *Excessive Appetites* was the result.

Moving to Birmingham

A: Now tell me how you came to leave Exeter.

JO: I left Exeter after 17 years for a mixture of reasons. I had applied for a chair at Exeter and they had turned me down, so I started to look for other jobs. Birmingham University was looking to appoint a new chair in clinical psychology. I was approaching 50 at that stage and I thought if I am going to move it is now or never. As you know, Birmingham had a reputation in Britain as being a rather dirty industrial place ringed by motorways. What actually happened when I got there was the exact reverse of what I was expecting. As soon as I got to Birmingham I fell in love with the place. However, the job of running the clinical psychology training course turned out to be very difficult.

A: But overall was Birmingham a good move?

JO: The foundation was being laid then for the next decade, which became one of the most rewarding times of my career with a small research group and a number of projects. I was invited by the Department of Health to set up what became our Untreated Heavy Drinkers Study, a longitudinal study of 500 people who were regularly drinking very heavily but who had not had any treatment for a drinking problem. I was able to pass over to someone else the job of running the large postgraduate course. The other large study has been the UK Alcohol Treatment Trial (UKATT), which allowed me to work alongside a number of people I had long known but had never had the opportunity to work with, such as Gillian Tober, Duncan Raistrick, Nick Heather and Christine Godfrey. Besides Heavy Drinkers and UKATT there is our family work, which goes right back to my PhD. I have had the great pleasure of running a small research group, with senior colleagues such as Sue Dalton, Alison Rolfe, and particularly Alex Copello, who has become my closest colleague.

A: Tell me more about the family work.

JO: That has been a theme of my research all the way through, from early London days in the late 1960s. A very significant event was a 6-month sabbatical which I took after 3 years at Exeter. After a month at WHO Geneva I went to Mexico for 5 months where I was attached to the Institute of Psychiatry in Mexico City, which is a WHO collaborating centre. I met there the person who was to become our main collaborator on the family work in Mexico over a number of years, and who has become a close friend, Guillermina Natera. That trip to Mexico was a very significant experience for me. Then I was contacted by someone from the Northern Territory in Australia. My close colleague Richard Velleman went out on one trip to the Northern Territory and I went out on another one and then with our help they trained six interviewers who interviewed Aboriginal family members affected by someone in the family who had an alcohol problem. Over the years I have become a great advocate of qualitative research. Some of those interviews with family members in Mexico and Australia and Britain were really rather extraordinary in providing detail which other research methods can not.[9]

A: And gambling continues to be an active interest?

There has been a great deal of change in the law in Britain just in the last few years and there are new forms of gambling, such as internet gambling, and more powerful gambling machines. I have become really interested in policy in that area.

A: People sometimes ask whether you are retired now: it certainly does not sound like it.

JO: I tell people that retirement for me is a 20-year process. I'm scarcely halfway through it so I hope you'll hear a lot from me yet!

Notes

1. Frank J. Persuasion and Healing: *A Comparative Study of Psychotherapy,* 3rd edn. Schocken, NY: Johns Hopkins University Press; 1991.
2. Orford J., Edwards G. *Alcoholism: A Comparison of Treatment and Advice, with A Study of the Influence of Marriage.* Oxford: Oxford University Press; 1977.
3. Orford J. *Excessive Appetites: A Psychological View of Addictions,* 2nd edn. Chichester, UK: Wiley; 2001.
4. Orford J. *The Social Psychology of Mental Disorder.* London: Penguin; 1976.
5. Jellinek E. M. *The Disease Concept of Alcoholism.* New Haven, CT: Hillhouse Press; 1960.
6. Pittman D. J., Snyder C. R., eds. *Society, Culture and Drinking Patterns.* London: Wiley; 1962.
7. Orford J. *Community Psychology: Theory and Practice.* Chichester, UK: Wiley; 1992.
8. Berridge V., Edwards G. *Opium and the People: Opiate Use in Nineteenth Century England.* Basingstoke UK: Palgrave Macmillan; 1982.
9. Orford J., Natera G., Copello A., Atkinson C., Mora J., Velleman R. et al. *Coping with Alcohol and Drug Problems: The Experiences of Family Members in Three Contrasting Cultures.* Hove, UK: Routledge; 2005.

22

Conversation with Shanthi Ranganathan

Dr Ranganathan founded and developed in South India a nationally influential centre to respond to alcohol and drug problems. What has given her work special interest and authority is her sensitivity to the Indian cultural context.

The Launch of a Life's Work

Addiction (A): You have been working in the area of addiction treatment and rehabilitation for over 25 years. Tell us about your family background and how you happened to get into this field during a period when the subject was relatively unknown in India.

Shanthi Ranganathan (SR): I come from a very traditional family. No one in my family drank. Also, during a decade or so following India's independence, when I was in my school and college, 'prohibition' was in force in this state of Tamil Nadu. Drinking alcohol was an offence punishable under the law. There were no bars or wine shops. To me, any one who drank alcohol was a villain or wicked. By the time I graduated, prohibition had been scrapped.

A: So how did you come to develop an interest in alcohol problems?

SR: I got married when I was 20. It was a traditional, 'arranged' marriage. I married into a wealthy household where drinking was considered quite common. When guests were entertained, alcohol was served. My husband started drinking at a fairly young age. Over a period of time, he became an alcoholic. We did not know how to handle this problem. My mother-in-law pleaded with him, shouted at him, and even stopped talking to him for some time. We did whatever we thought should be done, but he did not give up drinking. He would often give up drinking for a period of time and start again. At that point, we learnt that treatment was available in the United States; we took him to America for treatment. He was in a centre for 1 month and I attended a few sessions for family members. That was the first time I understood that addiction to alcohol was a treatable condition. I also observed that there was no centre available in the entire region not only in India, but also in other Asian countries. My husband died when he was hardly 33 years old. I had suffered in the process of being victimized by alcoholism. At the same time, I did not suffer too long to have become bitter about the whole thing, and I had the energy in me to do something constructive after his death. My in-laws were supportive. My mother-in-law felt that the family should do something to deal with the problem of addiction. We started the TT Ranganathan Clinical Research Foundation with funding from the companies owned by our family. The rest is all history.

The TT Ranganathan Clinical Research Foundation

A: How did the work of your Foundation then progress?

SR: We started the centre in a modest way in our own ancestral bungalow near the Santhome beach. It was a fairly big house. Before I started offering the services formally, I went to Hazeldon in the United States for training and I also visited several other centres. After coming back, I started offering help through an out-patient programme. I was not satisfied with the way I was providing the therapy. Hence, I went to Broadway Lodge in England, which was started by Hazeldon; I stayed there for a period of 1 month. I acquired a great deal more clarity on how to conduct group therapy and issues to be dealt with in counselling.

A: Then you broadened your programme?

SR: When we started receiving patients from other cities in India, we felt the need to start an in-patient programme wherein we could offer both detox and psychological therapy under the same roof. In 1987, we were able to build our own centre. Here the patients could undergo treatment along with their spouses. Now we have completed 25 years and what we have today are:

- A 65-bed primary care centre: the patients stay here for a month. We have a family ward where the spouse can stay for 15 days to attend the mandatory family therapy programme.
- A 20-bed 'after-care centre'—patients are admitted for 3 months.
- A vocational therapy unit—patients who have completed treatment, if they have no skills, are given computer training and family members receive training in tailoring. We have a packing unit wherein they learn work ethics—to arrive on time and leave on time, work with the team and take up responsibilities, an outreach centre for intravenous (i.v.) drug users—a community programme.

Besides this, we conduct treatment camps in villages. We have been conducting camps for the past 16 years in six villages.

A: Your centre treats mainly alcoholics or also drug dependents?

SR: Initially, we treated only alcoholics. In 1987, brown sugar (heroin) addiction showed up as a serious problem, and there was a need to accommodate these patients in our centre. At some point in 1999, we felt that there was a large number of i.v. drug users and they were HIV positive.

A: How many people has your programme benefited?

SR: Around 18 000 families. When we treat a patient, it is not only that patient who recovers. The entire family recovers from the trauma.

A: Your programme has total abstinence as its goal?

SR: Yes, we believe in total abstinence. Because of addiction, every area of his life will have been affected—strained family relationships, violence at home, loss of job and 'spiritual bankruptcy'. Some of them go back to alcohol or drugs, some of them do not make any positive changes in their lives. But we do not give up. We recognize some relapse as an inevitable part of recovery and conduct a relapse prevention programme. Any such major change is a process. It does not happen overnight. We provide follow-up support for a period of 5 years. After a year, we expect them to come back to the centre once in 3 months. We provide support to them. We help them to intervene.

A: What kind of people come to your Centre—poor, middle-class or rich?

SR: Addiction has no bar for religion, community or economic status or educational background. We receive patients from various economic backgrounds. We provide free treatment for those from the lower strata of society—conservancy workers, casual labourers, fishermen and the like. We have seven special rooms for those who can afford them. In the campsites, where the treatment is free, all of them are from the lower strata of society.

A: Do any particular class or classes of clients respond better?

SR: The typical 'middle class'. Their response is often gratifying. A clerk in a private firm or, for instance, a supervisor in a power supply undertaking or the manager of a hotel and so on. When they make an effort, there is a sea change in their life-style. I must say a good number from the lower strata also benefit.

A: In what way is treating addiction in India different from how they do it in other countries?

SR: In most of the Asian countries, the TC (Therapeutic Community) model is the method used by many centres. There are disadvantages to this model—the treatment period is too long (9–12 months). In India, they are not covered by any insurance. No individual can afford to stay in a treatment centre for a long period of time.

A: In India we do see much poverty. At the same time, the government itself is directly selling alcohol—as in our state, Tamil Nadu. Is it not frustrating?

SR: Well, this paradox has become a social reality. Alcoholism leads to poverty. In the entire country, there seems to be no organization, which is concerned about the policies related to availability of alcohol. The World Health Organization (WHO) has been emphasizing that the availability of alcohol has to be curtailed. Policy has never been looked into. Western countries face a declining market growth with regard to the sale of alcoholic beverages. So, most of the large liquor companies are focusing on India and

China who have a huge untapped population of non-drinkers. Recently, an organization has been launched called the 'Indian Alcohol Policy Alliance', which is part of the Global Alcohol Policy Alliance in England.

A: But your Foundation has an advocacy presence?

SR: We make our best endeavours to make the government aware of the implications of high availability of alcohol.

A: Have you faced any ethical dilemmas in your work?

SR: Yes. You know our programme has always been an abstinence-based model. When HIV became an issue with i.v. drug users from the streets, they were not willing to quit drugs totally. The option given was harm minimization. The dilemma began as to whether to adopt harm reduction strategies as an alternative to abstinence. We looked into harm reduction as an option in order to curtail the spread of HIV. After many deliberations, we decided to provide sublingual buprenorphine for i.v. drug users for a period of time so that they could be taken off i.v. use and when they are ready to go for abstinence, we provide them all support. We do see some improvements. We used to receive a large number of patients with abscesses. Now the incidence has reduced a great deal.

A: How do you measure the quality of your service?

SR: I must say it is difficult to measure the quality of service. The attributes on which we measure are various. But yesterday it happened. The patient had taken treatment in 1988. He has been sober for more than 13–14 years. Recently, his daughter fell in love with a boy 'outside her community' and wanted to marry him. He suffered many conflicts and had a relapse for a day or two. He immediately came to the centre with his wife and daughter, shared his problems and learnt to accept the situation. This happened 4–5 months back. He came back again yesterday. For him, to come back after several years to resolve his conflicts, we must be providing quality service. We do not give publicity to what we do. Our main referral is through old patients bringing new patients. To me, it is an indication of the quality of service.

A: You are a Hindu. But a large number of your counsellors and other staff are Christians.

SR: True. Many of them are Christians.

A: Your Centre, is it an all-women show?

SR: The majority of the staff and almost all professionals are women. The resident counsellors who take care of the patients during the night are men; ward boys in the detox ward are men; a few administrative staff are men. The entire patient population is men.

A: And this gender situation is satisfactory?

SR: Being a woman, I think we are a great deal more empathetic. We have not faced any problems so far with this mix.

A: Nowadays there are many religious conflicts in society. Does that create any problem in your Centre?

SR: So far, no. We do not talk about any religion or a specific God. All of us believe in a Higher Power. It is also important for the clients to get into a spiritual mode. We start the day with the serenity prayer. There are no religious conflicts in our organization.

A: When I was walking past your centre, I noticed several pictures of 'Gods,' both Hindu and Christian.

SR: In India, many of them pray to a specific God. The room where you saw the pictures is called pooja room. We hang the pictures of a wide repertoire of Gods belonging to the main religions. Whichever the God to which the patient would like to pray, he can sit quietly for a few minutes in the morning after a shower.

Highs and Lows

A: Two great moments in your life?

SR: As the President of FINGODAP—the body where all non-governmental organizations (NGOs) in the country are members, I visited several NGOs. When I visited, some were doing good work. Some had good intentions, but no skills or knowledge. I felt that there should be minimum standards of care for the entire country. We should provide some guidelines for the NGOs. Our centre as a team developed the documents. When we developed this, we had a meeting with 300 NGOs. To our surprise and satisfaction, the majority of them accepted the minimum standards of care. The government accepted the document and made it mandatory for the NGOs, who are receiving financial support from the Ministry of Social Justice and Empowerment. How do they achieve these standards? The next step was that the government established regional resource and training centres (RRTCs) in five regions. Organizations who have been working for a longer period of time and who have the expertise were chosen as RRTCs. Our centre is the RRTC for the South. Our role is to provide knowledge and skills and help them comply with minimum standards of care through training and on-site training in local languages.

A: Another high point?

SR: One of our clients who came as a young boy of 18 with multiple addictions, after 15 years, with sobriety and financial success, gave us a big donation to build one wing to provide vocational training to our patients and their family members. It was a touching moment in my life. The boy clearly said, 'I don't want my name anywhere in the building. It is one way of showing my gratitude.'

A: You have not mentioned the awards you had received. Don't you see them as your high points? What do they really mean to you?

SR: They do mean a lot. The Government of India honoured me with a 'Padma Shri' award in the year 1992, presented to me by the President of India. In 1999 Dr Kofi Annan, United Nations Secretary General, gave me the UN

Vienna Civil Society award at Vienna, in the very first year of its introduction. These two awards increased the visibility of our institution.

A: What have been the two most agonizing moments in your life?

SR: In the community project for i.v. drug users, many of them are very young people. In this group, 45% of them are HIV positive. They are young, the majority of them are married and they cannot access antiretroviral drugs. Sometimes when I go there, the staff talk about the death of one or two patients. It is very sad. Overall, this makes one feel sad.

A: Other difficult moments?

SR: In our second year of conducting camps in villages, we were conducting a camp at Kanyakumari—the southern tip of India. A patient with severe withdrawal symptoms was admitted. He had several medical problems and he went into delirium tremens and died on the third day. That was a very agonizing moment for all of us. At that time, the wife of the dead patient told all the other 24 patients not to leave the programme just because her husband died. It was the most touching as well as agonizing moment.

A: Most of your counsellors seem highly qualified with bright academic records and clinical experience—how do you retain them on salaries which, compared to industry, may seem unattractive?

SR: It is the grace of God that they stay with me. The work itself gives us much satisfaction. We work as a team, and at the same time we have a great deal of independence. We encourage the patients to celebrate their new birthdays—the day on which they quit drinking or taking drugs. They come with their entire family—wife, children, parents—and share sweets with us. They share with the new patients and are given a medal from the counsellor. The gratitude of the patient and improvements he has made gives us a great deal of happiness.

A: What part of work gives you a lot of joy?

SR: Attending camp programmes gives me a sense of fulfilment. In every 15-day camp, I try to spend at least 2 days. Once a year I am part of the team which is conducting a camp at a village called Manjakkudi. The interaction with the patients and the community. I have been going to the campsite for the past 17 years. Patients who were treated earlier also come back and share their joys and sorrows.

A: Your Centre does some publishing?

SR: So far, we have published four manuals for the Government of India, five manuals for the UNODC and six workbooks for the Colombo Plan. This work gives me a lot of stimulation.

A: Which part is tiring or boring?

SR: Administrative work, preparing reports for government, donor agencies, making the records available and so on. I think the creative components of my job form the 'artist' component. All these administrative procedures form the 'slave' component. Well, we have to do that also!

23

Conversation with Bruce Ritson

Dr Bruce Ritson was formerly Consultant Psychiatrist at the Royal Edinburgh Hospital and Senior Lecturer at Edinburgh University. He currently chairs the medical campaign group, Scottish Health Action on Alcohol Problems (SHAAP), which is hosted by the Royal College of Physicians of Edinburgh. He has had a long and fruitful research career.

Early Career

Addiction (A): Can I take you back to your medical undergraduate studies in Edinburgh in the late 1950s and early 1960s? Did you know that many years later you would be immersed in alcohol studies?

Bruce Ritson (BR): No. I was born in Elgin close by the territory of the Speyside malts. My father joined the army at that time, and we moved around a great deal before returning to Scotland and settling in Edinburgh. There were many breweries in the city at that time—the aroma of brewing drifting across the city was a daily occurrence. However, early in my undergraduate years I remember thinking I would like to be a psychiatrist. I was drawn to a subject where there were many unanswered questions.

A: Who were your teachers of psychiatry?

BR: Alexander Kennedy, who was a Professor of Psychiatry in Edinburgh. He was a brilliant lecturer, a charismatic figure. A little after that there was Morris Carstairs, who was particularly interested in social psychiatry and anthropology, and inspired an interest in a cultural perspective on mental health. He was the Reith Lecturer in 1962 and he had a big effect on me at that time.

A: Other than your teacher and the challenge of unsolved questions, was there anything else that attracted you to the subject?

BR: I was interested in how the mind worked.

A: Was there much teaching in your undergraduate course on alcohol problems?

BR: There was one memorable lecture from Professor Kennedy on 'Alcoholism' and drug addiction. It was really not such an issue at that time.

We learned about dependency and the risks of prescribing, more within therapeutics and pharmacology.

A: So you graduated MB ChB and stayed in Edinburgh at that stage?

BR: Yes, I undertook some general medicine and surgery. One of these jobs was in a ward where people who had taken overdoses came in for medical treatment, and that was interesting. That possibly began to influence me — not in addictions, but in psychiatry. I was interested in the circumstances that drove individuals to such desperate measures.

A: Your first psychiatric post?

BR: That was in the Royal Edinburgh Hospital in general psychiatry. Morris Carstairs was there at that time, as was Frank Fish, who had a deep understanding of phenomenology and German schools of psychiatry. I worked with Ian Oswald for a time. He was interested in the effects of various drugs on sleep.

A: Were there any opportunities at that time in addictions?

BR: I don't think it had established itself, really. There was no specific service at that time. The Nuffield Provincial Hospitals Trust in 1963 enabled Edinburgh to establish a unit for the treatment of alcoholism under the leadership of Henry Walton.

A: You wrote an article in a nursing journal[1] on setting up a specialized alcohol unit.

BR: Yes. The unit had already been established as an out-patient service and, like many innovative projects, it started in a hut next to the hospital. By the time I arrived the clinic had moved into a new building attached to the main hospital and had become an in-patient unit.

A: What was it called then?

BR: It was called the Unit for Treatment of Alcoholism, and was part of the academic department. Henry Walton was the consultant. It was quite a small team, but from the start it was a team of nurses, social workers, occupational therapists. I was very pleased to rotate there. It was a new service with excellent teaching, particularly in group therapy. At that stage I think that was my main interest, but it was then that my fascination with alcohol-related problems really started. While I was there, I got a research grant and that enabled me to stay on for another year and do an evaluation study:[2] the first of many which, looking back, was fairly basic. I learned a great deal from those patients—first the transformation to the sober self and then the struggle to maintain that state in the face of external as well as internal pressures. They were interesting people who recovered and you saw someone coming alive again, and that was nice. I know many relapsed, but you would get this sense of a huge change in someone. The follow-up study also showed me that many patients had lost contact, but it was not necessarily because they had relapsed catastrophically.[3]

A: Given that the Unit for the Treatment of Alcoholism pre-dated the concept of the alcohol dependence syndrome, were these people all alcohol-dependent, or was there a range?

BR: Most of them were alcohol-dependent and most were severely dependent. It is interesting when you say 'alcoholism.' It is a word I rarely use now. A strongly held view at that time was that people who were alcoholic had become so because of some underlying psychological problem. The focus was on finding an underlying psychic cause, which I do not think I would really go along with now. Sometimes there is an underlying cause, but often it is the outcome of chronic exposure to excessive drinking and the psychological harm is secondary.

A: Can you tell me more about the research training then available?

BR: I learned research by doing it and by discussing it with other researchers. There was not as much training in research methodology as one might like to have seen.

Experience in the United States

A: At quite an early stage you have a trip to the United States for a year to Harvard Medical School.

BR: That was a formative experience for me. With the help of Morris Carstairs and a scholarship I was able to spend a year at the Laboratory of Community Psychiatry at Harvard Medical School. The leader of the programme was Gerald Caplan. The students came from all around the world and the focus was upon community mental health, a field in its infancy at that time. It was concerned with the dynamics of decision making and dealing with stress in communities and organizations by providing consultation to workers at all levels, with the aim of improving their capacity to deal with their clients. It strengthened my interest in social psychiatry and the importance of political and economic factors in mental health. One of its founding ideas was the value of crisis intervention and the importance of helping people get through crises by working not directly with them, but with the agencies in the front line. Looking back on the community mental health movement at that time I think it achieved a great deal, but suffered from a lack of evaluation. It also failed to address the needs of individuals with severe mental illness, and in that respect was very different from community psychiatry in the United Kingdom, which emphasized rehabilitation and support for seriously ill patients. After I had worked at Boston I had time in California in a community mental health centre where there were quite a lot of psychotic people and, of course, the hippy culture and the drug scene was very alive. We saw many people with what were probably drug-induced illnesses. Philosophically, drugs to alter consciousness were talking-points. I came across patients who had been given LSD therapeutically but I do not think I would argue for that. Like many things, I do not think it was evaluated properly.

A: So the trip to Boston and California was very useful in seeing different systems and gaining new ideas.

BR: Yes. Another thing I should say is that as a student at Harvard and to a certain extent in Edinburgh, we were taught a lot of sociology which was a significant part of psychiatric training at that time, and now it has virtually vanished. It stayed with me as an important influence.

A: Famously, the 1960s is the era of so-called 'anti-psychiatry', and figures such as R. D. Laing and others came to prominence.

BR: Laing's work was more influential at the time in philosophy and art than in psychiatry, although he encouraged the clinician to pay attention to what the psychotic individual was communicating which was good practice. It was unfortunate that he made very many parents feel responsible for their children's illnesses, which did a great deal of harm. He was also against many forms of medication, which exacerbated much suffering. Among the 'anti-psychiatrists' Erving Goffman and Thomas Szasz were a much greater influence.

First Consultant Post

A: So, in July 1968 you return to the United Kingdom. You are soon to be in your first consultant post and that was an addictions-related job. Can you tell me about that?

BR: Yes. It was in England, which was new to me and it was in Nottingham. It was in one of, by now, a number of specialized regional addiction units. It served a large region and was based in Mapperley Hospital. The psychiatric service was very well known for community mental health in the British model. One of the things about working there was that it gave me a kind of independence. I worked very closely with some very talented probation officers. It certainly showed me what social work—when it was competent and well established—could really do. In that unit there were people with drug- and alcohol-related problems. It was the first time I had worked with drug addicts, who were becoming much more common.

A: Were you a full-time addiction consultant?

BR: No, I had responsibility for some general psychiatry. It was probably about 80% addictions. Only the extreme end of the spectrum of illicit drug misuse came to the clinic: mainly opiate dependence and psychotic reactions to hallucinogens and stimulants. Almost all the drug addicts were young but came from all social backgrounds.

A: Not a good network of addiction specialists?

BR: It was not huge. I was involved with the Alcohol Education Centre. D. L. Davies was a psychiatrist at the Maudsley Hospital and had the vision to see the importance of research and education for the development of this relatively neglected subject. He appointed Marcus Grant to direct the centre.

A: Were you aware of the work of Griffith Edwards?

BR: Very much so. In fact, I was already aware of him even when I was doing my research with Henry Walton. I visited Griffith. I was very impressed with him. The thing that struck me was that he had a team of researchers, quite an established team, and I was very envious of that.

A: Were you able to do much research yourself in Nottingham?

BR: We conducted some follow-up studies.

A: Was there any Alcoholics Anonymous or Narcotics Anonymous influence?

BR: I saw them as a resource, but we did not bring them in as part of the treatment.

Return to Edinburgh

A: You were three years in Nottingham and then you went back to Edinburgh.

BR: Yes, working as a general psychiatrist serving one of the sectors of the city with an in-patient ward attached to it, and a little bit of learning disability as well. I thought that it was a good idea to try to re-frame the services for people with a learning disability, so I did that for about 10 years. I remained interested in alcohol-related problems. I was chairman of Edinburgh and Lothian Council on Alcohol and conducted a research project with Cairns Aitken and John Hamilton evaluating the feasibility of decriminalizing habitual drunken offenders, which was a big issue at that time. Offenders were offered detoxification in a small ward in hospital as an alternative to imprisonment. The outcome[4] showed that it was perfectly possible and more humane to help habitual drunken offenders outside the criminal justice system. I learned then that cooperation and planning among professionals could be very fruitful until it came to hard cash and allocating resources.

A: Ten years later—what happens then?

BR: The consultant who had worked for many years running the unit for treatment of alcoholism thought he would like a move to general psychiatry. We did a swap.

A: Did you then become full time in addiction psychiatry?

BR: No, I still kept some sessions in general psychiatry and learning disability. When I inherited the alcohol clinic it was called the Unit for the Treatment of Alcohol, but fairly soon after we changed the name to the Alcohol Problems Clinic (APC). I was sole consultant for some years before Jonathan Chick joined me; that was a great help. That was the only change of name until after I retired, when it became the Alcohol Problem Service, with the in-patient part very generously re-named the Ritson Unit.

A: During this 20-year period in addictions, how would you characterize the trends in treatment?

BR: Looking at it from Edinburgh, I think the trend was increasing emphasis on out-patient treatment, and then on community outreach with community nurses. The in-patient unit began to be a detoxification unit for some, although most people detoxified at home. Some then stayed for an in-patient group programme lasting up to 3 weeks. In recent years we have had more day patients. The content of therapy has moved from predominantly psychodynamic to more cognitive–behavioural approaches. The changed emphasis was influenced by an evaluation study Jonathan and I conducted.[5]

External Roles

A: Can we talk about training and your involvement with the Medical Council on Alcohol (MCA)?

BR: The MCA has been important for me; it was a meeting place for clinicians working with alcohol problems and it has promoted education for undergraduate and postgraduate doctors. I have enjoyed writing a handbook with Marsha Morgan.[6]

A: There is also the Royal College of Psychiatrists. You were involved with the Faculty of Substance Misuse and you chaired it at one point. You were part of a campaign—if that is the right word—to try to have a separate specialist accreditation for addictions.

BR: Well, I am still in favour of it. When I was chairman it was quite a struggle to get a faculty established. We managed to move it from a section to a faculty and I think that was important. One major achievement by the college was producing *Alcohol Our Favourite Drug*, in 1986[7] which was a follow up to a college report published in 1979. I was chairman of a very strong team of authors.

A: You also had some involvement with the World Health Organization (WHO).

BR: Yes, in many different roles and places. I was involved in the International Community Response to Alcohol Problems Project,[8] which took place across three continents in Mexico, Zambia and Scotland. The Edinburgh arm of the study provided a baseline for a repeat study, where we were able to demonstrate that after a significant increase on tax on alcohol, heavy drinkers reduced their consumption even more than moderate drinkers.[9] I was then asked to coordinate a somewhat similar study in the WHO European region.[10]

A: Moving on, one theme throughout your career, shown in the books and articles you have written, is an eye on the bigger picture, seeing the epidemic growing and the importance of prevention and alcohol policies. We are in a very interesting situation now in Scotland, where you chair Scottish Health Action on Alcohol Problems (SHAAP), and also the Scottish Intercollegiate Group on Alcohol (SIGA).

BR: One of the things that has happened in Scotland in the last 10 years or so is the willingness of the medical profession to unite to tackle this problem. SIGA was formed to reflect this. First of all, our concern was to make sure that doctors were properly trained. It is essential that doctors and nurses in primary care and in hospitals know how to recognize harmful and hazardous drinking and respond appropriately. We drew attention to Scotland's appalling record in deaths from liver disease. Certainly, the present government recognizes (who could not?) that alcohol is causing huge harm to Scotland. Minimum unit pricing is something SHAAP also advocates.

A: There is one final area to discuss—your involvement as a medical adviser to the Driver and Vehicle Licensing Agency (DVLA). What are your thoughts on the legal limit for alcohol for driving and other measures?

BR: I was Chairman of the Alcohol and Drugs Advisory Committee for some years. I think we should have lowered the limit and come into line with almost all the other countries in western Europe.

Wider Interests

A: Can you tell me about your many interests outside the medical field?

BR: One interest that is not totally unrelated has been a concern about the damaging effects of 'total institutions'. This, along with a belief that none of us is all good or all bad, brought me to an interest in criminal justice and penal reform. I was chairman of the Scottish Howard League for penal reform for many years, and remain a member of the Scottish Consortium on Crime and Criminal Justice. I have a belief that the quality of the environment in institutions of all kinds is important for residents, staff and visitors. It is an important measure of a civilized concern for others and ourselves. This has led me to become Chairman of 'Art in Healthcare', which is a charity that provides artworks for health care settings. I have also been a very amateur painter for a number of years. I continue to play rather geriatric squash regularly and enjoy hill-walking when time allows.

Conclusion

A: I get the impression that you have been happy with the direction your career took.

BR: Yes, I have found it very stimulating and enjoyable. The patients I have worked with are often very dejected and rejected, and it is great to see them regaining control over their lives. As a discipline, addiction studies is wonderfully varied. I have always felt it important to avoid being drawn into entrenched positions of political or clinical certainties or becoming overwhelmed by deadening bureaucracy. There was always scope to move to another area of interest, plenty of ambiguity that I enjoy.

Notes

1. Ritson E. B., Collie A. W. The treatment of alcoholism in a specialised unit. *Nurs Mirror Midwives J* 1966; 123(5): i–iv and 123(6): v–ix.
2. Walton H. J., Ritson E. B., Kennedy R. I. Response of alcoholics to clinic treatment. *BMJ* 1966; 2: 1171–4.

3. Ritson E. B. The prognosis of alcohol addicts treated by a specialised unit. *Br J Psychiatry* 1968; 114: 1019–29.
4. Ritson E. B., Hamilton J., Griffiths A., Aitken C. *Detoxification of Habitual Drunken Offenders.* Scottish Health Service Studies no. 39. Edinburgh: Scottish Home and Health Department; 1979.
5. Ritson E. B., Chick J., Connaughton J., Stewart A. Advice versus extended treatment for alcoholism: a controlled study. *Br J Addict* 1988; 83: 159–70.
6. Ritson E., Morgan B. *Alcohol and Health: A Handbook for Students and Medical Practitioners.* London: Medical Council on Alcohol; 2003.
7. Ritson E. B., editor. *Alcohol Our Favourite Drug.* London: Royal College of Psychiatrists Tavistock; 1986.
8. Ritson E. B. Research and action: lessons from the W.H.O. project on community response to alcohol related problems. In: Babor T., editor. *Alcohol and Culture. Annals of the New York Academy of Sciences no. 472.* New York: NYAS; 1986, p. 33–45.
9. Kendell R. E., de Roumanie M., Ritson E. B. Influence of an increase in excise duty on alcohol consumption and its adverse effects. *BMJ (Clin Res Ed)* 1983; 287: 809–11.
10. Ritson E. B. *Community and Municipal Action on Alcohol.* WHO Euro series 63. 1995. Geneva: WHO.

24

Conversation with Michael A. H. Russell

Michael Russell came to Britain from South Africa. Over a professional life-time he has made varied and fundamental contributions to the study of nicotine dependence and has also done much to support and train a generation of younger researchers.

South African Origins

Addiction (A): I think you grew up in South Africa before you came to England?

Michael A. H. Russell: Yes, I was born in South Africa in 1932. My mother was English, and we used to come over to England almost every year. That stopped in the war, of course. I did all my schooling in Cape Town. I then managed to secure a place at Oxford to study law, but in my last term at school I did constitutional history, which I found so boring that I switched to medicine. I started at Oxford in 1952, then my clinical training at Guy's Hospital.

A: While you were at Oxford you were a bit of a sportsman, I think?

MAHR: Not a great one. I gave work the priority; but I was quite a good swimmer and got a half-Blue. I was also fairly good at rugby. I got as far as the Greyhounds (the second team). It was at Guy's that my rugby was really useful to me. I played for the first team for 3 years, and for United Hospitals—I am sure that is why I got good house jobs.

A: When you qualified at Guy's did you already at that time have a clear sense of where you wanted to go in medicine?

MAHR: No, in fact I went back to South Africa. I thought I might be a general practitioner (GP). So I went back there and did some junior doctor positions. This was in Groote Schuur, the University of Cape Town teaching hospital. The second one was in neuropsychiatry with Henry Walton. He was an inspiring teacher and he made me interested in psychiatry. It was in that time with him, only a 6-month appointment, that I found learning to understand people's thoughts, feelings and behaviour much more interesting than dealing with abortions or caesarean sections. I decided to do psychiatry. In those days psychiatry was a bit of a Cinderella subject—psychiatrists were not considered as important as physicians or surgeons—they were rather looked down upon. So what was necessary if you wanted a good position in psychiatry was to train as a physician first and obtain your MRCP (Member of the Royal College of Physicians). To obtain the MRCP in those days you needed a great deal of clinical experience. I did registrar positions at Groote Schuur Hospital for a couple of years.

A: By that time you had met your wife?

MAHR: Yes, Audrey was a nurse at Groote Schuur Hospital. We both decided we were not going to stay in South Africa. The political situation was unpleasant. In January 1964, we left South Africa to come to the United Kingdom. Three months later I managed to pass the MRCP. Then we decided to take a year off to travel, which was a wonderful experience. I secured a place to start training at the Maudsley in October 1965.

Arriving at the Maudsley

A: In 1965 Sir Aubrey Lewis was still at the Maudsley as Professor of Psychiatry.

MAHR: Yes, we had to come in on Saturday mornings then, when Sir Aubrey held a big seminar. Occasionally you had to present the topic and got challenging questions. You were not allowed to refer to notes, and there were no slides. Some people were terrified by that. The Maudsley training was very tough and competitive. I was lucky to be on Sir Aubrey's professorial Unit for my first 6 months, with Bob Kendell as my senior registrar (SR), and Mike Gelder, who recently retired from the Chair in Psychiatry at Oxford, was my consultant.

A: What was it that attracted you to smoking?

MAHR: I was aware, of course, that it was a major health hazard which we had failed to control effectively for many years. This was also the age of learning theory and behaviour therapy. I was so impressed with the effects of electric aversion on transvestism that I thought it might work on smoking. So I decided to do a pilot study[1] of its effects on smoking as the basis of my DPM (Diploma in Psychological Medicine) dissertation.

A: Were you yourself a smoker at that time?

MAHR: Yes, usually no more than 10 a day.

First Footsteps in Smoking Research

A: So that was your very first involvement with smoking as a subject for research?

MAHR: Yes. Both Griffith Edwards and Isaac Marks were enormously helpful as supervisors. Griffith also provided space for me in the Addiction Research Unit (ARU) and acted as Consultant in charge of the cases. I also had to learn about the typical problems of giving up smoking. For this I sat in at many sessions of the Smoking Advisory Clinic in Islington. My DPM dissertation would have been completed by July 1968 when I became a senior registrar, and I would have been reading avidly on smoking all this time. Griffith advised and helped me obtain a 3-year Medical Research Council (MRC) project grant to conduct a controlled trial of electric aversion therapy for smoking. The results were disappointing. It was in July 1969 that I completed my year as a senior registrar and joined the ARU as a research worker. The best advice Griff ever gave me was that to do good research you had to do it full-time, which I did, thinking it would be for only 3–4 years and look good on the CV for getting a consultant post at a teaching hospital. I wrote a review on 'Cigarette Smoking: The Natural History of a Dependence Disorder'.[2]

Unequivocal Identification of the Smoking Habit as Nicotine Dependence

A: Looking back, that was a truly seminal paper, because that was really a very clear and unequivocal statement that smoking was basically all about giving yourself nicotine. It was certainly a somewhat heterodox view at that time. Would you agree?

MAHR: Yes, it was certainly more forthright than the 1964 report of the US Surgeon General. But for me it was all there in print in 1967, in a volume of the *Annals of the New York Academy of Sciences.* There was a paper by Schmiterlow et al. using autoradiography following radioactively labelled nicotine given intravenously to mice. It shows the brain full of nicotine after 5 minutes; after 30 minutes it has all left the brain.[3] Thirty minutes after a cigarette is about the time a smoker begins to feel like another. Indeed, it was in 1967 that Lucchesi et al. showed that intravenous nicotine significantly reduced cigarette consumption compared with the saline control.[4]

A: You were satisfied in your own mind that the evidence pointed clearly to nicotine. So what did you feel was the next step?

MAHR: The priority was to find a measure of smoke intake. Initially we used carboxyhaemoglobin (COHb) as a measure of smoke intake, and of course for validating abstinence. I linked up with Peter Cole. He had a laboratory at St Bartholomew's Hospital which measured COHb. Indeed, our first joint study published in March 1973 was a demonstration of passive smoking using and exposing ARU staff during a weekly meeting at which one or two staff had reports to present.[5] Another thing we collaborated on with Peter Cole was CO yields of cigarettes. We did start looking at some titration studies quite early on in 1975, using CO as an intake marker and giving people cigarettes with high (3.2 mg) and ultra-low nicotine (< 0.3 mg) yields, and showing that they tended to smoke harder to compensate for the ultra-low-yield cigarette and substantially reduced CO intake from the high nicotine cigarette.

A: You set about developing a blood nicotine assay.

MAHR: It was Isaac and Rand's paper in *Nature* in 1972 showing exquisite measurement of blood nicotine that inspired me. Then we recruited Colin Feyerabend and persuaded the DHSS that measures of blood nicotine were necessary to validate abstinence. Colin published his first paper describing his method in 1975.

Building a Research Team

A: So you had the beginnings then of getting a research team.

MAHR: Yes. Julian Peto was one of Griffith's very superior statisticians and he helped me enormously with an analysis of the effect of price changes on cigarette consumption by men in Britain from 1946 to 1971.[6] For every 1% increase in corrected price, consumption fell by about 0.6%. Peto also helped me to develop a motivational typology of smokers.

Nicotine Replacement Takes Off

A: You were firing on all cylinders! Can I ask you about nicotine replacement, because that has been one of the major themes of your career? When did you first come across Ove Ferno?

MAHR: I came across him first at the Second World Conference on Smoking and Health, which was held at Imperial College London, in 1971. I can remember from the floor saying rather humbly that we ought to consider whether it would not be safer to focus on getting the tar down rather than nicotine down.

A: Did Ove have prototypes of the gum with him?

MAHR: Yes. I was not very impressed. It was 4 years later, during the Third World Conference in New York in June 1975, I recall going on a couple of long evening walks with Ove in the Central Park area, talking non-stop together. I was very impressed with Ove, his charm and modesty, and developed a deep respect for him. Following this meeting he invited me to visit Sweden, where I met some of his colleagues in Helsingborg and visited Westling's clinic in Lund. This certainly aroused our interest in the gum and we started to study it almost as soon as I got back.[7]

Clinical Trials with Nicotine Gum

A: So your involvement started quite early on before they decided to go for it as a commercial product?

MAHR: Oh yes. The company president and the scientific advisory committee had resisted supporting the gum for some 4–5 years, despite Ove's position as Vice President and Director of Research and Development for pharmaceutical research and for the medical department. In comparison with the 14% success rate at 1-year follow-up after psychological treatments, we found that a 1-year success rate of 38% was obtained by use of 2 mg gum. We went on to conduct a full-scale randomized double-blind trial. The trial was supervised by Martin Jarvis.

The Royal College Reports

A: Can I just go back a bit, because there is one thing I wanted to ask you about the period around 1970–71. That is, I believe you were involved in the preparation of the 1971 Report to the Royal College of Physicians, which was their second report on smoking. Was it Charles Fletcher who approached you?

MAHR: Yes, Charles Fletcher was always very nice and supportive of me, partly because there were relatively few people focusing on the kind of work with smoking that we were doing at the ARU. The smoking problem had become his major interest and he served as Secretary and was the moving force within the Committee responsible for the first RCP report, Smoking and Health, published in 1962, which had a major impact internationally. He was also secretary of the Committee for the second RCP report (1971), and the third report (1977). For the third report I was a member of the Committee.

Winning MRC Programme Grant Support

A: Lots of work, but what were you doing about funding?

MAHR: In early May 1978 one of the Medical Research Council's administrative staff phoned me and gave me about the biggest surprise I have ever had. She invited me to apply for an MRC Programme Grant. My last question was to ask why they were being so kind to me, to which she replied that someone important and powerful had recommended it. My first thought was that it might have been Charles Fletcher. Then I thought it might have been Griffith, who was incredibly helpful to me with putting the application together and transferring some of the staff funded on his grant to my proposed grant. Anyway, the proposal was approved by the Neuroscience Board of the MRC in June 1978.

A: The MRC then supported your work for 20 years.

MAHR: Yes indeed. Above all, it enabled us to recruit Martin Jarvis, who was awarded tenure when we obtained additional support from the Imperial Cancer Research Fund in early 1988.

The Impact of GP Advice

A: There have been so many areas where you have mapped out the territory in smoking, but probably your most cited paper was on simple advice from a GP to patients coming to see them in the course of their routine clinical load. Where did the idea for that study come from?

MAHR: I do not know how the idea came, but it was just apparent that there were many smokers to treat and also many smokers did not especially want treatment—they were not motivated seriously enough. Over a 3- or 4-year period it would be practically 90% of smokers would visit their GP. There had been some data from America that people listened to doctors more than other people, so it did seem that if it had even a small effect it would be very worthwhile. After the success of the trial of GP advice we tried to expand it to getting the gum used within general practice, so we looked at advice alone and compared it with advice plus nicotine gum. The gum given as well as the advice not only made more people try to give up, but it increased the success rate of those who did try. Then we became even more ambitious, because we wanted to see if we could change the prevalence in the practice populations by GPs doing different things.

A: Did it work?

MAHR: It did work, yes.[8,9]

Relationships with the Tobacco Industry

A: You must have come into contact with the industry in many different forms in the 1970s.

MAHR: Well, I valued relationships with them because they knew so much about tobacco, and quite a few conferences that one went to in America had tobacco industry people there as well. I formed quite a strong relationship with BAT (British American Tobacco), and they gave us help with some funding for enlarging the old prefab at 101 Denmark Hill, which the MRC knew about. It was not only me that mixed with them, it was OK to do it then. They had a place in Sussex, a lovely old house, and held conferences there.

A: Do you think they were more open in sharing their research data at that time?

MAHR: Yes. Certainly the proceedings from those meetings were published. As far as America goes, I did not have close dealings with them, but I certainly visited Philip Morris.

A: What would you say about government and its approach to smoking in the 1970s and 1980s?

MAHR: I was never very good on the policy side, somehow. It did not interest me so much, although it should have because that is really where you achieve things. No, I think I was more just an experimentalist and I did not really feel the need to push some of the theories I felt were right. I would just like to demonstrate the theory and then if people wanted to accept it or not that was hard cheese. Perhaps one reason I was not especially popular with government people was that I used to be fairly outspoken. We were not unduly aggressive. Ultimately I think we did function as a group. We all knew what each other was doing and thinking and all had a hand or say in things, and I think that makes a big difference. It was just great having such clever people around. I think our regular Friday meetings were important.

A: What happened at those Friday meetings?

MAHR: It was informal. It got everyone together, it was the end of the week; no one could actually submit a paper without letting all of us read it and give out comments. We were not dictators; it was group pressure rather than me having control of the funds and exerting the pressure. Tender people might have felt it that way.

Notes

1. Russell, M. A. (1970) Effect of electric aversion on cigarette smoking. *British Medical Journal,* 10, 182–186.
2. Russell, M. A. (1971) Cigarette smoking: natural history of a dependence disorder. *British Journal of Medical Psychology,* 44, 1–16.
3. Schmiterlow, C., Hansson, E., Andersson, G., Applegren, L. & Hoffman, P. (1967) Distribution of nicotine in the central nervous system. *Annals of the New York Academy of Science,* 142, 2–14.
4. Lucchesi, B., Schuster, C. & Emley, G. (1967) The role of nicotine as a determinant of cigarette smoking frequency in man with observations of certian cardiovascular effects associated with the tobacco alkaloid. *Clinical Pharmacology and Therapeutics,* 8, 789–796.
5. Russell, M. A., Cole, P. V. & Brown, E. (1973) Absorption by non-smokers of carbon monoxide from room air polluted by tobacco smoke. *Lancet,* 17, 576–579.
6. Russell, M. A. (1973) Changes in cigarette price and consumption by men in Britain, 1946–71: a preliminary analysis. *British Journal of Preventive and Social Medicine,* 27, 1–7.
7. Russell, M. A., Feyerabend, C. & Cole, P. V. (1976) Plasma nicotine levels after cigarette smoking and chewing nicotine gum. *British Medical Journal,* 1, 1043–1046.
8. Russell, M. A. H., Stapleton, J. A., Jackson, P. H., Hajek, P. & Belcher, M. (1987) District programme to reduce smoking: effect of clinic supported brief intervention by general practitioners. *British Medical Journal,* 295, 1240–1244.
9. Russell, M. A. H., Stapleton, J. A., Hajek, P., Jackson, P. H. & Belcher, M. (1988) District programme to reduce smoking: can sustained intervention by general practitioners affect prevalence? *Journal of Epidemiology and Community Health,* 42, 111–115.

25

Conversation with Hiroshi Suwaki

Hiroshi Suwaki is a Japanese psychiatrist who has made a contribution to alcohol research which has won him international respect. He has done much to build bridges of understanding and friendship between his country and the scientific communities of other countries.

Introduction

Addiction (A): Hiroshi, you are a distinguished Japanese psychiatrist, but the first thing a westerner will notice on meeting you is that you write and speak extraordinarily good English. How did you attain these skills?

Hiroshi Suwaki (HS): Thank you for your compliment. I was born in 1940 in a beautiful town, Kojima, located in the midst of the Seto Inland Sea National Park in the west of Japan. As you know, in August 1945 Japan laid down arms totally from the battle of World War II. A vivid memory around the year of 1945 is that there were many Koreans living together with us along the same street. They were tough people, amid the poverty after World War II, and we Japanese children learned from them how to obtain a little but precious money by rag-collecting or by raising pigs with hogwash. I still remember their names: Chonsu, Mansu and Heigan. In 1946, when I entered primary school, the era was undergoing a drastic transitional period of national ideology throughout Japan, from loyalty for the emperor to democracy. The characteristic portrait of General Douglas MacArthur, the Supreme Commander at that time, with his pipe and sunglasses, is still vividly preserved in my mind. After the War, we often had a chance to meet and talk to westerners, mainly Americans. At the same time, NHK (Japan Broadcasting Corporation) began to send us English conversation programmes on radio. At that stage in Japan, English became a compulsory subject in junior high school (age 12–14, compulsory education). In senior high school (age 15–17, non-compulsory education), English became as important a subject as Japanese and mathematics. In Kojima Senior High School, I joined an English conversation club and sometimes enjoyed talking with overseas American students. Luckily, I won the prize at the English speech contest in Okayama

Prefecture at the age of 16. At university age, I did not particularly practice to improve my English. On the university campus we sometimes saw westerners, but they were relatively few, compared to the present day.

A: So you came to the United Kingdom already with a good grounding in the English language.

HS: My English at that time was very much limited in its vocabulary and not satisfactory in daily conversation. During my first visit to London in 1978, Griffith Edwards kindly introduced me to alcoholism treatment units, therapeutic hostels, detoxification centres and so on, in Britain. There, I met Professor Neil Kessel, Dr Brian Hore, W. H. Kenyon and many other prominent people, and I was enlightened from the conversations with them. I think I was also able to develop my English through interviews with these people.

A: Do you read poetry or novels in the English language or just stay with the science?

HS: I do not read many novels in English, but for some short stories and essays written by Ernest Hemingway, Somerset Maugham, and so on.

Personal Background and Early Training

A: What sort of family background did you have?

HS: As I have just mentioned, I was born in Kojima (presently, within Kurashiki City). Both my father and mother were primary school teachers, and I had one brother and two sisters. My mother did not have enough time to take care of four children, so we were all brought up by our grandmother. She had a great talent for fashion designing and was a modern lady of progressive character. My grandfather was also a schoolmaster, but died at a relatively young age. My grandmother could reproduce a design from only one glance at a costume, and she was a real pioneer of the sailor-style dress, which became the widespread standard formal dress for schoolboys and girls in Japan. Later, as Kojima developed, this costume was produced there and Kojima is now noted all over Japan as the place for school uniform. She also instructed us grandchildren in the game of 'Go' and 'Shougi' (Japanese-style chess). My younger brother graduated from Tokyo University, and later he became professor of American literature at Musashi University, but sadly died at a relatively young age.

A: What made you choose medicine as a career, and then psychiatry?

HS: I think I had already determined to be a physician before high school age. Tekken Ishii, my grandmother's elder brother, was a warm-hearted outpatient clinician in a small town within 1 hour by bus from my house. chose to be a practitioner at his native place in Okayama Prefecture. He treated poor people without money or for small gifts, according to their means. In my childhood, grandmother often took me to his house whenever she visited. I think I decided to be a physician at that time. Until the internship I had a dream of being a surgeon. At my internship I met Dr Kiyoshi Matsuoka, a multi-talented surgeon, which resulted in the turning-point of my career from dreams of being a surgeon to subsequently becoming a psychiatrist. He had superb surgical skills with a broad range. I worked with him for 1 month and in this short time I was completely overwhelmed by his accurate and dextrous finger movement in his operations. After the operation, it was our common custom to bathe together in a large bathtub in the Japanese style and to enjoy relaxation and conversation. He seemed completely satisfied and happy with his surgical vocation. At that time, I realized I could never be a surgeon with such gifts as Dr Matsuoka had.

A: So how did you get to psychiatry?

HS: At the same time in Kochi, I worked once a week in Geshi Hospital and had accommodation and meals there. I met Dr Takamaro Geshi, a unique and prominent psychiatrist interested in alcoholism treatment, and Mr Harushige Matsumura, who is the first chairman of the All Japan Alcohol Abstinence Society. This fateful encounter with Dr Geshi and Mr Matsumura led me to devote myself thereafter to alcohol-related problems. A year later, I visited Professor Nikichi Okumura: he was the director of the Department of Neuropsychiatry, Okayama University Medical School. I then received my standard psychiatric and neurological training there. After I had received basic, standard training in the Department of Neuropsychiatry, Okayama University Medical School, I went to Kochi and again worked in Geshi Hospital for 1 year as a psychiatrist. Then I moved back to Okayama, and had a job at Jikei Hospital, a well-known psychiatric teaching hospital in Japan. There, I established a systematic multi-disciplinary treatment approach to Japanese alcoholics.

A: Generally, did psychiatry have high or low prestige when you first entered it?

HS: Fortunately, the era in which I entered psychiatry was a new epoch shifting from an old prestige into a new field of speciality comparable with plastic surgery, anaesthesiology or neurosurgery. Psychiatry or neuropsychiatry was newly regenerated as an attractive clinical field, covering a broad range of human life including biological, psychosocial and spiritual areas, for our entire generation.

Early Publications

A: So, as early as 1975 you published a sophisticated follow-up study of alcoholic patients.[1]

HS: I felt that long-term follow-up studies of alcoholics tell us the real stories of their lives, in which their life-styles and medical problems coalesce. Thus, 105 male alcoholics whom I had treated as physician-in-charge at Jikei Hospital were followed for an average of 27 months after leaving the hospital. The factors which proved significant to favourable outcomes were: age above

40 years, married state, Naikan therapy and continuation of after-care by group meetings and/or Danshukai (Abstinence Society).

A: Then in 1979 came a paper on affective disorders in alcoholism.[2]

HS: I reported on affective disorders among 121 Japanese male alcoholics treated by myself at Jikei Hospital. The incidence and clinical characteristics were comparable to those of the United States and Europe. This study was conducted just before DSM-III adopted operational diagnostic criteria. Nowadays I think the scientific validity of this paper was quite low.

Visit to the Addiction Research Unit (ARU)

A: In 1978–1979 you were a visiting fellow at the ARU, at the Institute of Psychiatry, London, and I know that you made a very favourable impression on the people who had the privilege of being your academic hosts. What led you to decide, at that time, to come to London?

HS: On 21–26 August 1977, the ICAA International Symposium on Alcohol and Drug Dependence was held in Tokyo and Kyoto. There, I noticed Professor Griffith Edwards for the first time; he delivered a very impressive invited lecture: 'Diagnosis, treatment and rehabilitation of alcoholics'. On this occasion, I myself presented two papers: 'Naikan therapy to alcoholic patients' and 'Danshukai (Abstinence Society) activities in Okayama Prefecture'. In 1978, I could obtain a grant from the Japanese Society for Research Promotion to visit overseas institutions, and I wrote a letter immediately to Griffith.

A: What was the content for you of the ARU experience personally and professionally?

HS: I came to Great Britain in October 1978, and stayed for 6 months. At the ARU, Griffith visited Bethlehem Royal Hospital Alcoholism Treatment Unit every week. I joined the small meetings to observe how he spoke to patients. I also met with the research staff.

A: What were your leisure experiences during that early visit to London?

HS: I enjoyed leisure time in London with my family—my wife, Sachiko and two sons, Mitsuru, aged 7 years and Makoto, aged 5 years. I bought a used car, and we enjoyed driving tours to the outskirts of London. We rented a flat in Wimbledon, a safe, quiet and convenient place. You had a much more mature, accommodating culture, living together in a multi-racial society. I had a strong impression that people in England behave more politely regarding their needs and feelings.

Kochi Medical School

A: When you returned to Japan, you were appointed Associate Professor at the Kochi Medical School Department of Neuropsychiatry. What is the role of neuropsychiatry in your country?

HS: In the late 18th century, many of the Japanese pioneers who introduced modern medicine into Japan went to Germany. They brought back to Japan biologically orientated psychiatry. Nowadays, however, dynamic psychiatry is also accepted widely in my country.

A: You held that position at Kochi from 1979 to 1986, and your published output developed further. You published, for instance, a review in the *British Journal of Addiction* in which you introduced western readers to Naikan and Danshukai.[3]

HS: Naikan is translated into 'self-observation method', which aims at the spiritual growth of oneself, regardless of any religious sect. Originally, Mishirabe (self-observation) was practised rigorously in Jhodoshinshuu Buddhism under conditions of fasting and sleep deprivation. Iinobu Yoshimoto modified this method into a practice in which ordinary people are able to take part, including good meals and good sleep. He named this method Naikan. This culturally congruent treatment is easily accepted and helpful to indigenous people. Danshukai is translated into 'Alcohol Abstinence Society'. We might be enlightened in a peer group by sharing the common goal of abstinence.

A: In 1981 you published a survey of in-patient alcoholics in two prefectures. One of your more striking findings was that nearly half these patients had been in hospital for a year or more.

HS: This survey was conducted in 1977–1979, when specialized alcoholic treatment units or hospitals still did not prevail across the country. Most of the alcoholics were admitted into traditional large psychiatric hospitals, and the duration of admission tended to be longer in that period.

A: In 1980 you attended an important World Health Organization (WHO) working group in Washington, which attempted to explore the applicability of the dependence syndrome concept to drugs other than alcohol.

HS: That was my first visit to the United States and I met many other prominent scientists. That was a great experience. Griffith chaired the meeting, and he arranged the report on alcohol- and drug-related problems.[4]

A: Then in 1985 came an important paper on alcohol-induced facial flushing in Japanese men.[5] What were your conclusions?

HS: Drinking behaviours and alcohol-induced facial flushing of 1646 Japanese men were analysed from their questionnaires. The results clearly indicated their low rate of alcohol-related problems.

A: Then a job move. From 1986 to 1991 you were Professor of Medical Psychology of Kagawa University Medical School. What were your strategies for maintaining international contacts and awareness?

HS: After visiting ARU in 1978, I joined the 1979 Rutgers Summer School of Alcohol Studies, recommended by Griffith, for 3 weeks. I do not think I had such a conscious strategy. I just wanted to grasp and understand the overall picture of this gigantic dependence problem, through meeting internationally prominent scientists.

Professor in the Department of Psychiatry and Neurology, Kagawa

A: From 1991 to 2005 you held a chair in the Department of Psychiatry and Neurology. How did your responsibilities change at this juncture?

HS: I was appointed to Chief Director of the Department of Psychiatry and Neurology. This department covers a broad range of clinical scientific and educational activities.

Current Responsibilities

A: So in 2005 you took up the job of Director of the Addiction Research Unit at the Sankoh Hospital. That sounds like a very appropriate appointment?

HS: Yes. Just before my retirement, I chose to come to Sankoh Hospital and continue my life work on addiction.

Looking Back, Looking Forward

A: Looking back, how has the place of alcohol changed in Japanese society over your life-time?

HS: Memories of my early life are fragmented and episodic, and memories concerning alcohol are very scanty. I was brought up in a family where no one had the custom of regular drinking. Later, my father took a small amount of sake (Japanese rice wine) as an evening drink. My father was a flusher, and my mother a non-flusher. She never drinks except on special occasions. I recall a memory that neighbours gathered and enjoyed sake at the Shintou-shrine festival in the rice crop season of autumn. In Japan, consumption continued to increase gradually until 1998 and then reached a plateau, spreading among young and female populations. Now, broad generations of young and old, male and female enjoy alcoholic beverages, especially beer, in my country.

A: What, over those years, has happened to the drug problem?

HS: The most distinctive feature of substance abuse in Japan is overwhelmingly, long-lasting abuse of methamphetamine and organic solvents. In the early half of the 1950s a large epidemic of methamphetamine abuse prevailed all over Japan, as the methamphetamine used and stocked in the military camps appeared in the public market. In view of such a catastrophic situation, from 1951 to 1956 the Stimulants Control Law has been administered rigorously. As a result, from 1957 to 1970 abuses of these substances seemed to have been extinguished (later, we called this period a 'lucid interval'). However, from 1970 to the present, 'Bouryokudan' (organized criminal groups) have smuggled these substances from Korea, Taiwan and other south-eastern countries, and a similar situation still continues.[6]

A: And solvents?

HS: As for solvent abuse, the origin is considered to be a subculture of indulging in marijuana or LSD in western countries. In the case of young

Japanese vagrants, they sniffed organic solvents. Solvents are cheap and easy to access for youngsters.[7]

A: In relation to both alcohol and drugs, do you see intentional and effective national policies as having evolved, or . . . ?

HS: I believe we should try our best with various measures to tackle these monstrous problems at all. At this point, I find myself to be somewhat pessimistic for our future. With regard to our normal daily lives, I think we should enjoy and develop healthy pleasurable activities of our own.

A: What should the rest of the world be learning here from the Japanese experience?

HS: For the past half-century, Japan has been influenced largely by western culture, including democracy and an individually orientated life-style. Today, I feel that Japan has been internationalized and westernized, perhaps like other Asian countries. In recent years many Japanese people have come to enjoy playing golf, baseball, tennis or playing Go, Shougi and so on. We do enjoy both work and hobbies somewhat enthusiastically, with great pleasure and satisfaction.

And Finally

A: Japanese colleagues sometimes seem by western standards to work almost punishingly hard. What hours do you expect to work most days? And how often are you able to take a holiday?

HS: As I touched on before, after World War II working conditions were also internationalized and improved. Average daily working hours are 8 hours, except for some businessmen or workers in private professions. Usually, we are able to take a holiday twice a week, mainly Saturday and Sunday.

A: Outside work what are your interests and relaxations?

HS: As my recent favourite outside sport, I enjoy playing golf with my elder son, Mitsuru (he is a psychiatrist) and with other close friends when we are able to meet together. My handicap now is 14. Mitsuru is my private golf instructor. And I enjoy my private life with my wife, Sachiko and my mother, Tomiko at Villa Dan-no-Ura, Kagawa Prefecture. Our two sons have now left Kagawa and lead their own lives.

Notes

1. Suwaki H. A follow-up study of alcoholics in Japan. *Psychiatr Neurol* 1975; 77: 89–106 (in Japanese).
2. Suwaki H. Alcoholism and affective disorder. *Int J Rehab Res* 1979; 2: 531–2.
3. Suwaki H. Naikan and Danshukai for the treatment of Japanese alcoholic patients. *Br J Addict* 1979; 74: 15–19.
4. Edwards G., Arif A., Hodgson R. Nomenclature and classification of drug and alcohol-related problems. *Bull WHO* 1981; 59: 225–42.
5. Suwaki H., Ohara H. Alcohol-induced facial flushing and drinking behaviour in Japanese men. *J Stud Alcohol* 1985; 46: 196–8.

6. Suwaki H. Methamphetamine abuse in Japan. In: Miller M. A., Kozel N. J. *Methamphetamine Abuse: Epidemiologic Issues and Implications.* NIDA Research Monograph, Number 115. Rockville, MD: NIDA (National Institute on Drug Abuse); 1991, p. 84–98.
7. Suwaki H., Nishii Y., Yoshida T., Ohara H. Backgrounds and prognosis of the adolescents with glue-sniffing. *Jpn J Alcohol Drug Depend* 1982; 17: 74–86.

26

Conversation with Ambros Uchtenhagen

Ambros Uchtenhagen, whose background before he qualified in medicine lies in philosophy and sociology, is a Swiss psychiatrist who from his base in Zurich has contributed to research, and to European thinking on drug policies. His research on heroin as a drug for treatment of opium dependence has shown a difficult research question can be rationally addressed.

Addiction (A): Starting your academic life you had a minimum of three major fields of interest, philosophy, painting and medicine; what was the background?

Ambros Uchtenhagen (AU): Well, I am not sure now myself, and at times it looked rather not much thought through, I always wanted to become a doctor and this had some relation to being often sick as a boy. I met many doctors, and they became a kind of important imaginative model for my future. So it was also agreed in my family that I would be a doctor. But then, in college, I realized that it was hard for me to cope with natural sciences, and my interests were completely different. I was not a very good student, but I had some reputation for writing philosophical essays, which made my teachers speechless, and then I took to painting; together with friends we studied technique of 16th- and 17th-century painting. I was painting all night, and during daytime it was difficult to follow college.

A: Then at university?

AU: Then, when I entered university, I surprised my parents by saying: 'I'm not going to be a doctor, I want to be an artist, and I want to study science of fine arts', which I did, including archaeology, because for me it also opened the door to travelling. After the Second World War frontiers were suddenly open, and we were hungry to see and learn and to reach beyond the restricted area we had been living in. So I went as a guide to archaeological sites in countries I had been dreaming of. But then I had a decisive encounter with a personality, which inspired me with a love for philosophy again. This was Ernesto Grassi, professor from Florence, guest professor in Zurich, a great humanist, and later on the editor of Rowohldt's Deutsche Enzyklopädie. At the same time we had a lecturer in sociology, René König, one of the first outstanding empirical sociologists here who also became one of the important personalities of my past. Philosophy and sociology were the main topics now, and I wrote a thesis on theories of power from Plato to Machiavelli.But at the same time, I got a feeling of living in an ivory tower, and the perspective of an academic career became really ambiguous. Of course, this had something to do with the person I was at the time. A hunger for 'real' life and human contacts was the main reason why I went finally to medical school in order to become a psychiatrist.I am quite happy with the decisions I have taken, especially when thinking that my professional career left room enough for continued active engagement in philosophy and in visual art.

A: Finishing medical school, did you plan something for your professional life?

AU: As already mentioned, I was determined to specialize in psychiatry. Even before going to Medical School, I engaged in reviewing brain research and psychotherapy for newspapers. Regarding research, I had a chance to conduct and publish some work with Manfred Bleuler on schizophrenia. We had a great deal of freedom to study whatever was of interest, we were not squeezed too much into predefined career models. If we missed some classes, it did not really matter, and we missed a lot. It was much easier to have this kind of combination of studies, in parallel even, than it would be nowadays.

A: You had your training in psychiatry in Zurich at a very exciting time in the Burghölzli hospital.

AU: The Burghölzli hospital was at that time a world-famous place for the advancement of psychiatry. But Bleuler himself was, apart from being an excellent clinician, also an extremely critical and sharp-minded teacher, so this was a very good place for learning, although for research purposes I could have imagined different places more advanced and less focused on traditional issues. Bleuler's research focused mainly on the long-term course and clinical characteristics of patients. This is also one of the reasons why my first substantial work (only partly published) was on the course and prognosis of addictive disorders.[1]

A: Do you remember special groups of patients that were of interest for you?

AU: Well, in the beginning it was schizophrenia. Schizophrenia was—and still is—such a fascinating condition. However, during the years I worked with Bleuler, I discovered that there was a completely disregarded other group of patients: alcoholics and people with other forms of substance dependence. Nobody really cared about them; so this became a main issue, as I always tried to focus on things which were neglected. Later on, in the last phase of my psychiatric activities, it was the same with psychogeriatrics, and I had the opportunity to set up a centre for in-patient, day-patient and out-patient care of psychogeriatric patients. Psychiatrists neglected alcoholism treatment and research. It was something to be dealt with by other people, mainly by non-professional organizations, by Blue Cross and Alcoholics Anonymous.

A: You then also started psychoanalytical training parallel to your clinical training.

AU: I made my analysis for very personal reasons, also for learning about psychoanalysis. But I think I also needed it. Trusting the judgement of my colleagues, they said that thanks to my personal psychoanalysis I became a kind of tolerable person. At the same time I wrote a book on Freud and psychoanalysis together with my analyst. It is still a readable book.[2]

A: The contribution of psychoanalysis to psychiatry.

AU: It has contributed much to complement, in a way, the statistical and biologically orientated trends in psychiatry. As a tool for therapy, however, I think it is debatable and it has its restrictions.

A: The first book I ever held in my hand edited by Ambros Uchtenhagen was a very thick one on group therapy and on an international meeting on group therapy.[3] What was your interest in this special approach?

AU: The efforts and resources needed for a few individual psychotherapies bore no relation to the need for help of a great number of patients. This is one of the main reasons why group psychotherapy had an appeal for me.

A: Ambros, after your medical education, you then started your clinical work in Zurich and continued in Zurich. What was the reason that you did not leave your home town for outside experience?

AU: Why did I stay in Zurich? I can think of a number of reasons. Bleuler definitely offered me very early opportunities for a career, and this of course was a temptation. Secondly, I had married at that time. Lilian had possibilities of her own to make a political career, which would have come to nothing if I had moved away. Also, I had to earn a living. It was not so easy at that time to find a paid post in another country. All this has contributed to staying here. As a kind of compensation I took to travelling in order to meet other people, to learn about their approaches, and then to bring the information home and see what use it was for my own work. Also, I was always a passionate reader.

A: Then?

AU: For 7 years I was chef de clinique with Bleuler. I started what I termed social psychiatry, with intermediate structures such as day- and night-hospitals, rehabilitation workshops, visiting patients at home and so on. I had the impression that under the very strict rule in our hospital, patients were controlled too much. I introduced a night-hospital, allowing patients to go out during the day to work or to school. It became a burden for Bleuler, because he had a great need to control everything. I was responsible for a service called 'family care'. Psychotic patients were given mainly to the care of foster families and visited regularly by myself and a small team of social workers. You can learn a great deal from your patients. A thing I learned with psychotic patients is to respect their refusal of therapeutic approaches. Making their own choices was not always helpful, but the start of a learning process which in the end was helpful. Learning from failure, learning from making the wrong choices is the same with addicts.

A: What is your view on this structure of psychiatry nowadays?

AU: When I started work in psychiatry, introducing psychotherapy into psychiatry was a big issue. The therapeutic milieu became a big issue. It helped many patients, but it has not fulfilled another hope of social psychiatry, namely to prevent psychiatric illness. So a certain dissatisfaction with the results of social psychiatry had contributed to the upsurge of a more biologically orientated one. Neither biological psychiatry, nor social psychiatry, nor psychological approaches alone will work in research or in practice. We need to learn how to combine these approaches. Perhaps we even need a type of new transdisciplinary specialist who is prepared to tackle this.

A: Was there something you can identify as being important in a very special way to your way of thinking?

AU: The World Health Organization. It gave me the opportunity to meet and work with many colleagues from many countries. This may have shaped my thinking more than any book or theory.

A: Ambros, you have had a very successful career, and you had a big impact on Swiss development in social psychiatry. Retiring, you started on a second, third or fourth career founding a research institute. Why did you decide to found the Zurich Institute of Addiction Research?

AU: During all my professional life until my retirement, I had a heavy burden with developing services, testing new therapeutic approaches, caring for staff and patients, being involved in committee work, becoming increasingly involved in health policy in this country, always at the expense of time for research. The need to satisfy my research aspirations really added to the decision to set up the Institute.

A: What was your famous or your favourite child in addiction research?

AU: What has received more attention than anything else was the heroin prescription project.[4] A few people were absolutely against such an experiment. So new alliances arose. It was a real challenge not only for this reason, but also because earlier experience with heroin prescription, the American experience, but also the British experience, was not so favourable.

A: Other favourite projects?

AU: We started over 20 years ago with the first national project on cohorts of heroin addicts from in- and out-patient treatment programmes and from prisons, compared systematically with a representative population sample in the same age group, regarding biographical background and evolution over 2 years.[5] It was the starting-point for a nation-wide collaboration with residential drug-free treatment institutions, with a shared protocol for client documentation and follow-up. However, there are more recent projects which were at the forefront of my interest: the European Union project on 'Evaluation of action against drug abuse in Europe', which was the opportunity to build up an expert network. The European version of the Addiction Severity Index is perhaps the most visible product of this effort,[6] but also publications and guidelines on prevention evaluation and treatment evaluation came out. Another offspring of that project—again at European level—was 'Adequacy in drug abuse treatment and care in Europe ADAT'.[7]

A: What were the main reasons in Switzerland to implement this feasibility study in heroin prescription and heroin assisted treatment in the middle of the 1990s?

AU: When we prepared that project in about 1991, it was the period when we had these highly visible horrible drug scenes in our cities. There were up to 70 dealer groups in our 'Needle Park' in Zurich fighting each other. We had an enormous number of drug addicts, coming mainly from the countryside or other regions, and from other countries as well. More than 80% in the open drug scene in Zurich were not from Zurich. Although we had already developed a well-diversified and abstinence-orientated therapeutic network, there still was a considerable proportion of heroin addicts who did not engage in treatment. The high visibility of the heroin problems has caused great concern in our country and encouraged politics and politicians to do something about it and to come forward with new initiatives.

A: And the heroin project?

AU: At that time, I was a member of the Swiss expert group on drugs. We went to Merseyside where John Marks, the new 'British guru' of heroin prescription, was working. We made a thorough review of all morphine and heroin prescription projects ever known. On the basis of this review, we came to the conclusion that it was worthwhile having such an experiment. I was charged to develop a first protocol.

A: Switzerland is a conservative country. Why do you think this approach was successful and accepted?

AU: One of the main reasons may be—and this is part of the Swiss character—that we do not like to be taught by others what to do. We want to use our own experience and to draw our own conclusions. This helped greatly. A second reason is that the problem was really out of hand, and no other country had a convincing answer to that challenge.

A: Looking back on the experience now of 6 or 7 years of heroin prescription, can you conclude what should be integrated into such services to make them more attractive?

AU: We knew from the start that it should not be a programme simply prescribing heroin. It should provide a comprehensive assessment, treatment and care programme, covering all needs of the patients. The problems of dual diagnoses and of polydrug-dependent patients were not met by us adequately. This is something for us and other similar programmes to deal with in the future.

A: What is your view on the cannabis debate?

AU: The interests of large numbers of cannabis users are mainly on the risk reduction side, that they should learn how to use cannabis—if they are determined to use it—so they do not have undue health and social risks. The Dutch coffee shops, according to our colleagues there, have resulted in separating clearly the markets for cannabis and the market for so-called hard drugs. I do not know if this would be the case here. We already have well-separated markets, and in particular a separate market for cannabis.

A: What is your view on the debate on controlled drinking?

AU: I grew up in a tradition where it was 'all or nothing.' You were completely abstinent, or you were due to relapse. The issue of controlled drinking has gained momentum only in recent years. The background is that we have learned that at least as much damage is caused by risky consumption patterns of alcohol, not by alcohol dependence. This concerns a much larger target group to tackle than those fulfilling the criteria of dependence. What can be offered for that target group is different to what can be offered to dependent people. Learning how to refrain from high-risk drinking patterns to more risk-free drinking patterns. Whether it is a valuable goal for those who are dependent is a completely different issue.

A: Looking at the future, what is your overall vision on addiction treatment and your overall view on addiction research?

AU: Research and treatment depend on each other. One answer is, we need a kind of proper monitoring in the sense of analytical epidemiology, so we always have updated knowledge of what is going on in real life with people using substances. Priorities will have to be made from a public health perspective. This is not feasible without updated knowledge about where most of the burden of disease and the burden of social problems are coming from. The second answer is that we always need new knowledge about what happens inside people. We must learn about the very subjective and qualitative aspects of substance use, and how it contributes to either coping with challenges in life or making them more complicated and severe.

Notes

1. Uchtenhagen, A. (1974/1987) Prognose und Verlauf der Toxikomanien [Prognosis and long-term course of drug dependence]. Abridged version: Langzeitverläufe bei erwachsenen Toxikomanen [Long-term course of drug dependence]. In: Kleiner, D. *Langzeitverläufe bei Suchtkrankheiten [Long-term Course of Substance Dependence]*, pp. 137–150. Berlin: Springer.
2. Bally, G. (1958) Die Psychoanalyse Sigmund Freuds. Unter Mitarbeit von A. Uchtenhagen [The psychoanalysis of Sigmund Freud]. In: Gebsattel, V. E., Giese, H., Hirschmann, J., Kretschmer, E., Matussek, P., Moreno, J. J., Müller-Suur, H., Schultz, J. H., Stokvis, B. & Wiesenhütter, E. Grundzüge der

Neurosenlehre *[Outline of Neurosis Theory]*, Vol. 3, pp. 1–15. München: Urban und Schwarzenberg; and Grassi, E., ed. Rowohlt's Deutsche Enzyklopädie. Hamburg: Rowohlt.

3. Uchtenhagen, A., Battegay, R. & Friedemann, A., eds (1975) Group psychotherapy and social environment. *Proceedings of the 5th International Congress for Group Psychotherapy.* Bern/Stuttgart/Wien: Huber.
4. Uchtenhagen, A., Dobler-Mikola, A., Steffen, T., Gutzwiller, F., Blättler, R. & Pfeifer, S. (1999) *Medical Prescription of Narcotics to Heroin Addicts. Main results of the Swiss National Cohort Study.* Basel/New York: Karger.
5. Uchtenhagen, A. & Zimmer-Höfler, D. (1985) *Heroinabhängige und ihre 'normalen' Altersgenossen. Herkunft, Lebenssituation,* Zweijahresverlauf im Quervergleich *[Heroin Addicts and Their 'Normal' Contemporaries. Background, Life Situation, Evolution Over Two Years in Comparison].* Bern: Haupt.
6. Blanken, P., Hendriks, V., Pozzi, G., Tempesta, E., Hartgers, Ch, Koeter, M., Fahrner, E. M., Gsellhofer, B., Küfner, H., Kokkevi, A. & Uchtenhagen, A. (1994) *European Addiction Severity Index EuropASI. A Guide to Training and Administering Europasi Interviews.* Luxemburg: European Commission Printing Office.
7. Guggenbühl, L. & Uchtenhagen, A. (2001) *Adequacy in Drug Abuse Treatment and Care. Ethical Aspects, Treatment and Support Needs, Professional Standards, Effectiveness and Economic Evaluations. Project of WHO Regional Office for Europe, Research Report, Addiction.* Zurich: WHO Research Institute (http: www.suchtforschung.ch).

27

Commentary

Ilana Crome

Clinicians and Clinical Scientists in the Addiction Field: In Praise of Leadership

Introduction

My task has been to reflect on the factors and features that might have had a bearing on the direction of professional careers of ten researchers who have been agents of change in the addiction field. They straddle many professions and disciplines. I have attempted to draw together common themes as well as articulate differences and areas of consensus. These interviews cogently voice hitherto unheard perspectives in choices and course of careers. The motivation derived from inspirational figures, the sense of self-belief engendered by family, friends, teachers and colleagues, a social statement about concern for vulnerable and marginalized populations, conviction about the potential significance of a particular sphere of activity, and the flexible deployment of multiple skills accumulated during education, professional training, and from experience, emerged as elements of the route to leadership.

Origins – Insiders Looking Out and Outsiders Looking in

This cohort of scientist/practitioners was born between 1932 and 1942. Most were born in the UK (Martin Jarvis, Tim Cook, Bruce Ritson, Nick Heather, and Jim Orford), and several were born overseas in South Africa, Iran, India and Japan (Michael Russell, Hamid Ghodse, Shanthi Ranganathan, Hiroshi Suwaki). International experience was a precursor for an understanding of the role of international science, as well as the social, cultural, and political matrix – in addition to the position of addiction within the family, psychiatry or psychology, community and society. Travel featured prominently in terms of personal and professional development eg obtaining further education, higher degrees and experience. Especially valued was the opportunity to spend significant periods in other countries to enhance research skills. Bruce Ritson spent time in the United States, Hiroshi Suwaki describes contact with 'westerners and found the English 'polite' and an accommodating multiracial society. Sweeping changes in Japanese and South African society both politically and patterns of substance use were alluded to by Hiroshi Suwaki and Michael Russell respectively. Tim Cook reminds us that at one time in the UK 'drinking was not regarded as too terrible'.

From Generation to Generation

Many born in the UK were 'grammar school boys' (Jim Orford, Martin Jarvis, Tim Cook, Nick Heather). Education was much prized by some progressive, talented, sensitive parents or grandparents who were educationalists themselves (Hamid Ghodse) or had not had the opportunity for further education (Jim Orford). Austerity resonated throughout the childhood of some (Nick Heather, Jim Orford, Hiroshi Suwaki) but the feeling that seeking higher education was 'for better off' people was not usual. Several strands about the importance of families came to light: the specific influence of family members (Jim Orford); the role of family in determining career choice (Ambros Uchtenhagen); family reasons for decisions around career choices eg marriage, children, partners' occupation and career, political affiliations; the support afforded by spouses; addiction in the family (Nick Heather, Shanthi Ranganathan); and finally, research into the role of family in addiction which lasted a life time (Shanthi Ranganathan, Ambros Uchtenhagen, Jim Orford). Hamid Ghodse has three families: his biological family and two 'adoptive' families!

Discrimination, Deprivation and Stigma

There was a distinct sense that this group of practitioners and researchers were drawn to understanding and supporting the 'undeserving poor – the 'public (crude spirit) drinkers' (Tim Cook) and mitigating 'social injustices' (Nick Heather). This was evident not only in their reasons for becoming involved in this area, but also specifically formed part of their research. Bruce Ritson's experience of community mental health strengthened interest in social psychiatry and in the social and economic factors in mental health. Bruce Ritson described the 'dejected and rejected' addicts, while Hamid Ghodse raised the need to destigmatize addiction treatment with professional objectivity, compassion and a non-judgmental style. In some places psychiatrists were 'rather looked down upon and not perceived as important as surgeons or physicians' (Michael Russell). Hiroshi Suwaki had observed his uncle treating patients for free and Shanthi Ranganathan lamented the poverty in India so she provides free treatment for the 'lower strata'. Tim Cook described 'employment as the back bone to recovery' which chimes with Jim Orford's struggle in 'giving up conservatism'. Ambros Uchtenhagen noted that 'no-one seemed to care about addiction patients. . . . . .neglected patients'. A tolerance for imperfection seemed to be a hallmark.

Arts or Sciences – Did it Matter?

Some career trajectories were more clearly defined than others but all perceived education as the driver of deeper meaning and the voracious desire to understand. Fascination about how the mind worked, in behavioural sciences, tolerance about uncertainty and ambiguity, unanswered questions, the debate and the challenge, the need for flexibility, the variety and the never ending stimulation are common themes.

The law graduate – Tim Cook was a law graduate. He changed to warden, prison welfare officer, director of hostels for homeless drinkers, took a degree in social policy, then became director of family service units, and finally Clerk of the City Parochial Foundation to benefit the poor of London. Although Michael Russell had planned to study law, before he left school he changed his mind!

Three psychologists – Both Jim Orford and Martin Jarvis could have done either arts or sciences. Jim Orford commenced study as an engineer, but although he had not read a psychology book, it 'looked interesting' and changed. He describes 'out of the blue' things as does Martin Jarvis who read Classics at Cambridge and then did a part time degree in psychology while working in the Bank of England's Economic Intelligence Department! He talks about 'Doing stuff I enjoyed without a grand vision' eg risk taking, computing, evoked potentials and cognition. So while Jim Orford was an engineer turned clinical psychologist while Martin Jarvis was a clinical psychologist turned epidemiologist, Nick Heather was a clerk, sales representative, signals operator turned experimental psychologist, clinical and research psychologist. A psychology degree at UCL ' changed my life' and he finally decided he wanted to do 'something meaningful related to psychology and that I could contribute and write'.

Five psychiatrists – by and large those who became doctors and later chose to specialize as psychiatrists had clearer trajectories and decided early on in their careers, and even in high school. Hamid Ghodse was a biologist with interest in human behavior turned psychiatrist and epidemiologist while Ambros Uchtenhagen's 'desire for real life human contact compared to ivory towers' was the main reason to switch to medicine and psychiatry which could incorporate the arts. Unlike Michael Russell, Hiroshi Suwaki found that psychiatry had high prestige, and that it covered the spectrum of spiritual, biological and psychosocial components. Michael Russell had thought he might do research for a few years and then become a consultant psychiatrist!

The 'artist' ie creative activities and the 'slave' ie administrative, preparation of reports for government, donor agencies, are Shanthi Ranganathan's apt descriptors of the compensations and demands of professional roles!

Perhaps it did not matter what their initial career intentions had been, because these were people with ingenuity, who took different approaches to an old subject by the cross fertilization of skills and expertise.

The Power of Inspiration – 'The Fateful Encounter'

Something about which they were in absolute agreement was the attraction of charismatic mentors. The authority of these towering figures in the early clinical and research training of practitioners and researchers was a persistent theme.

Hiroshi Suwaki perhaps captures that 'fateful encounter' with Dr Geshi and Mr Matsumura made him realize that he would devote his life to alcohol related problems. From an inspirational school teacher or family physician, to Turner and Towndrow (Tim Cook), some other individuals who shaped the professional lives were Morris Carstairs (Bruce Ritson), Henry Walton (Michael Russell, Bruce Ritson), Alexander Kennedy (Bruce Ritson), Gerald Caplan (Bruce Ritson), Linford Rees and John Reed (Hamid Ghodse), Robert Kendell and Michael Gelder (Michael Russell); Bleuler, Brassi and Konig (Ambros Uchtenhagen); Neil Kessel, Brian Hore, and William Kenyon (Hiroshi Suwaki); Don Bannister and Frank McPherson (Nick Heather). Bruce Ritson mentioned only one lecture on alcoholism during his undergraduate training: in his later career he played a major role in the Medical Council on Alcoholism becoming an important meeting point for students and doctors.

Griffith Edwards' Addiction Research Unit was the envy of researchers in the UK and abroad. His generosity in hosting, supporting was underlined many times over (Hamid Ghodse, Hiroshi Suwaki, Jim Orford, Tim Cook, Michael Russell). The immense significance of colleagues in the 'The Maudsley' and the Addiction Research Unit was mentioned by many. Though tough and competitive, the role of colleagues and collaborators in terms of friendship, support, advice, inspiration, reflection and consolation, could not be overestimated.

Transition to the Research World: 'Grasping the Overall Picture of this Gigantic Dependence Problem' – 'A Grand Vision' or 'Out of the Blue'?

Hiroshi Suwaki encapsulated a stance held by many: ' I do not think that I had a conscious strategy – I just wanted to grasp the overall picture of this gigantic dependence problem through meeting internationally prominent scientists'. Martin Jarvis described the 'stuff I enjoyed – no grand vision but a 'beautiful fit' when Mike Russell offered him a post on a clinical trial on smoking cessation. Jim Orford 'had a message from Griffith Edwards whom he had never heard of' – and who became a major influence in his life – he did his PhD on wives coping with husband's alcohol problems and has continued working on this topic ever since. The famous 'Family study' on the influence of family on treatment outcome was the initiation of work which stretched over his whole career. When Hamid Ghodse received a letter from St George's suggesting that he apply for a senior lecturer post and Michael Russell was surprised at a call from the MRC inviting him to apply for a programme grant as someone 'powerful and important' recommended him, there seemed instantaneous recognition that these were pivotal points in plans for career progression. Grand vision or not, with hindsight, all were poised to seek out prospects as they materialized, and provide leadership in their particular field by the formation of their own unit, or, in a few cases, several units. What were the settings for these projects?

Clinical Backdrop for Seminal Contributions

The clinical backdrop was the foundation for fresh, feasible and functional approaches to treatment and to launch beacon research units and services. The interviews pointed to the sheer scale of the problems and the variety of patients and settings in which addiction was being treated, or not. These included hostels for the homeless, young offender institutions, smoking services, community alcohol units, outpatient treatment, night hostels, day hostels, drug dependence units. In Edinburgh in 1963 Henry Walton established the Unit for Treatment of Alcoholism – a hut next to the hospital – which excelled in teaching and group therapy. In keeping with changing concepts its name was later changed to Alcohol Problems Clinic. Hamid Ghodse cites the extreme difficulty in establishing the Springfield Unit where he could admit anyone with complex 'medico-psychiatric' disorders. The move to less inpatient, more community and outpatient treatment, and from psychodynamic to cognitive behavioural was evident in the UK and Europe, though perhaps not India or Japan.

Experience in several psychiatric specialties was fairly common eg Bruce Ritson in general psychiatry and learning disability as well as addiction; Ambros Uchtenhagen similarly worked in psychogeriatrics; Hiroshi Suwaki worked as Director in departments of Medical Psychology, Psychiatry and Neurology, and an Addiction Research Unit. Practitioners learnt from, and gained clinical insights to test, from the patients in these settings. Bruce Ritson learnt about the 'sober self' from patients; the harshness of maintenance of sobriety; that loss of contact did not necessarily mean relapse; and that decriminalizing the habitual drunken offender, ie detoxification outside prison, was effective. Shanthi Ranganathan built her own comprehensive centre where couples could be treated and to have inpatient, aftercare, a vocational unit, outreach for IV users, treatment camps, and relapse prevention. These thoughts complemented those of Tim Cook who described the consequence of group decisions in the therapeutic community. The realization that partnerships between agencies could enhance effectiveness could sometimes be hampered by resource allocations struck a chord with the current UK environment.

Few interviewees described the physical environment. Bruce Ritson graphically described the breweries in Edinburgh, the 'hut next to the hospital' where the addiction service started; such was his interest in the quality of the environment for patient well being that he became the Chairman of Art in Healthcare. Shanthi Ranganathan initiated her service in an ancestral bungalow. Tim Cook talked about the need for well furnished conditions for homeless offenders. After all, the external environment may reflect and/or change the internal world.

The seminal studies which follow were crafted on a shifting landscape in addiction treatment and continue to inform research, practice and policy.

The Prize of Leadership – Innovation and Entrepreneurship

This was a new epoch for contemporary addiction research. Seminal contributions surfaced from this new style of addiction research which went well beyond what Hamid Ghodse called 'trial and error'. The roll call of the research generated by this group is as notable as it is enviable. They are people of great personal authority who were responsible for innovative and entrepreneurial transformation in their field of practice. They were 'their own men' or 'woman' and had the strength to be 'out on a limb' with current thinking or innovate where there had been little or nothing. This leadership fostered new plans by taking the initiative, even if it meant being radical, providing support and a degree of control, evaluation of the project, informing the relevant clinical, research or policy community.

They had taken on board the advice of Griffith Edwards to Michael Russell ' To do good research you have to do it full time'. There was acknowledgement that this area exemplifies the need for multidisciplinarity ie there is 'no single treatment intervention or theoretical approach that will answer the 'mystery of recovery'. Also there was increasing recognition that there are a diversity not only of drugs but other addiction behaviours and the commonalities and differences were beginning to be explored. It was the 'radical quality of the claims' (Nick Heather) and 'pulling things together in a bold new way' (Jim Orford) that was energizing. Some people developed several units (Hiroshi Suwaki, Nick Heather)!

This cohort developed the beginnings of a scientific approach to the study of addiction. Some of the key issues or methodologies became precursors for more recent work. They began the process of tackling the big questions: the course and natural history of addiction, epidemiological studies, addictive behaviours other than substances, harm reduction, the genetics of addiction, randomized controlled trials and quantitative indicators.

Smoking research was undertaken by Michael Russell and Martin Jarvis. Michael Russell described the natural history of nicotine dependence as 'heterodox at the time' and pioneered the research that clarified that dependence on nicotine was what drove smokers to maintain, indeed to titrate, precisely what they required whatever the vehicle of administration. They developed methods to use quantitative indicators eg nicotine, carbon monoxide, cotinine so that cessation could be estimated as could passive smoking. Michael Russell realized that because of the prevalence of the problem, GP intervention was crucial to success. Eventually the capability led to using these indicators in epidemiological studies especially in teenagers which demonstrated the rapidity with which nicotine dependence developed. They pioneered the first randomized controlled trials of nicotine replacement and nicotine gum thus demonstrating the advantages of combined psychological and pharmacological treatments. In addition, the value of brief interventions in primary care became a template for future studies in other areas such as alcohol problems. Although considered by some to be 'crazy nicotine advocates,' this work was, as described above, very extensive and not limited as Martin Jarvis stated "It is not just 'it's all the nicotine stupid'". The influence of price on smoking behavior was further indicative of the far-reaching implications of their research.

Alcohol research was the domain of Jim Orford, Nick Heather, Bruce Ritson, Hiroshi Suwaki, Ambros Uchtenhagen, and Tim Cook. Here too biological research flourished when Hiroshi Suwaki demonstrated that alcohol flushers had low levels of alcohol consumption. The risk related to pattern of drinking as well as to dependence was elucidated. Natural history studies on untreated drinkers and those with alcoholism and affective disorder, comparative epidemiological studies in Mexico, the UK and Zambia under the aegis of the WHO, as well as randomized controlled trials evaluating CBT for controlled drinking and the UK alcohol treatment trial that compared motivational interviewing and social network behavioural therapy, were some of the influential projects. The development of community based interventions by GPs and nurses, screening and intervention packs and self-help manuals originated at this time. The UK study that compared treatment as usual with a single session of advice altered treatment fundamentally. Later the international family project in the UK, Mexico and Australia offered another perspective ie the influence of family on outcome.

Drug research encompassed the assessment of opiate dependence by measuring pupil constriction, epidemiological studies in accident and emergency departments that became a prototype for national and international studies, and the heroin treatment trial was the first to use the avante-garde approach to study the impact of prescribed heroin on entrenched users.

Though harm reduction was initially framed as 'controlled drinking,' it began to be embraced in illicit drug misusers and more latterly as a possible option for cigarette smokers. Broadening the remit of addictive behaviours to include non-substance dependence such as gambling threw new light on the complexity of these behaviours and the relationship to psychiatric disorder. It is surprising the Institute of Psychiatry and Maudsley Hospital did not regard this as 'core business'.

The reward was in the triumph of innovation and entrepreneurship: to see connections so far hidden.

Visible and Invisible Awards and Rewards

Shanthi Ranganathan won the highly esteemed Padma Shri award and the UN Vienna Civil Society award. Her response was to highlight the celebration of 'new' birthdays ie when they quit by patients who returned to her service still abstinent and the joy and satisfaction of working with patients. Hamid Ghodse won may prizes for the development of the pupillometer to measure dependence. Difficult moments were not discussed in any detail though deaths of patients, 'learning from failure', demanding responsibilities, rejection for posts and stinging competitiveness, rang many a bell.

Policy Influence and Dissemination – Being Part of the Bigger Picture

A principal task of the cohort was to directly or indirectly influence policy even though they may not have considered they were 'any good at it' (Michael Russell): he did contribute to the influential RCP report on Smoking and Health in 1977. Martin Jarvis felt privileged to serve on several national committees over the last decade where his expertise has been greatly valued: Action on Smoking and Health; Scientific Committee on Tobacco and Health; Specialist Advisor for the Health Select Committee's enquiry into the role of the tobacco industry.

The World Health Organisation has been a focal point: Nick Heather studied primary care across Europe and Australia; and, Bruce Ritson's international study on drinking in Mexico, Scotland and Zambia. Bruce Ritson played many roles eg Chair of the Edinburgh and Lothian Council on Alcoholism; Medical Council on Alcoholism; Chair of the Faculty of Substance Misuse, Royal College of Psychiatrists where he struggled to get the Faculty accepted and remains in favour of a separate specialty accreditation. Bruce Ritson was committed to other policy roles eg Scottish Intercollegiate Group on Alcohol, Scottish Health on Alcohol Problems, Scottish Howard League for Penal Reform Scottish Consortium on Crime and Criminal Justice – and sought avoidance of entrenched positions and bureaucracy. The experience around the establishment of Rathcoole House became central to the establishment of the Habitual Drunken Offenders working party and documents such as the 'Community services for alcoholics'.

Shanthi Ranganathan, as President of FINGODAP (umbrella organisation for Non-Governmental Organisations), provided knowledge and skills and help with minimum standards of care through training. Her organization, through its advocacy role, regretted that the government directly sold alcohol and there was no policy to prevent the escalation of use, a sentiment constantly echoed.

Retirement 'So-Called' - 'Recovery' from the Penchant for Addiction Research Is Not an Option

All of the cohort did not nor have not 'retired' in the conventional manner. It seems to be a life-long commitment that never stops, so even while indulging in interests (eg walking, painting, music, football, reading), involvement with addiction studies has not been peripheral.

Hamid Ghodse continues as President of the UN International Narcotics Control Board: he is characterized as 'the village elder who knows everything that is going on in his village.' Jim Orford defined it as a 20 year process in which he is teaching, lecturing and writing: he now considers himself a writer. On retirement Ambros Uchtenhagen established a research unit where the integration of research and treatment and the future need for 'a transdisciplinary specialist.' He sees monitoring and public health; subjective aspects of addiction; qualitative research as the domains for future research as do many others.

These incomparable men and woman in their turn have become models and mentors for the next generation of clinical academics specializing in addiction. In my own case, Hamid Ghodse and Bruce Ritson, as well as Griffith Edwards, have played a major part of my life as friends, colleagues and as collaborators offering advice, reflection and supervision - selflessly.

Nick Heather stated that he would like to be remembered as a person who 'made a contribution to the understanding and treatment of addiction and alcohol – simple as that.' We are appreciative that this generation – where 'personalities, polices and funds perfectly come together' - continue to provide wise counsel to enhance our understanding of the 'the mystery of recovery'! But then, 'recovery is a huge battle.'

References

Conversation with Nick Heather. *Addiction* 102 (2007) 523–33.
Conversation with Martin Jarvis. *Addiction* 106 (2011) 260–6.
Conversation with Jim Orford. *Addiction* 106 (2011) 698–705.
Conversation with Ambros Uchtenhagen. *Addiction* 98 (2003) 389–96.
Conversation with Timothy Cook. *Addiction* 98 (2003) 1029–38.
Conversation with Hamid Ghodse. *Addiction* 102 (2007) 197–205.
Conversation with Shanthi Ranganathan. *Addiction* 100 (2005) 1578–83.
Conversation with Bruce Ritson. *Addiction* 105 (2010) 1346–54.
Conversation with Michael A.H. Russell. *Addiction* 99 (2004) 9–19.
Conversation with Hiroshi Suwaki. *Addiction* 102 (2007) 1722–9.

Part 4—Careers in Social Science and Epidemiology

28

Conversation with M. Douglas Anglin

M. Douglas Anglin is an American researcher who has made notable contributions to research on civil commitment, the efficacy of methadone maintenance and the natural history of drug dependence. His concern has always been with the relevance of such research to policy choices.

Getting into Drugs Research

Addiction (A): Dr Anglin, you were born and raised in a small town in Arkansas; how did events bring you to a career working in the drug addiction field?

M. Douglas Anglin (MDA): I frequently say that most of the drug abuse researchers from my era developed 'accidental' careers, in part as a result of the times (the mid-1960s to the mid-1970s), and a few individual experiences. I studied for my undergraduate degree at the University of Arkansas (chemistry, physics and mathematics) in the late 1960s, so drug abuse was on the rise, particularly in middle-class youth, as was a counter-culture style of thinking. Having spent all those years in that relatively small environment, I was very eager to move to a bigger venue and applied to UCLA, a major nexus for the counter-culture. After my first 2 years at UCLA in clinical and social psychology, I needed a job and the man who eventually became my dissertation chair, William McGlothlin, needed a research assistant. He had just been funded by that component of the National Institute of Mental Health (NIMH) that was responsible at the time for drug abuse research to conduct an evaluation of an offender rehabilitation program called the California Civil Addict Program (CAP).

A: What did that program entail?

MDA: This program entailed a 7-year court commitment to criminal justice based treatment for primarily heroin addicts that included an intensive and lengthy initial confined period (providing drug treatment, job training and educational advancement) with transition services and further treatment on release to the community for a lengthy parole period. Detected relapse to drug use resulted in a return to confinement, typically for short periods, and re-release with enhanced services and monitoring. This program was to be shown by our evaluation to be meaningfully effective in curtailing drug use, decreasing crime and arrests and, for many undergoing this long-term program, producing a re-entry to prosocial values and activities.

A: Do you feel that your earlier training (before working with McGlothlin) was useful in this new field that you were entering?

MDA: Incredibly, not really. I think my early training did give me the logical assessment and problem solving skills to lay out various parameters of issues in a way amenable to scientific inquiry. But the real basics for research and specifically for drug abuse research that would have been helpful, I learned only later, through my experience in the field, first with Bill and then on my own. Importantly, these included the slow development of trust with the collaborating agencies that you needed to work with. Typically, no matter what your credentials were, agency personnel still had to know you as a person in order to trust you before you could elicit optimal cooperation. Essentially, you need to gain that cooperation from the top down, because there were many ways the beleaguered civil service or non-profit staff could blockade your scientific efforts. More broadly, in this competitive grant-funded world, the scientific writing of articles and grant applications was not addressed by any academic training, and I had to learn these skills by emulating Bill McGlothlin.

A: Tell me about McGlothlin and the work you did with him.

MDA: Bill McGlothlin had started his own drug abuse research career at the Rand Corporation, under military funding, on the effects of hallucinogens on human thought and behavior. That was in the mid-1960s, and at UCLA during this period there was some active work going on in different areas. Psychiatry Chair Dr Jolly West and Psychology Chair Dr F. Nowell Jones brought Bill to UCLA with a joint appointment in psychology and psychiatry. By 1972, Bill had moved from studying the psychedelics to marijuana and then into heroin, which was the point I began working with him.

A: What kind of work did you start doing as the research person working with him?

MDA: This project gave me a tremendous breadth of experience. I had to learn something about the epidemiology and etiology of drug use, specifically heroin use, all of the history of prior interventions and why the CAP could be scientifically justified for evaluation, the evaluation methods and techniques to be applied and the general literature as well, not to mention statistical analysis techniques. I helped determine the evaluation design and develop the instruments, and I attended many meetings between the California Department of Corrections senior officials who had to approve the study, and the warden and research staff at the California Rehabilitation Center (CRC) where the records and files were maintained. I also supervised other research assistants and clerical and data entry staff, and I coordinated the statistical analyses. Later in the process I wrote reports and articles with Bill.[1,2]

The California Civil Addict Program Evaluation

A: CAP had some interesting similarities with what has recently been developed as 'drug courts'.

MDA: That is an apt comparison, except for the troubling loss in successful program elements over the years, especially in one primary tenet of behavioral intervention: adequacy of time frame. It has been very disappointing in recent decades to see services stripped down to clearly subthreshold levels for many with chronic drug problems.

A: There is currently movement toward adopting a more chronic care model of addiction treatment that sounds like a revisitation to a 30-year-old concept as seen in the CAP.

MDA: One of the things that Bill McGlothlin pointed out to me is that nearly every question about drug abuse and related behavior that could be asked had been asked, and some good thinking, as well as some really poor thinking, had been applied to most issues.

The Natural History of Drug Abuse

A: Your work with Bill McGlothlin evolved into some focused work on the natural history of drug abuse. Can you describe your development of that concept?

MDA: Our natural history work evolved from the long-term evaluation of the CAP, where we examined retrospectively the committed offenders' drug use and criminal patterns for an extended period based on self-report data and official records. The time-frame included from first heroin use through dependence development to program entry, and then for the ensuing 10 years.

A: You also developed at that time the idea of 'return on investment'?

MDA: By providing the scientific information in the natural history frame, we helped to bring into the policy arena the 'return on investment' issue. Our CAP results[2] showed an immediate and sustained return for the full 7-year commitment period. The first grant I had entirely written on my own proposed using the natural history methodology to study the interrelationship of heroin addiction, criminal and treatment careers of the CAP cohort for an additional 10 years. Without this timely support, I would probably have taken an entirely different career path. In later studies we examined the natural history of those dependent on cocaine, crack and methamphetamine, as these drugs became of national prominence due to epidemic increases in use.

A: The natural history approach is one that has been also developed by George Vaillant in studies on alcoholism; how did the construct that you developed differ from his, or are they similar?

MDA: I think there is a great deal of similarity between all natural history approaches for behavioral, and even medical, conditions that tend to persist. Bill McGlothlin, although his initial purposes were evaluation, set the scene for our natural history studies based on work by David Nurco.

A: So how did you take that idea forward?

MDA: Working with Bill I developed a series of dynamic forms that capture the elements in each period that distinguished it from other periods. This is a very demanding interviewing and data entry process, as capturing a person's life for 10, 20 or, in some cases, for 30 years and breaking that history into these defined segments requires careful development for each subject. We found that for many groups the pre-intervention behavior was similar, but the post-intervention behavior was affected by the kind of intervention, the way it was delivered and ancillary events such as attending self-help groups, employment, and so on.

A: What do you see as some of the major lessons from your natural history research?

MDA: Simply stated, drug dependence is a complex and multi-factorially determined behavior, with genetic, physiological, familial, social and other components. Hence, efforts to intervene had to address drug dependence from many and diverse points if you were trying to find a set of forces that when combined result in successful intervention. Further, this combined 'force' had to be of sufficient strength and applied for a sufficient period (and in the case of addiction, this might be for a life-time) to change the course of enough individual addiction careers to show effects in the aggregate.

Methadone Maintenance

A: You and Bill McGlothlin also conducted an early study on the value of community-based methadone treatment.

MDA: We took the instrumentation developed in the CAP evaluation and the concept of the addiction career and applied the methodology to the first methadone maintenance programs opened in several counties in Southern California in the early 1970s. In retrospect, our results could have easily been predicted: that the high-dose, flexible implementation in Los Angeles County had the longest client duration in treatment and the longest delays to relapse to heroin use, crime, arrest and incarceration.[3]

A: Did your findings have an immediate impact on treatment policies?

MDA: I was very disappointed after publishing these results and presenting them state-wide and nationally that policymakers did not adjust their program procedures to derive optimal benefit from opiate maintenance treatment. Rather, increasing conservatism about methadone maintenance developed so that by 1986, county boards of supervisors, in California and elsewhere, were voting to take methadone out of the publicly funded system.

A: You are known in the United States as one of the most articulate spokespersons for supporting the value of methadone treatment. Are you satisfied that methadone treatment has been optimally used in the nation?

MDA: Not at all—research results are usually disregarded when political images, such as a tough on crime stance, need to be preserved. In the case of methadone maintenance, the Nixon Administration jump-started such programs in the United States in about 1968, with direct funding through the Law Enforcement Assistance Agency. In this initial period, you had the support of the Presidency and the recently established Special Action Office for Drug Abuse Prevention combined with massive amounts of federal funding. At about the same time Congress passed the Narcotic Addict Rehabilitation Act, which promoted drug treatment generally and provided further funding for programs in the community and within the criminal justice system. Overall, there was a major shift of resources into the treatment of drug addiction through methadone maintenance and other programs.

A: But that momentum was not maintained.

MDA: That political momentum continued into the early and mid-1970s but faded thereafter, to be replaced by the increased criminalization and stigmatization that seems always to resurface towards addicts.

A: Looks like the research evidence was being ignored.

MDA: In my more provocative presentations, I would say society was guilty of ethical negligence, if not true medical malpractice, in removing a proven treatment, subjecting patients to health morbidity and mortality.

A: Why has there been such difficulty in gaining acceptance of methadone treatment by the criminal justice system?

MDA: In one of my last public appearances, I attended a meeting of legislative personnel, judges, probation and parole agency staff and staff of other law enforcement groups. It was quite clear that information alone was not going to change the law enforcement collective or common wisdom about methadone. The entrenched law enforcement philosophy against substituting one drug for another, despite the proven benefits, was a barrier to even considering the evidence.

Intervening with Drug-Abusing Offenders

A: You are one of the leading proponents of the fact that adequately delivered drug abuse treatment reduces crime and that the criminal justice system can be useful in promoting treatment participation. How did you become involved in that particular area of research and policy?

MDA: After Bill McGlothlin's death, I wrote and secured funding for a second follow-up of our CAP cohort. Our arguments were for a longer-term evaluation, 20 years post-treatment. In the aggregate, addicts coerced into treatment by the criminal justice system did as well or better in duration and outcomes than the so-called voluntary entrants.

A: The logical next step?

MDA: Bringing about some improved linkages and assisting in overcoming the inherent problems. Work that we had conducted over the past 25 years has led to an increasing acceptance by the criminal justice system for providing (drug-free) treatment to those on probation, to the incarcerated and, importantly, as a component of transition back to the community on release to parole.

A: It is certainly controversial with treatment providers when they are presented with evidence that coerced treatment works as well, or possibly better than, voluntary treatment. Have you given any thought to why your findings seem to contradict the intuition of clinicians?

MDA: Part of the reason is that there is always a tremendous disconnect between group-based research and the individual experience of clinicians. In the latter case, the presistence of relapse and recycling into treatment of many of their patients can undermine acceptance of more general, sample-based studies.

Informing and Influencing Drug Policy

A: Can you discuss your views as to why research data and findings have been less than successful in influencing policy?

MDA: In my work as a researcher on various projects, we would obtain the analysis results and see distinct findings that had direct policy relevance.[4] I had assumed, and was terribly disappointed to find otherwise, that policymakers and agency officials would attend to the results as an opportunity to improve policy and, especially, interventions. When this did not happen, and in my further experience where research was occasionally considered, I realized that the best a researcher could do was good, scientifically defensible work with the findings properly distributed both in presentations and publications. Thereafter, one had to be patient, waiting for broader changes sweeping the field to introduce accumulated research findings in shaping the discussion.

A: Over the decades has the relationship between science and policy in this arena strengthened or faded?

MDA: As multiple bureaucracies have evolved and their size increased, opportunity, efficiency, and immediate relevance of developing, implementing and evaluating infrastructures for ameliorating the problems associated with drug use has declined.

Training and Mentoring New Scientists

A: One of your major contributions has been the initiation and leadership of a long-term NIH/NIDA research training program that at various times has been the largest training effort that NIDA has sponsored. Do you feel that we are getting the best people into the field to carry on needed research activities, and how do you feel generally about the development of new scientists in this area?

MDA: I think for anyone to develop an extensive research career in the same era as I did, several incidental and coincidental factors helped shape that career. Over my own career, I worked with many different speciality topics within drug abuse: a sort of a matrix, if you will, that had dimensions of personal interest, opinions about important issues for the field, relationships with funders and opportunities for funding. As a result, the actual level of work being conducted at any one time in any one topic had to be flexible, a sort of 'background–foreground' issue. A psychosocial researcher needs the background in all of these topics: epidemiology, etiology, program development, program evaluation, the long-term nature of drug dependence and so on. Within this knowledge set, what rises to the foreground depends frequently on what can be funded or other opportunities that allow the construction of a scientific research project. Of course, all this should serve the field. As Bill McGlothlin said to me when I had writer's blocks in my first paper, it does not matter how much you understand the data or are enthralled by the results, you only see a social response to your findings by presentation, consultation, and publication.

A: Why do you think young researchers choose to enter this particular research field?

MDA: Most researchers of my era entered drug abuse research coincidentally, even accidentally. Even now, in upcoming generations, there still seem to be multiple links: personal experience, whether that is for yourself or your family, cases of successful mentoring, opportunities for jobs to develop your skills in this area and provide for a career, and others. Such motivating events still outweigh the number of students entering the field who have looked at it abstractly and proactively, deciding that drug abuse research is what they want to develop a career in.

A: And research generations have in due time to be replaced?

MDA: An emphasis on 'generational replacement' came to me relatively early and was personally imperative, as I had been diagnosed with HIV in 1985 and with AIDS in 1993. Thus, it was very important to me that the drug abuse research center that Bill had initiated and I had inherited and enlarged be sustained, even if my health prospects were time-limited. I had already been recruiting and mentoring a number of individuals, but most of these individuals were relatively close to me in age. In this regard, I think one of my premier contributions to the field is having recruited and mentored some fine researchers. We were awarded that first 5-year Institutional Training Grant (ITG) and now, 15 years later, we still accept and graduate several fellows every year; a proportion of these become committed to a career in drug abuse research.

A: Any summary thoughts you would like to offer as we wrap up the career portion of this interview?

MDA: Just one. All the research that is currently being funded has a time horizon associated with it. There is currently great emphasis on bench laboratory and clinical trials research: genetic, physiological and medication development and these areas are important. However, the time horizon from such studies for achieving a process or mechanism that can be applied to the majority of people with drug abuse problems is fairly distant. This lag is further delayed in the absence of a clear national strategy that promotes balanced funding levels and funding mechanisms for different research areas. On the other hand, research that is ecologically valid—meaning it has good potential for application in the extant prevention or treatment system—can provide more immediately relevant and useful information to promote beneficial change.

A: Dr Anglin, you have led an immensely busy professional life. Can you tell us something about your leisure interests?

MDA: Leisure activities became increasing circumscribed as events developed in my life. Before Bill McGlothlin died in 1980, I had compensated for a relatively sedentary and studious youth by learning to sail, ski, scuba-dive and even hang-glide. Assuming the responsibility for our research group and the time it took to establish my first individual grants eliminated my participation in all these except for skiing. Later, the HIV diagnosis caused me to become even more focused on legacy development, and skiing faded away as well. But I have been an avid reader all my life: fiction, biographies, science, and continue to do so, especially in periods of poor health. My particular interest is theoretical physics and cosmology.

Notes

1. McGlothlin WH, Anglin MD, Wilson BD. Outcome of the California civil addict commitments: 1961–72. *Drug Alcohol Depend* 1975–76;1: 165–81.
2. McGlothlin WH, Anglin MD, Wilson BD. A follow-up of admissions to the California Civil Addict Program. *Am J Drug Alcohol Abuse* 1977;4: 179–99.
3. McGlothlin WH, Anglin MD. Long-term follow-up of clients of high- and low-dose methadone programs. *Arch Gen Psychiatry* 1981;38: 1055–63.
4. Anglin MD, Hser Y. Legal coercion and drug abuse treatment: research finding and social policy implications. In: Inciardi J,. *Handbook of Drug Control in the United States*. Westport, CT: Greenwood Press; 1990, pp. 151–76.

29

Conversation with Walter Clark

Walter Clark has a background in sociology but classes himself as "researcher in the epidemiological mode." For most of his professional life he worked at the Addiction Research Group at Berkeley, California. His work has focused on the study of population drinking practices.

Addiction (A): Walt, what is your professional background and how did you become involved with alcohol studies and the Alcohol Research Group (ARG) at Berkeley?

Walter Clark (WC): My background and studies in graduate school at Berkeley had nothing to do with alcohol. When I entered the alcohol field I was studying under Irving Goffman, conducting observational research on people's behavior. I had begun my doctoral dissertation, and had passed my qualifying examinations. I was then hired by Ira Cisin as a research assistant to work in the California Drinking Practices Study that he and Genevieve Knupfer were conducting in Berkeley. This was supposed to be a summer job, but as you know, lasted much longer than that. After working with Ira and Genevieve for a while I left to work in Canada. I was offered a job as an assistant professor in a Canadian university and went there with the notion of finishing my dissertation and pursuing an academic career, which I did off and on for about 7 years. I never totally cut my ties with Ira and Genevieve. Still, at some time during that period I decided I did not want an academic career and had no intention of finishing my doctoral studies. I decided that I would become a researcher, more in the 'epidemiological mode' of description, and with much less emphasis on social sciences.

Early Alcohol Research in General Populations

A: What were you hired to do in this job with Genevieve and Ira?

WC: Ira was a statistical researcher, and Genevieve Knupfer was a sociologist and a psychiatrist. I had never thought about alcohol before other than as a consumer, and neither had these other people. Neither Genevieve nor Ira had had any previous interest in the study of alcohol, and in fact there were not many such studies in those days. One of my first tasks was to collect and review everything that had been carried out in research on alcohol use in general populations.

A: How did Ira and Genevieve share responsibilities?

WC: Genevieve had much more to do with the content of the questionnaires and what we should be looking at. Ira was concerned with drawing an area probability sample of the city of Berkeley. This task involved me going out and walking around blocks that had been selected randomly and noting every 'nth' house and writing the address down on a piece of paper. Later, I returned and knocked on the doors and obtained, where I could, the names of all the people living there and randomly selected one, who was to be interviewed. And then I became the interviewer. The sample was several hundreds large, but as time went by we had more interviewers and more research assistants.

A: How did you handle the data analysis?

WC: Once we had all the data in hand, one thing we could not do was key-punch all the IBM or Hollerith cards. None of us were good typists much less good key-punch operators, so we sent that out; but everything else was done by hand, and when the cards came back the data were analyzed by running the cards through a counter-sorter like decks of cards. We would then count the results that the sorter showed, and with a slide-rule and mechanical calculator write pages and pages and pages of percentage calculations of this. We occasionally did try more advanced analytical techniques such as factor analysis. It was a time-consuming effort. Eventually you reach the theological stage of trying to name what you think the factors mean. This would take 3 or 4 days and at the end of the calculations, what was uppermost in mind was the hope that all the mistakes that were most certainly made in these calculations did not distort the results too much.

A: Response rates?

WC: We thought a 90% response rate was just acceptable, and it was possible to obtain 95% or 96% with a good number of calls back at home.

A: What was the main purpose of the California Drinking Practice Study?

WC: I do not think that was very clear in anyone's mind. The hope was that we would find a normal distribution of alcohol use in a population and then something very different that would describe this population of people who were going to end up in clinics or dying or cirrhosis. It was all very exploratory.

Surprises in the Distribution of Alcohol Consumption and of Drinking Problems in the General Population

A: What types of studies followed the California Drinking Practices Study at the ARG?

WC: Much of my knowledge applies to the 1970s, the time after I came back from Canada to the United States. At that time the people at ARG which, by the way, was then called the Social Research Group, were Don Cahalan, Robin Room and some others. They encouraged me to come back on a full-time basis, which I did until I retired in the mid-1980s. Don had had an affiliation with Ira Cisin at the George Washington University. Ira then returned to that university to resume his career there, and asked Don to become the director of the alcohol studies being conducted at the time. I hired Robin to work as a research assistant for a summer job. Robin came to alcohol research after being discouraged with the study of English literature. When we met, Robin asked me for a job and being an honest man said 'but I know nothing about sociology'. I replied, 'don't worry about it, there's nothing to know'—I had become discouraged at that time with the social sciences.

A: And that search for a bimodal distribution?

WC: As the studies progressed we confirmed that we could not find a bimodal distribution for alcohol consumption. There were many abstainers, about 30% of US adults, which is a higher proportion than what was found in studies in Scandinavia, Canada, France, Britain and Germany.

A: The social contest for abstention?

WC: We began to learn that many people tended to associate in their lives with others much like themselves. They went to churches with people who did not drink, they went to parties, when they went at all, with people who did not drink. They did not very often have heavy drinkers among their friends and acquaintances. Reversing that coin, heavy drinkers reported that they associated with people who drank a great deal. When we were asking people about drinking, most of us were worried that they would not answer questions truthfully. The years went by and the studies being conducted described the uses of alcohol and also began to ask about alcohol problems. But asking about alcohol problems and drunkenness worried us even more. Were their comments on their behaviours accurate? That was a concern then as I suppose it is a concern now, and all the years in between. Some things led us to wonder. For instance, if we added up all the alcohol that people said they drank and compared it to all that was sold, there was a discrepancy with the summed interview reports accounting for only 50% of what had been sold. So, we knew that there was under-reporting.

A: And the accuracy of the reporting on problems?

WC: It was probably the case that the best single source of information that you could obtain was by asking the people themselves what they did.

A: Where did your ideas on drinking problems come from?

WC: Almost all our early questionnaires could trace their history to Jellinek's analysis of AA members. Jellinek's[1] book on the disease concept of alcoholism was also enormously useful because he described alcoholism, defined it, identified several types, and in so doing provided the field with a number of testable propositions. He described loss of control as marked by unintended, unwanted drunkenness.

A: What did you find?

WC: In the general population we found to our surprise that loss of control, blackouts and so on were not to be found only in middle-aged people. These symptoms were most common among young men. We also found that it was not a one-way type of process. These symptoms came and went; so loss of control might have been reported by someone at one time but not at a later follow up. The notion of a single progression, of a clear-cut disease, fell apart in our hands. There were alcohol problems, and serious ones, in great abundance but no single entity that could be identified clearly as alcoholism.

A: The research carried out at the beginning was very empirical and not theoretically oriented?

WC: That is right.

The Social Environment as a Regulator of Consumption and Problems

A: How did these two 'surprises', that is, the high proportion of abstainers in the United States and the distribution of alcohol problems in the general population, influence the overall direction of research in general populations?

WC: Do you recall that there is a book by Cahalan[2] and another by Cahalan & Room,[3] that focused not on alcoholism as a disease but on problems of drinkers and problem drinking? These two books were reflections of what was found in general populations: many alcohol problems, no clear-cut identifiable entity of pathology, but just a great deal of drinking that led to serious consequences. We began to think about under what circumstances different consequences would appear, which eventually led me and some others to look at the social circumstances of drinking. That is, what are the social forces that bring about this distribution of alcohol use, with its problems and with its benefits as well? This goes back to the mid-1950s and the work of Ledermann,[4] in France. As you know, he then made the outrageous proposition that if one knew the per capita alcohol intake for a population one could predict the proportion of alcoholics, or of cirrhosis deaths in a population. To everybody's surprise, it emerged that there was some relationship. There is a predictable relationship between per capita consumption and the rates of cirrhosis and all kinds of severe alcohol problems. The question then arises, why should it be true? After all, we can imagine a population in which there are many heavy drinkers and many light drinkers and a certain mean for that group. Or we can imagine a different population having exactly the same mean, but with no heavy drinkers and no light drinkers but everybody in the middle. That is not what is found in practice. Empirically, what is found is a distribution that rises rapidly towards the mean of consumption and then a tailing-off to the right, and in the tail of that curve consumption is higher and the problems are more abundant. Many people were wondering about the explanation for the regularity that seemed to underlie the distribution seen across different populations. We thought that there had to be something in the social circumstances of alcohol use that explained the mean consumption and the proportion of people in a population falling on either side of that mean, as well as the proportion at the tail end of the curve that contains most of the alcohol problems. So we began to be concerned with circumstances of use, with the norms governing these circumstances of alcohol use. How much was customary to drink at a party if you are a Californian, or a New Yorker, or a Norwegian or whatever. Let me put it this way. First of all, as everybody will recognize, there are social circumstances in which one should not be found drinking or perhaps not drinking very much, and there are some where it is perfectly normal to drink; and at least for some people, to become inebriated is perfectly acceptable. There is a range of expectations of how much one can acceptably use and how much is too much. These social circumstances that regulate drinking behavior can be described and are remarkably consistent in the population, becoming a kind of a social lid that keeps behavior within acceptable boundaries, with perhaps occasional lapses. That varies from situations that are very wet, in our terms, to ones that are very dry. We studied everything from spending a quiet evening at home, to how much is normal to drink when friends come over to visit, or how much is customary at parties or when you are going to drive a vehicle. In general, women are not supposed to be as drunk as men.

A: When you look back to the past almost 50 years, what do you see that is different in the alcohol research field now?

WC: Well, let us begin with the funding. Funding was a very difficult proposition in the 1960s, not only for us but for anyone interested in alcohol studies, because these studies were expensive. Also, we were competing with all kinds of other health-related projects funded by the National Institutes of Health or the National Institute of Mental Health for the same research dollars. The notion that you were going to have any funding on any continuing basis was not at all certain. No one counted on it. We thought in terms of a year's study, a 2-year study. This all changed little by little, but especially with the creation of the NIAAA, which led to funding on the level that permitted research centers, and people like us to exist and young people to enter this field with the reasonable expectation of spending their working lives in it in a successful way. Something of the same kind led to increased and sustained funding in industrialized countries all around the world at about the same time.

A: The birth of the alcohol researcher as a specialist?

WC: In the early years there was no one such as an alcohol researcher. By 1970, certainly there were people who defined themselves in that way and who were thought of as alcohol researchers as though it was a specialty occupation, a way of life. That is clearly the case now.

A: In a way, the field became much more structured?

WC: It became structured. It developed a culture of its own. It is a separate discipline, I think, quite separate from, for instance, psychology or sociology. Certainly, it is a specialty in the public health field.

A: Now let me gain your perspective on an area that has changed quite fast recently: the present ability to conduct quantitative analysis.

WC: I did not have a calculator for the first 5 years. We used slide rules, and all the information was contained on huge stacks of cards. As for multivariate analysis, even though the techniques were available, the time and money to do them simply made them impossible.

A: Do you think that all these changes are for the better?

WC: When I began, there were few good journals. Most of them were not very good and to gain an education was something you pretty much had to do on your own.

A: Other changes?

WC: Another change is in the nature of some debates in the field. Jellinek's concept of the disease of alcoholism no longer looks like a very useful theoretical scheme. Today, there are no people, as far as I know, who are arguing as they were in the early years, that a Freudian explanation of alcohol abuse was central to understanding this problem. There are no arguments, so far as I am aware, from the behavioral people arguing that alcoholism is simply a conditioned response. All these notions seem to me to have become attenuated.

A: Is there anyone that you think influenced your work more than anybody else during your career?

WC: No one person. There were many people who were important, but it was a network of people pretty much all over the country and later all over the world who were conducting the same kinds of things.

Notes

1. Jellinek E. M. *The Disease Concept of Alcoholism*: New Brunswick, NJ: Hillhouse Press; 1960.
2. Cahalan D. *Problem Drinkers: A National Survey*. San Francisco, CA: Jossey Bass; 1970.
3. Cahalan D., Room R. *Problem Drinking Among American Men*. Monograph no. 7. New Brunswick, NJ: Rutgers Center of Alcohol Studies; 1974.
4. Ledermann S. *Alcool, Alcoolisme, Alcoolisation*, vol. 1. Paris: Presses Universitaires de France; 1956.

30

Conversation with Joseph Gusfield

Joseph Gusfield has exerted a creative influence on the alcohol research field with a strong and repeated emphasis on how problems are socially constructed. His book, Symbolic Crusade, *is widely acclaimed as a classic of the literature.*

Background

Addiction (A): Joe, you have made major contributions to the study of addictions, especially alcohol addiction, in the course of your career. But your work always has taken on the issue from a somewhat different angle than most addiction specialists. That has been the creativity. You let us all see the issues in a different light. How did you begin to develop these perspectives?

Joseph Gusfield (JG): As a sociologist I have always been interested in how things become problems. I like to say that if I am pressed to the wall, and asked, 'How do you solve this problem', I say, 'Why do you ask?'.

A: Your training?

JG: I was a graduate student in sociology in the early 1950s. I had taken a course in which I had read an excerpt from a history of the Women's Crusades of 1873. A group of women in Hillsboro, Ohio, sat in front of taverns (saloons, as they were called then), protesting their existence and taking the names of customers. It interested me and somewhat later I took a course in social movements, which at that point was not a very major field in sociology, but I developed an interest in social movements. I read a book by Herbert Asbury (1950), who was the great-grandson of Bishop Asbury, the Methodist who was so significant in coming to the United States from Britain and developing Methodism in the United States. The book was called *The Great Illusion.* It was a semipopular account of Methodist history in the United States focused on the anti-alcohol movement. What interested me about the Temperance Movement and the later Prohibition Movement is the anomalous position of it intellectually. What were the interests that people had in regulating or prohibiting drinking, especially in the case of religious groups? Churches played a crucial role in these movements in both the 19th and 20th centuries.

A: What kind of experience and perspectives did you have before you got into academia that may have influenced your take on these things?

JG: I became interested in social science and history, particularly with a very good history teacher in my high school, under whose guidance I actually read Charles Beard's *Economic Interpretation of the United States Constitution* (Beard 1935) and Thorstein Veblen's *The Theory of the Leisure Class* (Veblen 1934).

A: For a high school that is pretty advanced.

JG: It was. But Mrs Lotz was unusual.

A: Where did you go to high school?

JG: Roosevelt High School in Chicago, a public high school. I entered the University of Chicago in September 1941. The date is very important because in December of 1941 Pearl Harbor occurred. My freshman year was a huge intellectual unfolding. The university was intellectually a very stimulating place and I had a year of their social science sequence. I was in the middle of the second sequence when I went into the army, and I was in the army for 3 years. I enlisted in the Enlisted Reserve, which gave me a few more months in college. When I got out of the army I went right back to college.

A: Where did you go with the army?

JG: I was in England, France and Germany as a medic in a rear echelon unit in an infantry division. My original intention when I entered the university was to be a chemist. Somewhere along the line I decided I really wanted to be a novelist and was interested in literature. Before I went into the army, my intention had been to take a Master's degree in economics and go to law school. But when I did get out, I thought I was much too old, all of 23, to go for a Master's in economics. On my return to the University of Chicago I was asked to teach the social science sequence at their downtown college.

A: Were you still an undergraduate at this time?

JG: Yes, I was technically an undergraduate, but they were very short of people and this was essentially a course for adults at downtown Chicago. I entered law school at the University of Chicago and at the same time I was offered and became an instructor and after graduation an assistant professor in the college, teaching social science. It was a 2-year undergraduate degree at Chicago in those days. In the college, I taught a required course. The first quarter consisted of social science classics such as Freud's *Civilization and Its Discontents* (Freud 1961) and Karl Marx's *Capital* (Marx 1932). Most importantly, we read Max Weber's *The Protestant Ethic and the Spirit of Capitalism* (Weber 1930). I think that was the book that influenced me most deeply. It introduced me to the role of ideas and the complexity of analyzing human action. At the same time I was taking a seminar in the law school on the sociology of law; I also read Weber's work on *Sociology of Law* (Weber 1954) and other classics on the sociology of law and on jurisprudence. I became very interested in all this. But I decided I really did not want to be a practising lawyer; that I really wanted to study further.. Again, I had a very great teacher, Malcolm Sharp, who was able to pose legal questions in both philosophical and legal terms.

From Law to Sociology

A: You then moved into sociology?

JG: I had to make a choice at the time between law or social science. For a while I had felt a little bit like a fish out of water. After leaving the law school I became a graduate student in sociology. I came to appreciate it very much. The department tended to emphasize the contextual aspects of human behavior rather than widespread theory or generalization. I liked the difference in ways in which people would look at things. What interested me about the Temperance Movement was precisely its paradox. Here was a movement that had an enormous impact on American politics, which led to a constitutional amendment and ultimately an amendment that revoked its original amendment. At the same time, it was hard for me to understand.

A: What was hard to understand about it?

JG: I came to it, like most Americans, with a quasi-Marxist perspective—an emphasis on economic motivations and meanings in history. Why should middle-class people make such a movement so vital?

Awakening Interest in the Temperance Movement

A: So you were fascinated by this problem?

JG: I set out to study one such group, the Women's Christian Temperance Union. Why the Women's Christian Temperance Union? First of all, it had been a leading organization in the later development of the Temperance Movement and it arose out of the very crusades that had influenced me in my reading earlier. Its national headquarters was in Evanston, Illinois, which is a close suburb of Chicago. It enabled me not only to interview people there but also to utilize their library so that I could carry out an historical study of that particular group.

A: So, this is what influenced you to pick this dissertation topic?

JG: Basically, it was that anomaly and the fact that nobody had really studied it.

A: You were studying moral movements and therefore taking morality more seriously than some sociologists, especially Marxists, would have done. Taking it seriously but at the same time showing that it does not represent the absolute truth about anything.

JG: Yes. A young graduate student at Berkeley, Harry G. Levine, later went on to study the movement and published a fascinating article on the discovery of addiction (Levine 1978). His view of the Temperance Movement was somewhat different from mine. He tended to see the addiction issue as much more important to the movement than I did.

A: More on health versus your sense that people's understanding of right or wrong was at stake.

JG: This distinction between, shall I call it, sin or sickness, has persisted and it has been central in my more recent writing, on cigarettes. Cigarette smoking begins with an emphasis on health, but certainly has moved also to a sense of morality about it.

Symbolic Crusade

A: So what you looked at was this moral crusade. Your book *Symbolic Crusade: Status Politics and the American Temperance Movement* is still a classic in sociology (Gusfield 1963).

JG: Well, I am glad to know it, although I think sometimes more highly of my later book on drinking and driving, but we can get to that in a while.

A: *Symbolic Crusade* still sheds a great deal of light on all sorts of things that we label status politics. So, tell me a little bit about the book.

JG: I saw it in many respects as an effort to develop and maintain the cultural dominance of the Protestant native rural culture in the light of immigration, cultural diversity and secularism, which was changing the American population. Not only is it not static, it is also full of conflict, so that there is conflict about culture. I saw the political issue of drinking as a symbolic issue, important because what was at stake in Prohibition was, to a significant degree, a question of whose culture is to be publicly dominant.

A: But you are talking about what today we call culture wars.

JG: People today are much more aware of diversity, and the television, the radio, have made us more aware of different points of view. Changes in the content of public moralities have raised the issues of diversity of culture into matters of conflict. Today I do not see a dominant culture but a struggle going on over what it is to be.

A: Let us go back to that first book. So, you finished that book and it was based on your PhD dissertation?

JG: I finished the dissertation in 1954. I went on to expand it into a study of temperance and prohibition. The book was published in 1963. So, it means it was finished about 1961.

A: What did you do after that?

JG: I must mention that in 1950 I left the University of Chicago. I took a position at Hobart and William Smith College in upstate New York. I finished the dissertation while there doing interviews. I interviewed not only people in Chicago, but I was now interviewing people in upstate New York. I discovered that there was a great deal of Agrarian radicalism in the United States, also connected to Temperance.

A Passage to India

A: But then you moved back to Chicago?

JG: While I was at Hobart and William Smith College, I also taught at the University of Chicago, back again as a visiting assistant professor. In 1955, I accepted an offer from the University of Illinois in Champaign-Urbana. But I decided in the late 1950s that I wanted to get out of my own culture. I applied for a Fulbright to India. I did not have to know another language. At any rate, in 1962 I went to India with my family. We have been back six times since then.

Involvement in the US Civil Rights Movement

A: In the meantime, of course, this was the 1960s. Society in the United States was boiling.

JG: Well, I was very much involved in the civil rights movement. I was the sponsor for SNCC (Student Nonviolent Coordinating Committee) at the University of Illinois and I also did go south for part of the Selma to Montgomery march. I was considered an historian by that time and I marched with the historians as a group. We marched to Montgomery, Alabama. That was, of course, a very searing thing, and very influential for me. It was a participation in a really emotional action—a really emotional movement. The war probably had more influence on me than any other experience. But the civil rights movement brought me out of the aloofness to which I generally still retreat.

A: So in 1966 you were asked to consider joining the faculty at the University of California, San Diego (UCSD).

JG: I wanted a department that would break with the emphasis on quantitative work. I wanted one that had much more of a concern with observation. I was also interested in historical sociology. I was interested in culture. I had, in the intervening year read things that again had a great deal of influence on my thinking. One was Claude Levi-Strauss's book, *The Savage Mind,* three books really (Levi-Strauss 1966). One was a book by Harold Garfinkel, *Studies in Ethnomethodology* (Garfinkel 1967), and one was a book by my later colleague Jack Douglas on *The Social Meanings of Suicide* (Douglas 1967).

Drunk Driving

A: How did you come to develop an interest in drunk driving?

JG: Shortly after I became chair at UCSD in 1970, I was approached by an organization which was then called the Urban Observatory to undertake a study of sentencing in drinking and driving cases. We conducted the study, essentially of sentencing. What we found was a high degree of recidivism. The sentences were generally very slight; we found that fines were light and jail sentences uncommon. After this research (Gusfield 1972) I decided to go on and conduct a study of a different kind. A book emerged, called *The Culture of Public Problems: Drinking, Driving and the Symbolic Order* (Gusfield 1981). It came from continuity with my past interest in symbols. It also came from my general sense—being in the army may have had something to do with it—of not understanding, not being able to see the big picture. It came from a great deal of experience with the difficulties of creating facts.

A: In the meantime you now had more faculty who would reinforce this general way of thinking.

JG: Yes, that is quite true. The ethnomethodologists were very quick to sense doubt about fact or things that became fact and that too was an influence.

A: This goes back to the earlier studies of temperance—the thought that drinking is a moral problem?

JG: Yes, it does indeed, and I am trying to articulate this. The symbolic order of the United States in its rhetoric carried the theme that all problems are solvable. Also, if there is a problem somebody must be at fault.

A: Were you involved directly with people in organizations and alcohol studies before this?

JG: In the 1970s, certainly the 1980s, I was very much involved. I was on the advisory board for the Alcohol Research Group, which later became the Social Research Group, which at that point had some affiliation with University of California, Berkeley. It later became a freestanding organization. So, I had a great deal of contact with those people. Harry Levine, who I have mentioned before, was involved. Robin Room, whom I think of as probably the dean of alcohol studies, was there. He has an omnivorous knowledge and understanding of alcohol studies. I was also involved at various times in advisory groups—research on alcohol prevention, for example, which came out of the Institute for Alcohol Abuse and Alcoholism in Washington.

A: And activist concerns?

JG: I did have many of what you might call activist concerns. Those concerns were largely, almost entirely, with addictions and with addicts—providing treatment facilities and assessing legislation. It sharpened my interests not in the policies, but the applied activities that went on. Despite my general criticism of the Bush Administration, I think the faith-based policy he wants to establish is a very good one, because I think these organizations have achieved a great deal. I am interested in the question of the differences between policy toward alcohol, policy towards what we call drugs and policy towards cigarettes. Why is the drug policy so punitive and alcohol and cigarette policies far less so?

An Active Retirement

A: When did you retire?

JG: I retired in 1991. My leisure has been a continuance and increase in my painting. In answer to what kind of painting I do, I say mediocre acrylic and pastel, bad watercolor and I do not know collage. We did a goodly amount of cruising, travel and gambling (Las Vegas). I look back at what I feel has been an interesting and satisfying life, much of it a result of the fine and stimulating people I have known.

A: Do you have any final thoughts about the advice you might give to young social scientists that are starting out?

JG: The tension is often very good. I do not think that harmony is necessarily good. Tension is often quite productive. But I cannot really give advice to the young. They will not take it anyway.

References

Asbury, H. (1950) *The Great Illusion*. New York: Greenwood Press.

Beard, C. A. (1935) *An Economic Interpretation of the Constitution of the United States*. New York: McMillan.

Douglas, J. (1967) *The Social Meanings of Suicide*. Princeton, NJ: Princeton University Press.

Freud, S. (1961) *Civilization and Its Discontents*. [translated from the 1930 original]. New York: W.W. Norton.

Garfinkel, H. (1967) *Studies in Ethnomethodology*. Englewood Cliff, NJ: Prentice Hall.

Gusfield, J. (1963) *Symbolic Crusade: Status Politics and the American Temperance Movement*, 2nd edn. Urbana, IL: University of Illinois Press.

Gusfield, J. (1972) *A study of Drinking Drivers in San Diego County*. Report to the Department of Health, County of San Diego, California.

Gusfield, J. (1981) *The Culture of Public Problems: Drinking, Driving and the Symbolic Order*. Chicago, IL: University of Chicago.

Gusfield, J. (1996b) Benevolent repression: popular culture, social structure, and the control of drinking. In: *Contested Meanings: the Construction of Alcohol Problems*. Madison, WI: University of Wisconsin Press.

Levine, H. G. (1978) The discovery of addiction. *Journal of Studies on Alcohol*, 39, 143–174.

Levi-Strauss, C. (1966) *The Savage Mind*. Chicago, IL: University of Chicago Press.

Marx, K. (1932) *Capital and Other Writings*. New York: The Modern Library [original publications 1867–1883].

Veblen, T. (1899/1934) *Theory of the Leisure Class*. New York: The Modern Library.

Weber, M. (1930) *The Protestant Ethic and the Spirit of Capitalism*, trans. Parsons, T. New York: Charles Scribner's Sons [original publications 1904–05].

Weber, M. (1954) *Max Weber on Law in Economy and Society*. [translated from the 1925 original]. Cambridge, MA: Harvard University Press.

31

Conversation with Ragnar Hauge

When the longest-serving alcohol and drug researcher in Norway celebrated his 70th birthday about 2 years ago, little changed. Rather than enjoying a well-earned rest, Ragnar Hauge—jurist, criminologist and for many years head of Norway's national drug and alcohol research institute SIRUS—remained at his post at the institute.

Early Years

Addiction (A): Could you tell us something about your childhood?

Ragnar Hauge (RH): I was born in 1933, at the peak of the depression when the birth rate was at its lowest ebb, which meant, conveniently as far as I was concerned, that there were fewer people to compete with in the job market. I grew up in Trondheim, Norway's medieval capital, not very far from the Arctic Circle, with long, dark winters and short, bright summers. My father was a lawyer, later a judge. During my first 5 years at school, Norway was occupied by German troops, and people were not allowed to form or join associations, the cinemas were boycotted, radio sets confiscated and for long stretches at a time, the school was closed either because it could not be heated or because it was requisitioned to house troops. After elementary school I went to grammar school and the natural thing for middle-class boys after that was to keep on studying. The University of Oslo, at the time the only university in Norway, presented the obvious choice. Since law lies in the family, that is where I ended up.

A: Do you have any special memories from your student days?

RH: The most important thing that happened to me during that period was getting married, and the birth of our first child. As far as studies are concerned, teachers and students today have much closer contact than they did back then. Studying law basically meant reading the literature and taking examinations. Lectures were the only form of tuition. There was this immense gap between the students and professors.

A: Did any of your teachers in Oslo have a formative influence on you?

RH: Not really. I did not even speak to a professor, as far as I recall, until I had graduated!

A: Has the nature of alcohol and drug-related problems changed since your student days in the 1950s?

RH: Very much so. People drank less then, young and old. Since 1955—when I started studying—registered consumption has doubled. Attitudes to drink are far more liberal today. At the same time, smuggling and personal imports from abroad—especially from Sweden—have risen sharply, so annual consumption today is probably at least three times what it was. When I was a student, the few restaurants in existence had to stop serving alcohol by midnight. There was only one nightclub in Oslo, and it closed at 3 in the morning. Today, there are a vast number of licensed premises. Drug use was virtually unheard of among my generation.

Criminology

A: What led you away from your father's path as a judge, and towards criminology?

RH: Towards the end of my law studies I had to choose an elective course. To tell you the truth, I was slightly fed up with law by then. I chose criminology as an elective because it was the only option in the social sciences, and it looked more interesting than those law subjects.

A: Did criminology hold a prominent place in Norway that early?

RH: No, on the contrary, criminology was hardly considered a study at all in its own right. The Institute for Criminology and Penal Law was set up in 1954 at the Faculty of Law, University of Oslo. I sat my law examinations and was invited to begin at the institute conducting research. In 1964 I was appointed associate professor.

A: Criminology today is considered largely a social science—why was the Institute under the Faculty of Law?

RH: The legendary professor of criminal law, Johs Andenæs, started the ball rolling. His vision was for the Institute to provide a link between law studies and social science.

A: Did he succeed?

RH: Yes, by and large.

A: The Institute of Criminology was seen as a rebellious outgrowth on the conservative law faculty. When did that start?

RH: It was there from the outset. Some of the issues being raised by the criminal law researchers were considered highly controversial. The studies on Norway's vagrancy laws, which handed down terms of forced labour to the homeless, are the best known. A destitute, homeless alcoholic could be sentenced to hard labour in a prison-like institution for anything up to 3 years.

A: What was it like for a young jurist like yourself to become part of that environment?

RH: It was challenging. There were exciting issues; there was a buzz in the air.

A: Did the environment draw you towards the left of the political spectrum?

RH: I am a pacifist, and before I started studying in 1955 I spent 18 months at a camp for conscientious objectors, digging ditches and forestry work. I belonged to a group of left-leaning socialists, although I was not active in a political party sense.

A: What was the situation concerning social sciences at that time?

RH: It was a groundbreaking period in the social sciences—including criminology. The next step was to develop the welfare state. The social sciences grew rapidly during the 1960s and became important university studies, including criminology.

A: The criminal as victim as opposed to the victim of crime—is that a false dichotomy?

RH: I believe criminological research, focused on the lawbreakers and social causes of crime, is a necessary and beneficial balance in a repressive period.

Perspectives

A: You are a citizen of a small country in terms of culture and language. Could we talk a little about your relationship to the world outside Norway? Unlike many other researchers in Norway, you write mostly in Norwegian. Why is that?

RH: It was a conscious choice to write in Norwegian. Much of what I have written is not for my colleagues, but for people with an interest in the issues.

A: Your first—and only—really extensive trip abroad occurred relatively early.

RH: I spent a year studying in England, 1961–62, and followed the first graduate programme in criminology at the University of Cambridge.

A: Did your stay there affect you?

RH: Yes, also in other ways than the purely academic. British criminology at the time was dominated largely by Hermann Mannheim at the London School of Economics (LSE), Max Grünhut at Oxford and, of course, Leon Radzinowicz at Cambridge—all of whom were refugees from the Continent before World War II. It meant that Continental European criminology dominated, with an emphasis on historical, legal and psychological approaches, about which I was already familiar, while I was interested mainly in the sociological perspectives developed in the United States. And, not least, it gave me an opportunity to get to know post-war English literature, published conveniently in paperback form, making it affordable to people like me with little money.

A: And outside influences more generally, what has been their legacy?

RH: When you live in as small a country as Norway, what scientists elsewhere are doing becomes especially important. Meeting specialists from abroad has been vital to me as, indeed, they are to other Norwegian scientists.

A: Are there any books from international research you would like to mention?

RH: I referred to my early interest in American criminology. Edwin Sutherland's *Principles of Criminology* (1960) opened the doors in that respect. It was a key textbook in the United States, and was available and read here in Europe as well. That book introduced me to the Chicago School.

A: You had written two books on youth and crime by the end of the 1960s. Are those findings still valid today?

RH: The thesis of these books (Hauge 1968, 1970) is that juvenile crime derives in many ways from association with peer groups which generate their own, idiosyncratic culture and norms. That, I believe, remains a pretty firm conclusion.

A: You coined the term 'majority misapprehension'.

RH: Yes. We asked youngsters how much they thought their peers drank, and we found that a large number of them believed their peers drank much more than themselves. They had a sort of feeling that others were 'big drinkers' and that they were the odd person out which, in fact, did not accord with what the others were reporting. The same seems to be true also for delinquency. Misapprehension of the majority's behaviour may therefore help to explain why young people may feel under pressure to disregard their own ideas of right and wrong.

Alcohol and Drug Research

A: You have spent a large part of your career at SIFA (National Institute for Alcohol and Drug Research), or SIRUS (Norwegian Institute for Alcohol and Drug Research), as it is known today. You started working at the institute before it had even been established. How did that happen?

RH: Nobody was taken on before the summer of 1960. A decision had already been made to conduct a comparative Nordic study of drinking patterns among the young, under the leadership of the well-known Finnish alcohol researcher Kettil Bruun. Nils Christie—who was chairman of the board—asked me if I would carry out the Norwegian part of the study. It led to the report *Drinking Habits among Northern Youth* (Bruun & Hauge 1963).

A: What prompted your interest in alcohol and drugs research?

RH: There were no signals at the time that a new professorship in criminology would be approved in the foreseeable future, so career prospects there were not particularly bright. SIFA was therefore a good alternative. I was director for a period of 13 years, 1975–88, and after that I stayed on as a researcher. From the end of the 1960s the drug problem became a major issue.

A: Are there any research projects at the Institute you would like to mention in particular?

RH: The most widely known projects are probably our annual surveys on young people and drinking patterns. They started as far back as 1960, and by 1968 illegal substances were included. In other words, we in Norway probably have the longest time-series in the world on substance use among the young.

A: In so far as we in Norway have had a state alcohol and drugs research institute, has that affected alcohol and drug policy making?

RH: Whether the Institute has had any impact on policy making is difficult to say. Government documents often refer to research from the Institute, but whether the findings actually shape policy or are used simply to underpin political decisions already made is a moot point.

A: In your recent writing you adopt a millennial perspective. Is historical awareness important?

RH: You are thinking about the book on law and alcohol in Norway from the High Middle Ages to today (Hauge 1998). I believe history has a great deal to teach us. The alcohol and drug sector, or parts of it, display remarkably short memory spans at times.

A: Political circles are calling increasingly for research to be practical—and that measures put in place in virtually all areas of social policy should be based on science. Is an alcohol and drugs policy based on empirical evidence possible?

RH: I find it difficult to imagine a set of reliable and universally valid approaches with the same sort of function as they have in medicine. We have to look for the explanation of crime or drug and alcohol abuse in the individual's personality and social conditions, and they vary from person to person. The likelihood of finding clear-cut, coherent measures which work for everybody—whatever their background—is, I contend, remote.

A: For many years now, you have been a university lecturer—do you enjoy teaching students?

RH: One foot in the university, and the rest of the body in research: it has suited me down to the ground—the best of two worlds.

In Public

A: There is a widely known 1984 cartoon drawing in which you and the drugs police chief are tugging at either end of a drugs statistics curve; you are trying to pull it down, and he is pulling it up. Does it bear any relationship to the efforts of the Institute to offset banner headlines in the press and statements from the police?

RH: In the 1970s and 1980 s the police pursued a vigorous anti-drugs policy. Oslo, with half a million people, had for a time the biggest drug squad in Europe. They tended to exaggerate, and paint a gloomy picture of the situation. It was interesting at the start, but I soon became tired of being made to sound like a drugs liberalist.

A: You have got yourself into the public eye regularly down the years. In 1992 you managed to irritate some members of the Storting's standing committee on social affairs—they even threatened to cut the Institute's budget in half because you were so liberal. What happened?

RH: It started when I spoke at a meeting attended by some members of said committee. I did not see my lecture as particularly controversial, but it aggravated those committee members so much they went back to the Storting and tabled a motion to cut the Institute's budget so drastically.

A: Recently, you got on the wrong side of the Minister of Justice with a proposal in a report issued by the Penal Code Commission, of which you were a member, to decriminalize drugs for own use. One would be forgiven for believing you enjoyed annoying the conservative establishment?

RH: As far as I know, I have only set out what has been my long-held view, i.e. that the manner in which the Norwegian judicial system treats substance users is nothing about which we have reason to be proud.

Looking Ahead

A: What does the crystal ball tell you about the situation 15–20 years from now?

RH: As far as alcohol is concerned, use will probably continue to increase. We are influenced by countries where consumption levels are substantially higher than ours, and I cannot really see us moving in the opposite direction to them. Our tough retail laws are poised to fall, thanks among other things to European Union (EU) regulations on free trade. In the case of other substances, cannabis is probably here to stay but in 20 years or so I do not think people will feel very alarmed about it. And, like today, there will be a lumpen proletariat of heavy users of opiates. The use of other substances is largely governed by fashion, and predicting anything here is probably futile.

A: If a young student wanted a career in research, and he asked you for your advice, what would you say to him or her?

RH: I would tell him to think twice! It is difficult to find a job today, and there are many people out there waiting. Many scientists spend their days drafting funding applications, but if they obtain funds it is only enough for low-paid, short-term projects. In my day the reverse was true—the social sciences were desperate for more people. They expanded; there were many jobs, and not enough qualified people to fill them.

A: What do you do when you are not doing research: do you have any hobbies to recharge the batteries?

RH: Work and family are the two mainstays of my life, along with holiday trips, watching movies and reading fiction.

A: You must enjoy your life as a researcher, as you choose to turn up at SIRUS every day?

RH: Yes, I enjoy the life very much indeed. and perhaps precisely because I am not a stamp collector, or play golf or cultivate roses, it was a logical step to continue doing what I have always done. I am privileged in so far as I have an opportunity to continue working. As long as SIRUS offers office space and the company of good colleagues, I intend to keep on coming here.

References

Bruun, K. & Hauge, R. (1963) *Drinking Habits among Northern Youth*. Helsinki: Finnish Foundation for Alcohol Studies.

Hauge, R. (1968) *Gjengkriminalitet Og Ungdomskulturer [Gang Delinquency and Youth. Cultures]*. Oslo: Universitetsforlaget.

Hauge, R. (1970) *Kriminalitet Som Ungdomsfenomen [Crime as a Youth Phenomenon]*. Oslo: Universitetsforlaget.

Hauge, R. (1998) *Norsk Alkohollovgivning Gjennom 1000 År [Norwegian Alcohol. Legislation through 1000 Years]*. Oslo: Rusmiddeldirektoratet.

Sutherland, E. H. & Creesey, D. J. (1960) *Principles of Criminology*. 6th edn. Philadelphia: J. B. Lippincott.

32

Conversation with Harold Holder

Harold Holder has made many important contributions to alcohol research, particularly in relation to public health aspects. From 1986 to 2002 he was Director of the Prevention Research Centre, Berkeley, California. He has been a key contributor to international policy review statements including Alcohol Policy and the Public Good *and* Alcohol: No Ordinary Commodity. *In 1995 he was a recipient of the Jellinek Award.*

Early Years

Addiction (A): Where did you grow up?

Harold Holder (HH): I was born in North Carolina, and grew up in the north-west corner of Alabama. My home town was Sheffield, and had maybe 15 000 people. The area became famous because Huntsville is nearby, where the US space program began.

A: You are a life-long student of community norms. Which ones did you grow up around in Sheffield?

HH: I wonder sometimes to what degree that heritage influenced my professional work. I grew up in the evangelical church. I was active in the church, did youth group activities and so forth. I learned to public speak in the church which prepared me for giving research lectures later.

A: Since you went to college at Samford University in Birmingham, Alabama, I assume your church was Southern Baptist?

HH: Yes. and there were many rules about drinking, card playing, dancing and even mixed gender swimming. The most active I ever saw the Baptist church in politics was wet–dry votes around alcohol. Because Alabama had local option (counties can vote wet or dry), alcohol elections were a regular part of church activity.

A: Dry county?

HH: Dry county, but then it was sometimes wet. So, yes, I grew up in that culture. I did not like small town norms and the scrutiny of behavior that I grew up with as a child, and that heritage influenced my preference to live in big cities. I never lived in small towns after that.

A: And your involvement in the Baptist Church?

HH: I left that too. What ended my church membership in 1969 was the Vietnam War. I could not align with the church's support of that war.

A: When you were a kid, were you interested in science?

HH: I was actually more interested in art and reading. I loved mathematics and did very well at it in high school. When I went to college, I even thought about being a math major but I could not see any future in that.

A: What was it about maths that you liked?

HH: Certainly the symbology and the precision. Not just measurement precision but the precision of statement.

A: Some people would say that a guy interested in precision is going to become a physicist and not a social scientist.

HH: Well, I was intrigued with the uncertainty of human behavior. I did not understand that until 10 years ago. There I discovered that physicists defined chaos as beginning a complex process at the same point each time but yielding different results. I said 'that is human behavior' and at that exact moment I understood what intrigued me about social science. In physics, one often has a model which yields the same result each time. In the social sciences we always know it is a stochastic or unpredictable (sometimes random) process.

A: Wonderful. Just to close on your early years, who influenced you the most?

HH: My father influenced me in terms of work ethic. He only had a fourth grade education. So, he liked all the education I obtained. But what I took most from him was a standard that whatever you undertook, you did to the best of your ability. So, I have often slowed things down when they could have gone faster just because of that value. My father was a very methodical craftsman as an electrician. He did everything carefully and then he moved on to the next task.

A: Any teachers who had a strong impact on you?

HH: The teacher who had the most influence was my high school track coach. He supported my compulsivity to get it done, to work hard, and to finish whatever you're doing.

College and Graduate School (1957–65)

A: Your education was in history, journalism and communications.

HH: I probably studied history because I was very interested in social processes and complexity. Journalism was interesting because I liked writing, and when I was an undergraduate, I believed I was going to be a newspaper reporter.

A: Do you ever wish you had become a journalist?

HH: No. I was headed toward research.

A: You went to college in the deep south at a time of pretty significant racial rumblings. Did that spill over at Samford?

HH: I was there when the freedom riders came through Birmingham, and they were beaten in the downtown bus station. I was actually not working that day, but I was a reporter for the newspaper that took the picture of the attackers with their pipes raised in the air as they beat people. It shocked me. I did not understand this enormous violence. I had grown up in a small town that was segregated but in my family I did not learn a great deal of overt racial prejudice. I took segregation as the way things were. I developed a real friendship with an African American young man about my age who simply went to a different school.

A: Did you drink as a college student?

HH: No. It was a Baptist school, so there was no drinking. I had my first drink when I was 25 years old.

A: I think of Syracuse as a pretty cold, strange place for a kid from Alabama. What made you want to move?

HH: Well, part of that motivation was my desire to get out of the South. I was offended and upset by the racial tension. I love my Southern roots, but I had to leave. I have been through that process three times actually, going back to the South, and then moving away. Syracuse was a change in so many ways. Upstate New York was full of immigrant families. I saw the world as much larger than I had experienced until that time. Another was the intellectual challenge. I immediately got into trouble by applying the same standards to graduate school I had used in undergraduate studies, that is, simply working hard. These professors were asking me to think. But after, I guess about 7 months, I realized that I was as smart as the people getting PhDs, and I really liked statistics and research design and methods. That was the end of my journalism career.

A: Were there professors at Samford and Syracuse who really shaped how you think?

HH: Not so much at Samford. The professor who influenced me the most was at Syracuse University.

A: Who was that?

HH: His name was William Ehling, an odd fellow in the Newhouse School of Communications. He was interested in systems, mathematical models and theory. I probably did the first mathematics-based dissertation through the School of Communications at Syracuse. Most of my professors thought this was a strange dissertation. I had to recruit committee members from outside, including two professors in mathematical sociology.

A: What was your connection to that field?

HH: I had taken classes in sociology, primarily in theory building. However, I had no interest in the great verbal theorists. People such as Talcott Parsons did not interest me because their theories were all words.

A: I hear two themes: 'I want to hear the evidence' and 'I want to hear the practical purpose of what I am learning.'

HH: These are my blue-collar viewpoints. Ideas per se do not interest me. It is the application of ideas to problem-solving that interests me and has driven my career. Syracuse was the first place that I began to experience my need for evidence. My dissertation illustrated where my career was going to go.

Early Career (1965–76)

A: After graduate school, you joined the faculty at Baylor University, in Texas. Did you want to go back to the South or did a good position for you just happen to be there?

HH: The latter. I am convinced that one of the influences on Baylor choosing me was my Baptist heritage.

A: Only 3 years later, you became an associate professor at North Carolina State University.

HH: What got me to North Carolina was not so much the university, but the State Department of Mental Health. The State wanted to know how to get alcoholics out of the hospital and integrated back into the community. Well, this was a natural systems problem. This was the early 1970s and systems approaches were new. This was my introduction to alcohol (Holder & Stratas 1972). I thought there must be something we can do with each community to reduce alcohol abuse, not only treat alcoholics.

A: General systems theory was one of the hottest things in social science in that period and you wrote about it (Holder 1966, 1969).

HH: I now think the premise is a little bit naive but it was very powerful at the time.

Mid-Career (1977–1987)

A: In 1977 you began a productive period in Chapel Hill. Tell us about the 10 years you spent at the Human Ecology Institute, including being its director for seven years.

HH: There was a group of us who said we need a think tank, a place that is not governed by state funding, a place to explore social challenges more freely, a non-profit organization. THEI was my first exposure to public policy as a vehicle of change.

A: You began writing about computer simulations during this period.

HH: My personal holy grail was to build a rigorously tested science-based computer model which States or local communities could use. At that time I learned from the increase in the US minimum drinking age that science with good politics makes a difference. So I began studies of alcohol policy in the 1980s and then built a whole part of my career around such research.

A: Toward the end of your years in North Carolina, you start writing about health insurance and cost offsets.

HH: Under research support from NIAAA, we performed a series of cost studies.

California Years (1987–present)

A: Who or what led you to come to Berkeley in 1987?

HH: The Prevention Research Center, as I perceived it, was in difficulty. I was concerned that the science standard of this center was not as high as it should be. I had a deep desire for the alcohol prevention field to have a strong science base. Since the early 1970s I had realized that treatment alone was not the answer and prevention was essential. At this time, no one in the United States was talking about methods of prevention, other than school education. Then I read the 'Purple Book' (the color of its cover) about taking a public health approach to alcohol prevention (Bruun et al. 1975). It changed my professional career. An outcome was my first book (Holder 1987), a sort of American answer to the Purple Book. As the new director, I wanted to bring that perspective to the Prevention Research Center (PRC). I wanted this center to be a true flagship for US alcohol prevention research. I wanted the very best prevention science to be undertaken here.

A: Of the people you brought in, who has brought you joy, personally, intellectually?

HH: When I first arrived, Genevieve Ames and Robert Saltz were already at the center. They were conducting good research. Joel Grube, who is now the center director, was a postdoctoral student here, and after seeing his capacity I knew we absolutely had to hire him. Paul Grunewald, who is now scientific director for the center, showed up and said, 'If you hire me, I want to be an apprentice.' Those were the perfect words for me to hear.

A: What is it that makes some alcohol research centers great and others merely good?

HH: First, if you are a director, it is very important that you do not get your ego attached to a certain hierarchy or structure. I certainly had my own ego attachments, but I was particularly taken with the success of the folks working with me. Not all center directors or leaders see it that way. If their name is not the first author on the paper, they think they have lost something. Second would be find good people and stick with them. Do not tolerate mediocrity; and then the third element for success is to have very high standards.

A: Turning to one of the best-known PRC projects, you conducted a 5-year community trial with alcohol problem prevention (Holder et al. 2000), which was a success in an area where the normative result is failure.

HH: I actually honor those other failures because I learned from them. I found that most community prevention trials lacked sufficient strength of intervention or dosage for a long enough time. To succeed in community-based prevention, one must honor both the complexity and dynamics of a local system and undertake highly visible, politically salient and scientifically based strategies. If these three ingredients are not present, you are unlikely to have much prevention effect at the community level. The key to success is whether both scientists and community members can work in a true partnership to stimulate system changes. This is neither top-down nor bottom-up.

Internationalism

A: What accounts for your long-term involvement in so many international projects?

HH: Probably because I was a blue-collar kid who never got to go to Europe. I did not start doing extensive international travel until the 1980s. Then I realized that Americans knew very little about alcohol policy, but there were three countries that knew a great deal: Finland, Sweden and Norway.

A: How did you become involved in major international projects such as *Alcohol Policy and the Public Good* (Edwards et al. 1994) and *Alcohol: No ordinary commodity?* (Babor et al. 2003)?

HH: Well, I was involved because this remarkable man in England, Griffith Edwards, invited me. I got to know Griffith through the first project, Alcohol Policy and the Public Good. I thought, this is someone I want to sit beside, to learn from. I remember it so clearly because my 90-year-old father made his first European trip with me for our first project meeting in London. I took my father to Griffith's home for an opening reception for the working group and Griffith and Sue were so kind to him. What I also appreciate about Griffith, who had a huge influence on me whether he realizes it or not, is his openness to different ideas. He is always interested in fresh perspectives and bright people. His openness taught me a great deal. And, he demonstrated that if you were interested in or committed to a certain cause that you could have an effect if you were persistent enough.

A: That leads naturally to a question about *Alcohol Policy and the Public Good.* It aspired to public policy relevance. Do you feel it had such an impact?

HH: I was pleasantly surprised by that book. I was somewhat sceptical that anybody would ever read a book written by a bunch of scientists. But Griffith set two standards. First, all our statements must be correct and scientifically accurate. If we do not know, say so. Secondly, the writing must be readable, and I think those two qualities made it a best seller.

Closing Thoughts

A: Some people have a hard time retiring. But you seem extremely happy to be fully retired. Am I misreading that?

HH: No, you are reading it perfectly! I think some people saw me as intensely attached to my work because I spent so many hours in research. However, I take my full identity from where ever I am in the moment, maybe because I was a blue-collar kid. I mean, I learned to work at a farm; I learned how to handle tools and build things. Now that I do not come into the office but once every 6 weeks or so, I have time to work in my garden (especially my roses); I build stone walls, I do sculpture. It is all perfectly satisfying.

A: And anyway, isn't paid retirement the dream of a blue-collar kid?

HH: That is true! But I still get invited to great conferences and have opportunities to help.

References

Babor, T. F., Caetano, R., Casswell, S., Edwards, G., Giesbrecht, N., Graham, K., Grube, J. W., Gruenewald, P. J., Hill, L., Holder, H., Homel, R., Österberg, E., Rehm, J., Room, R. & Rossow, I. (2003) *Alcohol: No Ordinary Commodity.* Oxford: Oxford University Press.

Bruun, K., Edwards, G., Lumio, M., Makela, K., Pan, L. & Popham, R. (1975) *Alcohol Control Policies in Public Health Perspective.* Helsinki: Finnish Foundation for Alcohol Studies.

Edwards, G., Anderson, P., Babor, T., Casswell, S., Ferrence, R., Giesbrecht, N., Godfrey, C., Holder, H. D., Lemmens, P., Mäkelä, K., Midanik, L., Norström, T., Österberg, E., Romelsjö, A., Room, R., Simpura, J. & Skog, O.-J. (1994) *Alcohol Policy and the Public Good.* Oxford: Oxford University Press.

Holder, H. D. (1966) General systems theory and education. Parts I and II. *Public School Forum,* 2, 23–27.

Holder, H. D. (1969) Mental health and the search for new organizational strategies: a systems proposal. *Archives of General Psychiatry,* 20, 190–217.

Holder, H. D., ed. (1987) *Advances in Substance Abuse: Behavioral and Biological Research (Supplement 1). Control Issues in Alcohol Abuse Prevention: Strategies for States and Communities).* Greenwich, CT: JAI Press.

Holder, H. D., Gruenwald, P. J., Ponicki, W., Treno, A., Grube, J., Saltz, R. et al. (2000) Effect of community-based interventions in high risk drinking and alcohol-related injuries. *JAMA,* 248, 2341–2347.

Holder, H. D. & Stratas, N. (1972) A systems approach to alcoholism programming. *American Journal of Psychiatry,* 129, 32–37.

33

Conversation with Rudolf Moos

Rudolf (Rudy) Moos is a researcher whose work over many years has had a particular colouring of creativity and sensitivity toward the complexities of the human condition. His works have thrown much light on treatment processes.

Early Years: Emigration and Immigration

Addiction (A): Before we talk about your professional career, tell me something about your early life.

Rudolf Moos (RM): I had quite a difficult time in my childhood. I was born in Berlin, during the rise of National Socialism. After living in Berlin for a few years, I was hidden in a car and smuggled out of Germany into Belgium in the dead of night. I lived in Belgium with relatives for a few months until it became possible to emigrate to England. I was separated from my mother and father during much of this time, so it was quite a stressful upheaval, and I had a hard time adjusting to all the changes.

A: How did you eventually get to the United States?

RM: At the beginning of World War II, I lived with my aunt and uncle in Birmingham, England, and I had some more problems at that time. London and other cities in England were being bombed, and the British decided that young children would be safer if they were evacuated into the countryside. So I was evacuated, but this entailed another separation from familiar people and surroundings. I became quite upset at this new change and was eventually taken back to Birmingham. Soon after, my parents and I obtained a visa to enter the United States. We were fortunate to be able to come directly to San Francisco, where we had a distant relative. It was then that I conjured up a Guardian Angel, who I thought must have helped me come through all these experiences.

A: How were the next years as you were growing up?

RM: I had a difficult time adjusting to the new circumstances. I was somewhat isolated and did not have many friends at school. I also was rather unruly and difficult to control. My family was quite poor at the time, and so I began to take odd jobs as soon as I could. My first job was to deliver newspapers; however, I was fired because I dumped all the newspapers into a neighbor's basement instead of delivering them. My saving grace was that I loved to read and I lost myself in historical and biographical novels. My high school experience was also not very pleasant. I was still not very well adjusted and had trouble fitting into school social life. I enjoyed my courses and did relatively well academically, but this was at a school where less than 5% of the graduates went on to university.

Rejuvenation

A: So what happened after you graduated from high school?

RM: At that time, there were not as many choices as there are now. I could not afford to go to Stanford. I went to the University of California and, at around that time, my life took a turn for the better. I first lived with a family and helped with housework and childcare, so I had essentially free room and board. I enjoyed a few of my courses, and I did moderately well and was intrigued by some of the content, especially psychology. I also adapted much better socially and was elected President of the Scholastic Honor Society.

A: What influenced your choice of graduate school and the field you specialized in?

RM: I was told I should go elsewhere to graduate school, but I had moved around so much earlier in my life that I was happy to stay put. So I stayed at the University of California and chose to pursue graduate work in clinical psychology. I chose psychology, because I thought it would enable me to study people and their motivations, to find out why some individuals were able to overcome severe life crises and live normal lives, and perhaps to apply my knowledge to improve the world. I had rather grand ideas about what I hoped to do.

A: What happened after graduate school? Where did you begin your research career?

RM: I took a postdoctoral fellowship at the University of California Medical Center in San Francisco that combined clinical and psychobiological training. I was always interested in the biological substrate of behavior. Mark Rosenzweig and David Krech had just shown that rats raised in enriched environments developed different brain structures and chemistry than rats raised in deprived environments.[1] I was fascinated by these findings, which supported my ideas about the importance of social context.

A: And next?

RM: Due to chance and luck (or perhaps it was my Guardian Angel), Stanford University Medical Center was just expanding and becoming more research oriented. The Department of Psychiatry was looking for a clinically trained research psychologist who was comfortable with biological concepts. I was offered a position and, true to my wish to settle in one place, I accepted and have remained at Stanford and the affiliated Department of Veterans Affairs (VA) Medical Center ever since.

Disorder and Recovery

A: How did your research get started after you came to Stanford?

RM: I had a keen curiosity about the harsh conditions of life, and the disorder and dysfunction that often seem to accompany them. As chance would have it, my first clinical experience was with alcoholic patients. This led me to ask why some people who become dependent on alcohol and drugs can stop using them and lead essentially normal lives; and why do some people who suffer from depression improve and manage to live free of apparent symptoms? Some colleagues chided me for asking the wrong questions.

A: You took this advice?

RM: I found support for my ideas in the concept that life crises are turning points, times of opportunity as well as risk.[2] I was fortunate when Erich Lindemann came to Stanford; I formed a bond with him and benefited from his wise counsel. I learned that many people are remarkably resilient. They manage to confront and transcend the most profound life crises and to lead healthy, productive lives. I thought the answer to this question would be a prize worthy of the chase.

A : What were some of the experiences that led to your focus upon social contexts?

RM: Personality theory and psychoanalytical thinking held sway when I was in graduate school. These theories posited that one could understand and predict what individuals would do on the basis of their personal predilections and characteristics. But I knew from my personal experience, and from the many stories I heard about the vicissitudes of life for family members and friends, that this was not true. I thought that these theories overlooked the role of the environment, or social context, as a key influence on human behavior. I quickly found out that these ideas were hardly new and that, more than 100 years ago, there had been a strong emphasis in psychiatry on moral treatment and the curative power of the social context. I was able to learn more from Maxwell Jones during his visits to Stanford.[3]

Treatment Environments

A: So you decided to focus your work upon social contexts. How did that research develop and progress over time?

RM: I focused first upon patients and staff in psychiatric programs, and I showed that they behaved quite differently in the varied settings in these programs, such as community meetings, group counseling and free time. Soon, I had an opportunity to test my ideas in an ideal naturalistic setting. I demonstrated what I already knew: people vary important aspects of their behavior in different situations.

A: What then led to the actual development of measures to assess treatment environments?

RM: Once I had shown that people's behavior varied a good deal from one context to another, I thought that the next logical step was to assess these contexts and find out how they differed. I chose to consider first hospital-based substance abuse and psychiatric treatment programs. This energized me to obtain comparable data on 160 programs all over the United States, and the results were comparable.[4,5]

A: How did you move from specific items that characterized treatment programs to identify the underlying dimensions of treatment environments?

RM: We used a combination of conceptual and empirical approaches.

A: When you conducted this work, did you think that these dimensions might be related to patients' outcomes?

RM: Yes. We looked first at in-program outcomes and found that patients in supportive and well-organized programs with moderate to high performance expectations were more likely to be satisfied and self-confident, and to become involved in program activities.[5]

Other Settings, Other Countries

A: How did this work evolve to focus upon other types of environments?

RM: As we were conducting our work on hospital-based treatment programs, patients were being moved rapidly into community programs. It seemed no patients would be left in hospitals and our laboriously produced assessment procedure would become extinct. Perhaps it was my Guardian Angel who convinced me to use this impending crisis as an opportunity to see whether our findings would hold in community programs.

A: How did you proceed?

RM: We followed the same procedures we had used earlier and found that residents and staff perceived apparently similar community programs quite differently. More importantly, the associations between community program environments and patients' in-program outcomes were comparable to those shown in hospital programs. For example, clients in more supportive and well-organized programs tended to be more satisfied and hopeful about treatment.[5]

A: Then you took these ideas even wider?

RM: We found out later that the same three sets of dimensions could also be used to characterize other types of settings, such as families, the work-place and social groups.[6] I had a grand thought that some of these idea might help to understand and improve these communities and perhaps the human context.

Into the Frying Pan: Alcohol Abuse

A: Over time your work began to focus more upon alcohol use and abuse; how did that come about?

RM: I thought it was time to find out more about how treatment influenced patients' outcomes. I could have focused upon any number of disorders, but there were several reasons why I chose to study alcoholism. Most importantly, I wanted to focus upon a prevalent disorder, which would make the work more broadly applicable. I also thought that the disorder should have a clear behavioral component, which would make it more likely that the social context would affect it. We recruited five diverse residential alcoholism programs and focused initially upon the treatment environment and its associations with patients' treatment experiences and treatment outcome. However, these treatment-related factors typically explained less than 10% of the variance in patients' outcomes.[7] So I turned my attention to the real world in which people live and began to focus upon patients' broader life contexts.

A: What did you find?

RM: The findings showed that patients with relatively severe disorders could improve. At a 10-year follow-up, more than half the surviving and successfully followed patients were in recovery. These findings confirmed my optimistic view of the world and my idea that people could always change for the better.

A: What accounted for these positive outcomes?

RM: Patients with fewer stressful life circumstances and more cohesive and well-organized families in the first 6 months after treatment, showed better outcome at 2 years.[7]

Into the Fire: Substance Abuse

A: Your work then broadened to focus upon other substance use disorders, and an evaluation of 12-Step facilitation and cognitive–behavioral treatment.

RM: We selected two of the most prevalent treatment orientations for substance use disorders; that is, 12-Step facilitation (TSF) treatment and cognitive–behavioral treatment (CBT). We studied more than 3500 patients, and we assessed them at treatment entry and discharge, and at 1-year, 2-year and 5-year follow-ups. We identified a direct connection between the quality of the work-place for staff, the quality of the treatment environment and patients' improvement.[8] We also found that participation in continuing out-patient care, and especially in 12-Step self-help groups such as Alcoholics Anonymous (AA), was associated with better outcomes. Individuals who obtained help in the first year after recognizing their alcohol-related problems had better 1-year and 3-year outcomes than did those who obtained no help.[9]

A: You have also been involved in studying older adults who have problems with alcohol.

RM: To address these issues, we initiated a study of late-middle-aged individuals. We assessed these individuals at baseline, when they were between 55 and 65 years of age, and followed them after 1 year, 4 years and 10 years.

We were surprised to find that about 25–40% of older women and men had high-risk drinking patterns.[10]

Stress and Coping

A: You had an interest in stress and coping. How did you continue to pursue that interest?

RM: In general, we found that people who rely more on approach and less on avoidance coping tend to be more successful in managing life crises and their consequences. People often show tenacious resilience and experience personal growth in the aftermath of adversity.[11]

Professional Context

A: How did your professional work-place and context affect you?

RM: David Hamburg was Chair of Psychiatry at Stanford, and he established a cohesive, goal-directed and structured social context. He mentored and taught me how to cope with some of the erratic excesses of academia. I collaborated with a group of experts on health care decision-making, and we applied to develop a Center whose primary foci were on screening and decision-making in health care. the Center for Health Care Evaluation. The Center has grown exponentially, has provided us with stable support for more than 20 years.

Colleagues

A: What about some of the personal relationships and colleagues who helped sustain your work?

RM: I have been lucky to have had long-term productive relationships with several superb colleagues and collaborators. Initially, there was Evelyn Bromet. These and other colleagues helped to provide a stable and supportive social context within which I flourished. Most importantly, my wife Bernice has been a source of comfort and advice throughout my entire career. Bernice is a computer programmer; we have worked together for many years. Now, more than 44 years later, we have six grandchildren.

Role Models

A: Were there other individuals or role models who influenced you?

RM: Yes. In addition to my mentors and colleagues, there were three important personal role models. I was named after my grandfather, Rudolf Moos, who was a very successful businessman. He founded the Salamander shoe business. I like to think that he was the model for my orientation to detail, organizational skills, and love of learning and history. He made a fortune, and then lost everything because of the hyperinflation in Germany in the 1920s. He exemplified a stubborn unwillingness to succumb to life crises. Uncle Paul was Grandfather Rudolf's brother. He was an iconoclast. He became a musicologist. I like to think that his example fortified my contrarian instincts. Albert Einstein was Grandfather Rudolf's cousin. My grandfather's mother was from the Einstein family; more importantly, my grandfather knew Albert Einstein quite well. I have heard personal stories about Einstein all my life and, in a very real sense, I owe my career to him.

Ongoing Odyssey

A: You are in your fifth decade of work. What is your main interest now and what do you intend to pursue in your future work?

RM: I have a renewed interest in active ingredients associated with effective treatments and stable remission. Quite recently, I have speculated about the role of four theories that may identify the main processes involved in the development and remission of addictive disorders. These are social control theory, which emphasizes the importance of bonding, goal direction and monitoring; behavioral economic theory, which emphasizes the role and importance of rewarding activities other than substance use; social learning theory, which focuses upon the importance of abstinence-oriented norms and abstinence-oriented models in recovery; and stress and coping theory, which emphasizes building self-efficacy and coping skills. More broadly, it is hard to conceive of an Ultimate Blueprint where structure begins with genes, when genes are subject to contextual influences such as natural selection and mutation. The Ultimate Blueprint must encompass an ongoing interplay between structure and function.

A: Finally, from a personal perspective, how would you sum up what you have learned from your research experience?

RM: I have been on an odyssey of quest, discovery and renewed quest. We know that personal resources and specific aspects of treatment, life context and appraisal and coping are important, and that all these factors are linked closely. We have made some progress, but the essence of why some people do better than others is still beyond our grasp. Each question we have posed has led to a set of intriguing but also more complex questions.

Notes

1. Rosenzweig M. R., Krech D., Bennett E. L., Diamond M. C. Effects of environmental complexity and training on brain chemistry and anatomy: a replication and extension. *J Comp Physiol Psychol* 1962; 55: 429–37.
2. Lindemann E. *Beyond Grief: Studies in Crisis Intervention*. New York: Aronson; 1979.
3. Jones M. *The Therapeutic Community*. New York: Basic Books; 1953.
4. Moos R. *Evaluating Treatment Environments: A Social Ecological Approach*. New York: Wiley; 1974.
5. Moos R. *Evaluating Treatment Environments: The Quality of Psychiatric and Substance Abuse Programs*. New Brunswick, NJ: Transaction; 1997.
6. Moos R. *The Social Climate Scales: A User's Guide*, 3rd edn. Menlo Park, CA: Mind Garden; 2003.

7. Moos R., Finney J., Cronkite R. *Alcoholism Treatment: Context, Process, and Outcome*. New York: Oxford; 1990.
8. Moos R., Moos B. The staff workplace and the quality and outcome of substance abuse treatment. *J Stud Alcohol* 1998; 59: 43–51.
9. Moos R., Moos B. Participation in treatment and Alcoholics Anonymous: a 16-year follow-up of initially untreated individuals. *J Clin Psychol* 2006; 62: 735–50.
10. Schutte K., Nichols K., Brennan P., Moos R. A 10-year follow-up of older former problem drinkers: risk of relapse and implications of successfully sustained remission. *J Stud Alcohol* 2003; 64: 367–74.
11. Schaefer J. A., Moos R. The context for personal growth: life crises, individual and social resources, and coping. In: Tedeschi R., Park C., Calhoun L. *Posttraumatic Growth: Positive Changes in the Aftermath of Crisis*. NJ: Erlbaum; 1998, pp. 99–125.

34

Conversation with Juha Partanen

Juha Partanen is a Finnish social researcher with strong international interests. His work has often focused on drinking and drinking problems but he has also been concerned with wider issues. For many years he has worked at the Finnish Social Research Institute for Alcohol Studies and was, for a time, its Director.

Starting Out

Addiction (A): Where did you start?

Juha Partanen (JP): I grew up in the country near the Russian border. I am basically a country boy, although I have enjoyed my stays in places such as Paris or Tokyo.

A: You came to Helsinki for university?

JP: Yes. I started my studies at the University of Helsinki at the age of 17 in 1954—statistics, mathematics and sociology. It was a great thing to find Ruth Benedict's *Patterns of Culture.*

A: That was almost 10 years after the war. What was the atmosphere like at the university?

JP: Politically very quiet, yes. Apart from my mathematics professors, the education at the faculty of political science was not very inspiring. There was practically no tutoring or guidance; one had to find things oneself. This is the reason that I have had several blind alleys in my career. For example, I spent several years in the 1960s trying to develop a logic of data analysis. But nothing came of it, and there was no one to tell me that the whole effort was totally futile.

A: What was your first job?

JP: This started before I was 10 years old, and it began with plants. Mathematics also came very early—it was almost as important as girls for me. Later on when studying mathematics, I realized that I lacked mathematical imagination. I suppose I like to deal with empirical things and raw data, not only abstract things.

A: So what were the first problems that you worked on concretely?

JP: I had some jobs, minor work, at the time I was studying. But then my first contact with alcohol research was when, as a young statistician, I was hired, more or less by accident, as a research assistant to an American visiting scholar, Peter Park. He was visiting the Finnish Foundation for Alcohol Studies in Helsinki. His research problem was to find out whether Jellinek's famous horseshoe model of the development of alcoholism fitted the careers of Finnish alcoholics (Park 1962). It did not.

A: Other early influences at that time?

JP: I met Kettil Bruun, who was secretary of the Foundation; but that was only a short-term job. I was still far more interested in mathematics and statistics, and very little in alcohol issues. I was an adjunct acting professor of statistics for one year at the university, and arranged a job at the Institute of Statistics at Stanford University. I spent most of 1964 there.

The Organization of Finnish Alcohol Research

A: 1964 was an exciting time to be in the San Francisco area?

JP: It was. There was the civil rights movement.

A: And when you reached home again?

JP: When I came back to Finland, I was offered a major project at the Social Research Institute for Alcohol Studies. The Institute had been founded in 1952 and administratively it was part of Alko, the Finnish Alcohol Monopoly, but it was an independent research unit. The idea was not so much to serve decision-making in Alko, but to provide an information basis for the discussion of alcohol issues in general. The Institute remained in Alko until 1995, when Alko lost its central position in alcohol policies, and we were transferred to STAKES, the National Research and Development Centre for Welfare and Health, under auspices of the Ministry of Health and Social Affairs. In addition to the Institute, there is the Finnish Foundation for Alcohol Studies, even more independent in its research policies.

A: How long did you stay at the Institute?

JP: The Institute became my home base for nearly 40 years, in daily contact with people such as Klaus Mäkelä, Pekka Sulkunen, Jussi Simpura, Marja Holmila and others. But the central figure, as long as he lived, was Kettil Bruun. Unfortunately, he died at the age of 61.

Twins, Restaurants and Marxist Theory

A: What was the major project you were hired for in 1964?

JP: Several years before the Foundation had launched a large multidisciplinary study on twins, and the Institute had collected a unique data set consisting of 902 male twin pairs. There was quite a substantial amount of information on their drinking habits, psychological variables, intelligence and a number of other things; but they had no one to analyse these data, so they hired me. Together with Kettil Bruun, I wrote the monograph entitled

Inheritance of Drinking Behaviour (Partanen et al. 1966). The main result was that the drinking variables showed a great deal of heritability.

A: Then, you started to conduct an observational study?

JP: I carried out some research on Finnish restaurants. In the 1960s most Finns never went to a restaurant. It was essentially an upper-class institution. Women were treated rather badly, and there were all kinds of controls. I conducted a population survey on the customers, and interviewed close to 200 restaurant managers. The people in Alko were keen on this silly idea that the restaurants could exert a civilizing influence on Finnish drinking. I carried out an analysis showing that the on-licence environment was much wetter than off-licence (Partanen 1975). That is why they went to restaurants. After that, I did not quite know what to do. But then in the 1970s came Marxist theory, and a study which occupied me for several years.

A: For that you were on leave from the Institute?

JP: I created a research group to study the state of democracy and equality in Finland. This period of my life lasted from 1971 to 1977. Although not directly involved in politics, we had to accept the fact that we were labelled as extreme left-wing activists. Altogether our project produced some 40 publications, among other things my Marxist-inspired analysis of advertising. Finally, I wrote a monograph with Jukka Gronow, a 500-page analysis of the Finnish political regime and its economic basis (Gronow et al. 1977). There were editorials, cartoons, TV debates and even pamphlets written to criticize us. A delegation led by the Archbishop to the Minister of Education asking that the financing of our project be cut off. Of course the Academy of Finland, keen on its independence, refused to do this.

A: Do you see it as having had an influence on Finnish society in the end?

JP: Not really, and, after these 30 years, it is more or less dated. The following year I was chosen to be head of the Institute for 5 years. I then took up the theme of alcohol education. It is almost unimaginable how free and independent we could be.

A: My impression from the outside was that there was also a tradition of encouraging people to have an interest outside alcohol?

JP: Yes. Going through the existing research literature, it became evident to me that alcohol education, as it is practised, simply does not work. I believed that it was important to take into account the media environment into which educational messages are inserted. One thing I did was to organize a seminar in which alcohol researchers and film experts discussed the content of some films (Partanen 1980). It was a very stimulating seminar, and it gave rise to eight articles altogether. I also published a few articles on whether one could make people understand and accept restrictive alcohol policies (Partanen & Montonen 1988).

A: Around this time you became interested in the developing world, but also more generally in alcohol on the international scene.

JP: Well, first it was Kenya, and that was another serendipitous affair. My ex-wife, a diplomat, was stationed at the Finnish embassy in Nairobi, and I wanted to visit her and our adopted daughter. So I presented a very modest, small-scale research proposal. I visited Kenya for 2 weeks at the beginning of 1985. The next year I spent some 4 months in Kenya. The idea was to interview relevant people in Kenya, and to write a report on the basis of the interviews. This very modest research idea began to grow. I then spent some 5 years, on and off, working on this topic (Partanen 1991). So I do not think that my analysis or my very modest suggestions have had any influence on alcohol policies in Kenya.

Heroic Drinking

A: But it was also about Finland in some ways?

JP: In some ways, yes. I tried to make a comparison between traditional drinking and the role of alcohol in the modern world. Some anthropologists have now claimed that there are societies, especially in Africa, where the use of alcohol is totally problem-free, and they have called it integrated drinking. I came to the conclusion that in reality there is no such thing. Problems are always lurking when alcohol or any other psychoactive substance is used. I have been fascinated by the notion of intoxication, or more generally altered states of consciousness, for a long time, and suggested various formulations to describe its character (Partanen 1983).

A: So any final conclusions from your African experience?

JP: The final theme was that African drinking presented a clear-cut contrast to the uses of alcohol in our modern world, and I characterized this contrast by introducing the notion of 'heroic drinking'. Heroic drinking for me means a kind of primordial pattern of drinking; it is a male affair. It is archaic, but also a persistent cultural form—there are still many uses for heroic drinking among contemporary young people: to assert their masculinity. Anyway, I presented *Sociability and Intoxication* as my dissertation in 1991, obtaining my doctorate at the mature age of 54 years.

A: It was granted with the highest distinction, which was the first time in 30 years in sociology at Helsinki.

JP: I had not needed a degree as I had no academic ambitions. But my dissertation work was of some use when I took part later in a collaborative project on alcohol policies in developing societies (Room et al. 2002).

A: Is there a problem with fitting national drinking behaviours into neat formats?

JP: In Denmark I would emphasize the ideology of tolerance they have there, and in the Netherlands the traditions of Christian charity, merchant-like pragmatism and social engineering, which they have also shown in drug issues. In Japan I emphasized the peculiar gender roles. I do not think there is any developed country in the world where the worlds of men and women are as separate as in Japan. I have spent nearly a year there on four occasions. It is still a mystery to me how such a highly developed society is able to deal so complacently with heavy male drinking.

Drugs as a Main Interest

A: So, after your dissertation?

JP: After that it was drugs, and that has been my main interest for the last 10 years. I was already interested in drug issues around 1970, when the first drug wave hit Finland. Since the 1990s, we have had a second drug wave: I have conducted some survey work, held several lecture series and written a number of articles in which I discussed the nature of the current drug problem and drug policies from a sociological point of view (e.g. Partanen 1998).

A: How would you like to see society deal with these problems?

JP: Some 20 years ago Kettil Bruun and Nils Christie pointed out the political uses of the drug problem—they termed it a 'suitable enemy' for the modern state (Christie & Bruun 2003). I think it is not an exaggeration to call this prevailing attitude towards drugs 'narcophobia'. It is quite evident that we cannot get rid of drugs. We have to learn ways to deal with their use, and the penalization of drug use does not make sense. What one should do in drug policies is to recognize the different uses of drugs, and to estimate the risks related to them. One should also recognize the informal controls among the users themselves and in their immediate environment—family and work, etc.—and encourage these kinds of control instead of simply official controls. I think one should apply similar policies to drugs as are applied nowadays to sex. People may choose their own forms of sexual behaviour nowadays, there are no uniform norms for it. The only way to suppress international drug criminality would be to legalize all drugs, in order to eliminate the private profit motive, but of course this is a totally utopian thought in the present circumstances.

Living in a Golden Age

A: So if you were being utopian, would you see an Alko for marijuana in Finland, a state corporation, and state stores?

JP: Why not? Or leave it to the medical profession, allowing users to obtain their supplies by prescription. But this will not happen tomorrow, no.

A: You are officially retired, but in fact still writing articles.

JP: Just little things, columns and poems.

A: Do you have any general thoughts, looking back?

JP: How should I say it? The fact is I have always been a rather lazy person, not very productive. I have felt that it is quite enough to put in one-third of the day for work. There are so many other interesting things in life. On the whole my life has been easy; but I have certainly been very fortunate in choosing the historical period in which I have lived. This period which the English historian, Eric Hobsbawm, has called 'the Golden Age of Mankind'—roughly the 30 years after the Second World War.

A: Tell me a little about the other interesting things that you have pursued.

JP: Well, my last four winters spent in Paris were a nice experience and there is, of course, this traditional trio, Wein, Weib und Gesang, which in my case has meant red wine, lady friends and chamber music. But I would like to add at least gardening and sailing, and outdoor life more generally.

A: You are quite a serious gardener?

JP: Semi-serious.

A: So we expect a little show in 2 months or so.

JP: I would say in a month, for the first one. The white rose of Finland.

References

Christie, N. & Bruun, N. (2003) *Den Gode Fiende: Narkotikapolitikk I Norden [Suitable Enemies: Drug Policy in the Nordic Countries]*, 3rd edn revised [1st edn 1985]. Oslo: Universitetsforlaget.

Gronow, J., Klemola, P. & Partanen, J. (1977) *Demokratian Rajat Ja Rakenteet: Tutkimus Suomalaisesta Hallitsemistavasta Ja Sen Taloudellisesta Perustasta [The Structures and Limits of Democracy: A Study on the Finnish Political Regime and its Economic Basis]*. Helsinki: WSOY.

Park, P. (1962) Drinking experiences of Finnish alcoholics in comparison with similar experiences of 192 English alcoholics. *Acta Psychiatrica Scandinavica*, 32, 227–246.

Partanen, J., ed. (1980) *Finnish Intoxication on the Screen*. Report no. 143. Helsinki: Social Research Institute of Alcohol Studies.

Partanen, J. (1975) On the role of situational factors in alcohol research: drinking in restaurants vs. drinking at home. *Drinking and Drug Practices Surveyor*, 10, 14–16.

Partanen, J. (1983) Toward a theory of intoxication. In: Room, R. & Collins, G. *Alcohol and Disinhibition: Nature and Meaning of the Link*, pp. 26–41. Research Monograph no. 12. Rockville, MD: National Institute on Alcohol Abuse and Alcoholism.

Partanen, J. (1991) *Sociability and Intoxication: Alcohol and Drinking in Kenya, Africa, and the Modern World*. Report no. 39. Helsinki: Finnish Foundation for Alcohol Studies.

Partanen, J. (1998) Merchant, priest and humble engineer: observations from Rotterdam's drug scenes. *Nordisk Alcohol- & narkotikatidskrift*, 15, 52–67 [English supplement].

Partanen, J., Bruun, K. and Markkanen, T. (1966) *Inheritance of Drinking Behavior: A Study on Intelligence, Personality, and Use of Alcohol of Adult Twins* (Finnish Foundation for Alcohol Studies. Publication 14).

Partanen, J., Bruun, K. & Markkanen, T. (1966) *Inheritance of Drinking Behaviour: A Study on Intelligence, Personality, and the Use of Alcohol of Adult Twins*. Helsinki: Finnish Foundation for Alcohol Studies.

Partanen, J. & Montonen, M. (1988) *Alcohol and the Mass Media*. EURO Reports and Studies no. 108. Copenhagen: World Health Organization.
Room, R., Jernigan, D., Carlini-Marlatt, B., Gureje, O., Mäkelä, K., Marshall, M. et al. (2002) *Alcohol in Developing Societies: A Public Health Approach*. Helsinki: Finnish Foundation for Alcohol Studies.

35

Commentary

Kerstin Stenius

Sons of the Golden Age

Many decisive conditions influencing the careers, choices and interests of researchers will change as the addiction field matures, making it difficult to learn from the life courses of previous researchers. Our older colleagues have met very different challenges than we. The material for this chapter is a set of seven inteviews (M. Douglas Anglin, Walter Clark, Joseph Gusfield, Ragnar Hauge, Harold Holder, Rudy Moos, and Juha Partanen) that feature careers in social science and epidemiology.

Still, as they tell us their stories and as the history of addiction research now stretches over several generations there are certain constants that make it meaningful. The balancing between different motives for knowledge production, the complex relations between politics and science, even the same research questions that have to be asked over and over again are all part of the play. For as the youngest one in the group, Douglas Anglin, puts it: a common insight today is that nearly every question has been asked and some good and some bad thinking has already applied to most issues.

Most of the researchers interviewed in this section had some experience or contact – even if not altogether positive - with what John Henry Newman described as the academic cloister ideal, the small, multidisciplinary academic community of masters and students where knowledge itself was a sufficient reward and its pursuit the sole proper purpose of academic life. True knowledge can not only be an instrument to change the world, but is an end in itself, according to Newman (1907).

In *The uses of universities* Kerr (2001) describes how academic communities following Newman's ideal, first in the US from the 1930s and somewhat later in most other countries, were succeeded by the modern university, a university "neither entirely of the world, nor entirely apart from it". This was a more democratic institution, but still during the 1950s and early 1960s a place for the privileged few. Gradually it was transformed into a growing "knowledge factory". Research became increasingly dependent on purchasers' demand for knowledge and closely linked to the industrial state's striving for economic growth. With those steps, universities ceased to represent a distant and independently critical force in society (Elzinga 1969). But this development also coincided with optimistic expansion of higher education, when sciences and especially social sciences became more prominent.

The unavoidable tension in social and behavioral research between chasing and enjoying knowledge for knowledge sake, and being useful, of analyzing and being of the world, is obvious in all interviews here. Our men of science have tackled this tension in different ways: some have had a more Newman-like approach, others stress usefulness as the prime legitimacy for their research. Being good social researchers, they all know that social knowledge is contextual, and social research is about concrete, historically situated phenomena. Theories should be applied and developed to improve the understanding of facts. In this way they have managed to produce knowledge that goes beyond their particular cases.

Big Questions and a Vast Land to Explore

Alcohol and drug research was institutionalised as a specialty only after the Second World War and the growth in the number of research centres was slow, but steady, until the 1980s (Morisano & Babor 2010). As Walter Clark notes, it was not until the 1970s that a US social scientist could easily define him- or herself as an alcohol researcher. Maybe this happened somewhat earlier in the Nordic countries.

The social and epidemiological researchers interviewed here have been among the first to be recruited to the new centres for social addiction research and some were active in setting them up.

They came into alcohol and drug research with a strong foothold in traditional, general disciplines; law and criminology (Ragnar Hauge), mathematical sociology (Harold Holder), psychology and biology (Rudolf Moos), statistics, mathematics and sociology (Juha Partanen), epidemiology and cultural sociology (Walter Clark), history and sociology (Joseph Gusfield). Only Douglas Anglin, the youngest was recruited, accidentally, as a young student directly into drug research.

"How things become problems" (Gusfield), "the intriguing uncertainty of human behavior" (Holder), "the logic of data analysis" (Partanen), "why some people are able to overcome severe life crises" (Moos): these are some of the big questions that our interviewees tell us they asked themselves, before entering the alcohol and drug field. And even if Juha Partanen now claims that his was an impossible question, and is annoyed that nobody told him so, one wonders if the researchers' background in more general disciplines stimulated bigger questions and was very good for the addiction research that they produced?

From today's perspective we can envy them, equipped with curiosity, intelligence, excellent theoretical training and the courage to ask big questions.

And even if they were country boys, the whole nation became their territory as they explored the terrain of alcohol and drug research. In these success stories, the constraints of established hierarchies and academic competition are almost absent. Cross-disciplinary research was natural. The world and international contacts must have seemed so much more exciting than today, but at the same time as the international addiction research milieu was very small.

"The social sciences were desperate for more people", as Hauge says about the early sixties in Norway. Funding for research was initially small, but it was a time of optimism and he and others joined in the construction of the new centres.

Many of the people interviewed have asked what one could call the second set of addiction research questions. Not only why some people become dependent, but why do some who are dependent get out of that situation? Not only why young criminals do not follow prevailing norms, but what are the norms that they do have? Not only why workers drank so much in the 19th century, but why abstention was so important for middle class people? Not only how one could move more drinking into civilizing and publicly controlled milieu of the restaurants, from the private sphere, but whether drinking establishments really are civilizing? They started out in a climate that was dominated by Jellinek's disease theory, psychoanalytical or personality theories, behavioristic theories about human learning, system theories and Marxist theories. They confronted these theories with reality, in a time that favoured radical questioning.

Several of these pioneers describe how they had to, or rather were allowed to, start their research work, as outsiders, by reading all the previous research on the topic and even learning some basic methodology. They were recruited because they were good and clever people, not because they were alcohol or drug specialists. Walter Clark describes how he recruited Robin Room: "being an honest man [he] said 'but I know nothing about sociology. I replied, 'don't worry, there's nothing to know'.

Most of them became members of small teams where there was cooperation across the disciplinary boundaries, and notably between medicine and social science, seemed to have been natural. For example, Rudolf Moos started at a medical centre, Juha Partanen with a twin study, where genetic explanations played a central role, Walter Clark was recruited by Genevieve Knupfer, a sociologist and psychiatrist. These interviews convey the enjoyment of scientific exploration in an egalitarian and intellectually stimulating atmosphere with a fair amount of freedom.

Most of them spent a lot of time outside their offices, interviewing the general public, setting up evaluation procedures in treatment units or local communities, or observing behavior in restaurants. One wonders, for instance, if Walter Clark would have stressed the important issue of underreporting of drinking in surveys, or been so pre-occupied by the norms of drinking situations if he had not met and interviewed hundreds of drinkers - and on the basis of these interviews had to name the factors produced by the analyses? Or if Douglas Anglin would have ended up with his ecological view of treatment without his long and close contact with treatment institutions?

It is obvious that a lot of hard work and persistence, even stubbornness, lies behind the research results produced by these researchers. Juha Partanen's scientific spirit seems to have moved from one topic to the next more freely than most. As the others look back they describe how one question eventually leads to another, fairly closely related.

Social Engineering in Radical Times

The addiction research centres in the Nordic countries were established in connection with the consolidation of the welfare states, as Ragnar Hauge notes, and with a particular aim to produce knowledge that could inform and lead to the solution of the growing social problems connected to the increasing consumption of intoxicants. The researcher's task was to ask and possibly answer questions that concerned the whole nation. Social engineering is a feature that is common to the US and the Nordic countries. As Gusfield puts it: "In the dominant rhetoric all problems are solvable - and somebody or something can be blamed".

The post war decades were a period of increasing democratization. Experiences of the war, of the Civil Rights movement and of 1968 influenced the perspectives on society held by most of the researchers interviewed here. The interviews give only a fraction of the picture. Joseph Gusfield was active in the Civil rights movement and continued as an activist in treatment issues. Ragnar Hauge spent 18 months in a work camp as a conscientious objector. Juha Partanen was publicly labeled a left-wing activist in the 1970s Finland. These experiences naturally colored the researchers' studies of problems and problem solving. Social power took a central position in their studies. Gusfield raised questions about who has the power to define drinking problems. Moos was concerned with norms and normal drinking rather than with the disease concept and Clark in his surveys questioned the labelling of some persons as deviant drinkers. Juha Partanen went so far as to study the entire capitalist regime in Finland.

For those who studied control, treatment or prevention, like Hauge, Moos and Anglin, integration of the homeless and poor, the marginalized drinkers or the persistent stigmatization of injecting drug users implied a questioning of the exercise of statutory power. These addiction researchers identified themselves with those whose interests were not prioritized in the building of welfare systems, or those who were unfairly blamed. Poor alcoholics and later drug users were obviously groups whose conditions did and still do point at the limits of the ideals of universalism.

Research and Political Influence

Public communication has been an integrated part of the research work for several of our interviewees. Ragnar Hauge has written more in Norwegian than in English. He writes for Norwegians with interest in his issues and is a very well known figure in Norwegian public life. Harold Holder stresses that scientific writing in the policy field must be readable for research to have any effect, and that success requires partnership between researchers and decision makers. Others, such as Douglas Anglin, seem to have been focusing more on interacting with professionals.

Given their preoccupation with improving the situation particularly for those with less power it is natural that some of them can tell stories of their conflicts with the political establishment. Ragnar Hauge is famous in the Nordic countries for his public advocacy for a drug policy based on facts rather than on fear and ungrounded wishes. Douglas Anglin fights for more methadone treatment and accuses the US society of ethical negligence and medical malpractice. Harold Holder's skepticism in relation to state funding made him move in the late 1970s to a non-profit organization, where research was freer. They have all gained respect by insisting on what today is called evidence-based policy.

These researchers were among the first in a new field, and lived through its most expansionist period. They have also experienced moments of great disappointment as they look back. We hear many variations on the theme: from "political decision makers only listen to suitable arguments", to "my work did not really have any influence on Finnish society" to "you must work in partnership with them if you want to get results". But I would argue that behind all these retrospective statements is the passion of serious researchers, who wanted and still want to make a difference in the world.

Concluding Remarks

In these reflections I have stressed the similarities between the interviewees more than their differences. Their personal and scientific temperaments are certainly very different, and in that sense have given many role models. But it is easy both to respect and like all these men, who seem to have enjoyed uncertainty and even conflicts. "Tension is often productive", as Joseph Gusfield says.

Juha Partanen feels like a lucky person, who lived his formative years as a researcher during what Hobsbawm calls the Golden Age of Mankind, after WWII until the end of the1970s; a period of relative harmony, social optimism and expansion in Europe and the USA. All in all, this seems like a group reporting on happy careers. In many ways, all of these researchers have been able to follow Newman's ideals: they have not been forced to early specialization and narrowly concentrated research interests. With enough resources, time and exiting networks they have been able to accumulate knowledge and wisdom.

They have asked really important questions, influenced our conceptualisation of the world and paved the way for future research.

Subsequent generations will want to continue the conversation these people have started, but will also have to secure conditions that will enable equally good discussion.

References

Elzinga, Aant (1969) Forskningspolitik I Sverige (Swedish research policy). In: Ambjörnsson, Ronny, Andersson Gunnar & Elzinga, Aant : *Forskning och politik i Sverige, Sovjet och USA (Research and politics in Sweden, the Soviet Union and the US)*. Stockholm: Aldus.

Kerr, Clark (2001) *The Uses of the University*. Fifth Edition. Cambridge: Harvard University Press.

Morisano, Dominique & Babor, Thomas (2010) The Global Infrastructure for Addiction Science: The Public Heath Perspective. Poster presented at the *Annual Meeting of the College on Problems of Drug Dependence*, Scottsdale, Arizona, June 13, 2010.

Newman, John Henry (1907) *The Idea of a University*. New York, Bombay & Calcutta: Longmans, Green, and Co.

Part 5—Clinicians and Clinical Research: American Contributions

36

Conversation with Sheila Blume

Sheila Blume has been widely influential in the substance misuse field in the United States of America and more widely at many different levels. She has, in addition, played an important role in enhancing professional interest in pathological gambling, its measurement and its treatment. Her career early exemplified many of the difficulties that women had to overcome in entering this field.

Early Years

Addiction (A): Your career has been an accomplished one. Tell me how it began.

Sheila Blume (SB): I was born in Brooklyn. My father was an engineer and a self-made man who had grown up in poverty, and my mother had also come from the slums of New York. They were very interested in education and opportunity. I as a woman had the good luck of choosing my own path and graduated from Abraham Lincoln High School, a very good public high school, where I met my husband, Marty. I attended Cornell University but never got my bachelor's degree. I applied to medical school after 3 years, which was unusual. My challenge in college was to decide on a career. After my sophomore year, I got to study invertebrate biology at the Woods Hole laboratory and see what laboratory research was like. During that summer, I decided that I would go into medicine. I found the biological research of the 1950s too slowly paced for me.

A: Was that unusual for a woman in the 1950s to apply to medical school, especially after only 3 years of college?

SB: Yes. I was influenced by a professor named Marcus Singer, bless his heart, who had come to Cornell from Harvard Medical School. I was auditing his course in neuroanatomy and he was asked to interview me for medical school. He was aware of my interest and motivation, and he talked me into going to Harvard.

A: By that time, you had decided that research was not the career for you because it took too long to get results—correct?

SB: Yes, well, pure research. Medical research was OK. Harvard was then in the tenth year of a 10-year experiment. The first year they took women at Harvard Medical School, in 1944, was very late, given the times. They were forced into it by World War II. The medical school had been admitting boys right out of high school while refusing women from the best colleges. We were most unwelcome.

A: How did you know you were not welcome?

SB: How would you like to be sitting in a giant lecture room and have a professor show slides of nude women in compromising positions, as a joke? Anyway, I graduated with honors, as did most of the women. Women were on top of the class, and we were resented for that, too.

Wanting Out of Boston

A: What got you through those times?

SB: Ahh . . . true love! In the fall of my first year, I met Marty again and we were married at the end of the school year. And we fell in love right away and we stayed that way. When we needed to relax, we had our favorite places. One was a Japanese garden in the Boston Museum of Art. That is how we came to be interested in Japanese art. When I finally completed my internship at Childrens' Medical Center, and he gained his PhD in physics, we wanted out of Boston. I did not want to climb the corporate (academic) ladder, which for women was so hard anyway. We met only one female professor in our whole 4 years at Harvard. Marty and I wanted to go as far away as we could, so we applied for Fulbright grants in Japan and we got them. Marty and I decided to go around the world on the surface—no flying. We wanted to see how big the world was and were gone for 3 years. Although I had mastered the 12 lessons in my Teach Yourself Japanese book, as I had never heard it spoken, I could not understand the language. But to my pleasure and amazement, after a few weeks in Japan I suddenly felt a switch in my head go 'click' and I could speak and understand Japanese.

A: What did you work on while in Japan?

SB: I did a study on hair color in phenylketonuria in Japan. It was a lot of fun and I got to travel all over the country.

A: What was it like being a woman in Japan at that time?

SB: It was weird. First of all, the Japanese language has various forms and there is no appropriate form for a western woman, so western women use a modified male speech. The graduate students, who were our friends and Marty's colleagues, were fascinated because they were still in arranged marriages. Love matches were rare. Having a career and marriage and children—I had a baby while I was there—was almost unknown.

A: How did your career path move toward psychiatry?

SB: I thought if I studied some psychiatry, I would learn what makes people emotionally healthy and more about parent–child relationships. I wanted to be a good pediatrician and understand psychiatry at the same time.

Psychiatric Training

A: Where did you decide to study psychiatry?

SB: I went to a large state hospital—Central Islip State Hospital. My career took a turn the first day of residency training, 9 September 1962. Everyone else started 1 July, but we had just returned from England. I found they had been assigning me patients since 1 July! It was a women's admission service. I had been taught nothing practical in medical school about psychiatry. Psychoanalysis ruled in those days. So I interviewed my patients and found a museum of mental illness—every possible disorder.

A: And what did you do next?

SB: I decided to pick the woman who was the most sick and the woman who was the least sick and spend a lot of time with them to learn. The woman who I thought was most sick was acutely psychotic, while the woman who I thought was least sick was an alcoholic teacher with six kids. She had been sleeping in her car in the school parking lot. Somehow her husband had her committed. The psychotic woman got well on thorazine.

A: The alcoholic woman?

SB: She and I set out like two babes in the woods to try to figure out what to do. After a couple of weeks, I went to the chief of service and said I needed some help, and he started me on my career with his two-word answer, 'Why bother!'. That was the attitude in 1962. I was also attending the New York School of Psychiatry as part of the residency training, where we were encouraged to use group techniques. I started a group for alcoholic women. That is how I learned about alcoholism—it was always a woman's disease to me. My patients taught me. The only help I got was from Marty Mann's book, *The New Primer on Alcoholism*. I learned about Alcoholics Anonymous (AA) because there was a male AA group in the hospital. I got them to admit my women patients.

Getting into Alcoholism

A: And what happened during the rest of your residency?

SB: I went to child psychiatry for my second year at Central Islip. But fate stepped in. Unbeknownst to me, New York State decided to start the first in-patient alcohol rehabilitation unit in the state at Central Islip because we had an established AA meeting. The Bowery (New York City's Skid Row) was in our catchment area so we had a lot of alcoholics. The rehabilitation unit was started in 1962. In 1964, I got a call from the director. Well, the psychiatrist who ran the alcohol unit had asked for a month's leave of absence. Of the over 100 psychiatrists on staff, nobody would go there as a substitute. Somebody remembered there was a resident who 'liked those people'. So he asked if I would do it and I agreed. That is where I met my first male alcoholic patient. I loved it for that month.

A: At the end of the month?

SB: I was called back to see the director. The doctor who had taken a leave of absence decided not to come back. The directorship of the unit was open. He was offering me the job. In 1966, we started the first women's unit in New York state. At first we had separate male and female units. We eventually integrated them.

A: What did you do about detoxification in those early days?

SB: Actually we also had the first detoxification unit in the state hospital system. So I ran a detoxification unit, a rehabilitation unit, a little quarter-way house and a day hospital.

State Responsibility

A: How did your career evolve into becoming Commissioner of Alcoholism and Alcohol Abuse for the state of New York?

SB: Our governor, Hugh Carey, was running for a second term. One of the planks of his platform was that he was going to re-organize the Department of Mental Hygiene, the largest department in government. He formed a task force of 10 people, of which I was one, to rewrite the law as part of his initiative in going for another term. I discovered the power of a word written in law. For example, the old law said the purpose of the agency was to provide services for the alcoholic. We added two words—'and family.' The governor was re-elected and the law was passed. However, he ran into some trouble. He needed someone to go up to Albany in a hurry—someone who was well-known, well-liked and who could bring the field back together. And that task fell to me. I had a 4-year stint.

A: What did you accomplish as commissioner that you are most proud of?

SB: I did a lot that I wanted to do: for example, changing the social services law. Previously, the definition of child neglect contained phraseology that if a parent was a habitual user of alcohol or drugs, he or she was by definition a child neglecter. So we changed the wording—I composed the wording myself. It was written to say that if the parent was in a program of recovery, purposely stated that way so that AA could be included, that there had to be specific evidence of child neglect in order to accuse the parent of neglect. You can do that in government. But you also waste a lot of time.

A: Other initiatives?

SB: Another thing that we did was raise the purchasing age for alcohol from 18 to 19 years old. We subsequently measured single car crashes and found a drop among drivers between ages 18 and 19, but not for other ages.

A: Another focus of yours has been pregnancy and addiction.

SB: I was always interested in women because their problems were routinely overlooked. When I got to Albany, fetal alcohol syndrome (FAS) was just beginning to be described. I chaired a task force that developed a public education initiative.[1]

A: After 4 years in Albany?

SB: I went to the National Council on Alcoholism (NCA) for about 6 months. Around that time, the New York State Medical Society was starting the Committee on Physicians' Health, so I began to work for them. Then I went to South Oaks Hospital, in 1984.

The Move to South Oaks Hospital

A: How did the opportunity at South Oaks come about?

SB: South Oaks was a privately owned psychiatric hospital on Long Island established in 1882. The director was very interested in alcoholism and drug dependence and he developed a training program for addiction counselors called the South Oaks Institute. I became director of the alcoholism, chemical dependency and compulsive gambling services (as well as director of the Institute). I found that in the private sector I could try things out and if they did not work that was OK, whereas in government you cannot say something does not work. I developed all kinds of programs.

A: How did you become interested in gambling addiction?

SB: As always, through a patient. I came to know him in the late 1960s. He was part of my study of Jewish alcoholics. After leaving the alcohol unit, he switched addictions and became a pathological gambler.

A: South Oaks is the namesake for the pathological gambling scale that you developed.

SB: When I arrived, South Oaks had just made arrangements with a professor at St John's University named Henry Lesieur PhD to do research on gambling. He felt quite rightly that there was a need for a screening tool, and I worked with him on developing one. We finally developed the SOGS (South Oaks Gambling Screen).[2] The SOGS is now available in 35 languages.

Alcoholism Among the Jews

A: Where else have you been a consultant?

SB: For years I was a consultant to Israel, mainly because of my interest in alcoholic Jews. I also became involved with JACS (Jewish Alcoholics, Chemically Dependent Persons and Significant Others) which was founded in 1980. I hated to read that Jews do not become alcoholics when I knew that was not true. I realized that Jewish alcoholics were not being diagnosed and treated. On our own, we started interviewing Jewish alcoholics until we had interviewed 100 subjects. We published our paper in 1980.[3,4]

A: What kind of response did this work stir up?

SB: When we first began to present our results, they hit like a bombshell.

Involvement in Professional Organization

A: You have been quite involved in many professional organizations. Can you tell me about those experiences?

SB: I joined AMSA [the American Medical Society on Alcoholism, which later became the American Society for Addiction Medicine (ASAM)] and found that it was the only place where I could meet with others who cared about what I cared about. I was on the board of ASAM for over 25 years. I was at the ASAM Board meeting at which we invented the term 'addiction medicine'.

A: How did you become involved in the American Psychiatric Association (APA)?

SB: I joined the Council on Psychiatric Services and became an activist vetting everything that they did to make sure alcohol and drugs were not overlooked.

A: You have been involved for a long time with the Rutgers School of Addiction Studies. What has that been like?

SB: In 1965, I went as a student to the Rutgers School of Alcohol Studies, headed by a sociologist, Dr Selden Bacon. The Summer School was a wonderful place. I have lectured there every year since.

A: Tell me about your connection with Iceland.

SB: I was invited as a consultant to Iceland at the 20th anniversary of their rehabilitation program. I suggested that they develop a compulsive gambling program, and they did so. I was then invited back to train staff. They honored me by making me a Knight of the Icelandic Falcon.

The Importance of Professional Writing

A: Writing has played an important part in your career.

SB: I have written many textbook chapters, for which I usually take my notes and flesh them out with references. I try to write without technical terms whenever possible, and I often meet people who tell me they have gained a great deal from my work.

Writing is so important. I consider my life a series of missions—to get women into treatment,[5] to attend to the special needs of women, to interest society and the professions in gambling problems. You never know when you write something where it is going to go—the Supreme Court, Iceland, Africa—you do not know.

A: Who has been most influential in your career?

SB: In addictions, being a woman was not so unusual because of Dr Ruth Fox, who was the first Medical Director of the National Council on Alcoholism. There was also Mrs Marty Mann, a recovering alcoholic who was the founder of the National Council.

A: How is retirement?

SB: I never wanted to work until I died. I worked very hard and there is much out in the world that I did not have time for. When I hit my 60s,

I started going to adult education classes in drawing and painting. I now get to do what I like to do. I can teach and consult in my own time. I travel a lot. I started writing poetry. I have written thousands of limericks as SheilaB for The Omnificent English Dictionary in Limerick Form (OEDILF.com). The project involves putting the whole English Dictionary into limerick form.

Notes

1. Blume, S. B. (1981) Drinking and pregnancy: preventing fetal alcohol syndrome. *New York State Journal of Medicine*, 81, 95–98.
2. Lesieur, H. R. & Blume, S. B. (1987) The South Oaks Gambling Screen (SOGS): a new instrument for the identification of pathological gamblers. *American Journal of Psychiatry*, 144, 1184–1188.
3. Blume, S. B., Dropkin, D. & Sokolow, L. (1980) The Jewish alcoholic: a descriptive study. *Alcohol Health and Research World*, 4, 21–26.
4. Vex, S. L. & Blume, S. B. (2001) The JACS study I: characteristics of a population of chemically dependent Jewish men and women. *Journal of Addictive Diseases*, 20, 71–89.
5. Blume, S. B. (1985) Women and alcohol: a review. *JAMA*, 256, 1467–1470.

37

Conversation with Roger E. Meyer

Roger Meyer is an American psychiatrist who, throughout a long and fruitful career as addictions researcher and research center director, has exemplified an interdisciplinary view. He has helped to position clinical research in the broad field.

Addiction (A): Tell us something about your personal background and early years?

Roger E. Meyer (REM): I was born and raised in New York City in a mixed Irish, Italian and Jewish neighborhood. My father had come to the United States from Germany in 1929 at the age of 23, having survived a childhood of lost parents, the stresses of World War I and the devastation caused by the massive postwar inflation in Germany. His extended family included a number of distinguished academic physicians. My mother was born in New York to immigrant parents from eastern Europe and trained as a commercial artist. I was born in 1938 and like so many sons of that time felt much riding on my talents and intellect in terms of charting a future for myself and a respected place for my family in America.

A: Education?

REM: I was admitted by competitive examination to one of the finest high schools in the city (Stuyvesant). I then chose a small liberal arts college in upstate New York. Hobart College was as different from my earlier years as one might imagine. New York State's drinking age was 18. I was 16, and had never had an alcoholic beverage. The drinking on the campus led to the deaths of several of my schoolmates from auto accidents or accidental overdose. For the most part, fraternities were the major drinking venue but I was very much outside that orbit. Apart from this social mismatch, Hobart College turned out to be the best possible choice for me, and I was admitted to Harvard Medical School upon graduation.

A: How did you become involved in research on the addictions?

REM: I discovered psychiatry as a medical student and observing the revolutionary changes then taking place in psychopharmacology and in community-based treatments. I saw psychiatry as an opportunity to do research, particularly clinical research. I completed an intensive medical internship in Seattle in 1963 and came out of the experience feeling like a physician. I then began a psychiatric residency back at Harvard in a very psychoanalytical environment. I saw psychoanalysis as reactionary. In my second year, I chose to do research in psychopharmacology, and in my last year I completed a 1-year advanced program in community mental health. During my first year of residency, I met Dr Gerald Klerman (my first role model in psychiatry). Gerry was an encyclopedia of information about psychiatry, psychopharmacology and the history of medicine. I had been accepted into the US Public Health Service (PHS) as an alternative to mandatory military service; and, with Gerry's support, I was invited to work in the addictions program at the National Institute of Mental Health (NIMH), which I saw as an opportunity to link my interests in public health and psychopharmacology.

Chance Favors a Prepared Mind

A: What was your experience at NIMH?

REM: My first 6 months at NIMH were a combination of a crash course in addictions, introductions to the leading figures in the field, and an orientation to government. I came under the influence of Mitchell Balter, a social psychologist, who became my first mentor in the addictions field. Mitch's interest in epidemiology led me to the rich literature in drug and alcohol addiction. Later, a site visit to the Addiction Research Center at Lexington introduced me to some of the greats of that time and place: Harris Isbell, William Martin, Nathan B. Eddy, Jack O'Donnell and, most importantly, Abraham Wikler (perhaps the most creative psychiatrist of his generation, and largely unknown to most of his contemporaries in the United States). In December 1966, I attended a meeting of the Association for Research in Nervous and Mental Disease in New York where I encountered state of the art science across the addictions field. I was hooked! I could now see a career path following models already laid out by the likes of Abe Wikler, Jack Mendelson and Jerome Jaffe; three psychiatrists who were able to conduct translational research, a rarity in psychiatry to this day.

A: And the next step?

REM: By January 1967, I was in the Center for Studies of Narcotics and Drug Abuse, part of a new Division of Special Mental Health Programs that also included the National Center on Alcoholism headed by Jack Mendelson. Our Center Director died within 3 months of assuming office. So, at the tender age of 29, I was named Acting Director of the Center, a program that, 7 years later, evolved into the National Institute on Drug Abuse (NIDA).

A: And what were some of the tasks that confronted you on taking up that job?

REM: During the summer of 1967, I was asked to get a better sense of the public health consequences of hallucinogenic drug use in San Francisco.

Later in the year, our Center was asked about rumors of carcinogenicity and teratogenicity of hallucinogens. We convened an expert, multi-disciplinary panel and its output became my first monograph.[1]

A: What else did this job entail?

REM: Our Center also had responsibility for funding extramural research, including Avram Goldstein's early work on the opiate receptor, reviewing a broad portfolio of clinical and basic research, and approving the use of hallucinogenic drugs in research. We were given the responsibility to develop the national marijuana program. We were also asked to develop community-based treatment programs for heroin addicts. Although it was strongly recommended that we focus our support for the latter effort through the nascent community mental health centers, we believed that this was not the right strategy because the vast majority of these centers lacked expertise in addiction. We ultimately selected six programs for funding, including those in New Haven (Herbert Kleber), Chicago (Jerome Jaffe) and New York City (Efren Ramirez).

A: Exciting times?

REM: It was a heady time: I testified before the Congress and was invited to advise the Pentagon on marihuana use in Vietnam, and our programs were well funded. But I decided that the best next step would be to learn about addiction at the ground level and not from the heights of government. In my training as a resident in psychiatry, I had never worked with an alcoholic or an addict; and I was intrigued by the possibilities for productive translational research on addictive disorders. I felt that I had acquired an excellent working knowledge of the contributions that multiple disciplines were making to advance our understanding of the pathways into and out of addiction, and the implications for treatment and prevention. It made me more aware that the basic sciences underlying psychiatry were much broader than psychoanalysis and must necessarily involve non-psychiatrists who were skilled in research methodology. That understanding guided me throughout my subsequent career as a researcher and research center director.

A: What did you do after you left the Center in 1968?

REM: I went to work at Boston University (BU) as the Deputy Director for Research Training in Psychiatry, funded by an NIMH training grant. I wanted to create a research program in addictive disorders. My overarching goals were to develop animal models of opiate addiction that could be used to screen new medications; and, to adapt the biobehavioral clinical research methods developed in the alcohol field by Jack Mendelson and Nancy Mello to my own studies of addiction.

Efforts to Create Clinical and Animal Behavioral Models for Translational Research

A: So you went back to Boston with the intention of developing a more empirically validated model of addiction?

REM: Yes, at BU I began my original research with Dr Steven Mirin (who was my first mentee) on the reactions of heavy and casual marijuana smokers to marijuana in a laboratory setting.[2,3] At that time, I also began animal studies, which were an important stage in my own scientific development[4,5] and in the later development of my first research center grant award. While I was still in the Department of Psychiatry at BU, Jack Mendelson relocated from NIMH to become Chair of the Department of Psychiatry at Harvard's unit at Boston City Hospital, which was right next door to the BU Medical Center. The National Commission on Marihuana and Drug Abuse had just released a Request for Applications for a study of the effects of chronic marihuana smoking. Jack suggested that we apply jointly to conduct the study at Boston City Hospital. Participation in the study launched a 7-year collaboration and life-long friendship with Jack, a long collaboration with Tom Babor at Harvard and then at the University of Connecticut, and my first hands-on experience with a behavioral analysis model of addictive behavior in humans that would lend itself to multi-disciplinary collaboration. With Jack Mendelson's strong encouragement, I left the department of psychiatry at BU and became associate professor of psychiatry at Harvard and Boston City Hospital.

A: What happened next?

REM: Those collaborations with Jack, and with Joe Cochin, and Conan Kornetsky at BU came together in a research center grant that I submitted for federal funding. The clinical core of the center grant involved biobehavioral studies of volunteer heroin addicts given 10 days' access to heroin while under treatment with a narcotic blocking drug or placebo on a research ward. Prior to our own work, interdisciplinary clinical research in the United States was largely limited to fixed-dose, fixed-interval, clinical experiments utilizing prisoner addicts at the Addiction Research Center at Lexington Kentucky.

A: What was the focus of the studies of heroin use by heroin addicts?

REM: The studies were designed to test Wikler's hypothesis that an individual treated with a narcotic blocking drug who is allowed to administer heroin will repeatedly challenge the narcotic blockade, exponentially increasing the behavior, until there is behavioral extinction. We saw no evidence of operant patterns of extinction as had been postulated by Abe Wikler.

A: Within the expectations of the time do you think that Lexington researchers were ethical when they administered addictive drugs to prisoners?

REM: By today's standards, the research would be considered unethical. However, that needs to be considered in the context of the then current practice in the United States. Prison-based research during the war and until the early 1970s became the bedrock of clinical research in this country. Indeed, until that decade, the principal objections to prisoner-based research was a concern that these individuals would be given special privileges or early parole.

A Move Toward Autonomy Leads to Administration

A: After your success at Harvard and Boston University, at the age of 39, you left Boston to become the Chairman of Psychiatry at the University of Connecticut.

REM: Starting in 1975, I was approached by a number of medical schools to become a candidate for chair of psychiatry. I hoped that by taking on major administrative responsibility, I would be better able to build and sustain a research program and to avoid the marginalization that I felt at McLean. At the University of Connecticut (UConn) I saw a magnificent facility and a virtually empty hospital. Applying some of the lessons learned in the heroin/naltrexone work, I felt that I could make an important contribution to alcoholism research and treatment; and, as a department head, I could help to bring addictions into the mainstream of psychiatry and of medical education. During this time, there was an announcement that the National Institute on Alcohol Abuse and Alcoholism (NIAAA) would fund its first research centers. Tom Babor, whom I had recruited to McLean as part of the clinical research program, and I sketched out a vision for an alcohol research centre. But, in that first round, we did not get funded. We re-applies and were then funded. We recruited Victor Hesselbrock. His wife, Michie Hesselbrock, was hired to be the site leader of our Typology project. And Jerry Jaffe indicated that he would be interested in joining our department.

Recruitments and Support for Young Faculty Create a Team

A: So by 1982, you had put together an impressive group of researchers and a significant research infrastructure.

REM: By 1980, we had also applied successfully for a post-doctoral training grant that extended our resources by enabling us to recruit some very bright young people to alcoholism research. Of the four centers that were funded in 1978 we were the only one renewed in 1982. By 1982, Tom Babor had agreed to relocate to UConn with the renewal of the Center Grant. Tom, Victor and I wrote about the organization of the Center at that time in a paper published in 2005.[6]

The Need to Rebuild

A: What next?

REM: During the summer of 1984, I spent a mini-sabbatical with Griffith Edwards at the Maudsley Hospital in London. The experience energized me and focused my interests on the Alcohol Dependence Syndrome and possible markers of severity.[7] Ovide Pomerleau and his colleagues assessed alcohol dependence severity across some established scales.[8] I began some strategic conversations with Herb Kleber, the director of the addiction research program at Yale. The emphasis at Yale was on drug abuse, which complemented our alcohol research center. Herb and I saw the tremendous opportunities in a full collaboration, and we asked Tom Babor and Bruce Rounsaville from Yale to chart some promising opportunities. Bruce and colleagues offered to work with us in the development of pharmacotherapy trials and to provide mentorship to a young psychiatrist, Hank Kranzler, to develop a pharmacotherapy program focused on buspirone at the UConn site. Stephanie O'Malley was his counterpart in a study of fluoxetine in New Haven. Most importantly, our program had expanded out beyond the Center grant to investigator initiated grants and major collaborations. Tom Babor and his team directed the project development and data analysis for Project MATCH.

A: Sense of progress?

REM: Between 1987 and 1992, I think the Center really thrived. There was a sense that the Center mattered. In 1986, I was named Physicians Health Services Professor as an endowed Chair. In 1987, the Dean asked me to add responsibility for the medical school's faculty practice plan to my administrative portfolio. By the late 1980s, I sensed myself moving from young Turk to elder statesman within what seemed like a blink of time. When I was elected President of the Chairs group in psychiatry in 1990 and President of the American College of Neuropsychopharmacology in 1992 (the first alcohol clinical researcher in either role), I felt that perhaps alcohol research was going 'mainstream.' By 1992, our Center grant was renewed for a fourth cycle, and the psychiatry department had become the top research department, on a per capita basis (in terms of NIH support) at UConn. The Dean asked me to add the role of Executive Dean to my jobs as Chair and Center Director.

A: That sounds like a superhuman work-load. How did you do it?

REM: By 1992, my three administrative jobs at UConn had worn me down a bit. In the fall of that year, I started a year-long sabbatical at the Center for Advanced Study in the Behavioral Sciences at Stanford. I went to California and tried to sort out where I should focus my interests. I chose to accept a position at George Washington University with broad responsibility for the entire medical enterprise (hospital, medical school and other health science schools).

A: How many years were you at George Washington and what followed?

REM: I actually spent just under 2 years at George Washington. We brought together an outstanding clinical, operational and financial team that generated the first 'profit' ($35 million) in a number of years from clinical operations. This enabled my boss to proclaim that as we were now profitable, we should sell off the clinical operations. I was offered the vice-presidency at another school in the Midwest, but my wife and I really loved Washington; so in 1997 I started a consulting business with three other partners to small and non-US-based pharmaceutical companies interested in developing CNS drugs in the United States

A: And as well as giving extraordinary service to your science I believe you have enjoyed a very happy family life?

REM: The key event that has gone unmentioned so far was my good fortune in finding the right life-time partner. With Sheila, over nearly 45 years now, we have been privileged to raise three daughters (each accomplished in her own right) and now to experience the joys of being grandparents. My children remind me that I never missed a breakfast or dinner with them when not on travel.

A: And satisfaction in professional achievement?

REM: I feel that I was privileged to enter academic medicine in the United States at a particularly good time. The research career goals that I set out to achieve as I was leaving NIMH in 1968 were achieved beyond my wildest expectations. The privilege of serving as a consultant to the White House was a special opportunity to affect policy. My friendships within the addiction research community have been very meaningful. I know of no other field of research in psychiatry where the physician researchers are as committed to a multi-disciplinary perspective or are as generous and mutually supportive. Most importantly, my former colleagues at UConn, especially my mentees, represent the real lasting contribution to the field. On reflection I see a continuing need to develop an interdisciplinary model of alcoholism that can only come out of models of interdisciplinary research that are perhaps yet to emerge.[9]

A: If we caught you on a rare day not working, how would we find you spending your time?

REM: Enjoying time with my family, biking along the Chesapeake and Ohio Canal, playing tennis, reading history and several daily newspapers, and a recent hobby: making slide shows of trips that my wife and I have taken.

A: Now a final question. If a young clinical researcher were to approach you today and say 'Dr Meyer, you have vast experience, tell me why I should make addictions and their frequently stigmatized patients my priority choice?' what would be your answer?

REM: We in the addictions field have clinical research and animal models that should be the envy of our colleagues in the rest of psychiatry. The young person should understand that to really know the field, one should be able to read a multi-disciplinary literature and to think outside the box created by American psychiatry and the DSM. You should seek to collaborate with biological, behavioral and social scientists. You should be capable of developing empathy for the struggles that patients and families go through in coping with addiction as a chronic relapsing disorder, and you should be able to provide hope and informed treatments (often repeatedly). There is no other area of psychiatry that has so much imminent promise.

Notes

1. Meyer R. E., editor. *Adverse Reactions to Hallucinogenic Drugs.* Report of a Conference held at the National Institute of Mental Health, Chevy Chase,

Maryland, September 1967 (with selected background papers). Bethesda, MD: National Clearinghouse for Mental Health Information; 1969.

2. Meyer R. E., Pillard R. C., Mirin S. M., Shapiro L. M. Administration of marihuana to heavy and casual marihuana users. *Am J Psychiatry* 1971; 128: 198–204.
3. Mirin S. M., Shapiro L. M., Meyer R. E., Pillard R. C., Fisher S. Casual versus heavy use of marijuana: a redefinition of the marijuana problem. *Am J Psychiatry* 1971; 127: 1134–40.
4. Meyer R. E., Cochin J., Miller J. M., Rosow C. The relationship between aggression and host differences in vulnerability to opiate addiction in the white mouse. In: *Report of the College on Problems of Drug Dependence*. Philadelphia, PA: CPDD; 1970.
5. Hindman R. D., Miller J. M., Meyer R. E., Cochin J. The effect of length of exposure to etonitazene upon drug seeking behavior. *Pharmacologist* 1971; 13: 262.
6. Babor T. F., Meyer R. E., Hesselbrock V. M. From collaboration to integration: the university of Connecticut Alcohol Research Center in concept and practice. *Bull Soc Psychol Subst Abuse* 1985; 4: 3–15.
7. Meyer R. E. Old wine, new bottle: the alcohol dependence syndrome. Psychiatr *Clin North Am* 1986; 9: 435–53.
8. Cooney N. L., Meyer R. E., Kaplan R. F., Baker L. H. A validation study of four scales measuring the alcohol dependence syndrome. *Br J Addict* 1986; 81: 223–9.
9. Meyer R. E. Finding paradigms for the future of alcoholism research: an interdisciplinary perspective. *Alcohol Clin Exp Res* 2001; 25: 1393–406.

38

Conversation with William R. Miller

William Miller is an American psychologist whose creative contributions have, over a professional life-time, exerted a profound personal influence on the substance misuse treatment field. In 1994 he was a recipient of the Jellinek Award.

Finding a Life Direction

Addiction (A): Early life?

William R. Miller (WRM): I grew up in Appalachia in a little coal-mining town in Pennsylvania, and went to college with the intention of going to seminary. Along the way I had the fairly common faith crisis of having a childhood faith that was no longer going to work for me and not yet having an adult faith that was viable. So I found myself in my senior year an agnostic, and it did not make sense to go to seminary. I had majored in psychology and so applied to graduate schools in psychology. I wanted to go to the University of Oregon, but did not get in. Instead I got into the University of Wisconsin, and I started graduate school there in 1969, attended for one summer semester, and then my number came up in the draft lottery. This was during the Vietnam War and I had already filed as a conscientious objector, so I worked for 2 years as a psychiatric aide at Mendota State Hospital in Madison, following in the footsteps of Carl Rogers, where he did his research on schizophrenia.

A: What happened after that?

WRM: After a couple of years of service I was ready to go back to graduate school. This time I got into Oregon, and I loved my graduate experience there. Hal Arkowitz was my first mentor. Back then in 1973 there were summer internships with the Veterans Administration. My wife Kathy, whom I met in Madison, and I both liked Wisconsin so we said, 'Let's go back to Wisconsin for the summer'. We chose the Wood VA hospital in Milwaukee. I toured around the hospital and there was this alcoholism unit being run by a psychologist, Bob Hall, who asked, 'What do you know about alcoholism?'. I said, 'Nothing at all'. He told me, 'Come on in, and learn something'. And I did.

It was just a blank slate for me. Bob got me to look into some new research from the Sobells, which had been released in a State of California report and was just hitting the journals. We tried out a little controlled drinking therapy at the in-patient unit and pretty quickly decided this was not the right thing for that population. But I thought, 'Now this is something you could do with people earlier, farther upstream.' I had taken a class from Ed Lichtenstein, who was very much emphasizing prevention and pulling people out of the river before they go over the waterfall.

A: This was in Oregon?

WRM: Yes, back at Oregon. Ed became my dissertation advisor. I wanted to work with earlier problem drinkers from the community, so I advertised for people who would like to learn how to moderate their drinking. We compared three different approaches for helping people to moderate their drinking. One of them was electrical aversion therapy. A second we called behavioral self-control training. The third condition was an all-out training approach combining methods from the Sobells and from Syd Lovibond. All three worked about equally well,[1] which is a finding I have replicated many times since then.

A: You wanted to look at problem drinkers who are further upstream, but that was not common thinking at that time. So, where did your idea come from?

WRM: Well, my training was behavioral and so I have always thought about drinking as a behavior, and it did not seem to me that alcohol problems came in only one flavor.

A: After graduate school, where did you do your internship?

WRM: At the Veterans Administration hospital in Palo Alto, California. I worked with John Marquis, and also did a neuropsychology rotation with Jim Moses. I had experience at the front door as an intake worker, but never heard whether I had it right or got it wrong. That is a theme that has stayed with me, that it is easy when you are in practice to operate in a feedback vacuum. I also did a couple of studies while I was on internship. One of them was with this self-help manual co-authored with Ricardo Muñoz.[2]

A: What next?

WRM: I thought I might go into a clinical role. New Mexico had this faculty opening. They offered me a job and I took it. We came here and never left. I have loved New Mexico; it has been a wonderful place to work, and so happenstance, once again, affected the direction of my career.

The Doorway between Religion and Psychology

A: You said you went to college planning to go to a seminary. Was that in your family?

WRM: No, not at all. I felt a personal calling to do this. It seemed to me that was what I was supposed to do, so it was quite a struggle to make the decision not to go to seminary. I found my way back into an adult faith a couple of years later. There was a point in my life, soon after I received tenure, where I again felt the tug, the doubt, and that was another struggle. What I came out of that with was the sense that I am on the right path. The fruit that has come out of my living in that doorway between religion and psychology has been wonderful. Being a person of faith and also a hard-nosed scientist in the addiction field, both just fit naturally with who I am.

A: Do you feel the door has ever swung back and hit you in the face?

WRM: No, quite to the contrary. Many wonderful opportunities for stimulating conversations with smart people have come out of that.

A: What was the draw of going to graduate school?

WRM: I have been fortunate to have great mentors every step of the way. They fired in me a curiosity about people and this interesting way of discovering new knowledge.

A: So the call for you in psychology was knowledge, in a sense. I am asking because you were at college in the 1960s, and for some people the call was for social action and social change.

WRM: Well, they are intertwined. In Madison I was a hippie radical, long-haired, bearded guy out in the streets so I sort of fit that stereotype of the 1960s. But honestly, I am not sure that either of those—scientific curiosity or social action—was the real call. It sounds very unhumble, but I have felt moved by God in certain directions. I feel as if there has been some intentionality to it.

Recurring Interest in Alcoholism

A: So you became interested in alcoholism on the summer practicum.

WRM: Yep. Just happenstance.

A: Lots of people meet people with alcohol dependence and they do not like them. What was the draw?

WRM: Knowing nothing, that summer I mostly listened. I immediately enjoyed talking to them and working with people with addictions. Then I began to read the literature and it said, 'Alcoholics are liars and they have this immature personality that it so defended that you can never get through. You've just got to hit them with a brick to get anywhere, and you can't trust them.' It puzzled me, because those were not the people I had been talking to. It just happened that I was trained both in behavior therapy and in Rogers' approach.

A: When was your first review on motivation published?

WRM: Well, it is more happenstance.[3] I went off with Kathy to Norway on my first sabbatical leave. I spent it at an alcoholism hospital near Bergen, the Hjellestad Clinic. They brought me in to lecture on cognitive behavioral treatment of alcoholism and addictions. The director of the center asked if I would also meet with a group of psychologists who were working there and have a conversation every other week or so. What they wanted to do was to role-play some of the more difficult cases they were seeing. I began verbalizing a set of decision rules that I had been using that I was completely unaware of, that had to do predominately with having the client make the arguments for change. And, also, eliciting their confidence and hope. I began writing down these decision rules as they were emerging, and gave it the working title of 'motivational interviewing.' I sent this to a few colleagues. To my surprise, Ray Hodgson wrote that he wanted to publish it in *Behavioural Psychotherapy*. It appeared in 1983.[4] I came back to New Mexico and began conducting some studies on brief interventions designed to elicit motivation for change.

A: Was it modeled after Griffith Edwards' advice condition from the advice versus treatment study?

WRM: Actually, I did not know Griffith's 'plain treatment' paper at the time, but when I read that description later it made a lot of sense. We were not the only ones finding that brief treatment made a difference. We wondered, 'If it does not always work, what is true of the studies where the brief intervention did work?'. That is where FRAMES came from. FRAMES is an acronym for six things that often appeared in effective brief interventions: giving people Feedback, emphasizing a person's Responsibility for change, clear Advice to change, and a Menu of options for doing so. The 'E' is Empathy; the 'S' is support for Self-efficacy. And that is where the Drinker's Check-up came from, which is a combination of the motivational interviewing style with giving people structured feedback from assessment.[5] Each study had a similar finding, which was essentially a doubling of the abstinence rate for people assigned randomly to the motivational interviewing session, in comparison to people receiving the same treatment program without an initial motivational interview.

A: What do you think the experience of empathy is doing?

WRM: I think Rogers had it right. I think the experience of acceptance is transforming and lets people look at their life in a context that is safe. The normal experience of ambivalence is to think about a reason why you should change, then to think about a reason why you should not change, and then stop thinking about it. I think that as people are enabled to talk about their present situation without immediately being given advice they literally talk themselves into changing.[6]

A: Your ideas have seized people's imaginations in a way that is really unusual. What is it in your ideas or in the way you have disseminated them that has made such a difference?

WRM: The verb that I use is that people seem to 'recognize' it. I was doing it without knowing it consciously, and thanks to my Norwegian colleagues, they literally called it forth from me.

A: What about Steve Rollnick's piece?

WRM: On my second sabbatical in Australia I met Steve, a South African who lives in Wales. We wound up writing the book together,[7] a book that the publisher says 'has long legs'. It disseminates with very little in the way of marketing.

A: I am wondering if you have some sense that you are tapping into an optimism and hope about humanity in this approach.

WRM: Well, it is certainly a way in which we want to think about ourselves and each other. I have never been a behaviorist. I have been a behavior therapist, but with a humanistic personal philosophy about human nature. As for a 12-Step approach, when I read Bill W [co-founder of Alcoholics Anonymous], I hear a great deal that is familiar in terms of how you work with other people—a patient, compassionate approach that is not blaming or judging. It is nothing like what the treatment industry created with '12-Step disease model treatment'.[8]

A: Let us talk about quantum change next.

WRM: That was another product of a sabbatical. I became interested in transformational change—fairly major shifts that happen over a relatively short period of time. I began wondering, 'Is this a real phenomenon?'. We had one small article in the Albuquerque newspaper describing this kind of experience. Many people called, and 55 people came in and finished a 3-hour interview. We recorded their stories and Janet C'de Baca and I tried to understand what we were hearing.[9] In 35 years of research this was the most fun I ever had with a study, and the most uplifting.

A: What were some of qualities that you identified?

WRM: A surprising thing about quantum change was they went through a one-way door and knew there was no going back. In some sense, that study still feels to me like the most important piece of work in my 35 years.

Pie as Far as You Can See

A: One of the other things that is characteristic of your career has been your collaborations. I would be interested in hearing how you think about collaboration.

WRM: Well, collaboration does not seem extraordinary to me. It is not even something that I was seeking out intentionally. It is just that I enjoy talking to people, and ideas arise in conversation and lead naturally to, 'Why don't we do something with this together?'

A: But in traditional academia people worry about getting credit for their ideas. How did you not worry about all those things about credit?

WRM: I have had more a sense of plenty than of scarcity. That mentality of 'I need credit for this and I need to be first' involves believing that there are only scarce resources around and I need to seize as much as I can for myself. My experience has been that when I collaborate, find ideas together and do things together, in Scott Tonigan's words, 'There's pie as far as you can see—so much pie, that you can't possibly eat it all.' It is how I came back to faith, really. I did not come back to an adult faith by having a brilliant light revelation; I came back to faith because it made sense to me to believe.

A: Science for you has been reinforcing?

WRM: It is an incredibly thin reinforcement schedule, and certainly in the beginning it is very thin. I think it takes that kind of passion and curiosity to sustain you through the early years, and I think that if you do not impart that to clinical psychology students there are so many other rewarding things they can do that they are not too likely to want to do science. I certainly did not start out to be a scientist. We caught it in the course of our training at Oregon. We came to understand that this is exciting and interesting and you can find partial answers at least to things you care about, and have fun doing it and get paid for it, for heaven sake! I cannot imagine a better career than I have had. I just cannot.

Notes

1. Miller W. R. Behavioral treatment of problem drinkers: a comparative outcome study of three controlled drinking therapies. *J Consult Clin Psychol* 1978; 46: 74–86.
2. Miller W. R., Muñoz R. F. *Controlling Your Drinking*. New York: Guilford Press; 2005.
3. Moyers T. History and happenstance: how motivational interviewing got its start. *Behav Cogn Psychother* 2004; 18: 291–8.
4. Miller W. R. Motivational interviewing with problem drinkers. *Behav Psychother* 1983; 11: 147–72.
5. Miller W. R., Benefield R. G., Tonigan J. S. Enhancing motivation for change in problem drinking: a controlled comparison of two therapist styles. *J Consult Clin Psychol* 1993; 61: 455–61.
6. Miller W. R., Rollnick S. Talking oneself into change: motivational interviewing, stages of change, and therapeutic process. *J Cogn Psychother* 2004; 18: 299–308.
7. Miller W. R., Rollnick S. *Motivational Interviewing: Preparing People to Change Addictive Behavior*. New York: Guilford Press; 1991.
8. Miller W. R., Kurtz E. Models of alcoholism used in treatment: contrasting A.A. and other perspectives with which it is often confused. *J Stud Alcohol* 1994; 55: 159–66.
9. Miller W. R., C'de Baca J. *Quantum Change: When Epiphanies and Sudden Insights Transform Ordinary Lives*. New York: Guilford Press; 2001.

39

Conversation with George Vaillant

George Vaillant is an American psychiatrist who has made unique contributions to understanding of substance misuse and recovery within a life-course perspective. He has repeatedly shown an ability to make exact science out of difficult material. His Natural History of Alcoholism *ranks as a classic of the literature and in 1991 he was a recipient of the Jellinek Award.*

Early Background

Addiction (A): George, you have made fundamental contributions to understanding of the human life course, so it's natural to start this interview with some questions on your early life and family background.

George Vaillant (GV): I was born in New York City, almost exactly 70 years ago. I spent my first 2 years of life in Mexico, the next 4 in Manhattan, the next 5 in Philadelphia and Peru, and then when I was 10 my father died and we moved to Connecticut. We lived in Connecticut until I was 16 and I went to high school, boarding school in New Hampshire (Exeter). My family then moved to New Hampshire and I went on to Harvard. Since then I have spent most of my life in Cambridge. For the last several years I have lived in America and Australia.

A: So you started off with experience of living in other countries. Was that important? Has it given you an edge of awareness?

GV: It gave me an enormous dislike of America's efforts to try to run other countries and lives. I mean, from age 10 on, I realized that Americans could be enormously unattractive outside their own national boundaries. But I do not think that perspective influenced my professional career.

A: You mentioned briefly your father and he conducted fundamental work on the Aztecs and wrote *The Aztecs of Mexico* (Vaillant 1940). You must have pride in his accomplishments?

GV: Enormous. In fact, I have been consciously competing with him and marvelling that I have usually got in more royalties from his books than I have from my own.

A: He had a very creative mind, didn't he?

GV: Absolutely.

A: Were you aware of his qualities as a child or have you only later discovered that truth?

GV: He had absolutely wonderful qualities as a friend and as an intellect. He was not a very present father: he regarded young people as rather boring and he was much more interested in people of his own age. He did not even like graduate students much. So as a father he was colourful and he had a sense of humour, but he was waiting for me to grow up and be interesting.

A: Did he introduce you to the Aztecs or was that not something he would talk to you about?

GV: The spring that he died, he was closeted in his study writing a book on Aztecs for young people. He gave me a section to read in draft, saying something like 'If you read this I'll give you $2', but there was no discussion. He would talk to my sister who was smarter than I was.

A: Schooling?

GV: I was an enormous failure at boarding school so I did not think anything very dramatically positive was going to happen to me. I did much better at college. My ambition on graduating from medical school was to be a psychiatrist in a community health centre. I certainly did not imagine that I would be a scholar like my father or even have an academic career. In medical school I thought research was rather silly and missed the point of patient care.

A: You went to Exeter, a famous boarding school, and did you then say, I want to go to Harvard and that was that, or was Harvard entrance competitive?

GV: Harvard was the only place I applied. In those days you had to be quite stupid at Exeter not to get into Harvard, Yale or Princeton. But to go to Harvard Medical School was by no means assured. Before entering medical school I had spent 4 years at Harvard majoring in history and literature. So in totality, I spent 8 years at Harvard. I was much more successful at Harvard than I was at boarding school, so that was good in terms of self-esteem, and I was vice president of *Lampoon* (the humour magazine).

A: Those 4 years at medical school, did you ever think, this is wrong for me, I will go back to epic poetry?

GV: Oh no. It was totally what I wanted. Even when I was studying history and literature, what I wanted to do was medical school, what I wanted was psychiatry.

A: Harvard at that time, was there a peer group to encourage intellectual growth? Was there good afternoon conversation on lawns?

GV: It never quite worked out that way. Everyone was smart and I hung out with bright people, but largely they were not talking about ideas.

Psychoanalysis from the Inside

A: You qualified in medicine in 1959 and then what happened?

GV: I did a year's internship and 3 years as a registrar in psychiatry and that was fun. My co-residents included Eric Kandel, Joe Schildkrout, Alan Hobson, Judy Rappaport and Paul Wender: all people who later achieved academic distinction. I never took a course in psychology or sociology. In the evenings a brilliant cardiologist named Mark Altschule taught us biological psychiatry. It was an underground effort. There was psychoanalytical dominance at our hospital.

A: Did you in any way lose faith at some point in the world-view of psychoanalysis?

GV: I thought that if I was going to criticize analysis I had to do it from the inside. Fifty per cent of psychoanalysis might have seemed like rubbish, but the other half was very valuable.

A: Can you give me a brief encapsulation of what it is about psychoanalysis which in your judgement can specially enhance our understanding of the human play?

GV: If you can see beneath the surface you see a great deal about what is highly relevant but invisible to most doctors.

A: Do you feel that psychodynamic theory has contributed to your understanding of alcoholism?

GV: Ha. I want to say in capital letters, NO! I think psychoanalysis has contributed enormously to my education and to human knowledge about human beings. I think almost everything psychoanalysis has said about alcoholism has been (180 degrees) wrong.

A: How much do you attribute to the addictive nature of alcohol?

GV: The short answer is, a great deal. The longer answer is that I really like the Diagnostic and Statistical Manual version III (DSM-III) distinction not because there is a black-and-white difference between alcohol abuse and alcohol dependence; but alcohol dependence, as Edwards & Gross (1976) suggest, is on a continuum and the abuse/dependence distinction does divide alcoholism into the top half or the bottom half (in terms of severity). Many social drinkers are a little bit dependent and social drinking to dependence is a smooth continuum. We want our Alcohol Use Disorders Identification Test (AUDIT) score or Michigan Alcohol Screening Test (MAST) score to make cutting points between health and illness, but that is no more possible than it is with blood pressure. But I really do think it makes a big difference whether someone is a little bit dependent or a lot dependent.

A: So come 1962, you finished your residency.

The Lexington Experience

GV: Yes, my idea was to avoid the draft and go to NIMH (National Institute of Mental Health), but the government's view was that they had better people to work in their laboratories than George Vaillant so I was consigned to the prison service in Oklahoma. I went back and said again, I want to go to NIMH—that is what you promised me when you had me sign up. The compromise was that I would go to Lexington. At that point I knew nothing about addiction so I saw Lexington as an opportunity to understand psychopaths rather than to understand addiction. In residency training we did not admit alcoholics or discuss their treatment, and in 1962 heroin addiction had not arrived in Boston.

A: How did Lexington turn out for you?

GV: Lexington was exciting. There was an extraordinary group of doctors coming through, people such as Herb Kleber, Everett Ellingwood and Jerry Levine; and Harris Isbell was there, someone who could see addiction from many different viewpoints. One would have lunch with him and try to learn.

A: Did you have contact with Abe Wickler?

GV: Abe was terribly full of himself. He had read everything and had all sorts of notions. I learnt from him something about conditioning theories. He was not in Isbell's league for me in terms of being a hero or a role model.

A: You had patient responsibilities at Lexington?

GV: My job was to run a small psychiatric unit where addicts who had psychiatric breakdowns were sent. I came to think that it would be terribly interesting to find out what happened to addicts 10 years later on.

Falling Toward the Life-Course Perspective

A: And that was how you came to set up an absolutely seminal study (Vaillant, 1966a, b, c, d) in the long-term outcome for Lexington opiate addicts?

GV: Yes, I did not have line responsibility for treating addicts, but that is when I set up the study.

A: Seems to me that you were at that moment moving in a highly George Vaillant direction. You were launched at that moment; in intellectual terms, you became you.

GV: When I was an intern I had a patient who had been called a hysteric, and had been studied by all of the great medical scientists in Boston to find out what was wrong with her and nobody had found an answer. I put together 20 years of her records and although that was never published, it sort of prepared me. I suddenly saw long-term follow-up as science, and no one else was undertaking it. The idea of using a telescope, not a microscope, seemed to me wonderful. It was a kind of effortless way to have people say nice things about one and have one's papers published. Although I was not a trained scientist, I was reinforced by having my first paper accepted without revision (Vaillant, 1962). When my papers on schizophrenia were accepted (Vaillant, 1962, 1964), it was a way of writing and being a detective.

A: Few people have approached alcoholism from the life history perspective. What does that add to our understanding of alcoholism?

GV: By learning longitudinal research you understood development. Alcoholics do not become alcoholics overnight. So, by being interested in cumulative records, which was a way of studying drug use over time, and being interested in life history, it turned out to be a very useful way to study patterns of relapse, recovery and also discovering what really happened over time. It turns out to be quite useful for the study of alcoholism. I think one of the great surprises of longitudinal research is you discover that people recover. When I first published that heroin addicts recovered in the *New England Journal of Medicine* (Vaillant 1966b), people wrote me that they just could not believe what I had said. The addicts who recovered did not recover because of treatment, they recovered due to other factors.

A: Does treatment have a role and is it in any way similar to what Alcoholics Anonymous does?

GV: Treatment has a very important role but it is probably not the role that many of the treaters think they have. Griffith Edwards once asked me: 'Your research shows that it doesn't make any difference. How do you reconcile that?'. I think my reconciliation is really epitomized by this. 'If you want to treat an illness that has no easy cure, first of all treat them with hope.

A: Pause there for a moment. Was having studied English literature or history at all relevant to this choice of research direction, or was that an entirely separate world of thought?

GV: Oh, probably history did affect my thinking.

A: Remind me, where did you publish the results of your Lexington follow-up of narcotic addicts?

GV: One paper was in the *New England Journal* (Vaillant 1966b), one was in the *Archives of General Psychiatry* (Vaillant 1966c). Many years later I summarized my findings in *Addiction* (Vaillant 1988).

A: On leaving Lexington, you picked up on the Glueck & Glueck control group, a sample of inner-city Boston lads, and you also secured access to the information that Harvard gathered on its students of the Kennedy generation at the time they commenced their studies. How did you achieve these coups?

GV: Well, what I wanted to do was to follow-up schizophrenics. Addiction was just a passing phase and I wanted to study recovery from schizophrenia, which was why in 1966 I went to Harvard and said, can I look at your 1940 schizophrenic students at their 25th reunion? But they said, back in 1941 Harvard student health did not have a psychiatric health service. They had no records of schizophrenics; but they did have this study—the Grant Study of Adult Development. So I said, OK, I will study them 25 years later. The Gleucks had been interested in follow-up of delinquents and I went to them and was admiring of them, and they were people who loved admiration. So both the Gleuck sample and the Harvard sample were sort of turned over to me when I was still an assistant professor at Tufts, because nobody at Harvard cared about this material. It all happened rather gradually. I was being a bit like a museum curator admiring a couple of private collections. I arrived as the right person at the right time. Or, put differently, I was unbelievably lucky.

A: But then you moved away from studying schizophrenia, away from studying illness, and turned more to the study of normality—is that right?

GV: Yes.

What Price Environment?

A: What understanding of the human condition, besides the importance of defence mechanisms, have these enormously long-term studies of yours given to you?

GV: A triumph of the continuance of biology, that the brain continues to evolve and does not stop maturing at age 5, as Freud would have had us believe.

A: Help me with this. How much of what happened to the inner-city lads or to the Harvard graduates was determined not by their brains, but by the state of the environments in which they lived?

GV: Alcoholism is alcoholism—male or female, rich or poor, Irish or French.

A: How many books have you published?

GV: There have been five (Vaillant 1977, 1983, 1992, 1993, 2002).

A: Which do you like best?

GV: Oh, *Adaption to Life* (Vaillant 1977), no question about it. Writing is something that I started doing in high school; not writing books at that time, but writing has always been my favourite hobby. What is wrong with so much academic writing is that it is all prose and no passion, and it is devoid of feelings.

A: What strikes me on reading your work is your very special capacity for compassion.

GV: It is a mixture of having a childhood with a great deal of care and consideration and one that had isolation in it—it really helps to have both.

A: You have had a long relationship with AA and have been appointed to their Board of Trustees.

GV: I am enormously grateful for that appointment.

A: Are there any books or pieces of music which have been particularly important for you?

GV: Probably *The Little Prince* (de Saint-Exupéry 1943) would be near the top of the list, and also Lee Robins's *Deviant Children Grown Up* (Robins 1966)—they are very different. Music is not part of my environment.

A: Are you still changing?

GV: I have taken a much more spiritual stance. My findings in the samples that I have looked at is that increasing spirituality is not part of everybody's vital development; but it certainly is part of my life development.

A: What would your advice be to a young person who said, Professor Vaillant, please tell me how I should prepare myself for a career in the addictions field?

GV: I would say, you want to pay attention to time as a dimension rather than see things only as static. Oh yes, and subscribe to *Addiction.*

References

Edwards, G. & Gross, M. M. (1976) Alcohol dependence: provisional description of a clinical syndrome. *BMJ,* 1, 1058–1061.

Robins, L. N. (1966) *Deviant Children Grown Up.* Baltimore: Williams & Wilkins Co.

de Saint-Exupéry, A. (1943) *The Little Prince.* New York: Harcourt Brace and Ward.

Vaillant, G. C. (1940) *Aztecs of Mexico.* New York, Doubleday.

Vaillant, G. E. (1962) Tuberculosis: an historical analogy to schizophrenia. *Psychosomatic Medicine,* 24, 225–233.

Vaillant, G. E. (1964) Prospective prediction of schizophrenic remission. *Archives of General Psychiatry,* 11, 509–518.

Vaillant, G. E. (1966a) A twelve-year follow-up of New York narcotic addicts. I. The relation of treatment to outcome. *American Journal of Psychiatry,* 122, 727–737.

Vaillant, G. E. (1966b) A twelve-year follow-up of New York narcotic addicts. II. The natural history of a chronic disease. *New England Journal of Medicine,* 275, 1282–1288.

Vaillant, G. E. (1966c) A twelve-year follow-up of New York narcotic addicts. III. Some social and psychiatric characteristics. *Archives of General Psychiatry,* 15, 599–609.

Vaillant, G. E. (1966d) A twelve-year follow-up of New York narcotic addicts. IV. Some characteristics and determinants of abstinence. *American Journal of Psychiatry,* 123, 573–584.

Vaillant, G. E. (1977) *Adaptation to Life.* Boston, MA: Little, Brown[also in German, Korean and Chinese translations] [Reprinted with a new preface in 1995 by Harvard University Press, Cambridge, MA].

Vaillant, G. E. (1983) *Natural History of Alcoholism.* Cambridge, MA: Harvard University Press.

Vaillant, G. E. (1988) What can long-term follow-up teach us about relapse and prevention of relapse in addiction? *British Journal of Addiction,* 83, 1147–1157.

Vaillant, G. E. (1992) *Ego Mechanisms of Defense: A Guide for Clinicians and Researchers.* Washington, DC: American Psychiatric Press.

Vaillant, G. E. (1993) *The Wisdom of the Ego.* Cambridge, MA: Harvard University Press.

Vaillant, G. E. (2002) *Aging Well.* Boston: Little Brown [also in Hebrew and Chinese translation].

40

Conversation with William L. White

For over 40 years, William L. White has contributed creatively to the evolution of the American treatment response to alcohol and drug problems. He has also established a reputation as a distinguished historian of this field.

Addiction (A): Tell us something of your personal background.

William L. White (WLW): I was born in 1947 to parents who met while both were serving in the US Army in World War II. My father was a construction worker and my mother a nurse. I had a large family with more than 20 blood, adopted and foster siblings who shared the close intimacy of a small rural Illinois community. My parents placed great importance on education, having both come from families in which such achievement was denied routinely by life circumstances. I was fortunate to obtain scholarships to Eureka College, a small liberal arts school in Illinois. It was there that I developed a love for learning and an early interest in psychology, sociology and history. There were several influences from these early years that shaped aspects of my subsequent professional life: a public service ethic inspired by my own family and a young charismatic president (John Kennedy), a deep commitment to social change spawned by the American civil rights movement, and a love of writing. As I began my professional life, there was also a sense that my young life had been lived inside a cocoon. I have spent more than four decades since appreciating anew what I experienced within that cocoon; at the same time I have fought to escape its limitations.

Finding the Addiction Field

A: Did you find the addiction field or did the addiction field find you?

WLW: I am one of a legion of people in the late 1960s drawn to an emerging treatment field in the United States out of our own personal or family recovery experiences. That background stirred my early courtship with the field, but other experiences generated my long-term commitment to this work.

A: Could you provide an example of such an experience?

WLW: My first employment in the field was in 1967 with the Illinois Department of Mental Health. During that era of deinstitutionalization, one of my responsibilities was to tour the back wards of aging state psychiatric hospitals to screen alcoholics and addicts for potential community placement. Those visits afforded me a poignant opportunity to witness the care of the addicted in the decades before the emergence of community-based treatment. The depraved conditions in those institutions stirred my activism, as did my interviews and reviews of decades-old charts documenting prolonged institutionalization, bizarre and near-lethal withdrawal procedures, coerced sterilizations, 'shock therapy', psychosurgery and drug insults of unending varieties. Forty years later, I can vividly recall the leather restraints and straightjackets, the hydrotherapy tubs, the over-crowded wards, the stench of urine and paraldehyde and the feeling of utter hopelessness that permeated those institutions. If I had entered the field only a few years later, I would have had no real sense of the horrid conditions that preceded modern addiction treatment.

A: What addiction treatment resources existed at the community level at that time?

WLW: There were fledgling alcoholism programs, therapeutic communities and methadone programs, but there were no specialized addiction treatment services in most American communities. In the cities in which I was working, I could not even get alcoholics admitted to local hospitals for treatment of acute trauma because of morality clauses in hospital by-laws that prohibited the admission of alcoholics. Institutional ownership of alcohol and drug problems in those years rested with the criminal justice system, so much of my early outreach work was in the city drunk tanks and the county jails. The only welcome sign and haven of comfort for the addicted in most cities was inside the meeting rooms of Alcoholics Anonymous (AA).

A: Is there an incident that typifies your early work during this period?

WLW: There is one that comes immediately to mind. I helped get a man released from the drunk tank of a local city jail, connected him to a local AA group and offered daily support to him and his family. He did amazingly well for a few months, considering the severity and duration of his alcoholism. It was the week of Christmas when, depressed over the gifts he was unable to provide for his wife and children, he sought the balm of an offered bottle. He was jailed later that day for public intoxication and hung himself during the night in the same cell in which I had first met him. Such suicides were common in those years. When I stood before his body and met later that day with his family, I was overwhelmed by my own ineptness and the meager resources I had been able to muster in my offer of assistance. There were no addiction-trained physicians, no detoxification units, no treatment programs, no trained addiction counselors. I was enraged that this man had to die in despair in such a despicable place. I think my commitment to spend my life working in this field began that day.

A: Your work to help found Chestnut Health Systems was an early product of that commitment. How did this come about?

WLW: I worked as a streetworker (what today we would call an outreach worker) and community organizer for the state mental health department and a local mental health center in the early 1970s. The needs I was witnessing as a streetworker, including my outreach in the jails and hospital emergency rooms, informed the types of services I was trying to organize. This led to helping to develop one of thousands of local alcoholism councils that were popping up in those years. Landmark legislation was passed in the early 1970s that channeled federal dollars through the states to local communities to plan, build, staff and operate addiction treatment programs. Our local council received word in 1972 that we would be funded to open the community's first treatment center. I was invited to work as a counselor at Lighthouse, which was later rechristened Chestnut Health Systems. Within months, I assumed the clinical director position. We visited Hazelden, where they shared everything about the inner workings of the Minnesota Model. We also drew from Chicago's Gateway House, a second-generation therapeutic community in those days.

A: In 1975, you made a decision to return to school.

WLW: In 1975 I decided, as an alternative to leaving the field, to get into the field even deeper. First, I was able to arrange a Master's program in Addiction Studies through Goddard College that allowed me to use Dr Ed Senay as my primary mentor. My professional maturation began under his guidance. The second decision I made was to expand my experiential knowledge by gaining exposure to different types of treatment. This led to my relocation to Chicago and a position with the Illinois Dangerous Drugs Commission. My work there provided an understanding of the larger state and national infrastructure of the field and expanded my knowledge and skills in planning, policy development, research and training. This led to my accepting a position as Deputy Director of the National Institute on Drug Abuse's midwest training center and an eventual transfer to Washington DC, where I gained exposure as a national trainer. During this time, I refined the presentation skills that would keep me on the lecture circuit for the next two decades.

A: In 1982, you returned to Illinois to direct a hospital-based addiction treatment program. How would you describe the state of treatment in those years?

WLW: This move was a conscious effort to deepen my clinical leadership skills, and it was a great time to do it. The early 1980s were the pinnacle of recovery as a cultural phenomenon in America—a time when it was cool to be in recovery. Twelve-Step programs were growing explosively. This period also marked the rapid commercialization of addiction treatment. The image of the field has still not recovered fully from such abuses.

The Lighthouse Institute and Early Books

A: What led to your return to Chestnut Health Systems in 1986 and the founding of the Lighthouse Institute?

WLW: Russ Hagen invited me to return to Chestnut to create a research and training division. I accepted and became the first staff person in Chestnut's Lighthouse Institute. I focused most of my time delivering addiction-related training and consultation services throughout North America.

A: Shortly after you returned to Chestnut you published your first book.[1]

WLW: It was a very personal form of sense-making. I had helped build some very innovative programs in the 1970s, but then witnessed some of those programs implode at the very time they were receiving considerable external recognition. I saw similar destructive organizational processes in my consultation work with many addiction treatment programs. There seemed to be a propensity for addiction treatment programs to become closed incestuous systems marked by charismatic leadership, ideological extremism, professional and social isolation, and abuses of power that injured both clients and staff.

A: How did you come to write on ethics?[2]

WLW: I felt we needed an ethics casebook that provided a model of ethical decision-making and used real ethical dilemmas to mark the ethical terrain of the field. My next book[3] and my broader work with the AIDS Foundation of Chicago were attempts to offer some personal response to the devastation of the early AIDS epidemic.

Slaying the Dragon

A: You are perhaps best known for *Slaying the Dragon*, your work on the history of addiction treatment and recovery in America. How did this work begin?

WLW: I had worked in direct services for almost a decade before stumbling onto the existence of earlier periods of addiction treatment. I felt somehow cheated that such knowledge had not been passed on to me and became curious about the early history of treatment and recovery support groups. I began researching this history in the mid-1970s. I hope there will be other histories that will surpass what I have created, but I am very pleased to have written the first comprehensive history of the field and to have published it in a way that it has remained affordable.[4]

A: You must have found that research quite enjoyable, to have sustained it over that many years.

WLW: It became one of the professional loves of my life. First, there was the excitement of historical discovery, particularly in the archival research, and my interviews with people such as Dan Anderson, Vincent Dole and David Deitch exerted a profound influence on my own commitment to the field.

A: Your contributions in writing the history of treatment and recovery in America have been blessed by some special mentors?

WLW: The most important of these mentors has been and still is the Harvard-trained historian Ernie Kurtz. I knew of Ernie's definitive history of AA and contacted him in the early 1990s with a request that he review the four chapters I had drafted on AA for *Slaying the Dragon*. That initial contact grew into a sustained mentorship of nearly all my subsequent history work.

A: How do you square your role as dispassionate scholar with that of activist?

WLW: There has clearly been tension between my aspirations for objective scholarship and my activist role in this movement. I am, without question, a historian with an agenda. My goal is to use history to change people's lives and to elevate the professional field that has been such an important part of my life.

A: How did you come to collaborate on writing a history of recovery among Native American tribes?

WLW: That project began when I first met Don Coyhis, the Director of White Bison, Inc. and leader of the Native American Wellbriety Movement. I mentioned to Don that I had encountered evidence suggesting Native American recovery circles dating to the 1730s—200 years before the founding of AA. I suggested that this history could contribute to the cultural renewal processes that were unfolding in Indian communities across North America and encouraged him to research and write this history. He, in turn, challenged me to help with the project. The book[5] debunks many of the 'firewater myths' that have stigmatized Indian communities. I am pleased that we have donated all proceeds from the book to the Native American Wellbriety Movement.

A: You publish your work in books and peer-reviewed journals, but you also invest considerable time writing for addiction treatment trade journals, recovery advocacy newsletters and writing papers that you leave in the public domain and allow to be posted on multiple Internet sites.

WLW: Contributing to the scholarship of the field is important to me, but I have tried to remain faithful to my primary audiences: people in recovery, recovery advocates and those working on the front lines of treatment. I think we underestimate the potential power of 'grey literature'.

Recovery Management

A: You have called for a recovery-focused redesign of addiction treatment. How did you come to develop this perspective?

WLW: I think of it as my epiphany in Dallas. In the late 1990s, I was interviewing a 94-year-old man with 54 years of sobriety in AA. During a break in the interview, he asked me about this 'research stuff' I did. I later reflected on his question a good deal and realized that my colleagues and I had spent most of our lives studying addiction and this thing called treatment, but that, from the standpoint of science, we knew very little about people's lives in recovery. It was at this point that I began to write about switching from pathology and intervention paradigms toward a recovery paradigm as the organizing center for the field.[6] McLellan and colleagues' seminal 2001 article in the *Journal of the American Medical Association* will probably stand as a historical tipping-point in this effort.[7] My colleagues and I at the Lighthouse Institute are particularly interested in the effects of post-treatment monitoring, sustained recovering coaching, and assertive linkage to communities of recovery.[8–10]

A: You have also been very interested in the history of Alcoholics Anonymous and other recovery mutual aid societies.

WLW: Often abandoned by family and society, people suffering from addiction have been reaching out to one another for mutual recovery support for more than 250 years.[11]

A: How did you come to take on the practice of administrative discharge?

WLW: At the time my colleagues and I first looked at this, 18% of all clients admitted to addiction treatment in the United States were discharged administratively, which is a euphemism for being kicked out—mainly for confirming their diagnosis via alcohol or other drug use. We have argued that discharging clients administratively from addiction treatment for alcohol and other drug (AOD) use is illogical and unprecedented in the health-care system.

A: You also challenged the use of 'Treatment Works' as the field's most central organizing slogan.

WLW: Addiction treatment is a godsend for hundreds of thousands of individuals and families, but its role in the recovery process is misrepresented to the public through the slogan 'Treatment Works'. Perhaps most importantly, the slogan 'Treatment Works' misrepresents the highly variable and complex outcomes of addiction treatment and shifts the focus (and responsibility for recovery) from the addicted/recovering person to the treatment professional.

And Finally

A: How have you kept such passion for this work over the past four decades?

WLW: I have watched closely those people who have made sustained contributions in this field and sustained their health through that process. I have tried to model my professional life on what I have learned from them. I found four things in the lives of these professional elders: centering rituals that helped them continually refine their goals and evaluate their progress, replenishment rituals that allowed them to interact with others who shared their aspirational values, a commitment to self-development and self-care of themselves and their families and involvement in unpaid acts of service to others. I have pursued these strategies imperfectly, but I suspect they are the source of my professional resilience. This is a field whose front lines can consume you through the losses you experience, but it is also a field that can reward you at the deepest levels. I do not know any other helping arena within which you can witness people completely transform their lives. Staying attuned to the reality of such transformations and the potential for such transformations in all those we serve is a well of replenishment from which we should all regularly drink.

A: What fills your life outside of your professional activities?

WLW: Very simple pleasures: love for my wife and children, work in my private garden, long walks through the lush foliage and beaches near our Florida home, constant reading and donating time to grass-roots recovery advocacy groups. I am now phasing-down my professional travel, and my wife and I are looking forward to increasing our visits to other countries.

Notes

1. White W. *The Incestuous Workplace: Stress and Distress in the Organizational Family*, 2nd edn. Center City, MN. Hazelden; 1997.
2. White W., Popovits R. *Critical Incidents: Ethical Issues in the Prevention and Treatment of Addiction*, 2nd edn. Bloomington, IL: Chestnut Health Systems/ Lighthouse Institute; 2000.
3. White W. *Voices of Survival, Voices of Service: AIDS Case Management in Chicago*. Chicago: AIDS Foundation of Chicago; 1994.
4. White W. *Slaying the Dragon: The History of Addiction Treatment and Recovery in America*. Bloomington, IL: Chestnut Health Systems/Lighthouse Institute; 1998.
5. Coyhis D., White W. *Alcohol Problems in Native America: The Untold Story of Resistance and Recovery*. Colorado Springs, CO: White Bison, Inc.; 2006.
6. White W. Recovery: its history and renaissance as an organizing construct. *Alcohol Treat Q* 2005; 23: 3–15.
7. McLellan A. T., Lewis D. C., O'Brien C. P., Kleber H. D. Drug dependence, a chronic medical illness: implications for treatment, insurance and outcomes evaluation. *JAMA* 2000; 284: 1689–95.
8. Godley M. D., Godley S. H., Dennis M. L., Funk R., Passetti L. Preliminary outcomes from the assertive continuing care experiment for adolescents discharged from residential treatment. *J Subst Abuse Treat* 2002; 23: 21–32.
9. Dennis M. L., Scott C. K., Funk R. Main findings from an experimental evaluation of recovery management checkups and early re-intervention (RMC/ ERI) with chronic substance users. *Eval Program Plann* 2003; 26: 339–52.
10. White W., Kurtz E. The varieties of recovery experience. *Int J Self Help Self Care* 2006; 3: 21–61.
11. Kurtz E., Kurtz L. *Mutual Support Resources. Faces and Voices of Recovery*. 2006. Available at: http://www.facesandvoicesofrecovery.org/resources/ support_home.php (accessed 20 November 20 2006).

41

Commentary

Jonathan Chick

Clinicians as Change Agents in the Addictions World

Sheila Blume, Roger Meyer, William Miller, George Vaillant, and William L White are the five contributions to this book on whose careers I have been asked to comment.

Here are five names that resonate strongly in the story of addiction treatment, particularly alcoholism treatment, in the last 40 years. At first glance their careers appear to have little in common except that each started in the United States of the 1960's. Achieving national and international distinction as they have was not rooted in a particularly privileged family background. Though George Vaillant's (George Vaillant) father was a distinguished anthropologist/archaeologist (an expert on the Aztecs) the others in this subset came from humbler families, winning scholarships into a good education in which they excelled. Poorer material advantages do not deter learning to think honestly and incisively, although in George Vaillant's materially more endowed upbringing, that had been a trait noted in his father. An obituary to George Vaillant's father's recorded his "clarity of mind and characteristic Gallic aversion to all forms of hypocrisy'.[1]

Some common factors would be found if we looked at the lives of lively contributors in any discipline: A love for learning, a thrill in new knowledge, having an inspiring mentor, and happenstance (to use William Miller's word) - being in the right place at the right time (with the correct credentials) or 'Chance favours a prepared mind' as the *Addiction* Editor interpolated. The careers of this Famous Five portray most of these ingredients.

('Famous Five': Author's note to Enid Blyton readers: In commenting on the lives of these 5 addictionists, only the faintest allusion is intended towards the travails of Julian, Dick, George [Georgina], Ann and Timmy who, in a world where ginger beer rather than whisky flowed and the diet was ham rolls, dedicated themselves to the search for the truth.)

Perhaps one should not expect such a cache of addictionologists to have much in their life trajectory in common: a psychopharmacologist (Roger Meyer), an epidemiologist (George Vaillant), a talented administrator – a mover and shaker - who could take over a large clinic apparently at moment's notice, and a few years later take a State-wide role, promptly changing the wording in two State laws (Sheila Blume), a street worker/counsellor who puzzled over how organisations worked and went on to re-write the wider philosophy of addiction recovery (William L. White) and a trail-blazing psychologist who could equally have entered the seminary (William Miller).

In the 1960s there was a homily circulating that the most important step for any alcohol researcher was "to leave the field before his reputation was irrevocably tarnished". It was a field sullied, so it went, by poor methodology, poor science, and completely unreliable data obtained from participants who usually lied; plus, the stigma of the subjects under study would soon rub off on to any researcher ingenuous enough to get involved.

This has changed. ... somewhat. The USA National Institutes of Health today have substantial funds for research in alcohol and drug research. Even a few pharmaceutical companies have risked their reputation and stepped in this stony research world thanks to it being seeded and fertilized by neuropharmacological ideas of bona fide clinical professors such as Roger Meyer. These individuals, and their generation, both benefitted from a widening acceptance of the need and value of addictions research and, of course, contributed to that change.

So what, if any, might be the common features of their careers, and do any of those features epitomise a shining career in addiction treatment and research?

Love of Writing

One unifying trait in our five might be a love, and a skill, to write. George Vaillant worked for the Harvard humour magazine *'Lampoon'*. Sheila Blume loved the chapters she wrote in textbooks, and in retirement has written 700 limericks for the *Omnificent English Dictionary* in Limerick Form. William L. White's history of the addiction treatment in the USA, *'Slaying the Dragon,'*[2] is widely read and William Miller's *'Motivational Interviewing'*[4] (with Steve Rollnick) is what his publisher calls a book with 'long legs' - it disseminates with very little in the way of marketing.

But care must be taken in making too much of that. Drawing attention to their writing skills as a common thread could be falling into the fallacy of selection bias – these names may have been sought after for the Interview partly because their writing and presentation skills made them known to *Addiction*.

Taking a Broad View

A cosmopolitan thread in their careers could link them, but this too might be an artefact of selection – these pioneers gained international recognition and so an overseas–based journal such as *Addiction* might have known them and sought them out for the Interview for that reason. On the other hand, their having experience across cultures could help us understand their common interest in addiction. As William Miller taught us in *'Motivational Interviewing'*, when helping behaviour change, it makes a difference if we are tolerant of others' ambivalence, and accept that others may hold views and values that, at a given point, may be very different from ours.

Here is how these addiction-specialists–to-be broadened their minds cross-culturally:

As a young researcher, Sheila Blume lived in Japan and learnt to speak Japanese. By age 10, George Vaillant had lived in three different countries. William L. White researched Native American traditions (discovering 'recovery circles' dating to the 1730s). Roger Meyer described being 'born and raised in New York City in a mixed Irish, Italian and Jewish neighborhood' - he would have heard stories of adaptation in troubled times to other peoples' culture and values. While William Miller does not describe how wide a world view you could get growing up in an Appalachian coal-mining town, and does not mention travel abroad in his early years, he recounts having a go at one point at transmuting into 'a hippie radical, long-haired, bearded guy'. (Fortunately for the international addictions treatment community William Miller has now given many training seminars abroad – one favourite used to be held on the Italian Ligurian Coast).

That readiness to take a wider view is a characteristic evidenced in their collaborative attitude to colleagues in other disciplines, an approach that has come to typify both clinical and pre-clinical research in addictions especially in North America. As Roger Meyer put it (Roger Meyer, like Sheila Blume and George Vaillant, was a Harvard trained psychiatrist): 'I know of no other field of research in psychiatry where the physician researchers are as committed to a multi-disciplinary perspective or are as generous and mutually supportive.' Team-work typifies William Miller's contribution: he says that he found that he did not 'need to be first' – he was completely satisfied with collaboration: His approach was 'Why don't we do something with this together' – he did not feel resources were scarce and had to seize what he could for himself.

Deeper Meaning

A theme emerging in these interviews is that recovery from addiction has a deep meaning for many, touching something beyond correcting chemistry or learning a new coping skill. Meeting members of Alcoholics Anonymous (AA) seems to have been a fairly early and influential experience for most of these five, though William L. White is the only one who hints that he might have come into the addictions field through a personal or family experience of addiction, which is a quite a common route by which people come to work in addictions research and treatment. George Vaillant in his longitudinal studies met men in remission from alcoholism without 'treatment', or if they had had treatment did not attribute their remission to that. He wrote from his view point as a psychoanalyst that one to one treatment for the alcoholic has inherent hazards and is often doomed to fail. Since transference in the psychoanalytical sense was likely, it was infinitely preferable for transference to occur not to an individual therapist but to a caring fellowship (and AA has proven that it will be there long beyond any therapist could survive, in terms of tolerance and patience as well as in terms of years!).[4] See also William L. White: 'The phrase 'Treatment Works' misrepresents the highly variable and complex outcomes of addiction treatment and shifts the focus (and responsibility for recovery) from the addicted/recovering person to the treatment professional.'

Spirituality (which the interviewer did not ask George Vaillant to define) was an important ingredient as time passed for some of the Boston boys and Harvard students who he followed through their lives,[5,6] and was also, George Vaillant says, for him. Like George Vaillant, William L. White places emphasis on the long view, the changes that people make through their recovery journey, and the importance of a shared community. AA certainly came to regard the process as lifelong, continually practising being on guard against those tendencies we all have at some time to harbour resentments, feel jealous, feel self-pity, yearn for status or allow our instincts (which may have had a biological function) to harm others.

Nevertheless the 'spiritual' approach to recovery was sometimes misused. It is striking that both William Miller and William L. White commented on the dangers borne in the rapid commercialisation of addiction treatment that occurred during their time, programmes that sometimes misused the Twelve-Step approach. 'The image of the field has still not recovered fully from such abuses', said William L. White. And William Miller told his interviewer that AA's 'patient, compassionate approach that is not blaming or judging, is nothing like what the treatment industry created with 12-step disease model treatment'.

Hope

Early in their careers, they saw the plight of institutionalised addicts, William L. White in the Illinois Department of Mental Health, Sheila Blume in the Bowery, New York, George Vaillant working at the United States Narcotic Farm Lexington; these experiences could have hampered seeing the possibility of any change in such apparently hopeless people. 'From its opening in 1935, the Lexington epitomized the nation's ambivalence about how to deal with drug addiction. On one hand, it functioned as a compassionate and humane hospital, an "asylum on the hill" on 1,000 acres of farmland where addicts could recover from their drug habits. On the other hand, it was an imposing federal prison built for the incarceration of drug addicts.' (George Vaillant).

However, that was not to deter an evolving sense of hope for addicts – and a conviction that that hope was to be communicated to the sufferers:

George Vaillant: 'If you want to treat an illness that has no easy cure, first of all treat them with hope.' His life-long studies showed him 'a triumph of the continuance of biology, that the brain continues to evolve and does not stop maturing at age 5, as Freud would have had us believe.'

William L. White: 'I do not know any other helping arena within which you can witness people completely transform their lives.'

Roger Meyer 'In coping with addiction as a chronic relapsing disorder, .. you should be able to provide hope....'

William Miller: '.... having the client make the arguments for change..and, also, eliciting their confidence and hope.'

Compassion

That early exposure to the harsher side of society's attitude to addiction seems to have spurred on several to choose that career. William L. White was sensitised: 'I could not even get alcoholics admitted to local hospitals for treatment of acute trauma because of morality clauses in hospital by-laws that prohibited the admission of alcoholics.' Sheila Blume had been identified as the one out of the 100 staff at the Central Islip State Hospital who 'liked those people', so she got the job at the alcohol unit. William Miller had been trained in Carl Rogers' psychotherapy approach where empathy was a hallmark ingredient of good therapy, empathy being what sufferers experience when they feel the would-be helper is trying to understand what they are feeling, believe and go through - it is non-judgemental. This, of course, became one of the five tenets of Motivational Interviewing.[3]

And so, compassion for those in the grip of addiction was a strong force in these careers. In these interviews neither the *Addiction* interviewers or the interviewees speculate on the roots of a compassionate nature. But note that none of these five reported losing their mother in childhood, and although George Vaillant's father died when he was 10 years old, he specifically mentions 'a childhood with a great deal of care and consideration.' William L. White, raised in a large family, told the interviewer that although it was like being brought up in a cocoon, he had 'spent more than four decades since appreciating anew what I experienced within that cocoon.'

Compassion does not judge. For Robert Burns, there was only one who had the right to judge!

Who made the heart, 'tis He alone
Decidedly can try us;
He knows each chord, its various tone,
Each spring, its various bias:
Then at the balance let's be mute,
We never can adjust it;
What's done we partly may compute,
But know not what's resisted.

Notes

1. *The American Anthropologist*, 47, 1945 589–602.
2. White W. *Slaying the Dragon: The History of Addiction Treatment and Recovery in America*. Bloomington, IL: Chestnut Health Systems/Lighthouse Institute; 1998.
3. Miller W. R., Rollnick S. *Motivational Interviewing: Preparing People to Change Addictive Behavior*. New York: Guilford Press; 1991.
4. Vaillant GE (1991) An alternative to psychotherapy. in Crome IB. *The International Handbook of Addiction Behaviour*. London: Routledge.
5. Vaillant, G. E. (1977) *Adaptation to Life*. Boston, MA: Little, Brown [also in German, Korean and Chinese translations] [Reprinted with a new preface in 1995 by Harvard University Press, Cambridge, MA].
6. Vaillant, G. E. (1983) *Natural History of Alcoholism*. Cambridge, MA: Harvard University Press.

42

Addiction Careers: Catalysts for an Interdisciplinary Field

Thomas F. Babor

Tinker, tailor, soldier, sailor, rich man, poor man, beggar man, thief,
Or what about a scientist, a clinician, or an addiction institute chief?
Oh it's such a lot of things there are and such a lot to be
That there's always lots of cherries on my little cherry tree.[1]

Why would anyone want to publish, much less read, a book on the making of professional careers in an academic field that calls itself "addiction"? Let me count the ways. First, the interviews and the commentaries in this book provide a wonderful history of an interdisciplinary field populated by a variety of creative people: basic scientists in pursuit of knowledge for its own sake, clinical investigators searching for new or better treatments, and applied researchers trying to solve difficult social problems. Second, the book's interview subjects are role models for the next generation of addiction specialists, and for this reason their personal biographies tell us much about the ingredients of a productive professional career. Finally, the book reveals the inside stories of how scientific discovery happens, and how science is translated into effective clinical practice and social policy.

The field of academic addiction science is a social construction as well as a cognitive construct. It exists in the minds of a rather complex network of perhaps 10,000 people worldwide who identify with it as part of their career identity. The field is built around institutions that help to define its roles and responsibilities. Professional societies, research centers, national institutes, addiction journals, and specialized treatment programs constitute the major ingredients of the addiction field's infrastructure, but as the interviews in this book demonstrate, addiction careers constitute its building blocks and its human capital.

The emergence of a cadre of career scientists devoted to the pursuit of knowledge about dependence-producing psychoactive substances is a 20th-century phenomenon (Babor, 2000), but the roots of this global network were planted firmly in the late 19th century. Then as now, addiction studies were driven primarily by a societal interest in the social, medical, moral and economic consequences of alcohol, and to a lesser extent, psychoactive drugs and tobacco. The first wave of addiction professionals surged and then receded in concert with the rise and fall of the global Temperance Movement. During a 40-year period (1875–1915) addiction specialists emerged from various areas of academia and medicine to advance knowledge about addiction problems. They operated by means of professional societies (e.g., the British Society for the Study of Inebriety), international meetings, scientific journals, and the publication of scholarly books. The demise of addiction studies followed the imposition of Prohibition legislation in the United States, Scandinavia, the United Kingdom and many other countries in the aftermath of the First World War. It was not until the 1940s that addiction studies and services regained a sense of identity and purpose, and not until the 1970s when it gained enough scientific respectability to be considered a legitimate part of society's public health response to addiction problems. By integrating itself with the postwar biomedical establishment (particularly psychiatry), the addiction field experienced phenomenal growth. That growth has been characterized by a number of "megatrends" (Babor, 2000, 1993) that help to explain the professional careers captured in this book.

As depicted in Figure 1, these trends include: (1) the emergence of public and private financing mechanisms to support careers in addiction research; (2) development of an institutional base consisting of research centers, specialized clinical facilities and related organizational structures; (3) the growth of professional societies to give the field a sense of identity and purpose; and (4) the rapid expansion of scientific communication outlets and publication opportunities to facilitate information exchange and dissemination. The final ingredient of the addiction field depicted in the figure is the result of all this effort. Although opinions will differ as to what constitutes the collective "products" of professional academic careers, as well as the purpose of a profession that until recently did not even have a name or an identity, from a societal perspective the tangible products of the addiction field can be measured in terms of scientific knowledge, evidence-based clinical services, and policy interventions designed to address the consequences of psychoactive substance use. Without career professionals to populate this infrastructure and develop its products, the addiction field would not exist. In the following sections of this chapter, each of these elements will be discussed in terms of how they influenced, and in turn were influenced by, the professional careers documented in the 36 interviews collected in this book.

Addiction Careers: Who Becomes an Addiction Career Professional?

"I became intrigued about substance abuse early on, because around me I noticed some of my fellow students and friends, who were very much like me,

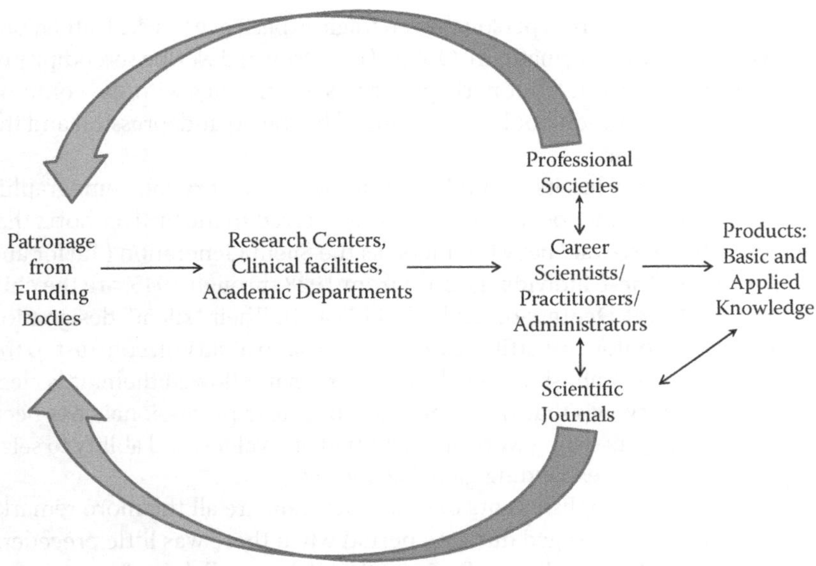

Figure 1. Career Professionals and the Infrastructure of a Specialist Field

being arrested for drug use, landing up in prison or, as it was called at the time, freaking out, and ending up on a psychiatric ward for a shorter or longer period of time. Throughout my life that question has kept me puzzling." Cees Goos

"I would like to say that it was altruism that motivated me to treat alcoholics, but the truth is that it was for more mercenary reasons." Richard Fuller

"Abe (Wikler) listened, frowned. He then said something like, 'that is a stupid idea'. Abe was blunt. About a week-and-a-half later he passed me in the hall, and said that we should talk a little bit about that experiment. He told me that after some thought it was a pretty good idea. In that experiment we demonstrated that the effects of morphine would normally impair reaction-time; however, in a conflict, morphine would improve reaction-time. That is how I became involved in the field of behavioral pharmacology." Conan Kornetsky

"Most researchers of my era entered drug abuse research coincidentally, even accidentally. Even now, in upcoming generations, there still seem to be multiple links: personal experience, whether that is for yourself or your family, cases of successful mentoring, opportunities for jobs to develop your skills in this area and provide for a career and others." Douglas Anglin

How do people select a career in an emerging field that for most of its existence had no name or identity? As suggested by these four personal accounts, the answer is as varied as the field itself. Personal experience with substance misuse, the influence of a mentor, the need to make a living, and the love of science are all mentioned in these interviews. Some developed their interest in addiction from personal, even tragic experience (Nick Heather, Bob Schuster, Shanthi Ranganathan). Others (Jim Orford) describe serendipity or "opportunity knocking." But perhaps the answer also lies with the common features of a generation doubly traumatized by the great depression and the Second World War.

Each generation has its own values, attitudes, behaviors and demographic characteristics. Some social scientists have referred to the birth cohorts that preceded the post-war "baby boomers" as the Silent Generation (Taylor and Keeter, 2010). These individuals, born from 1928 through 1945, are the children of the Great Depression and World War II. Their "silent" designation refers to their conformist attitudes and civic responsibility, in contrast to the subsequent anti-establishment baby boomers that followed them. It is clear from these interviews that this generation of career professionals has been distinguished by its strong work ethic, humanistic values, and ability to seize opportunities in an expanding global economy.

The career accomplishments of this generation are all the more remarkable because they emerged during a period when there was little precedent for either addiction studies or for interdisciplinary collaboration around a common public health issue. Beyond the fact that these individuals are a heterogeneous lot in terms of nationalities, socioeconomic backgrounds, and academic training, what they have in common is a determination to pursue knowledge about the nature, cure and prevention of addiction.

Patronage

"The move to research on cocaine was partly political, in the sense that there was a great deal of money available for work on cocaine. Crack cocaine was being discovered and there was much interest in cocaine as an abused substance." Michael Kuhar

"A few weeks after I arrived, I got a call from a congressperson who asked what I would do if NIDA had $60 million more a year. The NIDA budget, when I got there, was $85 million total. I called in my senior-level people and I said Okay guys, we have to have a proposal in two days to justify an increase of $60 million dollars. We got the $60 million dollar increase. That was an absolute joy, because suddenly we were able to start doing important research in new areas." Charles Schuster

"Treatment without science is witchcraft. We had to stop claiming rates of treatment success for which there was not the slightest shred of evidence. We had to make a better effort on the research side to communicate what we are finding." Enoch Gordis

How society allocates its resources is not only testimony to its values, it is also an indication of the career opportunities that attract young people into a profession or an emerging interdisciplinary field. Like other areas of academic science, the addiction field relies on patronage. In some cases the support and sponsorship comes from private sources, as when a philanthropist creates an endowment for a research center or academic chair. More often, however, the patronage comes from public sources. During the past 40 years a variety of funding mechanisms have provided support for the addiction research infrastructure, which in turn has made possible many of the professional careers described in these interviews. National research institutes, for example, have been developed in many high income countries to plan, support and conduct scientific research on addiction (Babor, 1993). Examples of such organizations mentioned in the addiction career interviews in this book include the Norwegian National Institute on Alcohol and Drug Research, the Indian National Drug and Alcohol Institute, and the US National Institute on Alcohol Abuse and Alcoholism. Many of these organizations have been established to support the development of scientific expertise with a public health orientation. In addition to the direct funding of research scientists, other functions include research training, public education and the coordination of international activities. The careers of many of the interviewees were nurtured by these organizations, and some of them (Enoch Gordis, Ragnar Hague, Charles Schuster, Robert DuPont, Leland Towle) played prominent leadership roles in them. The combination of categorical support for addiction research and academic freedom to engage in addiction science as a career has led to an information explosion in the addiction field (Babor, 1993, Babor et al., 2008).

During the same period, there has also been a steady growth in the provision of specialized medical, psychiatric and social services to individuals with substance use disorders (Babor et al., 2008). The number and variety of services has in many parts of the industrialized world increased dramatically in the past two decades, when many countries with alcohol and drug problems have invested in treatment services as part of a larger public health approach to substance misuse. Many of the clinical scientists whose interviews appear in this book have played a leadership role in the evolution of drug and alcohol treatment systems at the national level in countries like the United Kingdom (Jim Orford, Bruce Ritson), India (Shanthi Ranganathan), the United States (Charles Schuster, Douglas Anglin, Sheila Blume, William Miller), and Switzerland (Ambros Uchtenhagen).

Research Centers, Clinical Facilities and Academic Departments

"There was a group of us who said we need a think tank, a place that is not governed by state funding, a place to explore social challenges more freely, a non-profit organization. THEI (the Human Ecology Institute*) was my first exposure to public policy as a vehicle of change."* Harold Holder

"Throughout the first half of the twentieth century the few researchers and clinicians interested in addicting drugs and the treatment of those who developed problems with their use, with a few notable exceptions, were based in

the traditional academic departments of pharmacology, neurology, psychiatry, and psychology. One very notable exception was the US Public Health Service Addiction Research Center (ARC) at Lexington, Kentucky, where the researchers were actually government employees, some of them in the commissioned corps of the Public Health Service." Jerome Jaffe

"Lexington was exciting. There was an extraordinary group of doctors coming through, ..., someone who could see addiction from many different viewpoints. One would have lunch with him and try to learn." George Vaillant

At the core of the modern addiction research infrastructure is a network of research centers, clinical facilities and academic departments that provide a working environment for addiction professionals throughout the world. Although addiction research in many countries is conducted by independent scientists whose primary affiliation is to an academic department in a university or by clinicians who work in treatment facilities, in recent years there has been an expansion of specialized centers with the primary purpose of supporting alcohol, tobacco and drug research as well as professional training. These centers, now numbering more than 200 worldwide, provide dedicated facilities to groups of scientists and supporting staff so that long-term programmatic research can be carried out. The largest number of centers is located in the USA, the Nordic countries, the UK, Russia, Brazil, Canada, and Japan. Centers provide an optimal environment for researchers, one that is relatively free of administrative, clinical, and teaching responsibilities. Not only are the positions dedicated exclusively to research, the center also provides the prospect of long-term support, job security, and career advancement.

Because addiction is considered a new if not unusual career path for scientists in many disciplines, centers are often the only places where young researchers can apprentice. This is indicated in the comments of people like Konan Kornetsky who spent time working at the Addiction Research Center in Lexington, Kentucky USA. Another role of the addiction research center is to facilitate links with the community of scholars and with the general public. Research centers provide leadership and visibility to alcohol and drug research in the form of such activities as international collaboration, joint projects with other research centers, and consultation to governments. This is clearly indicated in the experiences communicated by Ragnar Hauge, who directed the Norwegian National Institute, which served both as a research center and a national resource for addiction policy.

A number of those interviewed (Hamid Ghodse, Jim Orford, Michael Russell, Martin Jarvis) mention the profound influence the Addiction Research Unit (ARU) in London had on their careers, not only in the training and support that was provided, but also the opportunity to work with seminal thinkers like Griffith Edwards. Like many addiction research centers, the environment of the ARU was multi-disciplinary, but with a social and behavioral orientation that attracted scientists from all over the world.

Journals, Books and Other Means of Communication

"Writing is so important. I consider my life a series of missions—to get women into treatment, to attend to the special needs of women, to interest society and the professions in gambling problems. You never know when you write something where it is going to go—the Supreme Court, Iceland, Africa—you do not know." Sheila Blume

"I think of contributions or papers as each being a 'brick' in the 'wall of knowledge.' Each finding or publication is a new brick added to the top of the wall. Eventually the wall grows and grows, and our own bricks become further down as new workers and their new bricks of discovery are added on top of our own." Michael Kuhar

"I read the 'Purple Book' (the color of its cover) about taking a public health approach to alcohol prevention. It changed my professional career. An outcome was my first book, a sort of American answer to the Purple Book." Harold Holder

These quotations speak to the importance and influence of scholarly writing in the addiction field. In addition to influential books, the peer reviewed journal article has become a fundamental building block of scientific communication in the field. The careers of most of the individuals interviewed for this book can be traced through their scholarly publications. As the field has grown and matured, there has been a concomitant growth in the number of specialty journals and the volume of scientific publications that have entered the world literature dealing with the pharmacology, biochemistry, neurobiology, psychology, sociology and epidemiology of substance misuse (Babor, 1993). Between 1900 and 1950, approximately 500 scientific articles were published per year on alcohol. Between 1950 and 1970, the number of publications doubled each decade. By the late 1980s more than 3000 scholarly publications on alcohol were appearing per year, and the trend has continued unabated during the 1990s. Part of this growth is reflected in the number of addiction specialty journals that publish articles on alcohol and other drugs. There are now more than 85 journals, most of which have been established since the 1970s (Babor et al., 2008).

Professional Societies

"I was Chairman of the Committee (Committee on Problems of Drug Dependence) *around the transition time. It was still an old boys' club in 1980. It was still not a membership organization when I became Chair. I lobbied to change that."* Lou Harris

"When I took over the Society it was limping along. I started to draw the threads together. It seemed to me that, first, the Society should have an annual meeting. The second thing was that we had a couple of endowed lectures, and it was logical to fit those into the annual meeting. I was particularly keen that we tried to get some educational programmes going." Malcolm Lader

Professional organizations are a major resource for scientists working in biomedical and psychosocial research. They distribute news and scientific information to their members, publish journals and newsletters, engage in advocacy for research, coordinate scientific meetings, and at times facilitate collaborative research. A recent internet search of specialty organizations dealing with addiction identified 38 societies whose mission statements suggested primary involvement in issues related to the misuse of alcohol, drugs, tobacco and other psychoactive substances (Edwards and Babor, 2008). The organizations, which have been established at both the national and international levels, are open to professionals of all disciplines who work in the addiction area, including treatment, prevention, research, policy and education. The British Society for the Study of Addiction (SSA) is a good example of a multi-disciplinary national society, as is the College on Problems of Drug Dependence (CPDD). The professional careers of scientists like Malcolm Lader (former president of SSA) and Lou Harris (CPDD) were devoted in part to reinventing the role of these organizations in the modern addiction field. These organizations, in turn, provide a means of networking and communication for their members. They confer prestige and often serve as advocates for professional issues like research funding and the training of scientists.

Accomplishments: Knowledge, Service, and Policy Products

"In terms of scientific accomplishments, one stands out. My laboratory published a paper in Science *in 1987 showing that the dopamine transporter was the receptor for the addicting properties of cocaine."* Michael Kuhar

"The prevailing view of alcoholism and drug abuse was that these were events that were largely the result of people being driven into this terrible life-style. Now all of a sudden we had monkeys pressing levers to obtain a drug. It is a perfect example of a methodological development producing a conceptual change: it was clearly the consequences, not the antecedents, that were maintaining the drug self-administration performance." Joseph Brady

"...the fact is that rational social policy which follows from the application of science- based interventions—for example—legal alcohol levels for driving, minimum age for drinking – has already saved thousands of lives. We cannot make that claim yet for either genetics or neuroscience. The benefits of genetics and neuroscience are largely for the future." Enoch Gordis

Scientific discoveries, new theoretical developments, and the application of scientific findings to the prevention and treatment of addiction-related problems are just a few examples of the "products" of addiction science. The pursuit of scientific breakthroughs to achieve a better understanding of addiction, or the application of addiction science to clinical practice and social policy, are the kinds of outcomes that the patrons of addiction science, be they governmental or private, expect for their investments. What do these addiction careers indicate in terms of the "return on investment?"

Seminal developments in neuroscience, psychopharmacology, epidemiology, treatment and prevention are described in one interview after another, often by the key players in discoveries and applications that in hindsight represent significant accomplishments both from a scientific and a public health perspective. In the 1960s and 1970s, Charles (Bob) Schuster and his behavioural pharmacology colleagues showed that animals would self-administer drugs, and that almost all the drugs that humans abused were self-administered by monkeys. According to Michael Kunar, this is a clear indication of an innate property of the brain that makes both humans and animals vulnerable to drug seeking and dependence. Although he did not discover the phenomenon of brain-stimulation reward, Conan Kornetsky and colleagues did develop new ways of measuring the reward threshold, finding that all abused drugs lower that threshold and increase the sensitivity of rewarding brain stimulation. Raphael Mechoulam found that the endocannabinoid system plays a role in the formation of emotions.

Sheila Blume developed a structured survey procedure that provides valuable diagnostic information about the severity of a patient's pathological gambling disorder, and William R. Miller developed a therapy technique, motivational interviewing, which has been used successfully not only for managing patients with substance use disorders, but also with patients in many other areas of medicine and psychiatry whose maladaptive behaviour interferes with their health.

Robert L. DuPont, former Director of the US National Institute on Drug Abuse, described how the crime rate associated with the heroin epidemic in Washington, D.C. was reversed over a period of three years by treating 15,000 addicts with methadone, which was developed in the context of clinical and pharmacological research on addiction.

Michael Russell and Martin Jarvis published studies in the early 1980's demonstrating for the first time the essential nature of nicotine addiction. This research showed, for example, that the dose smokers get is determined not by the cigarette product, but by the smoker's acquired needs. Research showing that smokers titrate the dose of nicotine to satisfy a biological need led to the development of nicotine replacement therapies, which have benefited millions of smokers by reducing the rates of lung cancer and coronary heart disease.

Addiction studies have often been at the forefront of advances in genetics, neurobiology, behavioral pharmacology, toxicology, psychology, sociology, epidemiology and clinical medicine. And the methods, theories and findings from all of these fields have been applied to the understanding of addiction, as well as its treatment and prevention.

Conclusion: No Regrets

"The research career goals that I set out to achieve as I was leaving NIMH in 1968 were achieved beyond my wildest expectations. The privilege of

serving as a consultant to the White House was a special opportunity to affect policy. My friendships within the addiction research community have been very meaningful. I know of no other field of research in psychiatry where the physician researchers are as committed to a multi-disciplinary perspective or are as generous and mutually supportive." Roger Meyer

"...the 'great men' approach is not the way to look at the evolution of the field. This field should be viewed as the product of an interaction between methodological developments and conceptual changes.... Well, the great men are agents. They just happened to be in the right place at the right time." Joseph Brady

"The ever-changing field involves economics, politics, history, biology and even religion. Whatever you are interested in, drug abuse has it. The best part has been the people, not just experts but everyone involved, including addicted people and their families, the real 'experts' in our field." Robert L DuPont

These are testimonials spoken from the hearts of career professionals who have no regrets. What, if anything, unites the seemingly diverse subjects of these interviews? For those who have read all 36, and the many other *Addiction* interviews that preceded them (Edwards, 1991, 2002), the thread is clear. They are all intelligent, creative people who cared profoundly about one or more aspects of addiction: a passion for science without neglecting its social value; a devotion to patients without uncritically accepting the conventional wisdom that addiction is incurable or not worth the effort to even try; an appreciation of institutions without allowing the bureaucracy to smother effective service and creative ideas.

And what is it about these parallel lives that defines the evolution of a specialist field like addiction? Most likely it is the network of clinicians, scientists, psychopharmacologists, and administrators who have provided the building blocks for institutions and a science base to justify public investment in addiction science. Martin Jarvis's description of the intrepid group of nicotine and tobacco researchers in the UK, which is echoed in style and substance in the stories of US neuroscientists and behavioural pharmacologists, provides a very clear example of the critical importance of interdisciplinary networks of career scientists in the development of scientific breakthroughs that have made a real difference in the lives of ordinary people. One is struck by the extent to which these stories suggest the vital interaction between science, clinical practice and social policy, whether it deals with opiate addiction, nicotine dependence or alcoholism. Given the enormous number of lives saved and human suffering prevented by these advances, would we be remiss in suggesting that these men and women are the unsung heroes of their age? In terms of their public health implications, one is tempted to compare them to the Royal Air Force pilots of whom Churchill said: "Never....was so much owed by so many to so few."

Note

1. Adapted from A. A. Milne, *Now We are Six* (London: E. P. Dutton & Company, 1927), pp. 19–21.

References

Babor, T. F. (1993) Megatrends and dead ends: Alcohol research in global perspective. *Alcohol Health & Research World, 17,* 177–86.

Babor, T. F. Past as prologue: the future of addiction studies. *Addiction* 95(1): 7–10, 2000.

Babor, T. F., Morisano, D., Stenius, K., Winstanley, E. L., & O'Reilly J. (2008) How to choose a journal: Scientific and practical considerations. In T. F. Babor et al. (Eds.). *Publishing addiction science: A guide for the perplexed* (2nd ed.). UK: Multi-Science Publishing.

Babor, T. F., Stenius, K, Romelsjo, A. (2008) Alcohol and drug treatment systems in public health perspective: Mediators and moderators of population effects. *International Journal of Methods in Psychiatric Research* 2008;17:(S1): S50–S59.

Babor, T. F., & Winstanley, E. L. (2008). The world of drinking: national alcohol control experiences in 18 countries. *Addiction, 103,* 721–25.

Edwards, G. (ed) *Addiction: Evolution of a Specialist Field.* Oxford, UK: Blackwell Publishing, 2002.

Edwards, G. (ed) *Addictions: Personal Influences and Scientific Movements.* New Brunswick, New Jersey, USA: Transaction Publishers, 1991.

Edwards, G. E., Babor, T. F. (2008) Addiction societies as valuable assets. *Addiction,* 103, 9–12.

Taylor, P., Keeter, S. *Millennials: A Portrait of Generation Next.* Pew Research Center Report. 2010.

Index

A

D

I

J

K

L

O

P

T

U

V

W

Y

Z

For Product Safety Concerns and Information please contact our EU representative GPSR@taylorandfrancis.com Taylor & Francis Verlag GmbH, Kaufingerstraße 24, 80331 München, Germany